Challenges and Opportunities of Corporate Governance Transformation in the Digital Era

Mikhail Yevgenievich Kuznetsov
Moscow State University, Russia

Maria Igorevna Nikishova
Financial University Under the Government of the Russian Federation, Russia

IGI Global
DISSEMINATOR OF KNOWLEDGE

A volume in the Advances in Business Strategy and Competitive Advantage (ABSCA) Book Series

Published in the United States of America by
IGI Global
Business Science Reference (an imprint of IGI Global)
701 E. Chocolate Avenue
Hershey PA, USA 17033
Tel: 717-533-8845
Fax: 717-533-8661
E-mail: cust@igi-global.com
Web site: http://www.igi-global.com

Library of Congress Cataloging-in-Publication Data

Names: Kuznetsov, Mikhail Yevgenievich, 1979- editor. | Nikishova, Maria Igorevna, 1942- editor.
Title: Challenges and opportunities of corporate governance transformation in the digital era / Mikhail Yevgenievich Kuznetsov and Maria Igorevna Nikishova, editors.
Description: Hershey, PA : Business Science Reference, [2020] | Includes bibliographical references and index. | Summary: "This book analyzes corporate governance transformation under the pressure of new technologies and economic changes"-- Provided by publisher.
Identifiers: LCCN 2019035789 (print) | LCCN 2019035790 (ebook) | ISBN 9781799820116 (hardcover) | ISBN 9781799820123 (paperback) | ISBN 9781799820130 (ebook)
Subjects: LCSH: Corporate governance--Technological innovations.
Classification: LCC HD2741 .C447 2020 (print) | LCC HD2741 (ebook) | DDC 338.6--dc23
LC record available at https://lccn.loc.gov/2019035789
LC ebook record available at https://lccn.loc.gov/2019035790

This book is published in the IGI Global book series Advances in Business Strategy and Competitive Advantage (ABSCA) (ISSN: 2327-3429; eISSN: 2327-3437)

British Cataloguing in Publication Data
A Cataloguing in Publication record for this book is available from the British Library.

Advances in Business Strategy and Competitive Advantage (ABSCA) Book Series

Patricia Ordóñez de Pablos
Universidad de Oviedo, Spain

ISSN:2327-3429
EISSN:2327-3437

Mission

Business entities are constantly seeking new ways through which to gain advantage over their competitors and strengthen their position within the business environment. With competition at an all-time high due to technological advancements allowing for competition on a global scale, firms continue to seek new ways through which to improve and strengthen their business processes, procedures, and profitability.

The **Advances in Business Strategy and Competitive Advantage (ABSCA) Book Series** is a timely series responding to the high demand for state-of-the-art research on how business strategies are created, implemented and re-designed to meet the demands of globalized competitive markets. With a focus on local and global challenges, business opportunities and the needs of society, the **ABSCA** encourages scientific discourse on doing business and managing information technologies for the creation of sustainable competitive advantage.

Coverage

- Core Competencies
- Differentiation Strategy
- Entrepreneurship & Innovation
- Value Creation
- Economies of Scale
- Value Chain
- Cost Leadership Strategy
- Ethics and Business Strategy
- Strategic alliances
- Resource-Based Competition

IGI Global is currently accepting manuscripts for publication within this series. To submit a proposal for a volume in this series, please contact our Acquisition Editors at Acquisitions@igi-global.com or visit: http://www.igi-global.com/publish/.

The Advances in Business Strategy and Competitive Advantage (ABSCA) Book Series (ISSN 2327-3429) is published by IGI Global, 701 E. Chocolate Avenue, Hershey, PA 17033-1240, USA, www.igi-global.com. This series is composed of titles available for purchase individually; each title is edited to be contextually exclusive from any other title within the series. For pricing and ordering information please visit http://www.igi-global.com/book-series/advances-business-strategy-competitive-advantage/73672. Postmaster: Send all address changes to above address.

Titles in this Series

For a list of additional titles in this series, please visit: https://www.igi-global.com/book-series/advances-business-strategy-competitive-advantage/73672

Leadership Styles, Innovation, and Social Entrepreneurship in the Era of Digitalization
Çağlar Doğru (Ufuk University, Turkey)
Business Science Reference • © 2020 • 447pp • H/C (ISBN: 9781799811084) • US $215.00

Business Reinvention for Ecosystem Value, Flexibility, and Empowerment Emerging Research and Opportunities
Soe-Tsyr Daphne Yuan (National Chengchi University, Taiwan)
Business Science Reference • © 2020 • 230pp • H/C (ISBN: 9781799815501) • US $155.00

Competitiveness, Organizational Management, and Governance in Family Firms
Cesar Camisón (University of Valenica, Spain) and Tomás González (University of Valencia, Spain)
Business Science Reference • © 2020 • 459pp • H/C (ISBN: 9781799816553) • US $225.00

Strategic Approaches for Conflict Resolution in Organizations Emerging Research and Opportunities
Siddhartha Bhattacharyya (RCC Institute of Information Technology, Kolkata, India)
Business Science Reference • © 2020 • 187pp • H/C (ISBN: 9781799817260) • US $195.00

Socio-Economic Perspectives on Vocational Skill Development Emerging Research and Opportunities
Ugochukwu Chinonso Okolie (Ebonyi State University, Nigeria)
Business Science Reference • © 2020 • 250pp • H/C (ISBN: 9781522541455) • US $195.00

Impact of Disruptive Technologies on the Sharing Economy
Ford Lumban Gaol (Bina Nusantara University, Jakarta, Indonesia) Natalia Filimonova (Vladimir State University, Russia) and Chandan Acharya (City University of New York, USA)
Business Science Reference • © 2020 • 350pp • H/C (ISBN: 9781799803614) • US $245.00

Achieving Peak Sales Performance for Optimal Business Value and Sustainability
Carlton Brown (University of Plymouth, UK)
Business Science Reference • © 2020 • 431pp • H/C (ISBN: 9781799816393) • US $245.00

Handbook of Research on Industrial Applications for Improved Supply Chain Performance
Jorge Luis García-Alcaraz (Universidad Autónoma de Ciudad Juárez, Mexico) George Leal Jamil (Informações em Rede Consultoria e Treinamento Ltda., Brazil) Liliana Avelar-Sosa (Universidad Autónoma de Ciudad Juárez, Mexico) and Antonio Juan Briones Peñalver (Polytechnic University of Cartagena, Spain)
Business Science Reference • © 2020 • 549pp • H/C (ISBN: 9781799802020) • US $345.00

IGI Global
DISSEMINATOR OF KNOWLEDGE

701 East Chocolate Avenue, Hershey, PA 17033, USA
Tel: 717-533-8845 x100 • Fax: 717-533-8661
E-Mail: cust@igi-global.com • www.igi-global.com

Table of Contents

Detailed Table of Contents

Reputation management is based on digital platforms and tools such as monitoring mass or social media, compliance facilities, and trade credit ratings. The digital instruments extensively utilize various methods of artificial intelligence, machine learning, and predictive analytics, including neural networks and natural language processing (NLP). The computational tools simplify managerial challenges, though assume their users to understand the whole scope and logical structures of data management. Opinions about a company, person, product, or a country are important, but financial consequences of reputational triggers are even more valuable. Reputation management merges with credit and compliance risk assessment both in regulation and in corporate practices.

We are increasingly living in a digital world, where companies attempt to adapt to a new context of Industry 4.0. The authors believe that artificial intelligence and the use of logarithms will alter the game of competition. Digitization is moving our economy away from "financial capitalism" to "data capitalism," and companies and their boards need to adopt the way they operate and steer the organization to new ecosystems where personalized service becomes part of the new digital strategy. Basically, it is not a battle of AI versus humans, but rather finding a way to enhance the collaboration of AI and humans in organizations. Despite the enormous potential benefits of AI, boards should not ignore the darker side of AI, namely the potential biasedness and sometimes unfairness of algorithms and privacy concerns and the ubiquitous cyberthreats. This is why proper data governance at the board level is needed. The authors suggest that this becomes a critical success factor to be addressed at boards, either as part of the risk management or strategic committee or as a separated digitization committee.

This chapter addresses the ethical values and responsibilities of corporate directors in the unfolding digital era. Explanation for directors of private or public companies in the digital era involves three principal dimensions. The first concerns the ethical values and responsibilities of any director defined independently of the company or industry or era. The second concerns the additional ethical responsibilities of a director in the digital era, which imposes further conditions on directors. These conditions are heightened for directors of high technology, digital era-oriented businesses. The third dimension concerns whether ethical values and responsibilities of directors vary across countries and legal systems. This dimension separates into legal standards for directors and cultural variations in attitudes and behaviors of directors and managers. The chapter offers real company illustrations for these three dimensions. The chapter recommends four solutions: better and better prepared directors, sounder regulation, and a more unified theory of ethics and responsibility.

Until recently, traditional automakers and digital companies have been working separately at their own pace, preserving their cultures and ways of doing business and driving innovation. In the early 2010s, younger generations of customers were spoilt by seamless ecosystems in digital and started wondering why they are still operating knobs while seated behind steering wheel. From this point, the process of interpenetration of two industries started, provoking transformation and cultural shifts in the traditional automakers industry. How far will it go? What are the main challenges of this transformation? What forms and principles of corporate culture will appear and dominate in the industry in the future?

The purpose of the present study was to find the answer to the following questions: How the growing digitalization will affect agency relations, an important element of corporate governance, and what preventive measures should be taken in this situation? Therefore, the impact of digitalization on opportunistic behavior and agency costs was reviewed. The analysis revealed that digitalization provokes reduction of information asymmetry, leads to a decrease in the initiative of top managers, thereby changing the preconditions of opportunistic behavior. On the basis of the ordinal approach, an original toolkit was developed, which made it possible to model the identified dependencies, transformation of the agents' utility in case the principals' demands altering, and to demonstrate ways to reduce agency costs by proper selection of candidates for top manager positions. In conclusion, by means of the developed toolkit, the methodological recommendations were suggested for selecting the agents during the process of recruitment, taking into account the impact of digitalization.

Since the time of the first corporations, shareholders have expected boards to manage corporate governance processes in the best way. At the same time, the era of digital technology can significantly increase the effectiveness of corporate governance procedures through automation of corporate governance procedures as business processes. The board of directors and the corporate secretary can rely on performance indicators and manage the effectiveness of corporate governance processes. This chapter discusses opportunities for improving the business processes, including automation and analytics. The author considers approaches to project management of corporate governance procedures automation and its limitations.

In order to detect evidence of fraud effectively, it is essential for the auditor to be aware of new and differentiated methods. Thus, the auditor can identify and assess the risks of material misstatement so that auditing is as reliable as possible. In this sense, the relevance of the application of the Benford's Law arises in order to demonstrate that the identification of situations of greater risk of fraud is appropriate in auditing. The objective of this study is to analyze the behavior of 27,058 Portuguese companies.

We live in a changing world. Disruptive technologies and digital platforms particularly are reshaping the world, making it more open and accessible on the one hand, but more fragile and uncertain on the other, rising risks of cybersecurity, personal data security. Do markets really need any kind of regulatory interventions under these circumstances? We see many cases where "state bureaucrats" impose restrictions on global companies based on digital platforms – technology champions. Are those actions effective, do they make sense in terms of global security, or it is only political game?

Foreword

Corporations and corporate governance of today have come of age. Since ancient times, Roman law recognized a range of corporate entities under the names *universitas*, *corpus* or *collegium*. In Medieval times, corporate arena expanded to include early trade guilds and livery companies as partnerships. Dutch and English chartered companies reflective of the mercantilism era were leading the colonial ventures of European nations in the 17th century. The abandonment of mercantilist economic theory in 18th century and the rise of classical liberalism and proliferation of laissez-faire economics have led to a corporate transition from being government or guild affiliated entities to encompass public and private economic entities free of governmental directions. Further developments in the 19th and 20th century have been marked by propagation of corporations operating under limited liability. The end of the 19th century witnessed the emergence of holding companies and corporate mergers. The 20th century, especially after the WW2, saw a proliferation of multinational corporations and global conglomerates.

In the late 20th - 21st century, the advent of computers, internet of things, digitization, artificial intelligence, and other disruptive technological and business innovations is bringing to life a multitude of new corporate forms and dynamics and fostering the Fourth Industrial Revolution (see World Economic Forum https://intelligence.weforum.org/topics/a1Gb0000001RIhBEAW?tab=publications).

The world is rapidly changing. Technological progress becomes so fast, that many business models, traditional industries, and even national and international institutions cannot keep up with the speed of change. At the same time, we still live in the world driven by the large corporate frameworks with centralized management, boards of directors, which try to set strategies and control companies through quarterly meetings, based on traditional reporting. Does the traditional corporate governance framework continue to be a sustainable and effective structure, or it will also transform under the pressures of disruptive innovations and changes?

These developments, the drivers and disruptors of today, as well as emerging trends and dynamics as relates to digitization of corporate governance are subject of exploration of this book. The reader may not find the exact final answers to these questions in this book, but it definitely raises fundamental questions about the viability and sustainability of the current corporate governance framework. How would the role of shareholders and other stakeholders change? What communication channels will dominate the future landscape? How digitization and AI could change the decision-making process? What are the legal, social, economic and other implications, as we as unintended consequences that could result from these changes?

An international team of authors gives the reader good food for thought not only on the future of corporate governance, but on the development of business and society.

Anatoly Zhuplev
Department of Management, Loyola Marymount University, USA

Preface

Corporate governance has been a sustainable, efficient concept for a long time. This model has been one of the main drivers of economic and social transformation of the world for the last several centuries, supporting several industrial revolutions. But today we are living in a new world, which is adapting to challenges of the new industrial revolution, which seems to be much more dramatic than the previous transformations, with high speed of transformational technological and social change. Will this concept be yet sustainable in the digital era, during the time of technological and managerial disruption and if so, how will this concept transform under the pressure of new economic, social and ecologic challenges? This book covers the main aspects of the topic: role of corporate governance in the society, corporate law transformation, technological shifts and their influence on decision making, including the dramatic potential of Artificial Intelligence, changing perception of human capital, evolution of the agency problem. The main objective of the Book is to analyze the main consequences and possible scenarios of corporate governance transformation under the pressure of new technologies and economic changes. This book will summarize the concepts, mechanisms, trends, forecasts of corporate governance development in the Digital Era. It could be the source of useful insights to corporate directors, owners, investment funds, consultants involved in the topic of corporate governance, as well as the students and research community of all over the world. In this brief introduction we would like to summarize the main ideas, covered in the book.

As Prof. Mark Fenwick and Prof. Erik P Vermeulen state, we live in the era of "the end of the corporation" as we knew it before. They describe an enormous and anxious discussion around the future of traditional business models and approaches to regulation. A traditional corporation focused on several issues, such as an accountable board and management, internal control and monitoring processes, transparent information disclosure about the financial position of the company, and responsibility for the interests of minority shareholders. The authors challenge the traditional approach to framing corporate governance primarily on creating shareholder value and agency costs, coming from incomplete contracts. However, the new reality, where business platforms and "ecosystem" business approach are winning the globe, dictates new forms of stakeholders' engagement, decision making and communication. New technologies, such as artificial intelligence, blockchain, and new social media are the drivers of this change. The authors express the main idea of this "ecosystem" organizational transformation - «the idea of delivering constant innovation via an open and inclusive process of co-creation». And the boards of directors, as one of the key mechanisms, should also change, by expanding their role and functions, including more interaction and engagement with stakeholders, and not only being focused on monitoring and compliance functions.

The next idea, refers to the changing approach to stakeholder's engagement in the digital era. Transformation of business models, appearance of "businesses as platforms", further development of social networks and digital culture makes it impossible for a nearly any company to be an "isolated island" and makes every player a part of dynamic network of stakeholders. For a long time in the corporate world the term "creating value" meant creating shareholder's value, with all the basic corporate structures, mechanisms and incentives serving this goal. But under the pressure of technological transformation and social changes during the last 30 years, the concept of the main corporate purposes has shifted. Michael E. Porter and Mark R. Kramer in their famous article "Creating shared value" stated, that companies "remain trapped in an outdated approach to value creation that has emerged over the past few decades. They continue to view value creation narrowly, optimizing short-term financial performance in a bubble while missing the most important customer needs and ignoring the broader influences that determine their longer-term success". This remarkable shift has been constituted in 2019, when the American business roundtable has approved the new Statement on the Purpose of a Corporation, which was signed by all the leaders of the corporate American world. The statement redirects the priorities of the corporations from shareholder value, saying that "Each of our stakeholders is essential. We commit to deliver value to all of them, for the future success of our companies, our communities and our country".

Building sustainable relations within this network of stakeholders becomes crucial for the long-term prosperity of the company. Stakeholders may have no direct impact on the company; however, their indirect influence could be quite powerful. Should they be a part of decision making then? Should some of them (clients, employees) have a vote on some decisions, or there should be other, informal ways of engagement?

And here we come to the second topic, which is closely related with stakeholder engagement -reputation management in the era of transition to digital platforms. Reputation becomes the "magic magnet", that keeps all the parts of the company network together, and in fact it becomes even more important looking forward. The reputation management technology itself comes through a big digital transformation. It is based on digital platforms and tools such - monitoring mass or social media, compliance facilities, and trade credit ratings. Different tools, such as artificial intelligence, machine learning and predictive analytics, neural networks and neutral language processing (NLP) become widely used in reputation management. In fact, reputation management merges with credit and compliance risk assessment both in regulation and in corporate practices. Transition to platforms require a new level of transparency – sometimes it means opening the company's systems to all third-party players, including competitors.

This is no longer a traditional approach to communication with stakeholders, with regular quarterly investors presentations and once a year annual report. Omni channel, integrated communication with extensive feedback becomes the most relevant approach to manage stakeholders' relations. With the further increase in the variety and complexity of digital communication tools for data distribution and processing, enterprises will transform their informational policies totally, trying to meet the expectations of various stakeholders - regulators, shareholders, customers, suppliers or vendors, employees. In the long-term perspective, enterprises could transform into "aquariums", becoming fully transparent in their goals, values, needs and value propositions, with easy access and active engagement and integration with their stakeholders' network due to a rapidly developing set of digital instruments.

The digital world of the future will rearrange the decision-making process as well. In the world, where companies try to adapt to a new context of Industry 4.0, competition will drive further implementation of Artificial Intelligence, first as a supportive tool for decision making ("alter ego"), and then, probably – as a human partner in decision making. Today many hi-tech companies make AI-driven technologies a big part of their strategies. For example, one of the strategic priorities for Google is "to embrace an AI-centric approach and solidify lead in machine learning".

As one the authors of the book mentions, this means, that moving away from "Financial Capitalism" to "Data Capitalism" companies and their boards will have to adopt to the new reality, where AI would become one of the most important partners in decision making. Probably, it will be a big challenge for organizational structures, HR policies, decision making, e.t.c. The main challenge for any board of directors would be finding a way to enhance the collaboration of AI and humans in organizations, at the same time balancing the risks, associated with the technology, such as the potential biasedness and sometimes unfairness of algorithms, privacy concerns, and the ubiquitous cyberthreats. That is why IT governance, at the board level has already become a necessity, and will become a critical success factor to be addressed by the boards in the nearest future. As we have discussed in some of the previous publications (Maria I. Nikishova, Mikhail E. Kuznetsov. Is Artificial Intelligence a New Dawn or Challenge for Corporate Decision Making? Managerial Perspectives on Intelligent Big Data Analytics. IGI Global. USA. 2019.), there are different expectations on the use of AI technologies. Some authors pay more attention to the risks associated with its use. For example, according to N. Bostrom (2016), the application of AI in management in general entails two major risks: loss of control over the technology and the risk of such technology being used with negative consequences for humanity.

That's why the strategies for the development of artificial intelligence (AI) in many countries have separate chapters with ethical principles in the development and application of AI technology. Today the most detailed ethical principles of AI are described by various public organizations and associations of AI developers, such as Asilomar AI Principles Institute of Electrical and Electronics Engineers (IEEE) or Montreal Declaration Responsible AI. The European Commission is developing the ethical principles of AI as well The newly published AI Development Strategy in Russia also provides a set of ethical rules for the interaction of humans and AI. Anyway, one of the most important dilemmas of the nearest future is to find the right combination of reasonable ethical limitations for the new technologies and balanced conditions, not to slow down or stop the development of the new technologies.

The agency problem, as always, is in the center of corporate governance transformation. The relations between owners (principals) and managers (agents) is traditionally characterized by a whole bunch of contradictions, and most corporate governance principles are set to resolve this agency problem. But what would happen in the digital age, when robots will become "new partners" of humans in decision making? How would it transform the agency problem? Will the agency costs reduce, driven by disruptive technologies, or there will be a new technological dimension of the problem? On the one hand, technology helps to reduce information asymmetry, helping to alleviate the agency problems and reduce agency costs. Interested parties can use large amounts of data in the digital form. Big data technologies make it easier to make informed decisions. On the other hand, the growing amounts of information and reliance on automated technologies could raise other problems and reshape the agency conflict, adding stakeholders (for example, users of a platform, with their concerns on their personal data) and algorithms, making automated decisions, as parts of the agency problem. In the extreme form, we could imagine AI empowered decision-making tools as beneficiaries, board members, managers of automated corporations, delivering goods and services for humans or machines. Or there could be other forms, with humans as agents, acting in the best interests of … machines? In that case the agency problem transforms from human-to -human into a more complicated human vs machine problem, adding a lot of new dimensions to corporate governance.

Fraud and internal corruption are classic examples of direct costs, coming from inefficiencies of corporate governance and auditing process. Good corporate governance is traditionally focused on fraud prevention on the top management level, as well as building effective internal control and risk management system. New technologies, based on big data utilization, suggest a lot of opportunities for internal control and risk management system enhancement. Application of Benford's law to fraud detection, given in the book, is one of such examples. But will anti-fraud, based on big data technology make it possible to get rid of internal corruption and fraud, and we will leave "in the best of the worlds"? Or it will just require new competences from "corruption professionals"?

And if we try to look into the future, as some authors argue, moral integrity and ethical values of directors become even more important in the new technological era. Honor, honesty, professionalism, and competence become crucial for not only IT giants such as Facebook, Amazon, Google, but for all industries and types of business. With further growing automatization of decision making, we will not get rid of moral dilemmas. Imagine, for example, a GPS navigator, trying to prevent a huge traffic jam, which tells us lie about the current traffic, giving us advice not to take a car, based on the mathematical assessment of the "general benefit". Or it should be personal benefit, or something in between? How the decision is made? Who is responsible for this decision – the navigator, the end user, the engineer? And in corporate governance we have tons of such dilemmas, balancing the interests of many stakeholders. One of the authors of our book states, that this makes it even more important to pay attention to the moral integrity, which is superior ultimately to legal compliance and in certain limited circumstances moral integrity may require even civil disobedience. But is this moral matrix universal? Will it change under the pressure of the new world? And how will it transform the culture of organizations?

As we know from Peter Drucker (although this saying has not been documented), "culture eats strategy on breakfast". But what if technological, especially digital transformation "eats" current corporate cultures, making them non-competitive? This dilemma is investigated in the chapter "the clash of cultures" based on the example of automakers industry. The process of integration, that started between automotive and IT industries is quite remarkable, provoking transformation and cultural shifts in the traditional automakers industry. What are the main challenges of this transformation? What forms and principles of corporate culture will appear and dominate in the industry in the future?

Rapid technological development rises another problem: the growing global influence of corporations. Empowered by new technologies, the largest transnational corporations become a real transformational power in the world, sometimes competing with states in terms of available resources and real influence. Could this competition lead to rebalancing of power between state governments and corporations? What is the role of regulators in the new reality, and what corporate governance instruments and approaches are applicable here? These questions are raised in the book and require further research.

We express our gratitude to all the authors of this book who investigated the challenges, opportunities, trends, and wrote about the future of corporate governance. The book consists of the following chapters:

Chapter 1, contributed by Prof. Mark Fenwick and Prof. Erik P Vermeulen, titled "The End of the Corporation: Transformation in Corporate Governance," describes the main challenges for modern corporations and features of fundamental transformation of corporate governance in the digital age. The authors emphasize the need to change business models, changes in communications, flexibility and adaptation to the digital environment, the need to move to an ecosystem models.

Chapter 2, contributed by Mikhail Y. Kuznetsov, Valeria Solovyova, Maria I. Nikishova, Maria Olshanskaya, titled "Stakeholder Engagement in the Digital Era," investigates the issues of stakeholders interaction in the digital age. The authors have identified the characteristic features and practices of the interaction of companies with various categories of stakeholders. The study analyzed key stakeholders of the companies, channels of interaction and significant topics for discussion. The authors note the importance of the process of managing interaction with stakeholders, balance of interests, building an understandable communication strategy in the process of digital business transformation.

Chapter 3, contributed by Olga Rink, titled "Reputation Management and a Corporate Identity: Transition to Digital Platforms," discusses trends in the development of corporate communications and reputation management in the era of digital technology. The author investigates the components of reputation as an asset, the main reputation risks in the era of digital technology development and organizational activities for reputation management.

Chapter 4, contributed by Prof. Peter Verhezen from Antwerp Management School, titled "What to Expect From Artificial Intelligence in Business? How Wise Board Members Can and Should Facilitate Human-AI Collaboration," rises the problem of the interaction of artificial intelligence and human in companies by emphasizing that it is not a battle of AI versus humans, it should be collaboration of AI and humans. Nevertheless, according to the author, despite the enormous potential benefits of AI, companies should not ignore risks and sometimes unfairness of algorithms and privacy concerns, and the ubiquitous cyberthreats. Therefore, the author offers recommendations for regulating the interaction of human and AI in companies.

Chapter 5, contributed by Dr. Duane Windsor, titled "Ethical Values and Responsibilities of Directors in the Digital Era," describes the trend of increasing demands on ethical values and responsibilities of directors in the digital age. According to the author, the sphere of ethical values and responsibilities of directors in the digital era expands and affects both private and state-owned companies, and therefore the author combines the ethical aspects of corporate governance, corporate social responsibility and stakeholder theory to explain this.

Chapter 6, contributed by Mikhail Bakunin and Mikhail Kuznetsov, titled "The Cultural Clash: Traditional Automakers vs. Digital Companies – Can They Work Together? Transformation of Business Culture in the Digital Age," discusses the main features and challenges of transformation and cultural shifts in the traditional automakers industry and argue that forms and principles of corporate culture will change in the digital era.

Chapter 7, contributed by Prof. Dmitriy A. Zhdanov, titled "Agency Cost Management in the Digital Economy," raises the crucial topic of the transformation of agent conflict in corporate governance in an era of rapid technological development. In connection with the digitization of the economy, there is a need to study how these processes affect corporate governance from the point of view of managing the opportunistic behavior of management and to study other corresponding trends.

Chapter 8, contributed by Sergey N. Endutkin, titled "Corporate Governance Efficiency: Automation of Corporate Governance Procedures," presents a solution for automating corporate governance procedures. The author considers corporate governance procedures as business processes that require optimization and automation in the digital age, because corporate procedures can both speed up and slow down decision-making processes.

Chapter 9, contributed by Adriana Nunes, Helena Inácio, and Rui Pedro Figueiredo Marques, titled "The Benford's Law for Fraud Detection: A Case Study of Portuguese Companies," presents a study of 27,058 Portuguese companies with different financial results, based on the application of Benford's law to identify evidence of fraud by auditors, assess the risks of misrepresentation and various correlations.

Chapter 10, contributed by Alexander A. Filatov, titled "Sovereign Bureaucrats vs. Global Tech Companies: Ethical and Regulatory Challenges," reflects on what corporate digital ecosystems are, how they are reshaping the world, on the implications and effectiveness of regulatory restrictions and interventions in the activities of global platform companies.

Mikhail Kuznetsov
Moscow State University, Russia

Maria Nikishova
CopCompetence, Russia

Chapter 1
The End of the Corporation:
Transformation in Corporate Governance

Mark Fenwick
https://orcid.org/0000-0001-8175-9008
Graduate School of Law, Kyushu University, Japan

Erik P. Vermeulen
Tilburg University, The Netherlands

ABSTRACT

Corporate governance is undergoing a quiet, but quick transformation. The rise of digital technologies is forcing companies to reconsider existing business models, but also how they organize themselves and structure firm governance. This chapter introduces the main features of the modern corporation and corporate governance, outlines how digital technologies are disrupting this business form, and describes the new business "ecosystems" that are emerging to replace the modern corporation. The chapter argues that in a networked age, all businesses need to "go digital." Companies need to become innovation machines, and this means that every firm needs to become a "tech" company and a "media" company. If they do not, younger and more agile competitors better attuned to the realities of the new digital world will replace them. For incumbents, the risks are existential. Established firms must adapt to the new digital environment by embracing the ecosystem model, or they will die.

INTRODUCTION

We are witnessing a quiet but quick transformation in corporate governance. The rise of digital technologies and social media are forcing companies to reconsider existing business models, but also how they organize themselves and structure firm governance. In this chapter, we introduce the main features of the modern corporation and corporate governance, outline how digital technologies are disrupting this business form, and describe the new business "ecosystems" that are emerging to replace the modern corporation.

DOI: 10.4018/978-1-7998-2011-6.ch001

Our conclusion? In a networked age, all businesses need to "go digital." Companies need to become innovation machines, and this means that every firm needs to become a "tech" company and a "media" company. If they do not, younger and more agile competitors better attuned to the realities of the new digital world will replace them. For incumbents, the risks are existential. Established firms must adapt to the new digital environment by embracing the ecosystem model, or they will die.

Compounding the challenge for incumbents, existing regulatory approaches are failing business organizations. In short, many corporate governance rules and regulations are programming institutions to be dysfunctional. There is an ever-widening gap or disconnect between regulatory strategies and the business needs of companies operating in fast-moving, technology-driven markets. Consequently, many businesses and other organizations are ill-equipped to meet the challenges of today's digital world. Instead, we need to design regulations that incentivize firms to establish the organizational structures and practices that will allow them to succeed. A new corporate governance focused on supporting a firm's capacity to innovate — as well as promoting compliance and risk management — needs to be developed.

BACKGROUND

Corporations & Corporate Governance

Corporations have dominated the global economy for at least the last 150 years, and there are good reasons to claim that the corporation is the most important institution in the world over this period (*Bakan, 2001*). After all, corporations have provided the basis for sustained economic growth and prosperity and have played a vital role in developing and disseminating new technologies and improving people's lives.

A modern corporation can be defined as a business organization characterized by a combination of three features.

First, a corporation is a creature of the law – it is formed by an act of incorporation – and, as such, the company exists separately from its owner-shareholders, directors, executives, managers, and employees. As an independent entity, a company can issue tradeable shares to investors, limit shareholder liability, and conduct business in its own name.

Second, a corporation is organized as a closed, hierarchical institution with a clear chain of authority flowing "downwards" from the owner-shareholders to the employees. A company uses authority-based management structures and is not governed by consensus.

Finally, corporations traditionally adopt a "linear" business model whereby the company gathers together various "inputs" (raw materials, components, or knowledge/information), which are then combined, thus adding value, before being sold as either a standardized product or service to a "customer," either another business (in B2B transactions) or a consumer (in a B2C transaction).

Understood in this way, the rise of the modern corporation is a relatively recent phenomenon, at least from a historical perspective (*Hadden, 1972; Wells, 2018*). The corporation did not emerge fully formed but rather developed over time as a series of contingent adaptations to changes in the social and economic environment. It was only in the latter part of the nineteenth century that these various elements combined. Any consideration of this history of the corporation reveals, on the one hand, a series of controversies, scandals, and setbacks, but, on the other hand, a gradual expansion in the availability of the corporate form as a means of conducting business and an increase in its influence over the economy.

In early modern Europe, trade was conducted by loose networks of traders. These relationships developed slowly into "self-protective organizations," backed by money-lenders (the origins of modern banks) who financed these business operations (*Micklethwait & Wooldridge, 2005*). The first European joint-stock companies were created by Royal Charters that granted a monopoly in a specific territory for specified activities for a specific period (*Brown, 2010; Gelderblom, 2013*). Joint-stock companies emerged in the sixteenth century — fifteen were operating in England by 1690 — however, none had more than a few hundred members (*Micklethwait & Wooldridge, 2005*). Moreover, there was no strong conception of corporate legal personality — rather, a corporation was seen as a creation of the sovereign and an instrument of government policy.

It was in the seventeenth century that this new business attracted greater interest, initially as a vehicle for financing European colonial enterprises. In this way, the earliest corporations were established as instruments of foreign policy and geopolitics, as much as business enterprises. The British East India Company and its Dutch rival, the Dutch East India Company (the VOC), fought over the right to trade with India and were supported by private armies in territories where they operated (*Stern, 2016*).

Take the VOC, for example. Over time, the VOC evolved into something like the current corporate form in that investors were issued shares, which could be publicly traded on the Amsterdam Stock Exchange (*River, 2017*). This combination of corporate shareholders and publicly traded stock is the basis of the claim that the VOC was the first public company. The primary advantage of this new corporate form was the ability to combine the economic power of a potentially unlimited number of investors. Traditional business forms, such as partnerships, which combined the economic power of a small number of people, who then ran the business together, were not suited to the more risky, large scale projects of the kind envisaged by the Dutch government and the VOC.

Nevertheless, the early history of the VOC was mired in controversy. Investors often expressed their dissatisfaction and frustration with dividend policies, the murkiness of the company's accounts, and the lack of disclosure and transparency (*Coolhaas, 1960*). Other problems for investors were the limited involvement of the main board of directors — the Board of Seventeen Lords (De Heren XVII) — which convened only a few times a year and directly reported to the Dutch government rather than to investors.

As such, the institutional design of the early VOC made this arrangement prone to fraud and deception, particularly regarding the state of finances and governance (*McCahery & Vermeulen, 2009*). In response to these shortcomings, the government obliged full and open disclosure of the VOC's accounts in 1622. Subsequently, the committee of nine and audit committee, an early form of a supervisory board consisting of "chief participants," was introduced in 1623 to advise management and were charged with inspecting the financial information of the VOC. One might say that, with these changes, the first "corporate governance" movement was born. The government forced information disclosure in order to bolster the control of investors. Nevertheless, such reforms could not solve the problems surrounding the complex and cumbersome management structure inherent to the VOC arrangement.

The success of the corporate form meant that by the early decades of the twentieth century, companies had become the key institution in the economy. Moreover, deep connections had developed between industry-driven economic growth and newly emerging welfare politics (*Zumbansen, 2011*). Corporations were seen as (and saw themselves as) public institutions that had an obligation to assist the state in mitigating the inherent inequalities that resulted from a capitalist market economy. As a result, large companies were actively involved in their local communities, not only as a source of employment and economic growth, but as provider of housing, of welfare assistance and as a source of entertainment for workers and the larger community (many European football clubs were founded by large companies, for example, PSV Eindhoven (Philips) or VfL Wolfsburg (Volkswagen).

Around the 1920s, however, differences began to develop between the United States and Europe. Whereas in the US, the role of finance became increasingly important in the organization and state regulation of companies, in Western Europe, "the company was embedded in a tightly regulated system of the company, employment, and social welfare law." However, such differences should not be overstated. Even in the United States, the social obligation of companies was never completely extinguished. Peter Drucker's account of GM, for example, emphasized the social responsibilities of US corporations in the 1950s, and a striking feature of this work, when read today, is that there is no discussion of shareholders or the company as an investment opportunity (*Drucker, 1946*).

By the 1960s, however, critiques of this social model of the company had started to emerge, particularly in the US. J. K. Galbraith's *The New Industrial State* argued that the corporation controlled its environment to such an extent that it transcended the traditional sources of "countervailing power" (*Galbraith, 1967*). The result was a shift from the corporation as a social institution to what John Kay refers to as the "empty corporation" (*Kay, 2019*). From the 1970s and 80s, the firm came to be seen as an investment vehicle, and the success of a firm was no longer judged by its broader role as a social institution and whether it was fulfilling diverse societal responsibilities. Instead, the success of a firm was now judged purely in terms of the return on investment delivered to investors. Various financial innovations, notably to securitization, accelerated this process as did the easing of restrictions on cross-border capital movements. There was a shift in the function of the financial industry from a source of capital to one in which such firms "serve themselves" (*Mitchell, 2011*).

The dominance of this financially driven view of the corporation resulted in a reconfiguration in regulatory models. In particular, it resulted in a renewed and myopic emphasis on the principal-agent problem. If the goal of the firm was shareholder primacy, ensuring that the firm (and, most importantly, its managers) acted in the best interests of shareholders. This logic has driven contemporary debates in corporate governance.

Following the logic of shareholder primacy, the primary goal of corporate governance today is to protect the interests of the shareholder/investor/owners of a company (*Berle & Means, 1932; Jenson & Meckling, 1976*). In practice, this has meant adopting regulatory measures that aim to ensure that *all* of the other actors within a firm act "as if" they were shareholder-investors. By better aligning the incentives of the various actors, firm performance — as measured by the share price — is improved, benefiting "all" of the stakeholders in a firm, as well as the public who (ultimately) benefit from the goods and services that a successful firm provides.

According to this view, executives, managers, and other employees are understood as being motivated by self-interest and of having an unhealthy disregard for the negative consequences of their actions on investors (and society). Increasing shareholder control over other actors within the firm – becomes the primary goal of corporate governance rules.

Several requirements are imposed on corporations. Investor confidence depends in large part on the existence of an accurate and useful corporate governance framework. Such an organizational framework traditionally focuses on four issues: (1) an accountable board and management, (2) internal control and monitoring processes, (3) transparent information disclosure about the financial position of the company, and (4) responsibility for the interests of minority shareholders (*Bainbridge, 2008*).

The takeaway? Corporate governance discussions have not really changed that much. The focus is still (as with the VOC) on reducing managerial misbehavior and maximizing the value of shareholders (the stakeholders who are taking the most significant risk). Moreover, the mechanisms for achieving this are more transparency and more supervision. However, framing corporate governance primarily in terms of shareholder value and agency-costs is incomplete and potentially misleading. It encourages box-ticking and an empty conformity. Managers are motivated to project an image of compliance while continuing as before.

Finally, it doesn't do anything to address the real needs of companies today, namely the challenge of navigating the digital revolution.

#Digital

Digital technologies are now turning the world upside down. Over the last three decades, an on-going series of technological developments have transformed economic and social life (*Ross, 2017; Simon & Schuster 2017*). Consider the following:

- The shrinking size, increased power, and diverse applications of personal computers and, more recently, smartphones.
- The global reach of communication networks and the new forms of social interaction and economic exchange that these networks have made possible.
- The availability of cloud databases containing vast amounts of information that can be processed by software algorithms for use across multiple social and economic settings.

The scale and impact of these technological changes justify talk of a "digital transformation." The result? #Digital is amongst the most pressing issues of our times. It is a fascinating but challenging time for business (*Fenwick & Vermeulen,* 2018; *Fenwick & Vermeulen, 2019; Fenwick & Vermeulen, 2020*). Industry boundaries are disappearing. New platform companies have emerged which operate across multiple industries (retail, transport, finance, healthcare, food, etc.) and use global communication networks to deliver new business models and disrupt incumbents. Social media empowers everyone and has transformed the meaning of communication and mass media (*Fenwick & Vermeulen, 2018).*

We cannot think in terms of traditional corporate structures anymore, as their boundaries have become more fluid and porous. Traditional corporate organizations with their departments, business divisions, and hierarchical relationships between the different groups of stakeholders are changing as companies adapt to this environment.

Business leaders understand that a new world needs a different approach. On August 19, 2019, the Business Roundtable, an association of chief executive officers of leading companies in the United States, clearly stated that "CEOs endeavor every day to create value for all our stakeholders, whose long-term interests are inseparable." This emphasis on "*all* our stakeholders" is significant. It reflects the emerging view that companies are not static hierarchies focused on the "primacy" of shareholders, but complex, dynamic ecosystems comprising diverse, interacting elements.

Think about it. Digital technologies have changed consumer behavior. Consumers do not appreciate mass production anymore, and brand loyalty is increasingly fragile. Digital technologies have made consumers way more knowledgeable and sophisticated (*Wu, 2016*). They will only stay if "products" offer them a meaningful and personalized experience. They expect data and data analytics to deliver these more sophisticated services, and "user feedback" and social media give them the "voice" to express their views and educate themselves about a company's performance.

The same can be said about employees. People are no longer satisfied with the prospects of becoming anonymous cogs in a hierarchical corporate machine (*Hoffman, 2014; West, 2018*). They are looking to maximize their personal potential by building a lifestyle and a sense of identity that revolves around doing things that they care passionately about. The digital transformation has created an unprecedented degree of choice. There are endless possibilities. Employees do not stay because it is hard to walk away. They stay if an "ecosystem" offers them the opportunity to engage in a meaningful life project through "work."

Finally, digital technologies are empowering investors in the ecosystems of the future, as well. Artificial intelligence tools that analyze website traffic and social media engagement offer institutional and other professional investors a better understanding of a company's growth opportunities and prospects (*McKinsey Global Institute, 2017*). A smart analysis of earnings transcripts helps investors capture and assess management sentiment.

Blockchain technology has the potential to substantially reduce the cost for companies to access capital markets, providing more investment opportunities and global liquidity to investors (*Filippi & Wright, 2018*). Smart contracts, computer program code, or protocol that automates the verification, execution, and enforcement of specific terms and conditions, will ensure the necessary compliance and security *(Corrales, Fenwick & Haapio, 2019).*

The result? A 21st-century company needs to cultivate and maintain one or more active and healthy ecosystems to engage with all stakeholders in order to stay relevant and competitive. This requires all companies to keep up with the latest technological trends. Of course, digital technology plays a significant role here in gathering feedback from stakeholders (*Fenwick, McCahery & Vermeuelen, 2019*). However, the quickest way to get instantaneous and consequential input is to encourage an open and inclusive dialogue with stakeholders, using different digital and social media platforms. The companies themselves have to step in and take a much more proactive role in creating such an environment in which all stakeholders feel valued.

Here are some concrete examples of this trend. Dutch multinational, Philips, has shifted its annual report into an interactive content experience for the company's broader stakeholder community, using various strategies and online platforms. Microsoft has appointed a Chief Storyteller to help stakeholders (including society) understand who they are, what they do, and why they exist. The move certainly helped Microsoft rediscovering its "soul." Other examples that increased stakeholder engagement and offered companies a window into different stakeholders' perspectives are: Jeff Bezos' yearly letter to the shareholders; "Millennial" representation on the board of Starbucks; the appointment of a social media influencer on the board of AirAsia to make the board more susceptible to the new generation stakeholders; and the use of Twitter as a business/communication tool by Anand Mahindra, executive chairman of Mahindra and Mahindra.

In the twenty first century, the rise of digital technology is transforming the world of corporate governance — but there is no "one-size-fits-all" approach. Artificial intelligence, blockchain technology, and social media can create unique ecosystems with different groups of stakeholders. How to use these technologies wisely is one of the most critical questions facing both companies and policymakers today.

One thing is for sure, companies need more digitally savvy corporate governance experts, and governments need to move beyond ideas and debates inherited from the seventeenth century. The pace and range of digital innovations, as well as the increased pace of innovation cycles, make it much more difficult for bigger, traditionally organized corporations to survive and flourish. Moreover, this sort of environment is not going to deliver a stable and fulfilling workplace, making it increasingly difficult for such corporate "dinosaurs" to attract the best talent needed to turn things around. The challenge for larger corporations is to transform themselves from corporations to something better suited to the challenge of "going digital" (*Fenwick & Vermeulen, 2015).*

It is in this context that we should consider the rise of the so-called platform business model, as the most significant adaptation to the new possibilities of a networked age. Here, we are talking about companies that operate a "social" platform (Facebook, Instagram), an "exchange" platform (Amazon, Airbnb), a "content" platform (YouTube, Medium), a "software" platform (GE's Predix, Microsoft's GitHub), or even a "blockchain" platform (Ethereum, EOS). Platforms come in diverse forms, but what is common to all platforms is that they make connections between "creators" and "extractors" of value and the platform generates a profit from making these connections, either by taking a commission or advertising (*Fenwick, McCahery & Vermeuelen, 2019; Moazed & Johnson, 2019; Parker, Alsyne & Choudry, 2016*).

At first, these new platform firms promised a more decentralized, efficient, and less formal style of business. However, as these tech businesses scaled into some of the largest businesses in history (so-called "super-platforms"), they have become shrouded in controversy and are now widely seen as problematic (*Galloway, 2017*). After all, remaining a sustainable and socially responsible platform can be difficult. As platforms scale — and particularly when they "go global" — they came to rely on hierarchical organizational structures associated with corporations. Furthermore, to sustain their growth, many went public, exposing them to the short term (quarterly) financial pressures associated with a publicly listed corporation.

Such structures make much sense as a strategy for managing the complexities of size. The problem is that a hierarchical organization can easily result in the bureaucratization of the platform, i.e., they can become closed, hierarchical, and overly bureaucratic. This type of organization worked well in an era of mass-production but is less suited to the dynamic business realities of today, particularly for platforms. A tension can emerge between the organization of a platform and what made it successful in the first place. The effect of this tension is that established platforms are unable to react effectively or quickly enough to the challenges created by fast-paced changes in markets, consumers, and technologies. The recent struggles of Facebook, as well as the image problems experienced by other large, well-known platforms (Amazon, Google, Uber, Wework), illustrate this risk of "devolving" into a more corporate style of organization.

While recognizing the validity of such criticisms, we must also acknowledge the innovation that platforms have delivered both to diverse stakeholders (most obviously, consumers and employees) and the global economy, more generally. After all, platforms have made an essential contribution to the creation of our new digital world. This is not surprising. The emergence of these new platforms and services has been one of the major economic developments of the last two decades. Perhaps, there is a more important lesson to be learned from the success of such companies.

At their best, what platform companies all have in common is that they empower and facilitate experimentation, collaboration, and co-creation amongst multiple stakeholders. These stakeholders include employees and investors, but also consumers, developers, content creators, other companies (both large and small), non-profits, educational institutions, governments, etc. As such, they point us towards a more fundamental shift in how the most innovative businesses organize themselves and structure governance, namely the emergence of what we describe here as "ecosystems."

Ecosystems

A business "ecosystem" – or ecosystem company - combines the following features:

- It leverages the unique opportunities of new digital technologies (i.e., software, big data, cloud-based databases, the Internet, social media, etc.) to deliver a meaningful experience to end-users.
- It adopts a flatter, fluid, and more inclusive style of organization involving collaboration with multiple partners built around a network of unbundled, high-performance teams focused on co-creation.
- It embraces a more open and transparent approach to communication and information management.
- It implements a new style of digital leadership that focuses on creating an environment that fosters and facilitates creativity, rather than supervising compliance and managing legal risk.

Together, these are the distinctive features of an ecosystem and distinguish it from the modern corporation *(*A brief note on methodology. The concept of an ecosystem developed here is based on the empirical study of the most successful technology firms today. As such, it represents an "ideal type" or composite of how a business needs to organize its operations and governance in a networked, digital age. References to specific companies in the following are not meant as blanket endorsements of those companies, but an acknowledgment that on the specific point cited that company has identified an interesting approach. In this respect, we hope to move beyond the "all or nothing" attitude that currently characterizes discussion of the most successful tech-firms*)*. In an age of hyper-competitive technology-driven markets, every company needs to consider reinventing itself as an ecosystem. Let's consider each of these features in turn.

Technology in the Service of Delivering a Unique End-User Experience

A technology-driven ecosystem is not simply a "company that uses technology." A technology-driven ecosystem adopts a business model that is characterized by economies of scale and network effects, deriving from the centrality of software in all of its operations (*Hagel, 2016; Campbell, Meyer, Li & Stack, 2015*). This allows (and requires) an ecosystem to collect user-generated data on a continued and systematic basis — which enables it to constantly improve performance and the end user experience. As such, in an ecosystem, the end-user is vitally important, and, in some sense, employees are "paid by the user" and not by the organization. The main strategic goal of a technology-driven ecosystem is to provide its users with a meaningful experience, as this is the only way to inspire trust and retain those users that are so essential for sustaining revenues.

To create value of this kind requires employees to maintain "zero distance" from the end-user / consumer (*Campbell, Meyer, Li & Stack, 2015*). This can be contrasted with the world of corporations and mass production. We are moving from a world of mass-market to personalization via interaction and interactivity in which mass-produced, one-size-fits-all manufactured solutions are replaced in favor of systems that able to produce a tailored niche experience.

Designing clear reputation systems, that help consumers navigate towards the best and right service providers. In a world of diminishing brand loyalty and where the costs of migrating to a new brand are so low, user engagement takes on an unprecedented meaning. This is the real lesson to be taken from the success of the most successful technology ecosystems. For instance, Airbnb or Amazon relies on the "wisdom of the crowd" — as established via an online platform and user reviews — to help consumers make decisions. A combination of software rating algorithms and consumer reviews have become more important than brand loyalty in establishing trust and shaping consumer choice in a digital age.

An additional advantage of this approach is that it reduces the need for traditional advertising and marketing. Instead, successful ecosystems rely on distribution generating "pull" dynamics (attracting more users via the delivery of a meaningful experience) rather than industrial "push" marketing, which relied on the skill of external actors, most obviously advertising agencies and marketing consultants.

A new attitude towards emerging technologies, such as artificial intelligence, sensors, and blockchain, is also important. Such technologies will further facilitate the organization of more and different types of ecosystem. For instance, in an Internet of Things environment, the user experience will be more and more dependent on technology and how it will increase smart connectivity between devices and convenience. Most discussions about ecosystems now revolves around the uses and possibilities of emerging technologies. This makes sense because smart technology is necessary to adequately coordinate people and assets and manage businesses.

Technology-driven ecosystems, therefore, need to exist in a constant state of high alert regarding technological change. And this requires a focus on emerging technologies that may not have any obvious or immediate connection to existing products or services. It is no longer enough to focus on incremental changes that are directly connected to existing operations. A much more open and broader perspective is required. Successful ecosystems do this by recognizing the value of all stakeholders in the value chain, treating them all as key participants in a constantly evolving value creation process, that connects them with developments across multiple technologies to provide innovative and contextualized solutions.

However, developing the right attitude towards technology and acknowledging the centrality of end-users is not enough. The success of an "ecosystem" depends on several other elements.

A Flat, Fluid, Inclusive Organization & Culture

Crucially in an ecosystem, there is a blurring of the borders between the inside and outside of the business (erasing the traditional separation between corporation and market) and the internal vertical divisions and horizontal layers of the corporation (erasing the traditional separation between the production department, marketing department, legal department etc., as well as the different layers of manager, employee, etc.). "Inside" the corporation traditional roles and identities (the manager, the employee, the user) are disrupted. In this way, the hierarchical and static structures of the modern corporation are unbundled, and we see the emergence of more fluid, dynamic identities and roles.

Within this flatter and more fluid organizational structure a crucial role is played by maintaining a network of unbundled high performance, entrepreneurial teams focused on collaboration and co-creation. Decentralized, high-performance teams are driven by a culture of entrepreneurship, and tech-driven innovation is the locus of this style of organization and innovation is situated in a set of loosely coupled, independent units (a network of microenterprises). This style of organization constitutes a network, in the sense that these teams are "small pieces, loosely joined." (*Weinberger, 2003*).

These teams become a site of creativity in which personal expression through responsibility and freedom is encouraged. The key idea is that it has become impossible to engineer a complex, innovative system from the top down. Settled identities of employee, user and companies are obsolete. The transformation of the organization and culture of a business is based on acknowledging that units, teams, and employees are expected to become permanently entrepreneurial. However, more than that, they must also become self-sufficient.

On this account, the true realization of the potential of employees is only be achieved through personal expression, responsibility, and autonomy. This occurs through process of imagination, experimentation, and learning. This also provides a more fulfilling employee experience than that associated with the routinized processes and procedures of a bureaucratized corporation.

Internal competition between these teams is also encouraged within the most successful ecosystems. Chinese company Haier is often cited in this context *(Hamel & Zanini, 2019*). Haier has divided itself into more than 4,000 microenterprises, most of which have less then fifteen employees. Procedures and processes replaced by innovation, creativity, and risk. In the twentieth century, low risk meant minimizing mistakes. In the twenty-first century, errors are embraced as they deliver learning opportunities, and learning is of key importance.

In a flatter and fluid environment, organizational culture becomes crucial. A "best-idea-wins-culture" needs to be embedded in the "DNA" of an ecosystem (*Fenwick & Vermeulen, 2015*). This means embracing the centrality of agility — the ability to move quickly and not spend too much time on any one thing and to retain ability to pivot fast and iterate. It means embracing luck and serendipity (*Hwang & Horowitt, 2012*). Here, the thought is that if you plan everything you cannot be lucky. Too much focus on one direction can become a hindrance. Smart disobedience takes precedence over compliance — you do not get success by doing what you are told. A new "anti-disciplinarity" and relentless commitment to excellence is required — "if you can do this elsewhere, you do not belong here." In short, we are in the world of "compasses over maps" and a successful ecosystem will understand this and adopt such an attitude in all aspects of its organization and culture (The principle of "compasses over maps" is most associated with the *MIT Media Lab, 2012*).

A company that is often cited as having been successful in creating this kind of organization and culture is Netflix (*Randolph, 2019*). In 2009, its founder Reed Hastings pointed out that too many companies have "nice-sounding" value statements, such as integrity, communication, respect, and excellence. However, he understood that these "values" are often not what is really valued within a company and, all too often, are just empty window dressing.

In a 124-page slide deck, Reed Hastings (and Netflix) outlined that the dynamic of this employer-employee relationship needs to be changed (*Heather, 2017*). Moreover, the quality of the working experience and environment now matters so much more. Of particular importance are opportunities for learning and capacity building. As was stated in the slide deck: The actual company values, as opposed to the nice-sounding values, are shown by who gets rewarded, promoted, or let go. This forward-thinking approach to culture helps to attract talented people as it offers them a much greater degree of freedom and responsibility. In the absence of this type of culture, the best young talent will leave. Inside Netflix, it is all about context, not control. The result is that every Netflix employee is treated as an entrepreneur. That the open culture is in the DNA of Netflix is also shown by its ability to attract creators. They are attracted by the creative (and financial) freedom offered by the Netflix platform.

In this way, ecosystems are built around the idea of delivering constant innovation via an open and inclusive process of co-creation. By "organizing-for-innovation" in this way, such ecosystems are radically different from the clearly defined, static roles and fixed hierarchies of traditional organizations.

Open Communication and Information Management

Many problems arise when a business fails to communicate properly with all stakeholders. For instance, YouTube's recurrent difficulties with its content creators have tended to be the result of poor communication. The best ecosystems understand that communication is not a one-way process of information disclosure but, instead, a more engaged, responsive, and open process that dialogue.

In a digital age, many alternative means can now be used for communicating. For instance, business leaders can interact with a company's stakeholders via an "annual letter." Such letters seem to work best when written in a personalized and honest style. A well-documented example of a company that has adopted this type of approach is Amazon. Jeff Bezos' annual letters to investors are considered a "must-read" for anyone with interest in Amazon (and ecosystem companies) (*Gregg & Groysberg, 2019*). What is perhaps most interesting is that these letters not only provide investors and other stakeholders with last year's performance and future developments and growth prospects but also include business advice and insights. It is not surprising that these letters attract enormous attention on social media. They have created significant hype, which makes communication even more personalized, open, and effective.

Genuine engagement, rather than information control, is the most effective approach. Social media and other online media (such as blogs) are becoming more and more important as a forum for disclosing information about a company, both internally and externally. There are many new opportunities and possibilities for more creative forms of information dissemination and sharing.

SOLUTIONS AND RECOMMENDATIONS

Digital Leadership

Finally, there is the question of leadership in a digital age. A key issue here the changing role of the board of directors (*Fenwick & Vermeulen, 2018*). More specifically, a board is expected to perform a more complex range of functions in a successful ecosystem and not be overly focused on monitoring and compliance functions. Of course, compliance remains important, but a board today needs to perform several additional tasks aimed at supporting executives and managers and helping to create an environment for key figures in the ecosystem to make better strategic decisions about the overall direction of the business (*Fenwick, 2016*).These new function are difficult, not least because of the uncertainties regarding the future direction of technology. So, boards need to become much more experimental in their composition. A more diverse expertise becomes importance, for example, relating to consumers, technology, and the Millennial generation, as well as individuals capable of playing "rebellious" roles such as influencer, disruptor, and storyteller.

To successfully transform into a well-functioning ecosystem, leadership is, of course essential. Business leaders should be visionary, entrepreneurial, and innovation minded. They should understand the "platform dynamics." Take Netflix again. When Reed Hastings "let go" of his Head of Communications for repeated use of a racial slur, he showed the importance of leadership. In a memo to Netflix staff, the founder CEO wrote:

I should have done more to use [a first incident] as a learning moment for everyone at Netflix about how painful and ugly that word is, and that it should not be used. I realize that my privilege has made me intellectualize or otherwise minimize race issues like this. I need to set a better example by learning and listening more so I can be the leader we need.

A company's success in becoming an ecosystem is dependent on its leadership and their ability to listen and engage. Business leaders should have a thorough understanding of the ingredients that make a company a successful and ecosystem company.

Ecosystems are not static. The world is constantly changing, and digital technologies are developing exponentially. Successful "ecosystems" can easily lose their appeal in a relatively short period. Also, traditional and social media are quick to portray platforms in a bad light. Particularly, the dominant and more centralized platforms attract much attention. Think Amazon and its treatment of employees, Facebook and the way it deals with privacy, etc.

Nevertheless, businesses that operate as ecosystems are still topping the most attractive employer rankings. Also, other businesses want to become part of such ecosystems. For instance, corporate executives increasingly refer to ecosystems in earning calls.

Moreover, more and more startups realize that by becoming part of an ecosystem company their growth potential and strategic possibilities will be greater than if they remain independent (*Fenwick & Vermeulen, 2016*).

To make this work, it is necessary for the ecosystem to take a different kind of leadership role. Leadership, in this context, means allows the startup to preserve its own identity and culture, whilst enjoying the benefits of being associated with a larger and more established firm (i.e., growing faster, exploiting synergies with other departments or businesses within the "ecosystem." Crucially, this opens the possibility of the startup influencing the culture and practices of the acquiring ecosystem. As illustrated by this possibility, ecosystem leadership involves maintaining a continued openness to change.

These then are the four crucial elements of any successful ecosystem. It should be noted that there is no "one-size-fits-all" model in this context. Ecosystems can take multiple forms ranging from slightly "tweaked" versions of traditional (hierarchical and closed) companies through to the (flat and open) blockchain-based "decentralized autonomous organizations (see *Figure 1*)." The "best" approach depends on the individualized circumstances of a business or organization.

But, this idea of a spectrum of possibilities connects to a final point on ecosystem organization, namely the constant danger of transforming (back) into, a company. Remaining a sustainable ecosystem can be difficult. As ecosystems scale – and particularly when they "go global" – they inevitably come to rely on hierarchical organizational structures. Such structures make a lot of sense as a strategy for managing the complexities of size. The problem is that a hierarchical organization can easily result in the bureaucratization of the platform, i.e., becoming closed, hierarchical and overly bureaucratic. This type of organization worked well in an era of mass-production but is less suited to the dynamic business realities of today. Constant vigilance is required in sustaining the ecosystem model, particularly in larger organizations that operate transnationally.

Figure 1. The Corporate Evolution

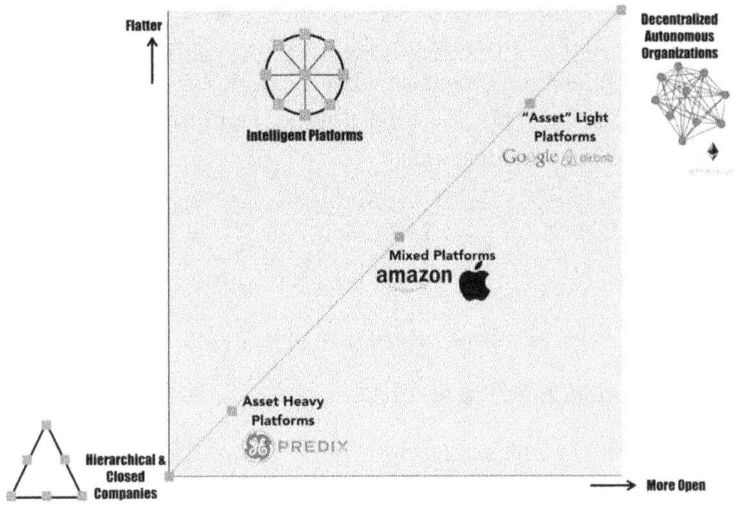

CONCLUSION

Unfortunately, however, many regulatory structures today are not fit for purpose. At least, if the purpose of regulation is understood as facilitating ecosystems and not preserving the corporation. Too much regulation incentivizes the wrong kind of organizational structures, culture, and behavior, and makes leveraging new technologies unnecessarily costly. As described in the first section, company law, including corporate governance, for example, has over recent decades embraced an "agency-cost" frame derived from the work of Berle and Means, and Jenson and Meckling (*Berle & Means, 1932; Jenson & Meckling, 1976*). Regulation has been designed with the goal of maximizing shareholder value and enhancing shareholder-owner control over the firm.

However, this approach does little to address a firm's need to organize for innovation and operate as a sustainable and socially responsible eco-system. Instead, most regulation creates a strong incentive for manager-agents to engage in formalistic compliance and adopt a short-term focus on financial metrics aimed at appeasing shareholders. The current regulatory framework distracts firms from doing what they should be doing to succeed in a networked age. Corporate governance results in costly bureaucratic and legalistic procedures that function as a drain on a firm's resources.

As such, current regulatory approaches and trends are failing business organizations. In short, too much corporate governance is programming institutions to be dysfunctional. There is an ever-widening gap or disconnect between regulatory strategies and the business needs of companies operating in fast-moving global markets. The result? Many businesses and other organizations are ill-equipped to meet the challenges of today's world. Instead, we need to design regulations that incentivize firms to establish the organizational structures and practices that will allow them to succeed. A new paradigm of corporate governance focused on supporting a firm's capacity to innovate – as well as compliance and risk management – needs to be developed.

There is currently an enormous amount of interest in emerging technologies and what it means for business and business regulation. However, the various stakeholders in the corporate governance space are moving at different speeds and in different directions. Everyone is aware that something important is happening, but there is much less agreement on what the digital transformation means for the future of business and business regulation. This is a crucial issue, as those jurisdictions that "get corporate governance law right" stand to benefit enormously.

REFERENCES

Bainbridge, S. M. (2008). *The new corporate governance in theory & practice.* Oxford University Press.

Bakan, J. (2001). *The corporation.* Free Press.

Berle, A., & Means, G. (1932). *The modern corporation & private property.* Transaction Press.

Brown, S. R. (2010). *Merchant kings: When companies ruled the world, 1600–1900.* Macmillan.

Campbell, D., Meyer, M., Xin, L., & Stack, K. (2015). *Haier: Zero distance to the customer.* Harvard Business School Case Study 115-006. Retrieved from https://www.hbs.edu/faculty/Pages/item.aspx?num=49076

Cooke, C. A. (1950). *Corporation, trust, and company: An essay in legal history.* Manchester University Press.

Coolhaas, W. Ph. (Ed.). (1960). *Generate Missiven van Gouverneurs-Generaal en Raden aan Heren XVII der Verenigde Oostindische Compagnie.* Gelderblom.

Corrales, M., Fenwick, M., & Haapio, H. (Eds.). (2019). *Legal Tech, Smart Contracts & Blockchain.* Springer.

Drucker, P. (1946). *The concept of the corporation.* Academic Press.

Fenwick, M. (2016). The new corporate criminal law & transnational legal risk. In M. Fenwick, & S. Wrbka (Eds.), *Flexibility in modern business law: a comparative assessment.* (p. 149). Springer. doi:10.1007/978-4-431-55787-6_8

Fenwick, M., McCahery, J. A., & Vermeuelen, E. P. M. (2019). The end of 'corporate' governance: hello platform governance. *European Business Organization Law Review, 20*(1), 171–199. doi:10.100740804-019-00137-z

Fenwick, M., & Vermeulen, E. P. M. (2015). The New Firm: Staying Relevant, Unique, & Competitive. *European Business Organization Law Review, 16*(4), 595–623. doi:10.100740804-016-0040-4

Fenwick, M., & Vermeulen, E. P. M. (2016). *Seven corporate venturing strategies to foster innovation.* TILEC Discussion Paper No. 2016/23. Retrieved from https://papers.ssrn.com/sol3/papers.cfm?abstract_id=2823008

Fenwick, M., & Vermeulen, E. P. M. (2018). Evaluating the board of directors. *European Corporate Governance Institute Law.* Working Paper No. 425/2018.

Fenwick, M., Vermeulen, E. P. M. (2019). Technology & corporate governance. *The Texas Journal of Business Law, 48*(1).

Fenwick, M., & Vermeulen, E. P. M. (2020). *The unmediated and technology-driven corporate governance of today's winning companies*. New York University Journal of Law and Business.

Galbraith, J. K. (1967). *The new industrial state*. Houghton Mifflin.

Galloway, S. (2017). *The four: The hidden DNA of Amazon, Apple, Facebook, & Google*. Random House.

Gelderblom, O. (2013). *Cities of commerce: The institutional foundations of international trade in the low countries, 1250–1650*. Princeton University Press.

Hadden, T. (1972). *Company law and capitalism*. Weidenfeld & Nicolson.

Hagel, J. (2016). The big shift in business models. *The Marketing Journal*. Retrieved from http://www.marketingjournal.org/the-big-shift-in-business-models-john-hagel/

Hamel, G., & Zanini, M. (2018). The end of bureaucracy. *Harvard Business Review*. Retrieved from https://hbr.org/2018/11/the-end-of-bureaucracy

Harwell, W. (2018). *Research handbook on the history of corporate and company law*. Edward Elgar.

Heather, A. (2017). Is this Netflix presentation Silicon Valley's most important document? *Mindtools*. Retrieved from https://www.mindtools.com/blog/netflix-presentation/

Hoffman, R., Casnocha, B., & Yeh, C. (2014). The Alliance: Managing Talent in a Networked Age. *Harvard Business Review*.

Hwang, V. W., & Horowitt, G. (2012). *The Rainforest: The Secret to Building the Next Silicon Valley*. Regenweld.

Jenson, M. C., & Meckling, W.H. (1976). Theory of the Firm: Managerial Behavior, Agency Costs and Ownership Structure. *Journal of Finance & Economics, 3*(305).

Kay, J. (2019). The Concept of the Corporation' (2019). *Business History, 61*(7), 1129–1143. Accessed 20 August2019. doi:10.1080/00076791.2018.1509956

Lawrence, M. A. (2017). Financialism: A (Very) Brief History. In *Understanding the 12 Technological Forces that Will Shape Our Future*. Academic Press.

McCahery, J. A., & Vermeulen, E. P. M. (2009). Corporate Governance of Non-Listed Companies Oxford University Press.

McKinsey Global Institute. (2017). *Artificial Intelligence: The Next Digital Frontier?* Retrieved from: https://www.mckinsey.com/~/media/McKinsey/Industries/Advanced%20Electronics/Our%20Insights/How%20artificial%20intelligence%20can%20deliver%20real%20value%20to%20companies/MGI-Artificial-Intelligence-Discussion-paper.ashx

Micklethwait, J., & Wooldridge, A. (2005). *The Company: A Short History of a Revolutionary Idea*. Weidenfeld.

MIT Media Lab. (2012). Retrieved from http://blog.media.mit.edu/2012/07/compasses-over-maps.html

Moazed, A., & Johnson, N. J. (2016). *Modern Monopolies: What it Takes to Dominate the Twenty First Century Economy*. St. Martin's Press.

Parker, G. G., Van Alstyne, M. W.,, ., & Shandgeet, P. C. (2016). *Platform Revolution: How Networked Markets are Transforming the Economy and How to Make them Work for You*. Penguin.

Primavera, D. F., & Wright, A. (2018). *Blockchain & the Law*. Harvard University Press.

Randolph, M. (2019). *That Will Never Work: The Birth of Netflix and the Amazing Life of an Idea*. Little, Brown and Company.

River, C. (2017). *The Dutch East India Company: The History of the World's First Multinational Corporation*. Createspace.

Stern, J. P. (2016). The English East India Company and the Modern Corporation: Legacies, Lessons, and Limitations. *Seattle University Law Review*, (39), 423.

Tricia, G., & Groysberg, B. (2019). Amazon over the years, based on Jeff Bezos's letters to shareholders. *Harvard Business Review*. Retrieved from https://hbr.org/2019/05/amazons-priorities-over-the-years-based-on-jeff-bezoss-letters-to-shareholders

Weinber, D. (2003). *Small Pieces, Loosely Joined: A Unified Theory of the Web*. Basic Books.

West, S. (2018). Meeting Millennial Expectations in Four Areas of Technology. *Forbes*. Retrieved from: https://www.forbes.com/sites/forbestechcouncil/2018/06/28/meeting-millennial-expectations-in-these-four-areas-of-technology/#3e7c9b244ffc

Williams, A., & Zumbansen, P. (Eds.). (2011). *The Embedded Firm: Corporate Governance, Labor, and Finance Capitalism*. Cambridge University Press. doi:10.1017/CBO9780511794537

Wu, T. (2016). *The Attention Merchants: The Epic Scramble to Get Inside Our Heads*. Vintage.

Zumbansen, P. (Ed.). (2011). The Embedded Firm: Corporate Governance, Labor, and Finance Capitalism. Cambridge University Press.

Zumbansen, P. (2011). *The New Embeddedness of the Corporation*. Williams & Peer.

KEY TERMS AND DEFINITIONS

Corporation: In this chapter, the term 'corporation' is used to refer to limited liability joint stock companies, both publicly traded corporations and private ('closely held') companies. As such, single proprietorships and partnerships are excluded from our definition of a corporation. The definition used here, therefore, differs from a broader, more everyday definition of a company as any organization that engages in business.

Empty Corporation: This is a corporation in which the relationships of the company are defined by contract and circumscribed by corporate law like the nexus of contracts; it denies the reality of the corporation as social unit.

Chapter 2
Stakeholder Engagement in the Digital Era

Mikhail Y. Kuznetsov
https://orcid.org/0000-0001-5657-8184
Moscow State University, Russia

Valeria Solovyova
TopCompetence, Russia

Maria I. Nikishova
https://orcid.org/0000-0002-8089-1899
Financial University Under the Government of the Russian Federation, Russia

Maria Olshanskaya
https://orcid.org/0000-0002-5792-500X
Moscow Open Social University, Russia

ABSTRACT

The chapter discusses the issues of corporate interaction of stakeholders in the digital age. The authors identified the characteristic features and practices of the interaction of companies with various categories of stakeholders. The study analyzed key stakeholders of the companies, channels of interaction, and significant topics for discussion. The authors note the importance of the process of managing interaction with stakeholders, balance of interests, building an understandable communication strategy in the process of digital business transformation.

INTRODUCTION

To survive in a constantly changing environment, today companies need to respond to all ongoing external and internal changes that affect the success of the business, quickly and accurately. The stakeholder theory, being a strategic management approach, enables companies and its executives to understand and manage these changes that impact not only the internal environment of the organization, but also

DOI: 10.4018/978-1-7998-2011-6.ch002

the external business environment. Despite its relatively short history, the theory of stakeholders has become widespread now.

The appearance of the first full-fledged theory of stakeholders is closely connected with the publication of E. Freeman's Strategic Management: A Stakeholder Approach in 1984 (Freeman, 1894). According to Freeman, the actions and activities of persons (a group of persons) that influence or are influenced by the company in achieving its strategic goals should not be ignored, and their impact, real or perceived, should be determined and taken into account in the decision-making process. Stakeholders may have no direct impact on the company; however, their indirect influence should also be considered. Stakeholders' impact and interests should be studied and analyzed to build and improve the company's strategy. This process is included in stakeholder management, which involves identifying stakeholders and maintaining their commitment. The key objective of stakeholder management is to create an environment for business to develop successfully.

In the era of communication development, the effectiveness of an organization depends on how well it is engaging its stakeholders. Stakeholder engagement helps the organization to increase its social capital, minimize non-financial risks and identify new opportunities for the company's development. Given that, understanding of key mechanisms of engaging groups of stakeholders allows large organizations to improve their performance, increase profits and create a competent, relevant and effective sustainable development strategy for the future and, therefore, achieve the entire set of goals and succeed.

Research Topic: stakeholder engagement in the digital age.
Research Goal: to analyze the practices of building corporate communication with stakeholders, to identify and describe the range of practices applied by large organizations to inform stakeholders / discuss companies' activities with stakeholders, based on information disclosed in public annual reports.
Research Target: formats of stakeholder engagement.
Research Scope: stakeholder engagement: a case study of 100 companies.

The research method is a desk study of annual reports of large European, Asian and North American companies for 2017–2018 of the Global Reporting Initiative (GRI) database.

Research Objectives:

- To study information disclosed by large organizations in their public annual (non-financial, integrated) reports on their interaction with stakeholders.
- To identify main trends and/or patterns/ distinctive features of stakeholder engagement by large organizations around the world based on the analysis of their annual reports.

STAKEHOLDERS' ROLE IN THE ERA OF DIGITIZATION

The role of stakeholders is growing significantly in the era of digitization. Here digitization means digital presentation of information, use of modern digital technologies resulting in increased economic efficiency.

PwC's study (PwC, 2018) showed that 41% of Board of Directors members consider the development and implementation of innovative technologies to be a key factor of the organization's success. They believe that investing in information analysis resources is the surest way to meet the changing needs of shareholders, consumers and other stakeholders.

Back in 1984, R. Freeman's theory of stakeholders (Freeman, 1894) gave attention to a tendency towards an increase in the number of stakeholders as well as their role in the organization's success.

According to the analysis performed by the Consulting & Analytical Center SustainAbility Ltd (O'Neill, 2018), organizations have recognized the importance of stakeholder engagement: taking their interests into account helps identify violations and develop successful business strategies.

Practices applied by organizations to engage stakeholders are very diverse, but there are several common areas:

1. *All stakeholders are important.* Although it is important to interact with all types of stakeholders, increased awareness of environmental and social issues makes organizations focus primarily on key participants in corporate relations, such as consumers, investors, etc.
2. *Increased attention to the satisfaction of mutual interests.* The strategies of many companies are shifting from one-way communication to a dialog.
3. *Varying degrees of control.* Organizations differ in their degree of stakeholder engagement centralization.
4. *Increased transparency.* Stakeholder engagement activities are disclosed in corporate information materials, including public annual reports.

What Role Do Stakeholders Play in Organizations' Activity?

Firstly, they help enhance and maintain the company's reputation. According to some organizations, close interaction with stakeholders is a kind of a 'license for success.'

Secondly, understanding the role of participants in corporate relations and considering their opinions and interests helps companies to foresee risks that could be missed if only an internal analysis was performed. This provides an undoubted advantage in the competitive environment.

Thirdly, such engagement could improve the decision-making system. There is increasing evidence that listening to different points of view contributes to making the right decisions and finding extraordinary solutions.

Summarizing the above, the authors can conclude that by engaging stakeholders and taking into account their interests, the organization maximizes its chances to achieve sustainable commercial success, as it increases its knowledge, which has a direct impact on planning, mitigates the risk associated with making individual and collective decisions, and multiplies the chances to solve systemic problems positively through cooperation.

According to external stakeholders, companies should adhere to the following principles in their operations (O'Neill, 2018):

Table 1. Classification of stakeholders by level of their impact on the company's target function (compiled by the authors)

Groups of stakeholders	Impact on the company's target function	Specific indicator of the stakeholder's impact on the company value
Government authorities	Interfere, regulate and control, at a legislative level, certain aspects of the company's activities	Volume of tax deductions
Professional public associations	Establish standards, guidelines and frameworks for relations between a business and a community of practice	Labor productivity, high-tech jobs
Consumers	Direct targeted influence	Sales revenue
Shareholders/owners	Make strategic decisions on how to carry out activities and develop the company	Cost of equity
Executives (top managers)	Impact on the achievement of the company's strategic goals	Profitability
Managers and employees	Direct impact on the quality and speed of managerial decision implementation	Labor productivity
Investors and lenders	Direct impact as a source of finance for the company's investment activity	Cost of borrowing
Competitors	Indirect impact on the necessity to develop competitive advantages	Market share
Suppliers	Direct impact on the company's costs	Cost of sales
Media	Impact on the public opinion and the organization's image	Market value of the company's stock

Source: Furta & Solomatina, 2010; Novozhilova, 2017

- Transparency: disclosure of information on significant issues of the organization's activities is a vital component of stakeholder engagement.
- Trust: building strong relationships depends on trust and mutual respect.
- Coherence: this refers both to the coherence in relations with specific participants in corporate relations and to the intra-company coherence in relations with various stakeholders.
- Ambition: system-level problems require companies to take a serious approach to finding solutions for engaging those stakeholders that may help move the system, even if it is difficult to work with them.
- Accountability: the main expectation of stakeholders relates to the demonstration of engagement results and consequences.

Digitization and the use of digital technologies by companies make these principles more feasible. To interact with a company, business clients often seek information about its activities and services. The more transparent the disclosed data is, the higher the level of trust and the likelihood of future relationships are. In this context, the companies' websites and the digitization of services provided by them are of great importance: the ability to communicate via the Internet or electronic centers, online payments, smart contracts, remote release of goods or provision of services (Russian Customs Academy, n.d.), if available, contribute to increasing the loyalty of consumers and other stakeholders.

A smart contract as a computer technology that performs specific operations without human intervention also makes it possible to control the supply chain and, therefore, mitigates the risks related to interaction with suppliers and changes their role (Khalin & Chernova, 2018).

Given that, the digitization process makes the activities of organizations more transparent. Greater transparency also facilitates information sharing and eliminates competition in its consumption, which expands the pool of stakeholders with different expectations and aggressive means to keep companies stick to their obligations and increases their role (Future 500, 2018).

The increased number of corporate relation participants owning minimal resources, but able to have a significant impact on the organization, forces companies to create/revise their strategies to eliminate unforeseen situations and to reduce risks.

Representatives of federal and regional authorities in the era of digitization can take control over organizations' activities to a new level of quality. Digital technologies enable remote and automatic transfer of data on financial and operational components of the company's activity, check taxes, etc., which also reduces the risk for interacting parties.

For example, a comprehensive assessment of material and industry indicators will almost certainly reveal new and unfamiliar problems or new and unfamiliar stakeholders. Such stakeholders include active stakeholders and minorities, advocacy groups, various communities studying environmental issues, problems of social stratification, the use of renewable energy, etc., as well as sponsors and various environmental funds.

According to the report prepared by Future 500, a non-profit consulting company (Future 500, 2018), the management of organizations is more than ever aware of the external pressure by stakeholders in the field of sustainable development. Therefore, companies must be more focused on these topics, paying attention to social and environmental issues, including rejecting plastic waste, stopping the manufacture of products containing chemicals that are toxic and dangerous to nature and humans, using green technologies in the supply chain etc. Maintaining a balance of economic, social and environmental priorities also helps attract investors.

From another point of view, the advantage of digitization is the exclusion of intermediaries, since manufacturers can sell goods / provide services via a website, and consumers can choose on their own (Khalin & Chernova, 2018).

Information technology development entails new IT risks, such as dishonest customers and consumers, digital fraud and piracy. Therefore, digitization requires that close attention should be paid not only to sustainable development management, but to information security management as well (Gordeeva & Petrova, 2018).

Summing up all of the above, it can be noted that in the digitization era, the stakeholder pool is increasing, which, first and foremost, is due to increased transparency of companies supported by the use of various digital technologies, such as fog computing, blockchain, neural networks, supercomputer, distributed registry technologies and etc. However, it does not seem possible to give an unequivocal estimate of stakeholders' role. According to the world's best practices, a corporate strategy that considers stakeholders' interests is an important factor of the company's competitiveness and business performance, that reduces the likelihood of unforeseen risks and improves the quality of decision-making.

To make their interaction with participants in corporate relations more efficient, organizations should pay special attention to sustainable development and stakeholder engagement trends in the digital era.

STAKEHOLDER ENGAGEMENT TRENDS IN THE DIGITAL ERA

Modern organizations are increasingly recognizing that stakeholder engagement is critical for developing successful business strategies.

Although interaction with stakeholders and their engagement in the course of the company's activities is quite common, there are no generally accepted best practices in this field, that is why many organizations are still trying to determine the right approach.

Stakeholder engagement is a process by which companies build and maintain dialog-based relationship with individuals and organizations. It can take various forms, including unilateral information disclosure, interaction via social networks, events, stakeholder advisory boards, partnerships, etc.

Previous non-digital methods for engaging stakeholders were quite expensive due to constantly recurring, labor-intensive processes, travel expenses, and time-consuming activities. The digital approach has reduced these costs (Future 500, 2018).

A specific element of stakeholder engagement is the ability to manage key groups of stakeholders at the individual level. Virtual environment enables engaging stakeholders as if companies met with them face-to-face while there is no need to buy plane tickets and leave the office (Tractivity, 2018).

All this makes it possible to track their preferences and needs with high probability and accuracy. This accuracy helps the company communicate the information a stakeholder is interested in, in a format which is convenient to digest and in which it is likely to be read and understood. For example, some stakeholders would not like emails since they prefer communicating in person (this can be done using videoconferencing or just a phone). Others will avoid social networks since they prefer traditional corporate means of communication, such as corporate mail. It can be noted that the digital approach allows companies to respond to emerging issues more quickly and always be in the know. Companies using new digital technologies to communicate with stakeholders are perceived by them as more advanced and future-oriented partners. Digitization makes it possible to improve the manufacturing and business activities and to increase the transparency of operations, performance, and, therefore, the competitiveness of the company.

There is a variety of ways to engage stakeholders. If any stakeholder wants to know more about a company and contact it, the first thing it can do is visit its official website or another service to get data and make initial evaluation (including by reading feedback about that company).

The most common way to interact with clients/customers is CRM systems. This software is used to automate client/customer engagement strategies, maximize sales, optimize marketing and improve the quality of service by storing customer information and the history of relationships with them, as well as to analyze results.

Another thing to be noted is cloud technologies (cloud computing): they also facilitate interaction among stakeholders and enable simultaneous work with the same data by several users, etc.

ELEVATE's LaborLink is a mobile technology platform that allows factory workers to raise questions about working conditions anonymously via their smartphones.

In the modern world, much attention is paid to social networks, such as Instagram, Twitter, Facebook, VK.com, Telegram, etc. They allow keeping track of stakeholders' opinions, especially potential customers, share the company's position on certain issues and events, as well as communicate through Correspondence (O'Neill, 2018).

In addition, online-forums, analytic and crowdsourcing platforms are often used to expand the pool of stakeholders and engage them.

IOT (Internet of Things), Big Data, social networks and many other tools, the number of which is increasing every year, are used in the modern world to optimize and improve the quality of interaction with stakeholders.

These technologies are valuable as they facilitate establishing trusting relationships through quick feedback and thereby help to promote the business's reputation in the eyes of each stakeholder.

In conclusion, the authors can say that the number of stakeholders is increasing in the digital era and their needs are increasing as well. New IT solutions can help the business to satisfy such needs. Such solutions may have several shortcomings, but, nevertheless, if a business is not good at applying them, it cannot win any trust and full attention of its stakeholders.

DYNAMICS IN DEVELOPMENT OF RELATIONS WITH STAKEHOLDERS

In the 2000s, during the transition from a command system of management to a market economy that required a new management style from the companies operating at that time, few top executives cared about stakeholder engagements. That statement can be indirectly confirmed by the fact that practice guidance on how to engage stakeholders came out only in 2002. In October 2002, participants in the UNEP annual consultative meeting with industry associations declared their desire to have a guidance that would help them to arrange a focused dialog with stakeholders. UNEP launched a study covering a dozen leading corporations (Scherbachenko, 2018). The results of the study showed that the approaches applied and the problems arising differ depending on the group to which the stakeholder belonged. However, according to M. Freeman's concept (1894), companies' senior top management should consider stakeholders' interest when developing the company's strategy.

In the 2010s, stakeholders' ability to impact the activities of companies increased. Companies began to disclose these aspects in their reports more often (most often in annual reports or in reports on sustainable development) and consider the opinions of various groups of stakeholders in their decision-making process. To perform analysis, companies usually use various techniques and models already outlined earlier in this study. Furthermore, companies may even create job positions or departments that are directly responsible for engaging stakeholders, which means that companies agree deliberately to increase their costs (payroll, consumables, office equipment, etc.) in order to ensure effective work in that field.

In 2012, the leaders of the world's largest companies were surveyed (PWC, 2013) to determine stakeholders' impact on companies' strategies. According to CEOs, the business strategy is notably impacted by customers and buyers (97% of respondents believe that this group, to a greater or lesser extent, impacts their business), competitors (90%), government (85%), employees (83%), supply chain partners (76%), lenders and investors (75%). Slightly more than half of respondents (53%) believe that the media do not play any or play just an insignificant role in determining the business strategy; 50% believe that users of social networks do not have any impact on business.

At the same time, 92% of respondents said that they are going to increase the engagement of social networks users in strategy development. This trend is expected to become stronger due to a rapid growth in the number of social networks users as well as to a significant increase in the overall number of Internet users.

Over the past five years, CEOs have become more focused on issues of sustainable development and, as a result, the role of stakeholders has increased. According to the study held in 2013 (PWC, 2014), most CEOs around the world noted an increase in trust displayed by their buyers (52%), partners (42%) and lenders and investors (43%). At the same time, top executives in the BRICS countries, Western Europe and the United States say that employees' confidence is falling: 9%, 14% and 15% respectively. 45% of CEOs from the United States report a decrease in media confidence while 56% — in confidence from the government and regulatory agencies. 30% of CEOs from Western Europe indicated a decrease in confidence from financial and credit organizations.

Digitization of business activities, including the automation of business processes, the use of cloud computing, mathematical modeling, blockchain technologies, neural networks and supercomputer technologies, helps simplify interactions and relationships between stakeholders, save time, reduce the negative impact of the human factor and increase the level of corporate culture, competitiveness and effectiveness of the organization as a whole. Digitization development entails a lot of limitations and barriers. According to the results of a survey conducted in 2016 (PWC, 2017), CEOs think the most important risk that could affect the management of stakeholders to be personal data compromise and violation of ethical standards (93%); cybersecurity system hacking with a damage to business information or the organization's main systems (91%); interruptions and failures in IT operations (90%); and risks associated with the use of social networks (88%).

Today, in the era of the digital economy, the mechanisms of interactions between various groups of stakeholders, shareholders and top executives is also changing. For example, in 2016 Hitachi Corporation announced the creation of an open platform for corporate process management (Mitchell, Agle & Wood, 1997). This platform facilitates engaging stakeholders in the company's activities. M. V. Dmitrievich (Dmitrievich, 2017) believes that companies may choose to include representatives of stakeholders in their board of directors within the period in question. Moreover, he thinks that the widespread use of artificial intelligence in business development and corporate governance processes may lead to the transformation of boards of directors into open virtual 'hubs' with stakeholders being involved in the decision-making process, as well as to potential conflicts of interest between stakeholders as the owners of digital tokens, and developers of intelligent systems.

ELECTRONIC CHANNELS FOR STAKEHOLDER ENGAGEMENT IN THE DIGITAL ERA

Interaction with consumers is the top priority of stakeholder engagement (Evseeva, 2012). Many companies have succeeded in this field; such interaction becomes one of the company's competitive strengths. CRM (Customer Relationship Management) system is a very useful technology to this end. It accumulates information about all aspects of interaction with customers, helps to get an insight into customer expectations and the ways to meet them, and find effective customer engagement methods. Information about customers is registered in the database as it is received by the company. This information is then transferred to the operational systems of companies, i.e. hotline centers or process management systems.

Customer data (their purchase history, preferences) accumulated and processed using this technology enable developing a unique offering that would likely to appeal to consumers. Where the customer flow is large, only information technology may help implement this approach. Such customer support reduces the company's costs, increases customer satisfaction level, strengthens their loyalty to the company and, as a result, the company's income goes up.

The strength of the CRM technology is the reliability and relevance of incoming customer data, which can be achieved through a constant stream of new customer data. Customer engagement methods will be effective if conclusions about their expectations are drawn based on relevant information. Employees should understand the value of customer data and constantly enter and update that information in the database.

The organization's strategic cooperation with its external stakeholders is beneficial to both counterparts. Using information received from consumers and other counterparts, the company strengthens its competitive advantages, maintains and develops its core competencies.

Trusting relationship between the organization and its stakeholders is its key success factor. The SRM (Supplier Relationship Management) system is intended to manage such interactions, which implies determining the company's relations with all suppliers, identifying their needs, developing long-term and productive cooperation with them and strengthening resulting competitive advantages of the organization. Effective interaction between the company and suppliers requires the ability to keep track of correlations between its activities and stakeholders' interests. Having determined this correlation, the company will be able to plan further cooperation with key suppliers.

The aspects important for customers include the quality of goods and services (Evseeva, 2012), a wide range of available products, flexible pricing, high-level service, attentive and respectful attitude of employees, etc. Employees want fair wages, job autonomy, opportunities for additional education, professional growth and participation in creative projects. Suppliers expect strict adherence to concluded agreements, long-term contracts, and financial well-being of their partner. Investors would appreciate the company's progress in key areas of its activity, financial standing, guarantees of return on their investments, etc.

At the same time, the company's interaction with stakeholders may take different forms (Accountability, 2005):

- studying the needs of stakeholders and exchanging information with them through CRM, organizing a system for proposals and feedback, publishing reports, statutory documents, social reporting in the media and on the Internet, providing the requested information unless such provision conflicts the interests of the company;
- making and performing agreements with partners and government authorities in various areas of economic, environmental, social and cultural activities;
- submitting proposals to the government authorities regarding the development of the regions where the company operates, etc.

A network of relations based on trust between the company and its stakeholders is a vital condition for enhancing their cooperation. The operation of such a network is ensured through forums, various conferences, portals that support sharing knowledge between all participants in such interaction.

The era of digitization opens the door to different researches. Data processing technologies and transparency heighten the focus on social and environmental issues. Advanced technologies (Deloitte, 2016) are used to analyze the needs of stakeholders in all areas of the company's activity.

1. Innovative environment analysis technologies for strategic decision making.
    - Big Data analytics to predict trends in the emergence / development of innovations and their impact on the market and the company's structure. For example, software that has information about M&A transactions made in the market and their consequences analyzes the external environment and helps make decisions regarding the appropriateness of a M&A transaction by providing a price estimate.
    - Big Data analysis to study consumers' needs.
    - The robot program monitors the activity in the startup market, studies new patents, and identifies a trend in technology development.
2. Support for local social institutions and business communities. An element of corporate social responsibility which involves, for example:
    - Financial support for representatives of small businesses and budget institutions;
    - Free-of charge transfer of obsolete equipment to social institutions;
    - Transfer of idle equipment and/or free rooms to local entrepreneurs for temporary use.
3. Information transparency for external audiences. Disclosure of beneficiaries, facts of the company's activity, photographs working and non-working moments, interviews with employees and other data previously known only by the staff are communicated via external sources (website, media, social networks). Information transparency enhances customer loyalty and promotes the employer's brand.
4. Use of the Pro bono approach. Pro bono professional services being rendered to increase corporate social responsibility. For example: legal services to non-profit organizations or private medical centers' free-of charge services to those in need.
5. Creation of jobs and development clusters. Placement of the company's assets in regions where they may have a socially significant effect in terms of creating jobs, developing intellectual potential of the local community, cultivating conditions for attracting investments to the region. The solution is aimed not only at increasing the reputation and customer loyalty, but also contributes to the development of corporate culture and motivates employees.

A developed system of communication between the company and its stakeholders plays a special role in the stakeholder engagement development: receiving feedback from stakeholders in written or other forms, using hotlines, holding conferences in various formats and at different levels, communicating in the virtual space, involving stakeholders in the study of problems and preparation of reports and plans, using focus groups, meetings, profile committees made up from representatives of stakeholders and the company, creating controlling groups, multilateral forums, alliances, partnerships, joint projects with the involvement of stakeholders.

Public companies are usually interested in timely and complete disclosure of information about all aspects of their activities to stakeholders. Information management is an essential aspect of stakeholder engagement in the digital era. The best management tools and practices in this area are as follows:

6. Infonomics. A concept involving effective information management, including volume optimization, increased usability, and reduced search and processing time. The following approaches are used:
    - The simple language rule: all communications (including correspondence) should be in layman's terms understandable to most employees.
    - The 'Occam's razor' principle means using the optimal amount of communication tools, for example: if intra-company communication can be carried out through 5 different channels (Lync, Email, WhatsApp, Viber and Skype), it is recommended to choose and go with any 2 tools in order to avoid the risk of information loss.
7. Community of practice. This involves creating thematic communities of hyper-focused experts (based on specialization, experience, education, area of interest, etc.) to ensure intra-organizational consulting support on an ad-hock basis (upon request). The composition of the community of practice does not depend on the functional, industry, hierarchical affiliation of its members.
8. Cloud storage technologies. They make it possible to create a corporate cloud-based data warehouse for storing/processing client requests, archival materials, project documentation, regular reporting and other information. The tool reduces operating expenses on IT support and accelerates data management.
9. Confluence platforms. A unified wiki type knowledge base is created across the organization, which allows generation of an unlimited number of workspaces to place wiki pages and logical organization of content (using tags, indexes, cross-references, search, hierarchy and other functionality). It makes searching for required information more convenient and promotes a more efficient knowledge sharing.
10. Use of modern communication channels. Mobile communication channels (WhatsApp, Viber, Telegram, etc.) are used to make business communication/decision-making quicker and less formal the tool helps create a unified information space within divisions/teams and make their interaction more effective.

The foregoing enables us to draw the following conclusions. One of the ways for a company to gain competitive advantages is develop its relations with stakeholders. Its efforts in this area can be facilitated by CRM and SRM systems that enable accumulating information about everything related to interaction with customers, provide insights into customers' expectations and effective ways to implement them and to engage consumers, employees, partners, investors, etc. Design-thinking can be also called a new, innovative approach to building companies' activity in cooperation with stakeholders, which is based on intuition and the ability to determine patterns and visual symbols, to develop ideas that are not only functional, but also emotionally significant.

ANALYSIS OF STAKEHOLDER ENGAGEMENT BY COMPANIES BASED ON THEIR ANNUAL REPORTS

To analyze the practice of building corporate communications with stakeholders and to identify a range of practices used by large companies to inform stakeholders / discuss the companies' activities with stakeholders on the basis of information disclosed in their public annual reports, the authors have analyzed 100 annual reports published in 2018 to 2019 in the report database of the Global Reporting Initiative (GRI, n.d.).

The study was an in-depth analysis of companies' interaction and cooperation with stakeholders, identifying the main groups whose interests are most closely connected with the activity of the company and can have the most notable impact on the efficiency and implementation of strategic goals. An important point was also to identify communication means and channels for maintaining an ongoing dialog.

In addition, a range of issues and problems most often covered when working with key stakeholder groups was identified in the course of the study.

The study has covered important stakeholder management issues:

- Identification of specific groups of stakeholders;
- Identification of mechanisms and channels used for communication and interaction;
- Creation a list of key issues raised during the above process.

The purpose of the research is to determine and describe the main trends in the spectrum of practices used by large organizations to inform various groups of stakeholders or get answers to exciting questions in the digitalization era.

The objectives of the study are to find answers to the following questions:

- Which type of stakeholders companies are interacting with?
- Which issues are usually discussed in the communication presses?
- What methods and channels are used to communicate?
- What mechanisms of interaction with stakeholders do companies use?
- What digital technologies are used to interact with stakeholders?
- How to build efficient interactions with stakeholders?

Filters used to select companies' annual reports for analysis (GRI, n.d.):

Sector: Agriculture, automotive, aviation, chemicals, commercial services, conglomerates, construction, energy, energy utilities, forest and paper, logistics, metals products, mining, railroad, retailers, waste, water utilities (17 sectors)

Countries: 96

Report Type: GRI – G4, GRI – Standards, Citing – GRI

Regions: Asia, North America, Europe

Report year: 2017, 2018

In general, the authors can note that today companies identify key stakeholders, analyze their interests in one way or another, evaluate their relationship with them, identify key issues and include interaction results related to such issues in their reports intended for a wide range of stakeholders. However, companies have not developed any unified mechanism for managing stakeholders yet. Companies apply

Table 2. Core results of the study of stakeholder engagement by companies (compiled by the authors)

Core groups of stakeholders	Key issues raised in the course of interaction with stakeholders	Main channels of impact	Comments
Suppliers/ vendors	• Bribery and corruption prevention • Quality of goods and services • Reputation • Ethical and business practices • Safe working environment • Logistics issues • Safety and stability of cooperation • Costs and deliveries	• Annual meetings • Seminars and trainings • Targeted visits • Supplier assessment • Visits to and audits of suppliers	Constant interaction and communication with suppliers strengthen trust and understanding between organizations. This, in turn, will help stakeholders to evaluate the company's actions and determine the area for development.
Consumers/ customers	• Quality of goods and services • Assessment of products • Reputation • Support for customers' activities • High-quality service • Reliability of information provided • Environmental balance	• Activities based on open dialogs, meetings with customers; Open Door days • Information stands • Qualitative and quantitative surveys • Cultural events • Services to customers through mobile applications • Customers' visits/ field trips to the company • Website • Loyalty program • Social networks • Report on sustainable development • Complaint handling	The effectiveness of the company's approach to engaging consumers can be measured based on feedback, comments, survey results, company perception ratings, which helps to find ways to transform its activities and improve its service quality.
Government authorities and regulators	• Regulation of law-based activity • Implementation of ethical principles and corporate culture • Equal employment opportunities • Environmental protection (climate change) • Analysis and control over industrial emissions • Stability of economic indicators • Respect for human rights • Cooperation between the private and public sectors • Improving standards and compliance • Gender equality • Modernization of equipment and work processes	• Conferences • Official dialogs • Monthly review and agency-level meetings • Public hearings • Meetings devoted to updated environmental regulatory requirements • Ethical programs • Industrial conferences and networking events	
Media	• Innovation • Organization's economic development index • Social programs • Maintenance of mutually beneficial and trusting relations with stakeholders • Improved procedure for identifying the company's risks and opportunities in connection with sustainability issues (Risk management) • Safety quality • Relevance of loyalty programs • Corporate social responsibility • Gender equality • Modernization of working processes • Reputation	• Website • Report on sustainable development • Promotional campaigns • Social networks • Face-to-face meetings with media representatives • Official presentations and open seminars • Press-release • Media monitoring • Interview	
Local communities	• Social and environmental responsibility (climate change) • Quality of life • Occupational health and safety • Infrastructure and development of communities • Respect for human rights • Development of communication channels • Compliance with industry's standards	• Agency-level meetings • Website • Public hearings • Membership in various industrial and professional associations • Trade fairs • Assessment of interactions • Social programs • Publications in media sources • Annual survey • Cooperation and collaboration with various educational institutions and laboratories	Cooperation with local communities help organizations to reveal issues and shortcomings and to review the company's policy. Organizations use both official and unofficial methods of interaction with communities
Shareholders/ investors	• Integrity of the company's assets and safety of its operations • Circular economy • Loan terms • Dividends • Financial indicators • Corporate responsibility and governance • Quality of services and products delivered	• Ethical programs • Face-to-face meetings • Official general meeting of shareholders • Briefings on sustainability issues • Presentations and publications of reports • Annual general conferences with shareholders • Meetings of analysts and investors • Information center • IR	

continued on following page

Table 2. Continued

Core groups of stakeholders	Key issues raised in the course of interaction with stakeholders	Main channels of impact	Comments
Employees	• Gender equality • Salary and remuneration level • Working hours • Equal employment opportunities • Environmental responsibility • Occupational health and safety • Opinions on management issues • Reputation • Ethics and corporate culture • Employment and career development opportunities • Organization's performance and accomplishments • Readiness for emergencies • Respect for human rights • Compliance with the terms of employment	• Complaint handling • Workshops and trainings • Official and unofficial meetings • Online-consultations • Monthly review meetings • Employee surveys • Publications and promotion in the media • Coordination meetings • OHS meetings • Masterclasses and workshops • Corporate website • Field visits to improve the employees' knowledge • Social programs • Annual meetings • Direct e-mailing	
Competitors	• Fair competition • Partnership in related industries • Economic development issues • Integrity constraint	• Participation in seminars • Face-to-face agency-level meetings • Monthly review meetings	
Strategic partners	• Rational use of natural resources • Control of quality of goods and services • Opinion on the governance and strategy to ensure sustainable development of the company • Global trends and changes • Corporate culture and values • Plans in relation the company's performance and accomplishments • Procurement of raw materials and their delivery cost	• Face-to-face business meetings • Monthly meetings to discuss trends • Membership of associations • Assessment of interactions • Business conferences • Strategy development and improvement • Social dialogs • Joint projects • Meetings to discuss existing projects	Organizations strive to implement the world's best professional standards. One of the priorities is maintaining relations with business partners in compliance with the Code of Conduct in order to improve the quality of services or goods produced.

Source: companies' annual public reports

the stakeholder management process fragmentarily; they have no single policy or strategic approach to stakeholder engagement.

Thus, the analysis of the relations between companies and stakeholders indicate that nowadays the approach to and practices of stakeholder engagement management are mostly based on traditional corporate communication tools.

SOLUTIONS AND RECOMMENDATIONS

As a result of the study, the authors come to the following solutions:

1. Most of the companies whose reports were covered by the study list the following key groups of stakeholders: suppliers/vendors, consumers/customers, government agencies/regulators, media, local communities, shareholders/investors, employees, competitors and strategic partners.
2. The vast majority (6 out of 9) of main stakeholder groups identified during the study are concerned about working environment issues (including corporate culture/ethics) and respect for human rights.
3. The majority (5 out of 9) of main stakeholder groups identified during the study are concerned about issues of environmental aspects of companies' operations.
4. The most popular and effective way to interact with the groups of stakeholders (for 9 groups out of 9) is holding various kinds of meetings, including face-to-face meetings, with representatives of these groups.
5. Researches (analysis) of the company's interaction with certain groups of stakeholders and interviews with representatives of such groups are other most common types of interaction between companies and groups of stakeholders (9/9).

6. All organizations whose reports have been analyzed rate high a transparent and regular dialog with stakeholders in order to ensure maximum mutual understanding of development issues, problems and opportunities. The management of most companies believes that stakeholder engagement in their activities helps them reduce the negative impact on areas that stakeholders are particularly sensitive to.
7. 99% of the companies whose reports have been analyzed maintain ongoing communication with their key stakeholders on all issues most relevant to stakeholders. The dialog topics are determined based on a constant analysis of internal and external social environments, considering strategic targets of the company and top priorities of stakeholders.
8. Though the overwhelming majority of companies whose reports have been analyzed pay much attention to stakeholder engagement, when asked to specify their engagement tools in their reports, they mainly list traditional communication channels such as various kinds of meetings, surveys, seminars, conferences, hotlines, etc., while new tools and channels for interaction that appeared in the digital age, including CRM, SRM, Big Data collection and processing systems, etc., are not marked by companies as specialized resources for managing relations with stakeholders.

CONCLUSION

Corporate social responsibility is the concept according to which the company undertakes to solve problems that relate not only to the external, but also the internal environment of the organization, including social, economic and environmental spheres. To build an effective company, including building a corporate social responsibility system, it is important to have a systematic approach in cooperation with stakeholders.

Stakeholder theory states that the purpose of a business is to create value for stakeholders, identify, select and reconsider them. In this case, there should be highlighted that according to this theory any group or individual who can affect or is affected by the achievement of the firm's objectives is meant to be regarded as stakeholder or stakeholder group.

Interaction with stakeholders should be based on the principles of respect for interests and cooperation, information transparency of company activity, regular interaction, compliance.

In the age of development of communication, the effectiveness of an organization depends on how well stakeholder engagement is built. Before building a detailed dialogue with stakeholders, it is necessary to analyze in detail the main requirements of stakeholders to the company and the expectations of the company from stakeholders and identify key stakeholders of the company. Stakeholder engagement helps the organization increase social capital, minimize non-financial risks, and identify new opportunities for the company's development.

REFERENCES

Accountability. (2005). *Stakeholder Engagement. The practical guide to organizing*. Retrieved from http://www.urbaneconomics.ru/sites/default/files/2528_import.pdf

Deloitte. (2017). *Researching Advanced Management Tools and Practices*. Retrieved from https://www2.deloitte.com/content/dam/Deloitte/ru/Documents/financial-services/russian/issledovanie-peredovyh-upravlencheskih-instrumentov-i-practik.pdf

Evseeva, S.A. (2012). Stakeholder theory as the basis of the concept of sustainable development of an organization. *Science and Business: Development Paths, 10*(16).

Freeman, R. E. (1984). *Strategic Management: A Stakeholder Approach*. Boston: Harpercollins College Div.

Furta, S.D., & Solomatina, T.B. (2010). *Stakeholder map - a tool for analyzing the business environment*. Academic Press.

Future 500. (2018). *Top 10 Stakeholder Engagement Trends of 2018*. Retrieved from https://www.future500.org/blog/top-10-stakeholder-engagement-trends-2018

Gordeeva, M.V., & Petrova, I.A. (2018). Project quality management in the context of the digitalization of the economy. *Step into the future: artificial intelligence and the digital economy. A revolution in management: a new digital economy or a new world of machines*, 33-35.

GRI. (n.d.). Retrieved from http://database.globalreporting.org/search/

Khalin, V.G., & Chernova, G.V. (2018). Digitalization and its impact on the Russian economy and society: advantages, challenges, threats and risks. *Management Consulting, 10*, 46-63.

Milovidov, V.D. (2017). Corporate Governance 2.0: Evolution of the Corporate Relations System in the Information Society. *Problems of National Strategy, 4*(43).

Mitchell, R. K., Agle, B. R., & Wood, D. J. (1997). Toward a Theory of Stakeholder Identification and Salience: Defining the Principle of Who and What Really Counts. *Academy of Management Review, 22*(4), 853–886. doi:10.5465/amr.1997.9711022105

Novozhilova, Y.V. (2017). Information and analytical support of integrated reporting: assessment of the influence of stakeholders on the change in created value. *Statistics and Economics, 1*, 43-50.

O'Neill, R. (2018). *Common Threads: Designing Impactful Engagement*. Retrieved from https://sustainability.com/wp-content/uploads/2018/11/sa-common-threads-full-report.pdf

PWC. (2013). *Stabilization Course*. 16th Annual Survey of the Leaders of the World's Largest Companies. Retrieved from https://www.pwc.ru/en/ceo-survey/assets/16th-ceo-survey-russia-rus.pdf

PWC. (2014). *Growth without acceleration*. 17th Annual Survey of the Leaders of the World's Largest Companies. Retrieved from https://www.pwc.ru/en/ceo-survey/assets/17th-ceo-survey-russia-rus.pdf

PWC. (2017). *Peering hopefully into the distance*. 20 Annual Survey of the Leaders of the World's Largest Companies. Retrieved from https://www.pwc.ru/ru/ceo-survey/20th-ceo-survey.pdf

PwC. (2018). *Achieving perfection.* Retrieved from https://www.pwc.ru/ru/publications/achieving-excellence3.html

Russian Customs Academy. (n.d.). *Digitalization of foreign economic activity.* Report of the expert of the Institutional Development Committee. Retrieved from http://rta.customs.ru/nrta/attachments/4628_Tsifrovizatsia_VED.pdf

Scherbachenko, P. S. (2018). *Management of interaction with stakeholders in Russian companies.* Retrieved from https://cyberleninka.ru/article/n/upravlenie-vzaimodeystviem-so-steykholderami-v-rossiyskih-kompaniyah

Tractivity. (2018). *Stakeholder Engagement: The Benefits of a Digital Approach.* Retrieved from https://www.tractivity.co.uk/blog/digital-stakeholder-engagement/

KEY TERMS AND DEFINITIONS

Stakeholders: Any persons or groups that influence and/or may be affected by the organization's activities, products or services and related indicators. They may include the government (state), suppliers, investors, customers, consumers, employees, local communities, non-government organizations, working groups, trade associations, competitors, etc.

Chapter 3
Reputation Management and a Corporate Identity:
Transition to Digital Platforms

Olga Rink
https://orcid.org/0000-0001-5977-6741
Moscow Institute of Physics and Technology (MIPT), Russia

ABSTRACT

Reputation management is based on digital platforms and tools such as monitoring mass or social media, compliance facilities, and trade credit ratings. The digital instruments extensively utilize various methods of artificial intelligence, machine learning, and predictive analytics, including neural networks and natural language processing (NLP). The computational tools simplify managerial challenges, though assume their users to understand the whole scope and logical structures of data management. Opinions about a company, person, product, or a country are important, but financial consequences of reputational triggers are even more valuable. Reputation management merges with credit and compliance risk assessment both in regulation and in corporate practices.

INTRODUCTION

The true mystery of the world is the visible, not the invisible

Oscar Wilde

The Chapter covers a growing intrusion of digital data technologies into the corporates' business. The digital solutions, on one hand, bring opportunities for better client targeting and engagement, and, on the other hand, open companies to the new reputation risks. While the reputation risk matters.

An increase in computing power and a variety of tools for data distribution and processing can transform company's informational practices and policies to match expectations of stakeholders. Regarding the information disclosure, the author makes a conclusion that both public and privately held companies

DOI: 10.4018/978-1-7998-2011-6.ch003

are quite transparent for external views within the existing trade credit infrastructure. Therefore, stakeholders expect a business governance to match the best practices of global corporate codes, including information disclosure, ethics, anti-bribery behavior and the others.

The author highlights that while information migrates from traditional information channels into the internet digital ecosystems, flooded with fake news and trash logics, businesses have to detect and distinct logically true facts from the massive digital *seagulls*, polluting the big data ecosystem with false and unverified patterns, messages, hashtags, and key words. This means processing big data is to be used very carefully for marketing campaigns as well as for defense purposes.

The Chapter includes the cases that link reputation management with monitoring of credit and compliance risks of a counterparty and outline a methodology of managing the risk of loss of business reputation in credit institutions and banking groups as a sample, applicable for many businesses.

This Chapter investigates key points of digital transformation and challenges for the senior executives, which relate to the basic principles and trends for communications, formal standards of disclosure, as well as reputation risk mitigation.

According to (Gupta, 2018), *companies go through digital transformation in three stages. The first stage usually involves technology to reduce cost and improve efficiency in existing business operations... In the second stage, companies open up their technology platform(s) to clients... In the third stage, companies tend to move to a platform strategy by opening up their system(s) to third-party players, sometimes even competitors.*

Digital platforms have altered the communications landscape. Research of digital transformation practices has been undertaken at MIPT in 2019. The interim results from a business sample of 92 filled in questionnaires representing diversified industries and positions *(Appendix 1, Figure 3, Distribution of business population by digital transformation stages (Source: MIPT, 2019), Figure 9 Industry Breakdown (Source: MIPT, 2019))* reveal that 48% of responders use third party digital tools for their business purposes; 29% participate in improvement of an own technology solution; 24% point out that their company's digital platform is now open to clients or third-party contractors.

95% and 87% of the responders use websites and e-mails, correspondingly, to communicate with their stakeholders *(Figure 4. 95% of business population use websites (Source: MIPT, 2019), Figure 5. 87% of business population use e-mail (Source: MIPT, 2019))*; 73% exploit social media as a communication instrument (*Figure 6. 73% of business population use social networks (Source: MIPT, 2019)*). 43% and 29% now offer mobile applications or chat-bots with embedded Natural Language Processing (NLP) solutions, correspondingly *(Figure 7. 43% of business population use mobile applications, 30% on watch (Source: MIPT, 2019), Figure 8. 29% of business population use mobile applications, 36% on watch (Source: MIPT, 2019))*. At the same time mobile tools (30%) and chat-bots (36%) are mostly being monitored for the future. Sometimes large organizations insist on their proprietary communication channels to be in use instead of open internet.

A consistent corporate reputation is a result of establishing and applying rules of information disclosure. Information disclosure, as a term, has long been associated with the corporate practices set up for listed companies and regulated by stock exchanges and the state departments responsible for securities turnover. Basics of the international and Russian approaches for disclosure are published in (Rink & Martyushev & Matovnikov & others, 2010).

The Chapter extends the book ideas for public structures to a definition of *Disclosure* onto any corporation, public or private, because the business landscape has become digital and transparent; regulators or creditors require and share more data to assess an arbitrary counterparty.

The methodology of corporate reputation management, proposed in the Chapter, refers to the extended framework of information disclosure and generalizes the author's own business cases and some public ones. The method was presented before in (Rink, 2013) and published in (Rink, 2014).

With the increase in computing power and increasing variety of tools for data distribution and processing, enterprises can transform their informational practices and policies to match the expectations of stakeholders such as regulators, shareholders, prospective customers, partners or vendors, as well as people employed by the companies. The broad external requirements make corporates focus on an integral system of reputation management, including the trade credit and compliance along with an interaction with media and employees, in order to keep their cash flow as a priority.

FROM MISS MARPLE AND ALGEBRAIC LOGIC TO BIG DATA BACKGROUND

Digital platforms widely use algorithms of pattern recognition and natural language processing. Logical assumptions and validity of mathematical models in use, let alone nuances of human perception, are to be accounted for and verified for making decisions.

"*One is so inclined to be trusting and take people at their own valuation,*" said Miss Marple, a favorite character of many in (Christie, A., 1930). In all her stories the nice and inquisitive Miss Marple sought out the suspect who has had both a motive and an opportunity. In modern terms she does profiling and finds out a hidden pattern, based on historic data and a collection of facts and rumors in her neighborhood.

"I don't know about it being absurd," explained Miss Marple.

The character uses none of digital tools, though follows simple rules of logics. In the era of big data and digital communications, it is important to keep the basis of processing information by computer technology in mind.

The **algebraic logic** is a branch of mathematical logic in which operations over statements are studied. Statements can be true or false (1 or 0); thus, the result of logical operations over statements can also be true or false.

For example, if

(1) A=B;
(2) B=C;
(3) C=D.
(4) Then A=D.

Suppose (1), (2), and (3) are true, then (4) is true.

However, if (1) or (2) or (3) is false, then (4) may be false. Or at least (4) logically does not result from (1), (2) and (3).

To illustrate the idea let two persons have different experiences, cultures and worldviews and assess the validity of some initial statements in their own way.

For example, let (1) be related to a religious, political, or cultural values. What – income, conscience or spiritual values – is more important? Each of the experiment participants has his/her own answer, or perhaps several options at the same moment.

Let (2) be evaluated by a technician, highly qualified in a very narrow field, which an arbitrary reader or a computer user may highly likely not be.

Let (3) require, in turn, a legal training to be understood.

Consequently, an average reader is unable to verify the statements (2) or (3) simultaneously and responds differently to (1); hence whether (4) is true is not clear. (4) may be true in the case too. But why, we may never know, because logic and arguments are not transparent to the evaluators.

Mathematics is slender; its rules are clear and convenient. But even mathematics gives only a rough picture of the world, which may differ from a reality.

The number of information sources is constantly growing. (1) may be available in the media, (2) is taken from a compliance database, whereas (3) is provided by an external supplier of counterparty checks.

And what if a corporate structure has not 3, but hundreds, thousands or orders of magnitude more statements to be analyzed?

This is the power of the contemporary big data environment. Might artificial intelligence (AI) replace a human to make such logical decisions?

Which are the areas where the AI may be as intelligent, gifted, and creative as Miss Marple to carry out a correct identification of a business or a person under an investigation to discover truth?

Indicative abstracts, patterns, factors, hashtags, ratings, or key words, and subsequent predictive analytics or an identification of a perceptive "look-alike" may form a public opinion, but not take, for instance, a *Black Swan event* of (Taleb, 2007) into account. To make an informed decision and navigate reputational matters managers investigate facts and strategies in details.

INFORMATION DISCLOSURE: MORE OR LESS

The OECD / G20 Best Practice and Disclosure for Public Securities Issuers

The best practice of corporate governance pays special attention to the equal treatment of shareholders, the role of stakeholders in management, including the relationship of shareholders and non-shareholders, disclosure and transparency, as well as the duties of the board of directors.

Advanced standards of corporate behavior ensure a high level of business ethics in relations between stakeholders and management, which affect the reputation and a long-term success of the company.

The presence of a corporate code of conduct has become a norm for public companies, both global and domestic, and a guarantee of compliance with the standards recognized globally.

The Chapter "Disclosure and Transparency" of the Organisation for Economic Co-operation and Development, OECD/G20 manual (OECD, 2015) states that *the corporate governance framework should ensure that timely and accurate disclosure is made on any material matters regarding the corporation, including the financial situation, performance, ownership and governance of the company.*

The principles of corporate governance in terms of disclosure and transparency mention the following material information to be disclosed:

1. Financial and operating results of the company;
2. Company objectives and non-financial information;
3. Major share ownership, including beneficiary owners, and voting rights;
4. Members of the board and key executives, including their qualification, selection principles, and if they are regarded as independent, and as well as their remuneration;
5. Related party transactions;
6. Foreseeable risk factors;
7. Issues related to employees and other stakeholders;
8. Corporate structure and governance policies.

To protect capital markets the codes are mandatory for issuers whose securities are listed on the leading stock exchanges on the "Comply or explain" principle. That means, all discrepancies must be explained.

Codes of corporate conduct are intended to play an important role in the company's innovative development and include the following sections:

- creation of the business's own code of corporate conduct in accordance with the local regulation and international recommendations;
- disclosure on at least an annual basis whether the company complies with the provisions of the recommended code of corporate conduct;
- compliance with specific provisions on the remuneration policy.

It is worth noting, that stock exchange listing rules in some cases provide that:

- the board of directors should approve a document defining the rules and disclosure requirements;
- the board of directors should approve a document on the use of information on a company's securities and transactions with them, a disclosure of which may have a significant impact on the market value of the issuer's securities.

Information should be prepared, audited and disclosed in accordance with high standards of accounting and reporting, financial and non-financial disclosure and audit.

Annual audits should be conducted by an independent auditor to ensure an objective assessment of how the accounts are prepared and presented.

The distribution channels shall allow free, easy and a cost-efficient access for interested parties to the disclosed information.

A regulation on the information policy (Disclosure policy) determines the composition of information and documents to be disclosed. When developing an information policy, a procedure for the formation, coordination and provision of documents or information subject to disclosure is regulated by internal documents of the organization, separate orders, as well as regulatory legal acts.

Information Disclosure is, thus, governed by the following norms:

- Applicable legislation;
- Business's regulation on information policy;
- Shareholders agreement (The clauses specifying how shareholders / investors participate in company's decision making);
- Internal regulations of interaction with stakeholders and among divisions of the company;
- Job descriptions;
- Local acts on the establishment of working groups for the implementation of a single task (preparation of annual reports, annual / interim general meetings and so on.)

The practice of creating a Disclosure Committee (Committee on information policy) is also in line with the best global and domestic corporate governance practices. A Disclosure Committee is a group tasked with reviewing all proposed disclosures prior to their release. Philips and Russian Tatneft, as examples, have the unit within their corporate structures. The powers of a Disclosure Committee may be the following:

- to submit recommendations for improving the organization's information policy, including information disclosure procedures, in order to ensure consistency of the disclosed information in accordance with the requirements of regulatory acts, internal documents of the organization, as well as the best corporate governance practices;
- to define materiality of the information to be disclosed.

There are two basic options for monitoring the activities of the Disclosure Committee. The Committee may report to the board of directors or to the executive board of the organization.

The composition of the Committee on information policy may include from 3 to 5 people, for instance, the executive responsible for the implementation of information policy, the officials responsible for financial matters (Chief Accountant or Chief Financial Director) and risk management, the company's Corporate Secretary, the executive responsible for internal control, and sometimes employees responsible for production or business development. Depending on the current strategy, the Committee on information policy may include an independent director or other experts.

In most cases, stakeholders want to see and hear the key executives, as they are usually the company's most influential figures. Participation in the investor relations process may take from 10 to 20% of the top management's working time (Rink & Martyushev & Matovnikov & others, 2010). The main stages of communication may then be the following:

- definition of a strategic framework for raising finance;
- preparation of the content for the disclosure documents;
- participation in the most important meetings with investors and analysts;
- speaking at public conferences and to the press.

A purpose of information disclosure is to reduce the direct communication of the top management with the investment community.

Apart from annual and quarterly reports, the Russian disclosure rules (Bank of Russia's regulation N 454-P, 2018) define the requirements for formats and content of material facts and corporate actions, standardized over 50 existing types of material facts to be disclosed by the securities issuers. In 2018 *National Settlement Depository (NSD), Russia's central securities depository, and Interfax's Center for Disclosing Corporate Information launched the Single Disclosure Window into commercial operation. This service gives issuers the ability to disclose material facts via information agencies' news feeds and to inform NSD's Corporate Actions Center about corporate action*s (NSD, 2018).

A few exceptions not to disclose 18 types of the data are though made recently for sanctioned companies to avoid "secondary" sanctions for their counterparts (RBC, 2019).

Disclosure Regulation for Non-Public Companies

Despite the informational environment and the securities market infrastructure become more digital and consistent, the number of publicly listed companies lowers. WFE (2019) exhibited that *only the Americas saw an increase (37.3%) in the number of IPOs on 2017.*

- New listings through IPOs and investment flows through IPOs were down 14.5% and 12.1% on 2017. This was due to a decline in the number of IPOs in the Asia-Pacific (-22.7%) and EMEA (-22%) regions.
- *Despite recording a decline in overall listings and investment flows, the Asia-Pacific region accounted for over 50% of global IPO listings (60.2%) and investment flows (50.8%). Hong Kong Exchanges and Clearing (HKEX) recorded the highest number of IPOs globally due to a surge in the number of technology companies coming to market.*
- *Other **non-IPO listings** were down 23.3% on 2017. This was entirely due to a 60.9% decline in the number of non-IPO listings in the EMEA region. In the Americas and Asia-Pacific regions, non-IPO listings were up 1% and 12.9% respectively.*
- *In the EMEA region, listings and investment flows fell in the presence of uncertainty stemming from Brexit negotiations, trade tensions, volatility in oil prices and economic instability in some markets. In Europe listings and investment flows fell on most markets except Deutsche Börse and Euronext.*
- *There was a marginal decline of 0.3% in the **number of listed companies***

Thus, while public institutions disclose formally more information, the number of the listed corporations decreases due to economic and political factors.

Meanwhile non-public entities and the whole business population disclose formally more and more data and become essentially more transparent for a credit assessment and raising finance.

Oversight structures and national regulators now elaborate and implement Open Data initiatives that have already made over 30,000 official sources on commercial population world-wide available for processing. The data are

1. financials and debt triggers like trade data,
2. ownership,
3. bankruptcies,
4. governance and management,
5. business areas,
6. production facilities,
7. patents and trademarks,
8. human resources,
9. court filings,
10. news coverage,
11. sanction lists etc.

As a consequence, a credit investigation, including risk assessments, is now available on over 300 million businesses globally (Dun & Bradstreet, 2019).

Julian Guthry for (Wired, 2019) opened up a case, when a credit report led a foundation into an investment: "*So she [a researcher] read the Dun & Bradstreet research report on the software company, which was based in Silicon Valley. The company sold antivirus software and was growing quickly. It had a good product and apocalyptic viruses were predicted to take down computers across the globe.*"

Run over the report more closely, the researcher concluded, *"Hot co; anti-virus products; 2.5mm users; shareware; $7mm 1990 with $6mm pretax; 4,000 major corp users; excellent prospect; doing due diligence.*"

Even if a company is not public by its business type, it is very likely quite transparent for external views within the trade credit informational infrastructure. Therefore, stakeholders expect a business governance to match the best practices of global corporate codes, including information disclosure, ethics, anti-bribery behavior and others.

GLOBAL COMMUNICATIONS AND DIGITAL *SEAGULLS*

Digital Platforms Compete with Mainstream Media for Users' Attention

Appearance of internet and digital platforms radically alters the media industry. The audience of traditional news sources noticeably concedes to internet ecosystems.

Speaking of the Russian market as an illustration, in May 2019 over 320 mn internet users of browsers accessed to Yandex. The social network Vkontakte (VK.ru), Google, Mail.ru were requested by 182 mn, 132 mn, and 122 mn users of browser correspondingly. Russia Today holding, Komsomolskaya Pravda Digital (KP.ru), and the State Broadcasting Company VGTRK (Vesti.ru) remain among the most influential mainstream media with some 49 mn, 45 mn[1], and 44 mn internet readers, manifoldly less than the core digital platforms have today *(Figure 1. TOP digital platforms and media holdings by Yandex Radar, May 1-31, 2019, refer to Appendix 2 for the tables).*

The cross-device audience of the internet resources varies from 46% to 61% depending on the media. Whereas 10 hours 28 minutes 24 seconds of the average time spent on Yandex, as a digital platform, significantly exceeds 9 minutes 48 seconds spent daily on Russia Today, for example, in May 2019.

Figure 1. TOP digital platforms and media holdings by Yandex Radar, May 1-31, 2019

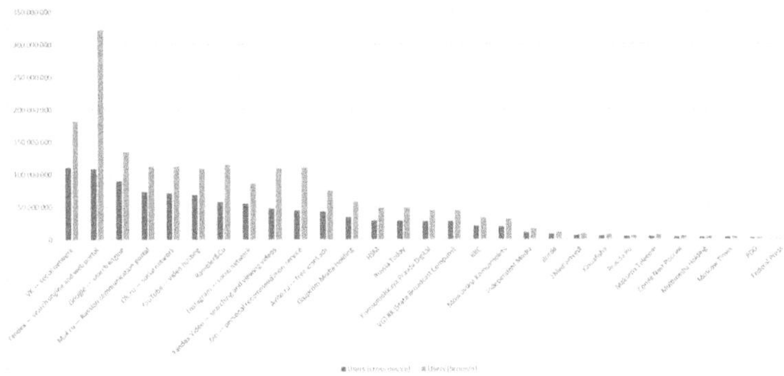

In March 2019 Mediascope Web-Index assessed the internet-audience of the Russian Federation aged 12-64 as 102 mn by their own embedded counter.

Both the ratings — Yandex and Mediascope — are applied to organize marketing or influence campaigns, though they have different purposes and user identification tools.

Business Models Evolve

Any media customer is a content consumer. His / her time is limited, and their attention is very selective, since the users are tempted by the abundance of information. Both brands and the media need noteworthy and visually interesting content to compete for their clients.

As a result, business models of the content production evolve.

- A profitability of the usual monetization models — subscription and advertising — drops for the traditional media (efficiency though depends on a source). Former print, broadcasting or electronic press may now offer a credit or compliance assessment, corporate or personal ratings and scorings, automatization of news coverage and many other services. Thomson Reuters and Interfax may be named as the examples.
- A "going offline" trend nowadays replaces an earlier "going online". Professional providers of news focus on commercialization of personal off-the-record communications with their customers and organize club activities or conferencing. The Bell or Vedomosti demonstrate the practice, for instance.
- 4 major components — content, hardware, software and telecommunications — maintain global circulation of content. Technological giants of the hardware and software industry — Apple, Microsoft, Sony, mobile operators — enter the digital production industry to supplement core products with data services or content manufacturing. For example, Sony Music Entertainment is *a global recorded music company with a current roster that includes a broad array of both local artists and international superstars.*
- Any user of a digital platform has become a content supplier with a zero threshold to entry spreading news and opinions. Independent investigators are increasingly creating their niche media on Youtube, Medium, Telegram, Yandex.Zen, WeChat etc.

Digital platforms mostly benefit from the business models that work well in the big data environment. They have a content of different authors and earn on advertising, software or hardware, as well as gateway solutions. The content-driven development has led to that digital services replace product-oriented business models everywhere in many industries.

Truth Versus Clickbait

It is key, that the reduction of the mainstream media' importance only to the true and material facts is at the heart of the press freedom.

Both in the United States (by the First Amendment to the US Constitution) and the Russian Federation (by the Constitution of the Russian Federation, 1993), as examples, freedom of the press is legally protected by the State Constitution. The free press clauses protect *the right of individuals to express themselves through publication and dissemination of information, ideas and opinions without interference, constraint or prosecution by the government.* In addition, propaganda or agitation instigating social, racial, national or religious hatred and strife as well as censorship are not allowed.

Nevertheless, circulation of information is subject to wider restrictions for various communication channels, state and commercial secrets, personal data etc.

Reverting to a nature of the news, if a dog bites a human being, then it's not a piece of news. If a person bites a dog, then a content supplier may cover the fact, as it's not only news, it's a sensation, "clickbait" in a modern term that describes a web content aimed to generate a revenue from online advertising, especially to the detriment of the quality or accuracy of information.

The authors of the "clickbait" news resemble *seagulls*, who are *clever*, represent *a carefree attitude, versatility, and freedom* in Native American Symbolism (onekindplanet.org), *resourceful, inquisitive, and intelligent, demonstrating complex methods of communication and a highly developed social structure, have a worldwide cosmopolitan distributio*n (Wikipedia on Gulls), though sometimes *'10 times' more polluting than humans* (TheJournal.ie).

(Regulation of the digital economy in France and Europe, 2017) overviews legal principles for digital *Collaborative economy websites* as a countermeasure against the digital *seagulls* or "fake news":

A fairer and more effective European digital economy also requires greater transparency and greater loyalty on the part of digital platforms: search engines, social media websites and price comparison websites. Three decrees were signed on 5 October by Bruno Le Maire and Mounir Mahjoubi with a view to tightening the transparency and loyalty obligations.

In the future, the platforms will have to specify their listing and classification criteria, and especially

- *in what way the amount of their remuneration is a factor in the order in which content is presented;*
- *whether or not the consumer opinions they publish have been verified, and according to what conditions.*

Consequently, whether a piece of the news is true or false, verified or not, and may it be an argument for decision making or not, remains an important question for global communications. At the same time, information consumers can't be held captive by pure facts. The facts are not only stubborn, but also evidential, when they are taken in connection with each other. Workers of either press or of any data source must both fix the facts, and verify, achieve the validity of the whole material.

Table 1. Search marketing: contextual and targeted advertising platforms

Content Optimization
https://Wordstat.yandex.ru or https://keywordseverywhere.com, https://trends.google.com as examples
v
Advertisement and Re-Marketing
Yandex Direct, Google Adwords
v
Analytics and Conversion
Yandex Metrika, Google Analytics

Business consumers have to detect and distinct logically true facts from the massive digital *seagulls*, polluting the big data ecosystem with false and unverified patterns, messages, hashtags, and key words.

DIGITAL MARKETING AND CONTENT MANAGEMENT

Digital platforms capture a great amount of users' time (Appendix 2) and now define what will be watched and read. Content manufacturers compete for an attention of their audience; whereas digital platforms are now the main environment to deliver a content and connotations.

Google, Facebook, Yandex, VK, WeChat or Badoo, live over their "Golden age", dictate commercial terms for mainstream media and brands, and take a significant share of the profits. Instead there is an opportunity for targeting digital messages to a specific audience as precisely as possible due to valid analytics on a campaign performance.

Digital communications are personalized and therefore an integral part of a persona marketing strategy for a business oriented to either retail or corporate clients. The experience-centric scenarios of interaction with potential clientele replace billboards, print advertisement, and banners on internet. Marketing affords are concentrated on various messages for their efficient groups of clients.

Digital platforms collect data about consumers: how much time do they read the article, how many times do they download a piece. That is, an identified person becomes a "lead", which, without knowing it, falls into the sales funnel and turns into a potential customer responded to the marketing campaign.

Technically a digital database is collected in the following sequence: identifying a peer, collecting its profile, enriching the collected information from the other available sources, and finally calculating a score or attributing the peer to a market segment. Then sales pass through the data base according with identified interests, patterns, and scenarios of interaction.

To identify a targeted person digital infrastructure may use cookies (including those used to identify the user), location, phone, citizenship, age, behavioral scenarios, purchasing characteristics, worldview, political and religious preferences, psychological portrait, interests, race, company, position, technological characteristics and other traces.

In order to identify a business, one may use a registration number or a tax number, company's name, telephone and location, international identification codes, owners and corporate links.

Channels of persona marketing may be computers and tablets, smartphones, digital TV, mobile applications, Web sites, social networks, interactive screens in metro or offline stores, self-service terminals, POS-terminals, game console, LANs and others, and are limited by the efficiency, budget, fantasy and customer's technical abilities.

For the search marketing, first, a business tunes its content and trade scenarios to match with the potential clients' requirements and interests (*Table 1. Search marketing: contextual and targeted advertising platforms).* Digital marketing patterns may be direct and "look-alike", simple and many-factorial. Say, whose who search a fitness center in an area may be also a target audience for healthy food. Or opinions, as a factor of choice, may lead to the sales of a financial service.

"Banners no longer work, banks need a result that is achieved without media advertising, due to the target action. Banks.ru users send 300 thousand applications for loans per month, place 3 billion rubles on deposits," says an owner Filipp Il`in-Adaev in interview to (Skrynnikova Anaslasiya, May 30, 2019).

In the context of digital marketing ROI (Return on Investment) is calculated as the ratio of profit to money invested in the promotion. Extensive analytics on conversion for every pattern, scenario, and content allows corporates to monitor and improve marketing campaigns.

ROI = (Revenue – Cost) / Cost × 100%

Digital platforms facilitate efficient trades, though the new trade models are therefore sensitive to the platforms' tariffs and the other their terms and conditions.

REPUTATION MANAGEMENT AND CREDIT ASSESSMENT

Business reputation management is closely connected with monitoring credit and compliance risks of a counterparty.

The nature of reputation risks has been extensively explored since the global financial crisis in 2008, which is associated with the bankruptcy of Lehman Brothers, one of the oldest and largest financial institution. The causes of the crisis and their ethical aspects are analyzed by (Norris, 2010) and (Whalen).

Due to the adoption of the Basel III standard and the relevant regulatory requirements of the central banks, the method of reputation risk management is mostly relevant for financial institutions, but its general ideas can be also applied to non-financial structures.

Risk managers of major European organizations assessed reputational threats as the most significant of all possible (Economist Intelligence Unit, 2005), while the most important factors of the reputational risk were speed of information dissemination through international communication channels and strengthening of regulatory requirements.

Reputation management is often associated solely with monitoring media or social networks for negative reviews or publications.

On practice, the procedures for assessing business reputation, managing the risk of reputational loss not less, and perhaps even more investigate credit and compliance risks, as they require verification of beneficiaries in the sanctions, anti-corruption or anti-money-laundering lists.

The current international problems caused by the introduction of trade restrictions and sanctions, changes in political and economic regimes, and, hence, variations in the regulatory environment, are the cause of many risks, among which reputation risk can be singled out, because it is affected by objective and subjective factors.

Reputation or Goodwill as an economic value is taken on the balance sheet only at a moment of changing owners of an enterprise (Pro-appraisal.ru). Public companies, whose shares are sold and bought on the stock exchanges or over-the-counter market, may be the examples. Capitalization and liquidity of such companies increase in the presence of high demand, while their physical assets may not grow.

For public companies their business reputation (goodwill), as an indicator to the market demand, either good or bad, may be defined as a difference between capitalization and assets. Thus, an impact of the reputational factors on a market may be followed and predicted using the disclosure and capitalization management tools.

Goodwill arises when an enterprise receives stable and high profits, its return on assets (or equity) is above the industry average. The value of the business exceeds the value of its net assets as a result.

Representatives of different companies shared interesting observations from their practice during one of the Financial Communications and Investor Relations Alliance (ARFI) disputes on May 29, 2010 (Rink, 2014), moderated by the author:

- reputation risk is a sort of a discount for management, since quality of guidance and leadership improves reputation;
- it makes sense to manage reputation of not only the company itself, but also of the services or goods it provides;
- a regular reputation audit is an important basis for reputation management; the ratio of negative and positive data should not be the only performance indicator;
- in order to manage reputation, first an identification of the possible risk factors is necessary to avoid their execution and a subsequent crisis.

G20 and the Basel Committee on banking supervision have carefully examined the causes of the 2008 financial crisis, its systemic risks and underlying factors. The interim advisory documents (Basel Committee on Banking Supervision, 2009 and 2011) point to the following important areas of the reputational risk:

- Reputational risk can be defined as a risk arising from negative perceptions by buyers, counterparties, shareholders, investors and regulators that may affect the bank's ability to maintain existing or establish new business relationships and gain a continued access to funding;
- Reputational risk, usually through implicit mechanisms of influence, can lead to increased credit, market and legal risks, as well as liquidity risks, each of which, in turn, can adversely affect the profit, liquidity or capital of the credit institution;
- Bank managers must adopt appropriate internal regulations (policies) to identify sources of reputational risk when entering new markets, launching products or activities. In addition, stress testing procedures should take reputational risk into account; so that management has a clear understanding of its consequences.

The final version of Basel III does not mention any reputational risks. The "Monitoring" Chapter of this document focuses on independent standardized instruments for counterparty risk analysis (credit and compliance risks), and notes the following:

Figure 2. Reputation Check in a fragment of a Dun & Bradstreet sample report

Maximum Credit

2000 EURO per month.

Informants' advice granting of credit to be a fair trade risk.

Reputation Check

Trade Reference Source	Reference Type	Payment Ability- Description
Suppliers within and outside the industry	No Complaints	Good

Business History

Date	Event Name	Old Value	New Value
01/01/2008	Authorized Capital Changed	5000.00 CYP	8550.00 EUR
01/01/2008	Paid-up Capital Changed	5000.00 CYP	8550.00 EUR
01/01/2008	Nominal Values of Shares Changed	1.00 CYP	1.71 EUR

Capital

Authorized Capital	8,550.00 EUR	**Asked**	0.00 EUR
Nominal No Of Shares	5,000.00	**Issued No Of Shares**	5,000.00

- To understand the main aspects of requirements to liquidity, banks should frequently study possible inconsistencies in contractual relations... This approach is useful to compare risk profiles of different institutions and identify banks' and regulators' time, when an extra liquidity may be of a demand.
- Market monitoring tools as the sources of operational signals about possible liquidity issues include... additional data on legal entities to assess the entities' financial condition and methods of financing.
- Banks must define their own capital requirements to calculate a counterparty credit risk under various scenarios.

In parallel with assessing their counterparts, many organizations monitor negative reviews on the press and social networks, as well as a direct feedback from buyers, suppliers or employees. Media monitoring has already been automated: starting from tracking references to your company and the competitive environment and ending with the creation of press clipping and reporting. A corporate may automate a distribution of press releases, receive data on a deliverability or a performance. Globally the number of such services increased from hundreds in 2011 to thousands in 2019. Only the Russian Federation counts dozens of the monitoring facilities.

However, this control is only a part of measures to address the broader challenge.

The verified reviews of a press coverage for counterparts are gradually becoming part of the credit and compliance reports and are often included in the "Reputation check" section along with the other sections (Figure 3. Reputation Check in a fragment of a Dun & Bradstreet sample report).

COUNTERPARTY ASESSMENT, BIG DATA AND ARTIFICIAL INTELLIGENCE

AI — statistics, machine learning, and natural language processing — are widely applied for modelling credit & reputation risk indicators. Variations in these risk indicators, calculated based on mathematical models, instead of raw data (including negative publications), often lead to the corporate deciding to change the terms of cooperation with contractors.

The variables or predictors, influencing the scoring risk indicators, can be both financial and non-financial.

The author's study on the criteria for investing in innovative companies, public and non-public, revealed that a quarter of all the factors are financial, and three quarters are non-financial (Rink, 2005).

The scoring models developed by the Interfax group and Dun & Bradstreet to assess the risks of various companies, including small and medium-sized businesses, take from 30 to 150 financial and non-financial indicators into account (Rink, 2013).

As shown by the financial crisis of 2008, risk managers need to not only identify partners (counterparties) whose risks are subject to systematic monitoring, but also monitor their beneficiary holders, as well as to count on the risks of groups of companies. This challenge has brought together global and regional leaders in business information and services for credit managers and compliance professionals. It is equally important to learn how to predict bankruptcy for the next 6-18 months in order to avoid the recurrence of such large-scale crises.

Such problems are being solved now. Thus, the unique international identifier of legal entities and individual entrepreneurs D-U-N-S, developed by Dun & Bradstreet at the request of the United Nations in the 1960s, is used to identify contractors. The UN, other supranational bodies and major financial and non-financial institutions are actively using D-U-N-S in their work.

The peculiarity of this identifier is that the number assigned to the company remains assigned to it after the termination of the organization's activities, which avoids duplication of numbers and the associated confusion. The ability to track corporate relationships and, accordingly, to analyze risks for groups of companies is an important advantage of this identifier.

For example, in all countries to calculate a probability of bankruptcy, called as the Failure Score, different data series are used due to differences in legislation, disclosure conditions, etc, though similar techniques are used to make it easier for users to work with comparable indicators.

The more open and complete is the external information environment, the more relevant is the correct identification of business units and the calculation of complex risk indicators for not only the contractors themselves, but also for their beneficiaries.

Reverting to the risk of loss of business reputation and taking the complexity of this problem into account, it is worth emphasizing that the measures taken should not be limited to the preparation of reputation reports and evaluation of negative information in media. The implementation of credit policy, receivable accounts management, compliance control and a financial monitoring remain the focus for reputation management of domestic and international companies.

SOLUTIONS AND RECOMMENDATIONS

Approaches to the reputation management were considered in (Regan, 2008). The author identified the main functional sections that a policy of risk management should include.

Close methodical recommendations are given in the regulation of the Bank of Russia N° 242-P ("On the organization of internal control in credit institutions and banking groups") dated December 16, 2003, the letter of the Bank of Russia N° 92-T ("On the organization of legal risk management and the risk of loss of business reputation in credit institutions and banking groups") dated June 30, 2005, as well as later documents.

Reputational Risk refers to the risk of losses due to an impact of reputational risk factors on the organization.

The fact of a reputational risk is an execution of a reputational risk factor:

- information;
- actions of employees or third parties;
- other facts that can negatively affect the business reputation.

To manage reputation, an organization must

- formulate goals and objectives of the reputation risk management;
- establish procedures for identifying, monitoring and assessing this risk;
- identify measures to maintain an acceptable level of the risk and to minimize it;
- distribute the powers of the participants in the reputational risk management process.

Reputational risk factors include

1) Legal violations and financial monitoring
   a) non-compliance of the organization, its affiliates and subsidiaries, as well as the business owners to the legislation, constituent and internal documents, the order of business turnover, and the principles of professional ethics;
   b) non-performance of contractual obligations to creditors, customers and the other counterparties;
   c) failure to effectively counteract anti-bribery measures, the legalization (laundering) of proceeds of crime and the financing of terrorism, as well as other illegal activities (AML / CFT) carried out by unscrupulous clients, contractors and/or employees.
2) Conflicts of interests of clients and contractors, shareholders, management bodies and/or employees. Risk factors are associated with the lack of mechanisms in internal documents to effectively manage these conflicts, as well as to minimize their negative consequences.
3) Ineffective compliance control and non-compliance with the "Know your customer" rule (KYC). Risk factors are related to complaints, lawsuits from clients and contractors and/or the application of measures of influence by regulatory and Supervisory authorities. The KYC report should contain data on legal entities or individuals, including information on sanctions imposed by state bodies and international organizations on the country of the legal entity's location, the legal entity itself and its management, as well as information on anti-corruption expertise (verification of public officials).

Compliance procedures touch the lists of the following departments

- The EU blacklist;
- Her Majesty's Treasury (UK);
- The Committee on sanctions of the UN Security Council;
- Foreign Affairs and International Trade Canada;
- Australian Department of Foreign Affairs and Trade;
- The Ministry of Foreign Affairs of Great Britain;
- The US Treasury office of foreign assets control (OFAC), (list of special categories of citizens and persons subject to blocking);
- The CIA list of politically exposed persons;
- Other regulators.

4) Violation of the "Know your employee" rule and employee qualification requirements:
   a) non-compliance of business reputation of candidates for management positions with the requirements established by Federal laws;
   b) shortcomings of the personnel policy in the selection of personnel.
5) Incorrect disclosure of information:
   a) violation of disclosure rules established by legislation and internal regulations;
   b) negative perception of information by clients, staff, shareholders, creditors, government authorities, media, rating agencies, audit companies and other partners, as well as lawsuits, published opinions / reviews, etc.
6) Negative perception by shareholders, counterparties and related parties in connection with
   a) shortcomings in risk management, organization of internal control system, including for AML / CFT purposes, risky investment and market policy, high level of operational risk;
   b) negative facts regarding the business reputation of clients, staff, shareholders, creditors, government authorities, media, rating agencies, audit companies and other partners, including lawsuits.

The given structure of the reputation risk factors testifies to the complexity of the reputation management process. Various divisions of the organization such as departments of financial monitoring, information disclosure, people management, risk management, legal and compliance departments are involved in reputation management; and their roles in this process are equally important.

REFERENCES

Bank of Russia. (2003). *Polozhenie Banka Rossii ot 16 dekabrya 2003 g. Nº 242-P «Ob organizacii vnutrennego kontrolya v kreditny`x organizaciyax i bankovskix gruppax»* (in Russian). Retrieved from http://base.garant.ru/584330

Bank of Russia. (2005). *Pis`mo Banka Rossii Nº 92-T «Ob organizacii upravleniya pravovy`m riskom i riskom poteri delovoj reputacii v kreditny`x organizaciyax i bankovskix gruppax»* (in Russian). Retrieved from http://base.garant.ru/585600

Bank of Russia. (2018). *Polozhenie o raskry`tii informacii e`mitentami e`missionny`x cenny`x bumag* (N 454-P, approved on 30.12.2014 by the Bank of Russia) (Zaregistrirovano v Minyuste Rossii 12.02.2015 N 35989) (in Russian). Retrieved from http://www.consultant.ru/document/cons_doc_LAW_175536/

Basel Committee on Banking Supervision. (2009). *Consultative Document. Proposed Enhancements to the Basel II Framework*. Retrieved from http://www.bis.org/publ/bcbs150.pdf

Basel Committee on Banking Supervision. (2011). *Basel III: A Global Regulatory Framework for More Resilient Banks and Banking Systems*. Retrieved from http://www.bis.org/publ/bcbs189.pdf

Christie, A. (1930). The Murder at the Vicarage. Academic Press.

Economist Intelligence Unit. (2005). *Reputation: Risk of Risks*. Retrieved from http://www.acegroup.com/eu-en/assets/risk-reputation-report.pdf

Fronin, V. (2018). *Vladislav Fronin: V CzK o publikacii ne znali!* (in Russian). Retrieved from https://www.kp.ru/daily/26918/3965399/

Gupta, S. (2018). *Driving Digital Strategy: A Guide to Reimaging Your Business*. Harvard Business Review Press. Retrieved from http://en.wikipedia.org/wiki/Intangible_asset

Guthry, J. (2019). *The woman who saved John McAfee from an epically bad deal*. Retrieved from https://www.wired.com/story/the-woman-who-saved-john-mcafees-biscuits/?fbclid=IwAR0HXX0093NMMXco4mz41zvsmoCy33SH7bFxGhp6HLk8lyApquTze1x_tgM&mbid=social_fb&utm_brand=wired&utm_campaign=wired&utm_medium=social&utm_social-type=owned&utm_source=facebook

International Regulatory Framework for Banks (Basel III). (n.d.). Retrieved from http://www.bis.org/bcbs/basel3.htm

Mediascope. (2019). *Mediascope Webindex as of March 2019* (in Russian). Retrieved from https://webindex.mediascope.net/report/general-statistics?byGeo=1&byDevice=3&byDevice=1&byDevice=2&byMonth=201903&id=88155&id=16571&id=12285

Norris, F. (2010). *Demystify the Lehman shell game*. Retrieved from http://www.nytimes.com/2010/04/02/business/02norris.html?_r=0

NSD. (2018). *NSD and Interfax Launch New Product – the Single Disclosure Window Service*. Retrieved from https://www.nsd.ru/en/press/ndcnews/index.php?id36=634082

OECD. (2015). *G20/OECD Principles of Corporate Governance*. Paris: OECD Publishing. Retrieved from https://onekindplanet.org/animal/seagull/

Pro-appraisal. (n.d.). *Ocenka delovoj reputacii* (in Russian). Retrieved from http://pro-appraisal.ru/drugie-vidyi-otsenki/otsenka-delovoy-reputatsii-goodwill

RBC. (2019). *Kompaniyam i bankam razreshili zakretit` 18 vidov danny`x iz-za sankcij* (in Russian). Retrieved from https://www.rbc.ru/economics/11/04/2019/5cae1ee29a7947722c3e75bd?fbclid=IwAR23Jd9pw0GSZ8oU0jR_YrdJC1ntkX4q745w96eNxnbonS31COKnMbG9MYw

Regan L. (2008). A framework for intergrating reputation risk into the enterprise risk management process. *Journal of Financial Transformation*, *22*, 187–194.

Regulation of the digital economy in France and Europe. (2017). Retrieved from https://www.gouvernement.fr/en/regulation-of-the-digital-economy-in-france-and-europe

Rink, O., Martyushev, S., Matovnikov, M., & ... (2010). *Organizaciya svyazej s investorami. Rossijskaya i zarubezhnaya praktika*. Moskva: Al`pina. (in Russian)

Rink, O. L. (2014). Upravlenie reputacionny`mi riskami: uravnenie s neskol`kimi neizvestny`mi (in Russian). *Moskva: Upravlenie finansovy`mi riskami*, *4*(40), 242-248. Retrieved from https://www.slideshare.net/olgarink/ufr-4-20141

Rink, O. (2005). *Technologies and Innovations. Criteria for Investment Appraisal* (Unpublished MBA dissertation). Kingston Business School.

Rink, O. (2013). *Reputation Management and a Corporate Identity*. Theses of a speech at the ComFest 2013 conference "Communication Unlimited", Mumbai, India. Retrieved from https://www.slideshare.net/olgarink/2013-10-17-arfi-reputation-management-short-32437868

Skrynnikova Anastasiya for VC. RU. (2019). *Iz SMI v servis s vy`ruchkoj 1 mlrd rublej v god: e`volyuciya «Banki.ru»* (in Russian). Retrieved from https://vc.ru/finance/67676-iz-smi-v-servis-s-vyruchkoy-1-mlrd-rubley-v-god-evolyuciya-banki-ru

Taleb, N. (2007). *The Black Swan: Second Edition: The Impact of the Highly Improbable*. Random House.

The Constitution of the Russian Federation. (1993). Retrieved from https://www.dnb.com/about-us/data-cloud.html

The WFE Communication Team. (2019). *The World Federation of Exchanges publishes 2018 Full Year Market Highlights*. Retrieved from https://www.world-exchanges.org/news/articles/world-federation-exchanges-publishes-2018-full-year-market-highlightspressrelease

TheJournal.ie. (2016). *Seabirds '10 times' more polluting than humans when it comes to dirtying Ireland's beaches*. Retrieved from https://www.thejournal.ie/seabirds-polluting-humans-beaches-2698817-Apr2016/

Whalen, P. (n.d.). *Lehman Brothers and Repo Accounting*. Retrieved from http://sevenpillarsinstitute.org/case-studies/lehman-brothers-and-repo-accounting

Wikipedia. (n.d.). *Gulls*. Retrieved from https://en.wikipedia.org/wiki/Gull

YandexRadar. (2019). *Top Online Projects in Russia.* Retrieved from https://radar.yandex.ru/top_list?month=2019-05

KEY TERMS AND DEFINITIONS

Business Reputation: A qualitative assessment of the company's activities as well as the actions of its owners, affiliates, subsidiaries, and affiliates.

Digital Marketing: A general term used to refer to the targeted and interactive marketing of goods and services to attract potential customers and retain them as consumers by using digital technologies. The main advantage is the measurability of its results.

Goodwill: An intangible asset associated with the purchase of one company by another. Specifically, goodwill is recorded in a situation in which the purchase price is higher than the sum of the fair value of all identifiable tangible and intangible assets purchased in the acquisition and the liabilities assumed in the process. The value of a company's brand name, solid customer base, good customer relations, good employee relations, and any patents or proprietary technology represent some examples of goodwill.

Information Disclosure: Ensuring the availability of material information about a company or a person to any number of interested parties in accordance with a procedure guaranteeing the data retrieval and receipt, including: information that the [company, person] is obliged to provide in accordance with the requirements of the applicable legislation; information that the [company, person] provides on its own initiative or at a request of a stakeholder.

Reputation Risk: The risk of losses due to an impact of reputation risk factors.

ENDNOTES

1. In 1990 the gazette with its 22 mn circulation (Komsomolskaya Pravda, 10.12.18 22.02) had the largest media audience in the Soviet Union

APPENDIX 1. DIGITAL TRANFORMATION PRACTICE, RESEARCH ON A SAMPLE (MIPT, 2019)

Figure 3. Distribution of business population by digital transformation stages
(Source: MIPT, 2019

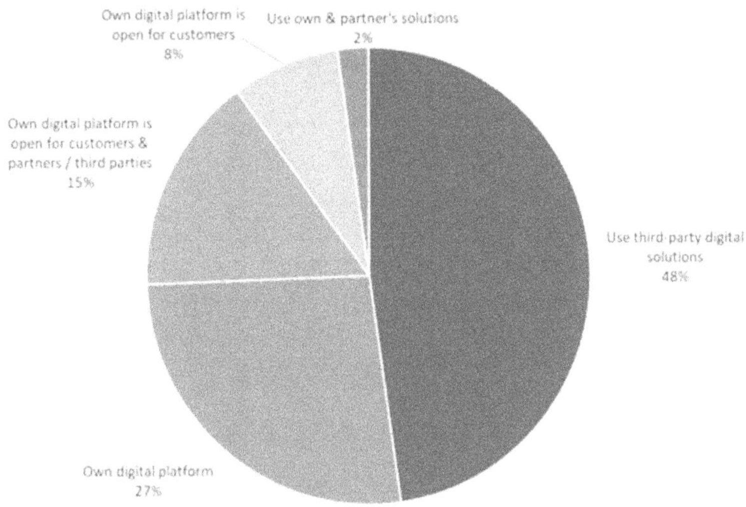

Figure 4. 95% of business population use websites
(Source: MIPT, 2019)

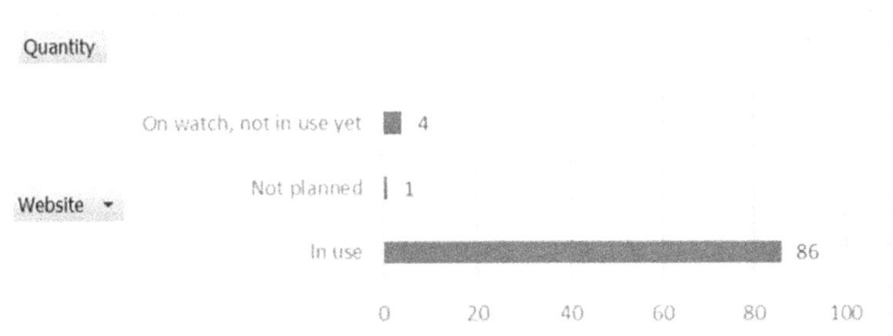

Figure 5. 87% of business population use e-mail
(Source: MIPT, 2019)

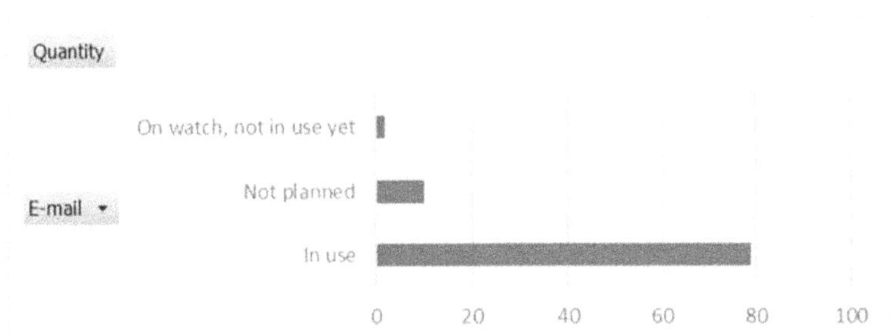

Figure 6. 73% of business population use social networks
(Source: MIPT, 2019)

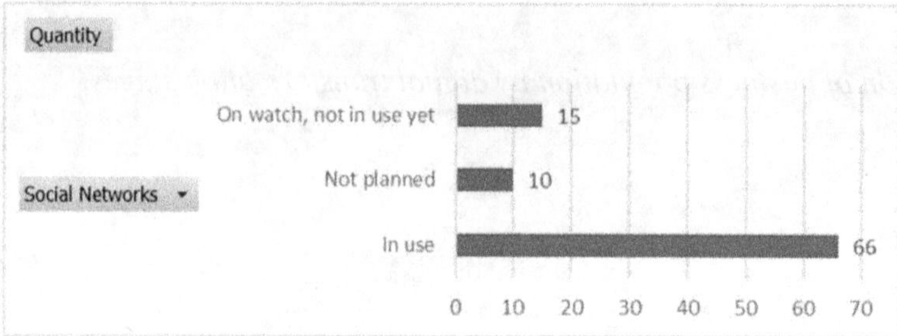

Figure 7. 43% of business population use mobile applications, 30% on watch
(Source: MIPT, 2019)

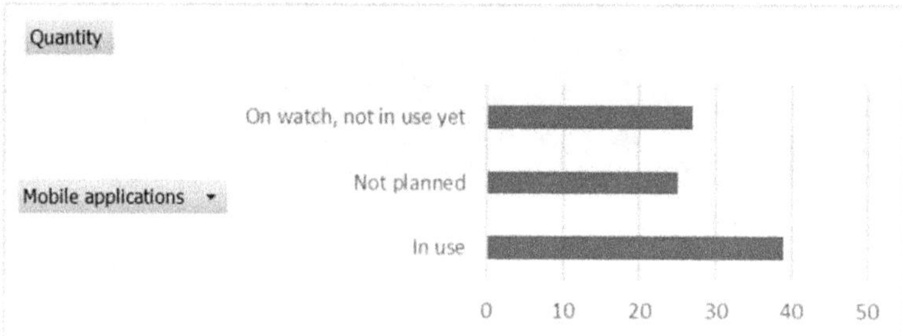

Figure 8. 29% of business population use mobile applications, 36% on watch
(Source: MIPT, 2019)

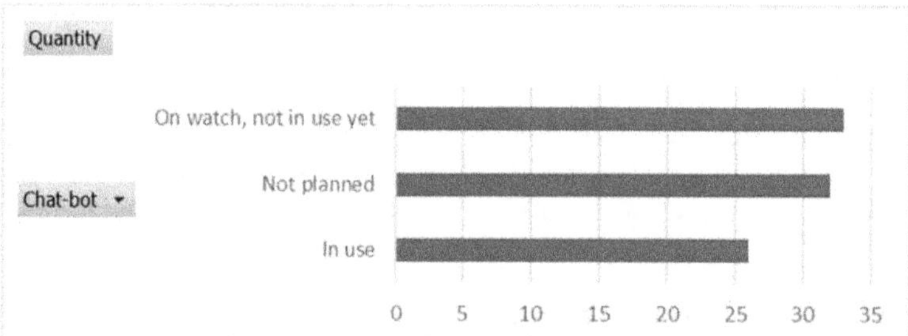

Figure 9. Industry Breakdown
(Source: MIPT, 2019)

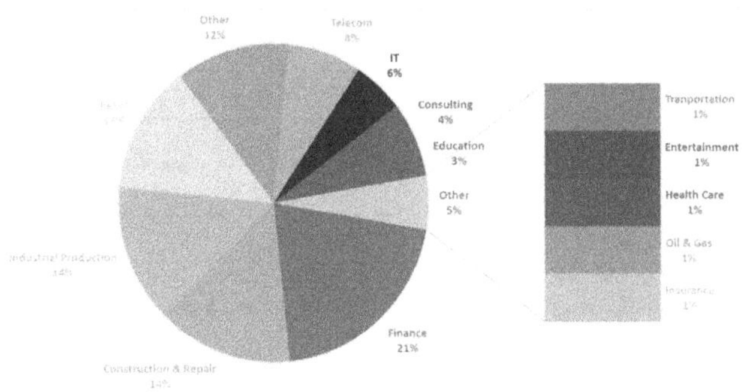

APPENDIX 2. DIGITAL MEDIA AUDIENCE

Table 2. TOP internet projects by Yandex Radar, report period: May 1 – May 31, 2019

Resource name	Resource type	Users (cross-device)	Users (browser)	Average time	Percentage of app users	Daily audience
VK — social network	Social networks	111 000 000	182 000 000			
Yandex — search engine and web portal	Portal	108 616 228	322 537 100	10:28:24	61,02%	45 390 910
Google — search engine	Portal	89 700 000	135 000 000			
Mail.ru — Russian communication portal	Portal	73 200 000	112 000 000			
Ok.ru — social network	Social networks	71 400 000	112 000 000			
YouTube — video hosting	Videos	68 800 000	109 000 000			
Instagram — social network	Social networks	55 100 000	86 000 000			
Yandex.Video — searching and viewing videos	Videos	47 343 029	109 435 400	00:42:03	0,00%	6 983 932
Zen — personal recommendation service	Communities	44 780 291	109 796 350	04:47:52	46,92%	10 255 755
Avito.ru — free want ads	Aggregators	42 393 513	75 203 500	01:07:56	50,36%	7 672 818

Table 3. TOP media holdings by Yandex Radar, report period: May 1 – May 31, 2019

Name	Users (cross-device)	Users (browser)	Average time	Daily audience
Rambler&Co	57 571 974	114 347 950	00:29:50	9 001 101
Gazprom Media Holding	34 267 782	57 235 300	00:16:24	3 660 319
HSM	28 902 908	48 193 950	00:16:50	2 802 905
Russia Today	28 212 960	48 625 750	00:09:48	3 375 911
Komsomolskaya Pravda Digital	27 868 679	44 652 250	00:06:48	2 449 247
VGTRK (State Broadcast Company)	27 857 175	43 922 150	00:06:15	2 623 292
RBC	20 228 848	32 899 150	00:12:26	2 073 359
Moskovskyi Komsomolets	19 349 755	30 829 750	00:05:21	1 685 839
Independent Media	11 086 763	16 364 600	00:03:53	744 259
Burda	8 031 252	11 007 650	00:03:44	420 568
1Mediainvest	6 348 867	8 962 600	00:02:57	386 450
Kinoafisha	5 651 101	7 610 700	00:03:00	275 226
Pravda.Ru	4 316 188	5 760 750	00:01:27	211 406
Maksima Telecom	4 236 828	6 897 900	01:18:24	856 684
Condé Nast Россия	3 796 827	5 324 000	00:02:57	194 105
Multimedia Holding	3 281 017	4 386 600	00:01:56	161 334
Moscow Times	2 839 447	3 936 300	00:02:06	124 032
PDG	2 357 155	3 224 700	00:02:55	102 460
Federal Press	1 009 798	1 338 200	00:01:04	41 195

Table 4. Russian monthly audience aged 12-64 excluding Yandex etc. (Mediascope Web-Index, March 2019)

		Russian Population 100 000+, 12-64
		Reach, thousand
Russian population 100 000+, 12-64		53 207
Internet Users	Desktop&Mobile	46 929
Internet Users	Desktop web	34 313
Internet Users	Mobile (web & apps)	41 946

Table 5. An assessment of the Russian monthly audience aged 12-64 of internet resources, in thousands. (Mediascope Web-Index, March 2019)

Projects	Monthly Reach, Desktop&Mobile
Google	44 857.5
Mail.Ru Group	44 533.4
Yandex	43 608.9
Facebook	41 514.6
Sberbank	34 815.4
Alibaba Group	25 940.1
Rambler&Co	25 505.2
Avito	23 264.4
Wikimedia foundation	22 840.7
Rakuten	22 021.9

Table 6. Russian monthly desktop audience aged 12-64 of internet resources, in thousands. (Mediascope Web-Index, March 2019)

Population of the Russian Federation 0+, 12-64			101,765.6
Internet users		Desktop web	55,462.9
Google Sites	Youtube.com	Desktop web	40,614.6
Mail.Ru Group	Vk.com	Desktop web	38,967.5
Google Sites	Google (ru+com)	Desktop web	38,311.5
Mail.Ru Group	Mail.ru // Post. internal pages	Desktop web	30,856.7
Mail.Ru Group	Mail.ru // Main page	Desktop web	25,958.6
Mail.Ru Group	Odnoklassniki.ru	Desktop web	23,422.2
Avito.ru	Avito.ru	Desktop web	18,067.0
Mail.Ru Group	Mail.ru // Answers	Desktop web	16,548.0
Mail.Ru Group	Mail.ru // News	Desktop web	12,307.0
Rambler&Co	LiveJournal.com	Desktop web	11,271.5
Kinopoisk.ru	Kinopoisk.ru	Desktop web	10,850.6
RIA Novosti	Ria.ru	Desktop web	10,808.0
Rambler&Co	Gazeta.ru	Desktop web	9,699.7
Komsomol'skaya Pravda	Kp.ru	Desktop web	9,599.6
VGTRK / State TV Company	Vesti.ru	Desktop web	8,974.6
Mail.Ru Group	Mail.ru // Moy mir	Desktop web	7,850.4
RBC	Rbc.ru	Desktop web	7,626.1
Rambler&Co	Lenta.ru	Desktop web	7,250.4
Mail.Ru Group	Mail.ru // Lady	Desktop web	7,178.4
Mail.Ru Group	Mail.ru // Cloud	Desktop web	7,148.4
Gismeteo.ru	Gismeteo.ru	Desktop web	6,895.6
Russia Today	Rt.com	Desktop web	6,754.5
Mail.Ru Group	Mail.ru // Search	Desktop web	6,680.4
Iz.ru	Iz.ru	Desktop web	6,560.7
Rossiyskaya Gazette	Rg.ru	Desktop web	6,525.0
Ivi.ru	Ivi.ru	Desktop web	6,313.2
Sportmail.ru	Sportmail.ru	Desktop web	6,186.1

Chapter 4
What to Expect From Artificial Intelligence in Business:
How Wise Board Members Can and Should Facilitate Human-AI Collaboration

Peter Verhezen
Antwerp Management School, Belgium

ABSTRACT

We are increasingly living in a digital world, where companies attempt to adapt to a new context of Industry 4.0. The authors believe that artificial intelligence and the use of logarithms will alter the game of competition. Digitization is moving our economy away from "financial capitalism" to "data capitalism," and companies and their boards need to adopt the way they operate and steer the organization to new ecosystems where personalized service becomes part of the new digital strategy. Basically, it is not a battle of AI versus humans, but rather finding a way to enhance the collaboration of AI and humans in organizations. Despite the enormous potential benefits of AI, boards should not ignore the darker side of AI, namely the potential biasedness and sometimes unfairness of algorithms and privacy concerns and the ubiquitous cyberthreats. This is why proper data governance at the board level is needed. The authors suggest that this becomes a critical success factor to be addressed at boards, either as part of the risk management or strategic committee or as a separated digitization committee.

INTRODUCTION

We are increasingly living in a digital world, where companies attempt to adapt to a new context of Industry 4.0. We believe that Artificial Intelligence and the use of logarithms will alter the game of competition. In such a changed environment where digitization is moving our economy away from "Financial Capitalism" to "Data Capitalism", companies and their boards need to adopt the way they operate and steer the organization to new eco-system where personalized service becomes part of the new digital strategy. Basically, it is not a battle of AI versus humans, but rather finding a way to enhance

DOI: 10.4018/978-1-7998-2011-6.ch004

the collaboration of AI and humans in organizations. However, despite the enormous potential benefits of AI, boards should not ignore the darker side of AI, namely the potential biasedness and sometimes unfairness of algorithms and privacy concerns, and the ubiquitous cyberthreats. Hence why proper data governance at the board level is needed. We may suggest that this becomes a critical success factor to be addressed at boards, either as part of the Risk Management or Strategic Committee or as a separated Subcommittee – for instance Digitization Committee.

BACKGROUND

Today, a majority of people are communicating via social media leaving digital traces which provides the "new oil" - or data – used by organizations that claim to facilitate the quality of our daily life. Indeed, our world is being dramatically influenced and driven by big data. In 2000, about 25% of all data were digitized, about 18 years later, 97% of all data are digitized in one form or another. In the future, data-rich markets will offer individual choices without the constraints of inescapable cognitive limitations.

A majority of people in the developed but increasingly also in emerging markets now communicate via the prevailing channels of social media – be it Facebook, WhatsApp, Instagram, Snapchat, Twitter, LinkedIn to name a few, which are all powered by digital data and algorithms. In the future, data-rich markets will offer individual choices without the constraints of inescapable cognitive limitations. Indeed, data are fast combining the new oil. We could easily argue that we are moving from a *finance capitalist system* to a form of *data capitalism*, facilitated by the growing internet traffic or network effect, massive data sets, and the enhanced processing data capacity or analytical power of computer. One of the consequence of this data capitalism lies in the curious shift from causation – as scientists have looked for through appropriate statistical methodology – to correlation where data "speak for themselves", without necessarily understanding the why behind the correlation. Current (narrow) AI applications are not able to generate causal relationships, as UCLA computer scientist and mathematician Judea Pearl argues (2019). AI today remains an algorithmitization of supervised data, allowing to recognize (sometimes complex and ambiguous) patterns in a speedy and efficient manner, whereby this non-causal analysis and mere correlations are often fast and reasonable cheap. But this narrow artificial intelligence cannot answer the why behind any mathematical equation, and AI cannot reflect yet how humans think in terms of general purpose. The human brain observes and continuously searches for causal links from limited data, based on a certain assumed model – which is quite different of how AI algorithms operate today.

But what is Artificial Intelligence (AI)? Is AI the branch of computer science that is concerned with the automation of intelligent behavior? We all can agree in principle that **intelligence** is the ability to deploy novel means to attain a goal – which are extraneous to the intelligence. In other words, intelligence is the ability to accomplish complex goals. The distinction between specialized intelligence and general intelligence helps clarify the difference between the specialized abilities of today's learning machines or (narrow) AI and humans' more general abilities. **Artificial Intelligence** is the overarching science that is concerned with intelligent algorithms, whether or not they learn from data. The adjective *Artificial* refers to intelligent machines that fullfil certain objectives, and more particularly, machines that learn to apply statistical techniques to supervised data that allows them to find patterns in complex big data in a much faster and intelligent manner than humans. This obviously lead to a number of advantages when these data analytics are applied to our current life as in voice or image recognition. **Machine learning** is a subfield of AI devoted to algorithms that learn from data (Husain, 2015; Finlay, 2018). Artificial intelligent machines are "smarter" – faster and better – than humans in terms of certain kinds of specialized knowledge or intelligence. But it remains very specialized knowledge about a certain specific domain and AI cannot compete with humans in terms of general purpose thinking and creative processes for which human executives are so sought after (Brockman, 2019; Ford, 2018).

IBM's Watson may have beaten the human champion at Jeopardy, but it can't play any chess game at all. A Tesla car may (sort of) drive autonomously, but that car cannot autonomously pick up a box at the near Carrefour center. Building some form of intelligence out of pure information technology based on digital data without human components is what people normally refer as "artificial intelligence". IT researchers Davenport and Ronanki (2018) distinguish 3 types of ***Artificial*** Intelligence: (1) *Process Automation* with robotics and cognitive automation (counting today for about 52% of the "AI-applications"), (2) *Cognitive Insights* that allows better predictions which will be our focus (roughly worth 35% of today AI-applications), and (3) *Cognitive Engagement* as in natural language processing chatbots and intelligent assistants (mounting to about 13% of the total AI practices). AI can help is in improving our innovative insights and reduce our biases in our presumed rational thinking, but AI improves our cognitive prediction abilities. "Artificial intelligence" does not actually bring us intelligence but instead a critical component of intelligence, namely *prediction* in a cost-efficient manner (i.e. AI will make prediction cheap). Prediction – i.e. "if-then" logical intelligence - is the process of filling in missing information. Prediction take digital information you have, data, and use it to generate information you don't have. For instance, statistical regression minimizes prediction mistakes on average which is a powerful tool with relatively small data sets. With the vast amount of personal data, however, digital devices will learn more about us than we may know about ourselves, enabling us "to better predict" and thus allowing us to make better and smarter decisions by reducing uncertainty. Not surprisingly, Google's CEO Sundar Pichai sees a shift in Google from "searching and organizing the world's information to AI and machine learning".

As the cost of prediction continues to drop, we'll use more of it for traditional prediction problems such as inventory management because we can predict faster, cheaper, and better (Agrawal, 2018). At the same time, firms start using prediction to solve problems that have not historically been thought of as prediction problems. For example, we never thought of autonomous driving as a prediction problem. Traditionally, engineers programmed an autonomous vehicle to move around in a controlled environment, such as a factory or warehouse, by telling it what to do in certain situations—*if* a human walks in front of the vehicle (*then* stop) or *if* a shelf is empty (*then* move to the next shelf). But we could never put those vehicles on a city street because there are too many *ifs*— *if* it's dark, *if* it's rainy, *if* a child runs into the street, *if* an oncoming vehicle has its blinker on. No matter how many lines of code we write, we couldn't cover all the potential *ifs*. Today we can reframe autonomous driving as a prediction problem. Then an AI simply needs to predict the answer to one question: What would a good human driver do? There are a limited set of actions we can take when driving ("*thens*"). We can turn right or left, brake or accelerate—that's it. So, to teach an AI to drive, we put a human in a vehicle and tell the human to drive while the AI is figuratively sitting beside the human watching. Since the AI doesn't have eyes and ears like we do, we give it cameras, radar, and light detection and ranging (LIDAR). In a way, machine learning does induce theories – a set of constraints on what the world would be, not necessarily a complete description of it - from data. The AI takes the input data as it comes in through its "eyes" and looks over to the human and tries to predict, "What will the human do next?" The AI makes a lot of mistakes at first. But it learns from its mistakes and updates its model every time it incorrectly predicts an action the human will take. Its predictions start getting better and better until it becomes so good at predicting what a human would do that we don't need the human to do it anymore. The AI can perform the action itself as long as the infrastructure is available

Figure 1. Wise Decision-Making
Source: Verhezen, P., (2018): Wising Up enable Managers to be commercially savvy, to make reasonable smart decisions, but also to commit to responsible behavior that distinguishes smart from wise leadership:

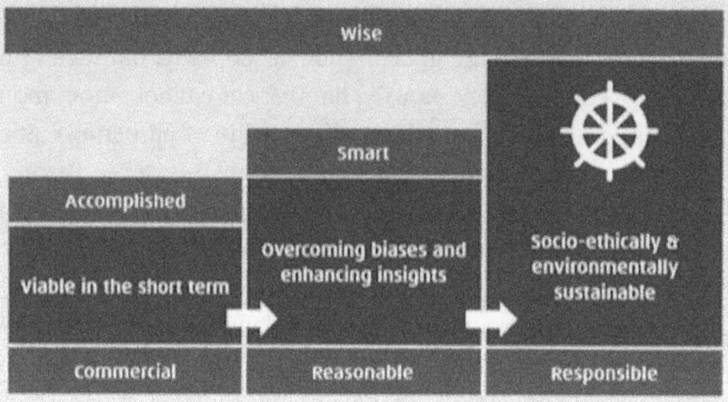

which means that high-speed connectivity is continuous and of good quality - requiring a 5G network. Businesses are expecting that we are close to a tipping point in materializing this idea of automated cars in geofenced situations and for ships. In non-geofenced circumstances autonomous driving – e.g. non-rectangular logically built cities as you often find in Europe – autonomous driving may face a number of serious technical challenges that may delay full autonomous driving for a while.

But this progress of better "prediction" leaves us with a crucial question: who does own the data and how can these personal data be used by organizations? Indeed, we should acknowledge the fact that today, more data means less privacy; more speed means less accuracy, and more autonomy means less control. More expected accuracy means less *explainability*. There are trade-offs to be decided upon. And let us not forget the simple heuristics that if "data or the application is free, then you are the product". The real customers are those who are willing to pay for access to knowledge about us (derived from these data), so that they can persuade us to purchase a product or influence us. Moreover, "datafication" is not value-neutral either – as we will argue – and using data still requires theory building on which they depend.

The power of this "dataficated" reality, be it biotech, nanotechnology, robotics, cyber-technology or Artificial Intelligence systems will have a huge impact on everyday life; it records all our movements, human interactions and financial transactions, all stored in the 'cloud'. This new reality within *Industry 4.0* will facilitate our life and possibly enhances it. This transactional improved efficiency will likely result in more sustainable solutions. But at the down side, this *Industry 4.0* will also be managed and possibly manipulated by a few multinational quasi-monopolies, and in worst scenario, the global inter-connectivity could also result in systemic failure.

Businesses need competent and smart employees and managers; increasingly, business is in need of wise leadership to deal with the ambiguities of the enormous global challenges. We believe in the enormous benefits of digital innovative technologies, in particular AI from which deep learning machines is a well-known example. However, wise leadership will need to find an integrated balance between these undeniable positive opportunities by AI and the darker side of AI.

(*cf.* http://www.verhezen.net/images/papers/VERHEZEN_2018_Amrop_AI_and_Wise_Leadership_181010.pdf)

Indeed, we believe that wise decision-making is only possible when managers make smarter decisions, by reducing their biases and potential errors on the one hand, while probing creativity and enhancing environments where innovation can thrive. Our belief is that Deep Learning Machines and Artificial Intelligence as in improving cognitive insights can help humans to make better decisions by reducing errors and by enhancing innovative tools and economic efficiency. Uncertainty, errors, and human biases (i.e. human irrationality) could potentially be significantly reduced by having artificial intelligent machines using the availability of big data to improve predictions or to find for the human eye or brain hidden patterns. Similarly, the tools – be it digital automation or cognitive engagement - that originate from artificial intelligence can be easily incorporated in innovative products and services or employed in robotics to take over repetitive boring or extremely dangerous work.

However, managers and corporate leaders cannot ignore the potential negative implications of artificial intelligence that may jeopardize quite a number of jobs and employment (London, Cui & Whigley, 2019). The social implications could be enormous in certain industries and areas. Moreover, the ethical implications of smart machines could be devastating if not handled properly (Burkhardt, Hohn, Wigley, 2019). At the other hand, the non-financial objectives and intangibles as expressed in the notion of ESG (Environmental, Social-Ethical and Governance objectives) can be improved and assisted by collaborative efforts of smart engineers and managers with artificial intelligence that significantly improve decision-making, taking into account certain stakes beyond mere profitability that are more socio-ethical and ecological sound. Our organizations could benefit from using AI applications in the decision-making process to become more responsible. Having a better understanding of what could happen in the future, based on the power of predictive AI applications, could help to nudge decisions in a certain more sustainable direction. It could inform executives to make a better selection of scarce raw materials, or extend the lifespan of electronics through predictive maintenance, or automate and improve e-waste recycling infrastructure through the combination of image recognition and robotics. Researchers believe that artificial intelligence tools could contribute to a more circular economy by taking advantage of abundant data in 3 major ways: (1) design of circular products, components and materials whereby iterative machine-learning-assisted design processes allow for rapid prototyping and testing, (2) operating of circular business models – product-as-a-service and leasing that increase product circulation and asset utilization through better pricing and demand prediction, predictive maintenance and smart inventory management, and (3) optimizing circular infrastructure where AI can help build and improve the reverse logistics infrastructure required to close the loop on products and materials by improving processes to sort and disassemble products, remanufacture components and recycle materials (Schouteden & Sturges, 2018). Indeed, AI could assist human decision-makers with better models and scenarios for climate change or weather forecasts. In case of natural disasters, AI could assist rescue workers to enhance the [efficiency of] disaster recovery efforts, by mapping and analyzing digitized struck areas, and possibly come up with better or faster rescue solutions.

The use of AI does not necessarily need to result in devastating unemployment as long as wise leaders foresee and prepare themselves and the community for a world where both humans and smart and extremely fast machines will be able to collaborate. And last but not least, corporate governance of organizations embracing big data will require proper data governance and guarantees that negative outcomes with the use of AI – be it cyber breaches or unethical decisions or privacy concerns – will need to be limited.

We here will briefly explain some of the potential benefits of artificial intelligence, after which we also focus on the darker side of deep learning machines powered by AI. Good AI should be distinguished from bad AI. Finally, we will conclude by indicating how smart human decision-makers could collaborate with AI, and why wise leadership and wise boards are needed to monitor and direct the organization towards such beneficial and appropriate collaboration, while not ignoring and preventing or minimize the darker side of AI to materialize.

The Potential Benefits of Artificial Intelligence

Just consider the GPS lead systems that are behind guiding autonomous driving cars or virtual assistants like *Apple's Siri* and *Amazon's Echo*. These tools are reflections of the way we have been thinking and talking. Artificial Intelligence, today, is functioning by brute force using millions of samples, using re-inforcement learning based on little pieces to approximate a desired function. *Vanguard*, an investment service company, uses cognitive technology (or a form of AI tool) to provide customers with investment advice at a lower cost than their competitors. Its Personal Advisor Services system automates may traditional tasks of investment, while human advisors focus on higher-value activities.

A majority of people in the developed but increasingly also in emerging markets now communicate via the prevailing channels of social media. Facebook, Instagram, Snapchat, Twitter, LinkedIn to name a few, are all powered by digital data and algorithms. *Amazon*, for instance, looks for unique patterns in the data they receive from customers which reveal the preferences of these customers. Identifying such patterns enables Amazon to statistically deduce customers' wants and needs without having to ask them directly. The data approximately tell what you and I want. The data do not know why we prefer one thing over another; it just "sees" that we choose one over the other, indicating some hidden patterns of our preferences. But that is sufficient for Amazon to feed the preferences-matching algorithm and search for the products [potential] customers are most likely to purchase. Artificial Intelligence seems to be a functional new tool that provides intelligence unavailable before. Or does it? Could it also be that Artificial Intelligence is only the newest fad in town: every organization is eager to put forward the enormous benefits of this newest digital technology, without really knowing how to turn this abundance of data in real changing business models. However, Amazon seems to know what it is doing: it just opened to the public a physical grocery store without check-out lanes or cashiers. You'll fill up your bag, walk out the front door, and get a receipt minutes later for everything that is in your bag: no human interaction is involved in the transaction.

Quite a number of companies are already taking advantage of big data and its prediction power. *Aviva*, a private global insurance company, is now able to predict insurance claims not based anymore on a detailed report of the health of its subscribers - who may have given blood and urine examples costing the company USD 125 per person for the analysis – but on credit reports and consumer marketing data which cost only USD 5 per person on average. Those data on the life style of people taking an insurance now function as a proxy to predict the health of these customers.

Banks can detect credit card fraud by looking at anomalies, and the best way to find them is to crunch all the data – big data - rather than a sample. The card network uses information or data about past fraudulent (and nonfraudulent) transactions to predict whether a particular recent transaction is anormal and possibly fraudulent, and preventing actual fraud or future illegal transactions.

When a mall operator uses advanced analytics to select tenants, optimize mall layout, and determine rents, its revenues can rise by 20 percent, according to a McKinsey survey. With its ability to enable personalization and customization at scale, AI can be a powerful differentiator for consumer-facing businesses. It improves precision and speed-to-market, and increases and enhances the potential for interactions, engagement, and transactions. Companies such as *Spotify* playlists, the *Facebook* newsfeed combine human and computer expertise to create new services and enable people to discover and engage with content and brands in new ways.

A few organizations use AI for personalization better than the listed fashion online organization *Stitch Fix* or the movie streaming giant *Netflix*. These organizations basically personalize their offers to individual customers by applying a sophisticated algorithm that is using continuous conditional probability calculations - which is the chance that one thing happens, given that some other thing has already happened. Conditional probability is how AI systems express judgments in a way that reflects their partial knowledge. And personalization algorithms run on conditional probabilities, all of which must be estimated from big data sets in which you as an individual are the conditioning event. Real problems are framed in terms of conditional probability (if-then logic) to solve them. Computers do not understand why you are watching a particular movie, but they are great at crunching data, i.e. tabulating vast databases of subscribers' movie-watching histories from a ratings matrix to estimate conditional probabilities of individual movies' preferences - discovered organically by AI. In other words, digital economy is about suggestions and thus conditional probability, translated into prediction, rather than search.

In AI, recognizing a pattern means fitting an equation to data through *supervised learning* (i.e. the algorithm detects interesting features in data where the end game is a predictive model of some sort). The big breakthrough in AI was the introduction of the use of neural networks for estimating prediction rules from data. The misleading notion of "neural network" is a complicated equation with a lot of parameters that is capable of describing very complicated patterns in data. These neural networks work incredibly well across a range of prediction tasks, from language to images to video. However, despite the initial excitement for AI using *reinforced learning*[1] – because this kind of learning resembles more how we humans think through trial and error – the number of successful reinforcement learning based solutions in (narrow) AI is tiny compared to the number of supervised learning ones - over 95% of the AI cases (Finely, 2018).

Other examples are governments that understand having sensors affixed to bridges and buildings to watch for signs of wear and tear could and is preventing potential disasters to occur. The cost of collecting and analyzing the data that indicate when to take early action is lower than the cost of an outage. Note that these predictive analytics may not explain the cause of the problem (the why), it may only indicate that a problem exists (the what). *General Electric* and *Rolls Royce* both have implemented big data analytics into their commercial jet engine business to predict more accurately when to replace expensive parts or when to optimally start maintenance of the jet engines, allowing those firms to apply new business models by leasing or renting power to the airplanes instead of merely selling engines.

Indeed, computers have significantly improved at image and voice recognition and speech synthesis. Computers can now detect tumors in radiographs earlier than most humans. Medical diagnosis and personalized medicine will improve substantially. Transportation by self-driving cars – where transportation is transformed into a prediction problem - will keep us safer, on average. And hopefully, we can sort out the ethical challenges regarding the use of this new kind of digitized intelligence.

Figure 2. Collaboration between humans and machines
Source: Interpretation by Verhezen, P. (2019) of model by Schoemaker & Tetlock (2017)

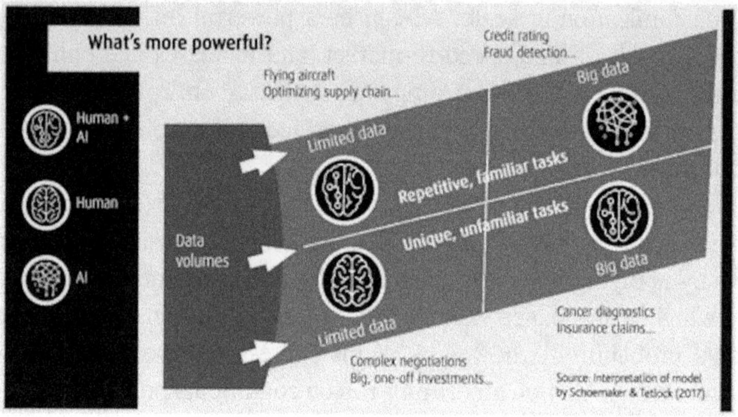

Now that everything becomes increasingly "datafied", it looks like we can measure most aspects of human life, and with those powerful machine-learning techniques, we now can build ecosystems (Lohr, 2015). Well-known examples are weather- and traffic-prediction models which are being extended to predict the global climate and plan city growth and renewal. MIT professor Sandy Pentland and his team for instance, researches to how human behavior and ecosystems interact; this "social physics" looks at patterns of cultural behavior and develops mathematically accurate predictions how people make decisions. At present, organizations are trying to influence conscious processes and explicit knowledge. Yet, Pentland's research indicates that sociometric data show that unconscious processes and tacit knowledge are potentially even more important in determining the behavior of organizations. Let us summarize our understanding of using AI to make smarter decisions so far:

The progress in AI will in many cases be exponential rather than linear. Already the progress in a wide range of applications (e.g., vision, natural language, motion control) over the last 12 months was faster than in the 12 months prior, according to McKinsey and the Boston Consulting Group. The level of investment is increasing rapidly. The quality- adjusted cost of sensors is falling exponentially. And the amount of data being generated is increasing exponentially. In most cases, when AIs are properly designed and deployed, they're better predictors than humans are. And yet we're often still reluctant to hand over the reins of prediction to machines. For example, there have been studies comparing human recruiters to AI-powered recruiters that predict which candidates will perform best in a job. When performance was measured 12, 18, and 24 months later, the recruits selected by the AI outperformed those selected by the human recruiters, on average. Despite this evidence, human recruiters still often override the recommendations provided by AI system when making real hiring decisions. Where Artificial Intelligence have demonstrated superior performance in prediction, companies must carefully consider the conditions under which to empower humans to exercise their discretion to override the AI. The organizations that will benefit most from AI will be the ones that are able to most clearly and accurately specify their objectives. Remember that today AI is at its best within very specific domain of expertise, assistance or automation. We're going to see a lot of the currently fuzzy mission statements become much clearer. The companies that are able to sharpen their visions the most will reap the most benefits from AI. Due to the methods used to train AIs, AI effectiveness is directly tied to goal-specification clarity. What makes AI so powerful is its ability to learn. Normally we think of labour as being learners and of capital as being fixed. Now, with AI, we have capital that learns. Companies need to ensure that information flows into decisions, they follow decisions to an outcome, and then they learn from the outcome and feed that learning back into the system. Managing the learning loop will be more valuable than ever before.

The way one can make individuals and groups smarter, the way one can make a more "humanized AI", will work only if feedback is truthful. In other words, data must be grounded on truth. However, manipulative advertising, propaganda and "fake news" destroy the usefulness of social sampling and data in general. We need data that we all can trust and we also need fair, data-driven assessment of public norms, policy and government based on trusted data about current conditions. Only under those circumstances, the individual and especially societies' overall fitness and intelligence can improve or can be "trusted".

Obviously, data-driven markets offer compelling advantages, and innovation and progress should not be stifled by irrational emotional fears or too stringent regulations. But the shortcomings and ethical challenges should not be ignored, especially the concentration of data and the possible systemic failure. And in case real artificial general intelligence would become a reality, a "matrix"-like intelligence, we really should be concerned about the malicious consequences of such super powerful machine-related intelligence. What interests us here is the importance of transparency of information and its algorithms to reduce potential information asymmetry. In other words, can data governance control artificial intelligence?

The Darker Side of Artificial Intelligence

We can assume that in most cases, the aim to use data and algorithms can be a force of progress and good use. Algorithms are used to help us better understand the world. Algorithms underlying artificial intelligence are only as good as the big data input. Indeed, algorithms are programmed to collect and categorize a vast amount of data points in order to identify patterns in a user's online behavior that could allow recommendations and more precise predictions. The algorithmic identity in any application gets more complex with every social media interaction, the clicking or likewise ignoring of advertisements, and the financial status as derived from online payments. Huge amounts of digitized data are now available. The more people share their personal information and preferences on social media – and people feel empowered to do so -, smart entrepreneurs will definitely take advantage and initiate new algorithms that embrace the enormous amount of data in cyber-space, and commercialize them in one form or another, or in best scenario initiate new insightful patterns that could help common good. Would it be too farsighted to put the argument forward that the intentional accumulation of "like it" on *Facebook* is nothing else as the product of an algorithm that rewards attention-seeking and shock value? What could undermine the benefits of AI? However, some entrepreneurs like Elon Musk, the CEO of *Tesla* and *SpaceX*, and the late Cambridge physicist Stephen Hawking claim that general AI and smart machines may become "our biggest existential threat" as a species. We discuss a few of those negative issues that is mostly inherent to big data analytics.

Biasedness

Facebook's algorithm decides what information to show us on the basis of the choices we already have made. This filter algorithm used by Facebook may create a filter bubble or echo chambers, even for initially unbiased people. The filter model picks up small initial differences and exaggerates them until the other side of the argument is lost. And we do not mention even the spreading of untrue rumors that become fake news which has become a source of constant entertainment. As in a kind of post-truth world.

The popular *Tinder* application for instance uses algorithms to romantically link people together is an example of what can be described as "amplified biasedness" by the machine learning. Tinder is one of the fastest growing social networking apps on a global scale with users in 190 countries swiping 1,6 billion pictures and generating around 20 billion matches every day. This location-based dating application plays a game-changing role in the dating world. However, we should not ignore how the biases of Tinder algorithms is a reflection of our society and how we analyze and perceive humans. Despite the personal swiping choices we make in finding a romantic partner, this online dating application seems to be reinforcing racial prejudices. Depending on how an algorithm is programmed – and Tinder's "magic" black box is not revealing how it functions -, the users' online behavior and the set of data it is given to process the intended matching process, certain cultural aspects will be highlighted, visualized and prioritized while others are left out or rendered invisible. This kind of algorithms are not value-free and reflect the cultural and individual preferences and human biases as in a darker shadow, not exactly expected from a cold presumably objectively calculating machine.

It should not surprise us that the specific workings of algorithms remain rather elusive, as developers and data scientists rarely provide the coding of the underlying programs in the name of technological neutrality and objectivity and in order to preclude unnecessary competition. But we can derive some basic features of the Tinder application: since each user expresses individual preferences, the system provides personalized recommendation which are obtained through collaborative filtering and algorithmic calculations. Tinder's "algorithm of desire" all boils down to ranking people according to their desirability – based on "skill levels". Nobody wants to be rejected. Tinder complied with this psychological insight by keeping the left swipes unknown to the users. Similarly, the right swipes are kept secret as well, and sometimes matches are not shown to slow down the very desirable people – the "winner should not take all" [desirable…] - to give people with lower raking a chance, and thus keep Tinder in the game. Not exactly neutral, is it. But psychologically, you could describe it as smart but not necessarily wise business thinking.

Humans are now constantly bombarded with personalized recommendations based on our online behavior and data sharing on social networks as *Facebook, Twitter, Amazon, Spotify* and *Netflix*. Machine-learning algorithms paired with AI is designed to develop in a manner – attempting in mimicking the human process of learning (seeing, remembering and creating a pattern in one's mind) – that allows Tinder's AI-paired algorithm for instance to develop its own point of view on people. The AI system does not know why it is recommending a particular match, but has strategically learned to develop a "thinking" (i.e. finding correlating patterns) that could resemble human intuition. The system identifies languages and words that share a common context which could potentially indicate similarities, potentially resulting in swipes that are clustered together reflecting perceived preferences through these embedded vectors of the participants' likes. Unfortunately, such algorithms also reflect the darker side of our culture: embedded biasedness. Apparently, studies reveal that Black women and Asian men are potentially marginalized and possibly discriminated in such online dating environments. With all the dare consequences. If initially several Caucasian matches were "successful" for instance, the algorithm will continue on the same biased trajectory. Confirming a "statistical commonality" according to gender, class or race in supplying a meaning for those categories, will be "learned, analyzed" and conceptualized by the algorithm. Not exactly the most neutral manner to advertise your "assets". Admittedly, the data points remain hidden in the black box and cannot be overridden by any external critical remark or research, but it reinforces our suspicion against presumed cold speedy machines and its algorithm that are advertised to be neutral and objective. The opposite is true.

Specific biases in the used criteria and variables in these algorithms are either unexamined or remain unconscious and unaware by the data designers, enhancing our point that we should be worried to blindly trust these algorithms. And here we face a paradox: machine learning AI pretends to be neutral and provide better decision-making options whereas in reality the underlying criteria and variables of these algorithms – often based on detecting personal preferences through behavioral patterns to come up with recommendations - are nothing else as a mirror to our societal practices, potentially even reinforcing existing biases. Indeed, societal biased garbage in, biased garbage out. The game of speedy and more precise predictions is not so objective as being proclaimed by the owners of these apps. Even if we or those owners have the best intentions, those intentions too could be easily (socially or personally) biased.

Unethical Use of Data and Fairness

Datasets could easily be turned into unethical use as *Facebook* has shown during the US elections in 2016. *Cambridge Analytica* used a personality model – the big five personality traits test - in its promotional material to send specific political tailored messages and ads catered to people and undecided voters with a specific profile to influence the US elections. What about Google possible decision to drop "do not evil" in its mission statement mid 2018, allowing the possible road to be opened for a watered-down version of a Google search engine – aptly labelled Dragonfly which blocks or self-censures sensitive topics regarding human rights for instance – to consider a re-entry into China's huge consumer market. Moreover, artificial intelligence is more like advertising intelligence where big corporations have got better at collecting consumer data, filter and package them and sell them back to these consumers in the form of recommendations.

We can easily argue that the code of algorithms is not value-neutral – it contains many judgments about who we are, who we should become, and how we should live. In case we would be asked to choose a software solution, will we be subtly influenced to buy from a particular online vendor and will we be affected by the vendor's (subconscious) prescriptive norms and values. What if these values are less than benevolent? The business ethicist Edward Freeman highlights this ethical conundrum by asking what will happen when a self-driving car under certain unfortunate circumstances – where an accident cannot be avoided – will need to make a (algorithmic) decision by making a choice about whether to sacrifice its occupants or risk (possibly fatally) harming passengers in other cars or pedestrians. How to implement robo-ethics or address ethical challenges with respect to AI? "How to guide developers to write this code", Freeman is asking. Keeping in mind that facts are distinct from values, we can conjecture that from an evolutionary perspective, our genes and memes attempt to survive. If we attempt to bring ethics into machine learning, it leads to a whole series of Trolley problems. At what number of people in line for death should the computer or GPS system decide to shift a moving trolley to one person? It remains an ethical challenge for most humans to make a fair and just decision. Obviously, we could also turn the whole Trolley problem by questioning who has given pedestrians access to the rails. These kind of judgments about moral and ethical choices are just as important as they always have been.

Even if a data set is accurately reflecting historical facts, it does not mean that these data are [ethical] fair, especially if it can proven that history itself was not necessarily fair. We should question whether an algorithm is fair, whether AI is doing things that humans believe are ethical. Bringing ethics into AI, one needs a human-in-the-loop approach as in an "open algorithm", not a black box.

An example of unfair use of data here is "predictive policing or profiling". Researchers like David Sumpter (2018) argue that commercial software that is widely used to predict recidivism is no more accurate or fair than the predictions of people with little to no criminal justice experience. At best, algorithms may match the accuracy of humans in this exercise, but just much faster. So while these models are far from perfect, they can be useful speedy tools. Admittedly, studies by Professor Philip Tetlock from the Wharton School found out that the average "expert" was 'roughly as accurate as a dart-throwing chimpanzee'. However, experts who were able to continuously include new info/data in their probabilistic reasoning, created bell-shaped curves in their head and drastically improved their predictions. But still it is hard to beat the collective wisdom. And here algorithms basically reflect the collective data on which that wisdom could be derived from.

There is not necessarily an equation of fairness, and the normative notion cannot be fully derived from descriptive logic. This brings us to David Hume's is-ought problem whereby there is a deep gap between what is (a scientific objective reality) and what ought to be – i.e. an ethical question of how we want to live and what kind of society do we want. Hume's dichotomy between "is" and "ought" implies that what ought to be cannot be directly derived from what is, and therefore aspiring ideals cannot really be bridged by algorithms. On the contrary, algorithms may reinforce "old ethical habits and norms". Only conscious and mindful humans – who hopefully can be considered wise decision makers – can put forward what kind of society we want to live in, what kind of life we want to strive for. Moreover, research by Ernest Fehr and others with the Ultimatum tests for instance indicate that the notion of fairness seems to be inherent to human thinking. What society we would like, what we consider as 'fair', our aspirations are norms set to make it a better world. Using the factual data of what is in the world does not make it a good "prescriber", only a good "recommendation engine in perpetuity". No change should be expected from such (commercial) thinking, unless we explicitly bring in these values and norms that aspire for a better and different future. Science does not provide the answers to normative [ethical] questions.

The Dictatorship of Data & Paralyzing Privacy

We can easily fall into the trap of the fetish of quantification and data. However, the quality of underlying data can be poor or even biased. It can be mis-analyzed or used in a misleading manner. And worse, data can also fail to capture what it purports to quantify. And consequently, we may attribute a degree of truth to the data which it does not deserve. Many thinkers have argued that creative brilliance does not depend on data[2].

The increasing reliance on data may also lead to the risks of a "tyranny of algorithms" where unelected data scientists and data experts are running the world. The incredible power of *Google*, *Amazon*, *Facebook*, *Apple*, *Microsoft*, *Baidu*, *Alibaba*, *Tencent* and others cannot be overstated. They currently control the data, and thus they control AI. Can we trust these organizations that they do the right thing, always? Not quite. The shadow of Big Brother seems to start looming over the use of our social media.

Moreover, the internet has made tracking easier, cheaper and more useful. However, the internet and big data also threatens our privacy. The *Cambridge Analytica* debacle – which used data from Facebook to influence the US elections and possibly the Brexit vote – shows that through access of personal data, companies and individuals (having access to these data) can influence human's behavior through personalized messages and advertising in a way never seen before. We believe that individuals should own and control access to their personal data, instead of the application providers. Moreover, in non-democratic states, or even in nominally democratic ones, government know things about their citizens that was considered fiction during Orwell's *1984* time. And obviously, the prospect of AI for malicious military purposes remains frightening.

Moreover, research demonstrates that rating just 6 obscure movies (out of the top 500) could identify a Netflix customer 84% of the time; if one knew the date on which a person rated the movies, the accuracy rate apparently increased to an incredible 98%. Hence why in an era of big data, the three core strategies long used to ensure privacy – (1) individual notice and consent, (2) opting out, and (3) anonymization – have lost much of their effectiveness. It is obvious that privacy is under attack from all sides. To what extent should the power of the internet and AI firms be clipped and constrained to secure the privacy of the individual?

Probability and Punishment

Big data threaten to imprison us – perhaps literally – in probabilities. For instances, the use of big data to conduct "predictive policing" may seem to be sensible, but it also stigmatizes certain socio-racial groups further. Using big data analysis to select what streets, groups, and individuals to subject to extra scrutiny, simply because an algorithm pointed them as more likely to commit a crime. For instance, US Homeland security's FAST (future, attribute screening technology) and other foreign Western government agencies try to identify potential terrorists by monitoring individual vital signs, body language and other psychological patterns. If these data and analyses are misused, it can lead not only to discrimination against certain groups but also to "guilt" by association. Punishing people before they do something bad negates the very idea of the presumption of innocence – the principle upon which our legal system as well as our sense of fairness is based. We should acknowledge that thinking bad things is not illegal; doing them is. Guilt is only possible when someone actually committed an (illegal) act or crime, not thought of it, or may have a higher probability to potentially commit a crime because of a specific social-economic background.

Predictive analytics predicated on mechanical objectivity comes at a price. Indeed, in the courtroom, objectivity, trade secrets and judicial transparency may pull in opposite directions. Mechanical objectivity is not the same as ethical thinking. Nor is such objectivity necessary reflecting the essence of scientific thinking or discovery. And such probability thinking also deprives us from a free will and erodes the fundamental notion of human dignity.

What Kind of Intelligence do Smart Computers Have? Is Singularity Near?

The arrival of neural networks made computer even more intelligent. Neural nets, whose basic design was directly inspired by our brain's architecture, have scored some spectacular successes in game playing, and patter recognition. Face recognition in *Apple*'s iPhone X uses neural networks to uniquely identify its owner's face. Convolutional neural networks, a form of regression model used to predict, is used for face and voice recognition. This principal component analysis uses the data to classify people, rather than relying on our preconceptions. Such component analysis and similar mathematical approaches underlie most of the algorithm used to classify behavior. Machine-learning, or self-learning or deep learning attempts mimicking our human brain - learning by itself – enabling the computer device and algorithm to learn "automatically" without us telling them what to do, or what patterns to pay attention to. Computers seem to become smarter by the day. Will AI out-smart us?

Whether AI will make humans subservient or obsolete, or whether AI will become a beneficial enhancement of our abilities to enrich our lives, the effective outcome of these different scenarios remains hard to predict at this point. *Tesla* uses neural networks in its car vision system to warn about potential collisions. *Google* has made great progress in the quality of its translations. The structure of these neural networks means that the algorithms are good at identifying objects in picture, putting together sounds to make up words and recognizing what to do in a game, but not yet beyond those tasks. When *IBM's DeepBlue* was able to defeat the world Chess champion Kasparov in 1997, it was considered a considerable step to the computer becoming "intelligent". However, while a computer could win a high profile chess game, and 20 years later, *IBM's Watson* won from the champion in a more complicated Go-game, which was an impressive engineering feat, but it is a highly specialized algorithm. It took AI less than three years to find solutions to beat the human champion because the human brains don't have the processing power to consider so many moves ahead. *DeepMind*'s Alpha Zero – bought by Google - works by playing hundreds of millions of games itself, pruning mistakes that led to losses, and elaborating on strategies that lead to wins. Such systems involving generative adversarial network techniques that generate and observe data. However, at the other hand, let us not ignore the fact that it is still proving difficult to get a robot arm to pick up a cup of water. These 'smart' machines are smart only in their specific domains. Present-day data engineering is still far away from matching the power and versatility of neurons and their synapses of our brain. Artificial Intelligence cannot yet make their own plan – as a conscious being can.

Current AI machine-learning algorithms are, at their core, rather simple and straightforward. Some may even describe these computers as dumb fast machines on steroids, using "stupid little neurons" as basis. AI is doing descriptive statistics in a way that is not science and would be almost impossible to make into science. At this point, AI is doing descriptive statistics in a way that is not science and would be almost impossible to make into science. At their core, the current algorithms are "dead simple stupid"; they work by brute computing force – "if you use reinforcement learning of credit-assignment feedback, you can get those little pieces to approximate whatever arbitrary function one wants", according to MIT social physicist Sandy Pentland. Despite the remarkable advances in computing, the hype about Artificial General Intelligence (AGI) – i.e. a general intelligence computer that will think like a human and possibly develop consciousness – smacks to science fiction, according to Venki Ramakrishnan, the 2009 Nobel Laureate for Chemistry, an idea that is supported by many other researchers. And he is not the only skeptical scientist regarding AGI. We do not have sufficient neuroscientific knowledge yet to understand what exactly consciousness[3] is, or how we remember a phone number, or the reasons why we suddenly loose memory, how exactly neurons interact. Deep learning machines and AI cannot answer the "*why*" question yet. We have no idea which parts of the brain – if the brain at all – are responsible for human consciousness. It seems that we tend to underestimate the complexity and creativity of the human brain and how amazingly general it is, compared to any digital device we have developed so far.

When Max Kurzweil – who quipped the notion of 'singularity' in his 2005 publication - declared that computers will become as intelligent as humans by 2035 – based on the power of exponential improvements as we have seen over the last 30 years - the spirit was out of the Pandora box. Max Tegmark (2016) at MIT refers to the view among AI experts that AI systems will probably (over 50%) reach overall human ability (AGI) by 2045, and very likely (with 90% probability) by 2075. From reaching human ability - singularity – it will move on to superintelligence in 2100 (75%). Again, there is no scientific proof for these inferences. Informed guesses at best. At such a point of singularity, computers will become as and likely more powerful than human intelligence; humans should progress to a stage of becoming "trans-human" – a cyber-human (electronically enhanced) or neuro-augmented (biological-genetically enhanced) human, or a *homo deus* - in order to remain relevant in a world where we may compete with Artificial Generally Intelligent machines. To some singularity is seen as an opportunity whereas others emphasize the dangers. It is true that most discussions around AI is focused on a narrow weak interpretation of AI (as in machines controlled by humans), and limited attention on the potential dramatic transformations that Artificial General Intelligence (AGI) may bring. Oxford philosopher Nick Bostrom coined the notion of "superintelligence" that may see humankind as a potential threat. However, as MIT Prof Brynjolfsson expressed it, any future depends on the choices we make. The near or further future is not different: "We can reap unprecedented bounty and freedom, or greater disaster than humanity has ever seen before". The future, however, will be an ever more demanding struggle against the limitations of our brain and intelligence. Singularity, on the other hand, is the point at which computers becomes as smart as us. With a rapidly changing ecology of intelligence and rapid evolution of machine-learning, we may need to consider the probability and advantages of an evolution towards cyborgs and superminds, above and beyond the *homo sapiens*.

According to these AI enthusiasts, the real risk with AGI is not malice but competence. Admittedly, a super-intelligent machine should be extremely good at accomplishing its goals. As long as these goals are aligned with ours, no problem. In case they are not, big trouble can be expected. Hence why the importance of bringing the "ought" or ethical dimension in the equation without further due. As a number of AI experts admit, postponing ethical critical thinking on AI until after goal-aligned AGI is built would be irresponsible and potentially disastrous. A super-AI machine lacking a moral compass would be like an unguarded projectile on steroids (that could seriously harm us). Safety engineering and ethical thinking is more than needed. We would not send humans to the moon without all precautions that safety engineering could think of. Similarly, we should not build super-computers or machine superintelligence (although we are still decades away for such an achievement, if at all) without in-built safety mechanisms to guide actions in an appropriate manner.

Intelligence tests of AI should build on Alan Turing famous "imitation game" test. A computer passes the Turing test, or imitation game if it can fool a human, during a question and answer session, into believing that it is, in fact, a human being. We are a long way from achieving this feat. Humans are very good and creative in connecting the dots of different frameworks, that can result in new innovative thinking or inventions. Our current algorithms are not yet very good at doing so.

According to the philosopher Daniel Dennett, Alan Turing could not foresee the uncanny ability of superfast computers to sift mindlessly through big data if which the internet provides an inexhaustible supply, and find probabilistic patterns in human activity that could be used to express "authentic"-seeming responses into the output for almost any probe human would attempt to decipher whether the computer is smart enough to fool us as authentic human. In other words, in such a case, the computer would outsmart and fool the human, without necessary being able to become more intelligent than humans. Hence why Dennett describes a plausibly multidimensional "computer-agent" more like an amygdala or cerebellum than a real mind; at best such a computer could be defined as a special-purpose subsystem that could play an enormous supporting role, but not "remotely up to the task of framing purposes and plans and building insightfully on its conversational experiences" that could resemble the general intelligence of a human.

Moreover, current machine learning systems operate almost exclusively in a statistical or model-blind mode. In that sense, current systems remain rather opaque and focus on the what (if) question to execute a specific task. The Oxford quantum physicist, David Deutch – who conceptualized the notion of quantum computing - believes with the late philosopher Karl Popper that human-level intelligence and thinking tout court lie in the ability of creative criticism, interleaved with creative conjectures allowing humans to learn one another's behaviors, including language and extracting meaning from one another's utterances. The power of AI may be impressive but the G of AGI still remains elusive. It is that aspect of general creativity that leads to innovation that is a truly human characteristic. Add the ability to ask normative and thus ethical questions and to feel empathy and compassion (a form of emotional intelligence), and humans still have some distinctive competitiveness over "intelligent" machines.

Crucial in understanding the limitations of current (narrow) AI is the fact that our world knowledge is often expressed in causal terms, something that is not really done by current neural networks or deep (referring to the different layers like in neural brain network) learning machines. These machines are currently more about finding statistical regularities in complex patterns, but not really organizing that as objects that can have various kinds of causal impacts on other objects. Artificial General Intelligence would be the kind of intelligence that is contextualized, situationally aware, nuanced, multifaceted and multidimensional while also having the flexible learning abilities that humans have, which goes beyond supervised learning of big data (where computers excel over humans), unsupervised learning, reinforcement learning, virtual learning and other various kinds of learning. Not feasible in the near and medium time ahead – despite the enormous efforts of some genius researchers!

As mentioned a few times, computers are not able to answer the *why-question* which implies self-conscious and understanding causal networks. Today, Artificial Intelligence uses big data to operate or to conform to the (Bayesian) logic of probability and logic of proportions. Causal thinking altogether definitely escapes the current AI algorithms. A Bayesian network can only tell us how likely an event is, given that we observed another information; but it cannot answer counterfactual questions. Bayesian networks is basically the mathematical transformation of information or conditional probabilities without causality (e.g. given that I know, what is the chance that x occurs). It only identifies associations between variables, that may indicate correlation or regression, but it does not answer of possible causation. The computer scientists and mathematician Judea Pearl argues that the human brain is not just wired to do probability problems but to do causal problems – something the computer cannot (yet) (2019).

Our intuitive causal reasoning – we explicitly or implicitly use models - often clashes with the logic of probability and statistics in general. Whenever we see patterns, we look for a causal explanation. AI algorithms driven computers, on the other hand, are good at optimizing a specific task, but currently unable to understand cause-and-effect relations. AGI will need causal models, as it should become a

Figure 3. Including a moral, ecological and social sustainability dimension in decision-making
Source: Verhezen, P., (2018): Normative ethical questions (MQ) is inherently a human feature, besides emotional intelligence.

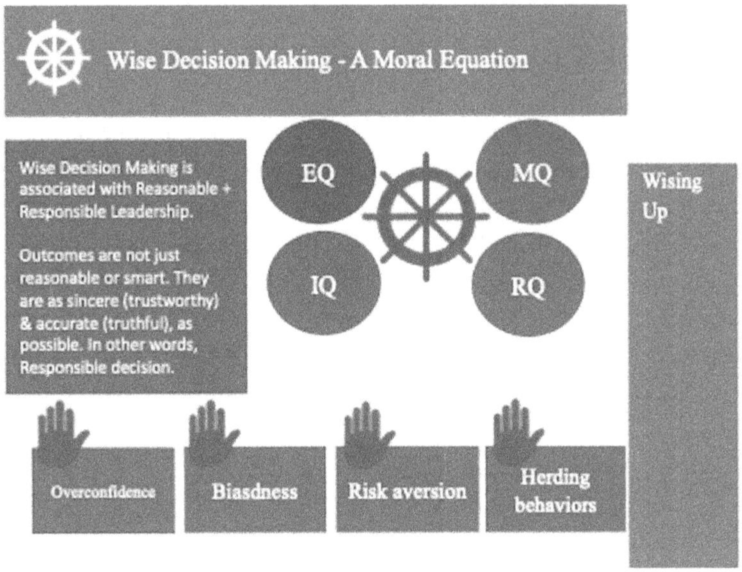

machine that can reflect on its actions and learn from past mistakes. UCLA Professor Judea Pearl (2019) believes that the algorithmitization of counterfactuals – he introduced the necessity of causal thinking in the AI-field - will be a major step toward understanding these why questions and making consciousness and agency a computational reality. Well, I guess that it all depends how we define and understand consciousness and mind in humans and how we ever may or may not be able to transfer these to computers.

Some researchers like Pearl believe it is possible to build a "moral causal thinking robot' in the distant future. We still assume that some form of consciousness and self-awareness is necessary to be able to think morally and care for others. Till then, a moral robot remains science fiction.

Boards Steering Towards Humans Collaborating with Artificial Intelligence, While Emphasizing Strict Data Governance

Can humans still compete with fast computers or are we losing the battle with powerful machines? Should we trust computers? How should one address the numerous risks and address the darker side related to Big Data and AI, while still be able to benefit from the speed and potential accuracy of AI (be it cognitive insights, cognitive engagement or digital automation)? Human society is a network just like the neural nets trained for deep learning, but currently the "neurons" in human society are still a lot smarter. Some artists have described the current form of AI as "artificial stupidity". But we should not underestimate the enhancing "creativity" of AI either.

We here focus on some *governance solutions* and *smart decision making* that are related to (1) privacy concerns, (2) biases in predictive recommendations, and (3) the audit of black box algorithms on the one hand. That some jobs will disappear with the increasing applications and growing predominance of AI cannot be denied. However, we recommend **wise corporate leadership** to accommodate these new innovative tools in the form of AI and deep learning machines, and stimulate collaboration between smart humans and intelligent machines where applicable and possible.

1. Governance that requires more Accountability and Responsibility

In order to reduce the risks of the darker side of AI, we suggest a more stringent data governance for those who use data provided by people who often have been unaware of the potential misuse of their privacy. We therefore suggest to enhance the accountability of organizations using these data to their commercial benefit. Secondly, we believe that recommendations in sensitive areas as justice or the medical field should not undermine the basic principle of human dignity and the principle that people should not be judged unless strong factual proof is available. And finally, we also believe that more transparency is needed to reduce the risks related to these AI "black boxes", by having gatekeeping third party certification that could enhance the trust in AI and its use of big data.

a. From Personal Privacy to Firm's Accountability

Although consumers and individuals should provide their consent in the use of their personal data, we suggest to be less focused on consent as such, but make the data users – i.e. the organizations using or selling those data – accountable for what they do with the data. It concretely means that the burden of responsibility is shifted from the public (and the aggregation of individuals who may have consented on the use of their data) to the effective users of data who actually benefit most of these secondary data use.

Another method is "differential privacy" which implies that the data are deliberately blurred so that a query of large data set only reveal approximate and not real results. The EU's General Data Protection Regulation (GDPR) has imposed strict rules to protect privacy. These privacy principles have been copied by many countries across the world. In addition, EU regulation is convinced that digital firms cannot lock out competition, such as *Microsoft*, *IBM*, and lately *Google* and *Facebook* have attempted to do for which they all were fined. And we do not even focus on the Chinese AI related organizations which are less bridled by privacy regulations; since the Chinese communist party here play a role that is questioned in the West. The rule in Western democracies imposes equal treatment of anyone, including rivals, who may use their platforms. The weekly *Economist* claims that that European regulations want consumers to control their privacy and how their data are monetized. The ability of European consumers to "switch creates competition that should boost choice and raise standards." The challenge is to make GDPR less clunky, and to avoid Europe to become a tech enclave, cut off from the mainstream, and allowing the (geopolitical) rivalry between US and China to create tech giants who will continue to act in an oligopolistic fashion.

b. Propensity of recommendation versus Innocent till proven guilty

Allowing governments to take predictive action because certain big data analysis suspecting someone is not good enough since it undermines the human dignity and the foundations that one is innocent till proven guilty. Not the other way around.

Indeed, the more we may switch to holding people accountable for their possible actions based on data-driven interventions and predictions with the intention to reduce the risk in society, the more we categorize or stigmatize certain groups, and the more we devalue the ideal of individual responsibility which we believe remains a fundamental human right.

Moreover, by pushing people to take certain decisions based on recommendations basically denies people's responsibility for their actions since it destroys their fundamental freedom to choose their own behavior, though admittedly often (unconsciously) influenced by peers and social pressure.

c. Audit of Algorithm or more transparency on Black Box

So far, most AI proponents have emphasized the positive practical consequences of artificial intelligence. However, the real danger lies in the fact that scientists do not really understand the "black box" behind the algorithm. The new machine-learning programs may have recognized patterns via deep neural networks and subsequent practical useful conclusions. But we have no idea how the computer or algorithm came up with the inference or conclusion. And the larger the data set, the more difficult it will become to understand and to analyze – even with the help of computers – these predictive conclusions. Does this mean that we will become completely dependent on the computer? It reminds me to the incredible and *hineinsight* misplaced faith in the practical wisdom of mathematical quants when calculating the "exact" value of these collateralized debt obligations – securitized risk tools – which partially caused the global financial crisis in 2008, bringing us to the brink of a real and complete global disastrous meltdown.

If we solely rely on the accuracy and "objectivity" of the conclusions prepared by black box algorithms, the more we ignore the reasons behind. Instead we strongly argue to bring back the notion of explainability, the why beyond the mere what. Explainability should not be sacrificed as the mimetic lamb in the name of more accuracy. In other words, we suggest that trust in AI can only be achieved by increasing more disclosure about the algorithm and the underlying prediction system. Hence why the introduction of "algorithmist" who acts as a reviewer of big data analysis and predictions in an impartial and purely confidential manner, could be sensible. In other words, a form of external certification is needed to create trust by a third party endorsing the reliability, replicability and accuracy of the AI algorithm. For instance, in the case of AI driving cars, AI diagnosing patients and in AI "robo" investing, some form of certification should become mandatory. And although ideation, creativity and innovation are often described as thinking outside the box, it does not justify secretive black boxes for nobody seems to be accountable.

We also could enhance transparency by using the new Blockchain technology - a P2P database in the absence of any central authority governing its use – currently applied for the rather volatile cryptocurrency Bitcoin. The central ledger system allows all participants to see every transaction by every other participant and encryption ensures no [chain of] block can be forged. In its essence, Blockchain is a disintermediation of trust with the use of mathematical guarantees. Our rather perceived subjective notion of trust is expressed as a computationally guaranteed property of the Blockchain system. In other words, blockchain provides an example of how a human ideal of trust is translated into mathematics and encrypted algorithmic code.

Figure 4. Wise leadership: Integrating Human Intelligence and Artificial Intelligence
Source: Verhezen, P. (2019) as published in http://www.verhezen.net/images/papers/VERHEZEN_2019_Wise_Decision_Making_and_AI_2nd_Paper.pdf

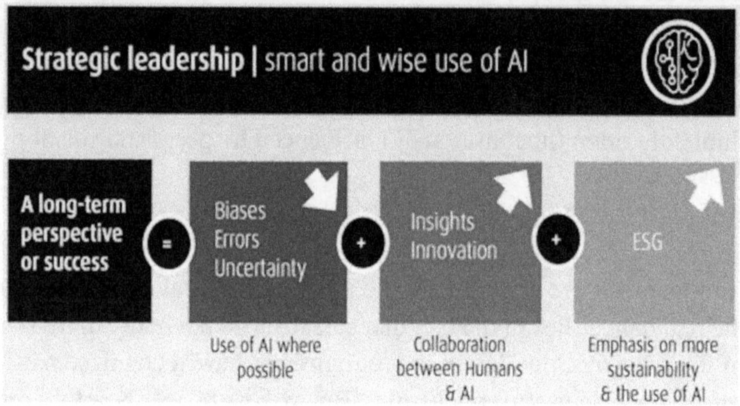

2. Future Collaboration between Humans and AI-learning machines

Digital tools and artificial intelligence in particular will enable humans to make better decisions when properly applied. We may not fully understand or control our destiny, but at least we have a chance to bend it in the direction of our own values which we feel are worth living for. The future is not just something that will happen to us – completely deterministically – but is likely something that we can and hopefully will build.

Nonetheless, the AI revolution that we can expect will be on scale of a real industrial revolution, hence why the notion of "*Industry 4.0*" was quipped. There will be beneficiaries but unfortunately also some losers in the process. Those jobs that need social interaction won't disappear immediately, those which are repetitive and can be optimized using data will be replaced by smart computers. Humans and AI are collaborating to improve five elements of business processes: (1) *Flexibility* (as in Robotics in Auto-manufacturing, Software to improve Product design, Software development estimates), (2) *Speed* (as in Fraud detection, aggregate patient data assisting in cancer treatment, Video analytics that enhance public safety), (3) *Scale* (as in Automated applicant screening in Recruitment, the use of bots in improving customer service, monitoring systems), (4) *Decision-Making* (as in diagnostic applications in equipment maintenance, real time Robo-advisors in financial services, Disease prediction) and (5) *Personalization* (as in wearable AI devices that improves the guest experience, wearable sensors to improve health care, and AI analytics in retail fashion). It seems that human-machine collaboration enables organizations to interact with employees and customers in new more effective ways.

Automation that eliminates a human from a task does not necessarily eliminate them from a job. One cannot deny that computerization, robotization and digitization have been responsible for considerable losses in blue-collar jobs in the last two decades. The physical labor that is at risk of being replaced by computers include tellers, cashiers, garment factory workers, fruit harvesters, assembly line inspectors and labor. Receptionist, bartenders, caterers may survive in the medium term but over a longer period, also their jobs will be at risk for being replaced by very smart machines. Presumably, elderly home caretakers, hair stylists, physical therapists will be able to keep their jobs which require a high level of dexterity within an unstructured environment. For the time being, aerospace mechanics, taxi drivers, plumbers and house cleaners may sustain their job for a little while longer.

However, lately the white-collar jobs are also under siege. Accountants, many legal and medical professionals, insurance adjusters, financial analysts and stockbrokers, travel agents, personal tax preparer, basic translators, and telemarketers all may disappear within years as result of ever more sophisticated machine-learning programs. Criminal defense attorneys, CEOs, psychiatrist, PR directors and social workers will likely keep their job because of the required social interaction and creativity or strategy based cognitive work required. Scientists, medical researchers and artists likely will sustain their job as well in the medium term.

Despite all the pessimistic forecasts of what jobs would be technically possible to do with machines, the actual job losses or resulting unemployment levels will likely much smaller. Some estimates forecast about 9% of jobs in the USA and Europe are at risk for being automated. PWC researchers find instead that 38% of jobs in the US *could* be at risk of automation by the early 2030s. The actual replacement is likely much lower, around 10-15%.

However, AI algorithms will be to many white-collar workers what tractors were to farmhands: a tool that significantly increases the productivity of each worker and thus shrinking the total number of employees required. Algorithms already exist; those ambidexterious robots still need to be invented.

In the long run, the biggest effect of automation and robots driven by algorithms is likely to be on workers in developing nations that currently rely on low-cost labor for their competitive advantage. Foxcon is taking a lead in automating and replacing blue workers in China. The question then becomes whether these Chinese factories in the global supply chain remain low cost and competitive. Probably, the low-cost advantage may disappear.

It will be an interesting but also challenging question how autonomous car will share the road with pedestrians, human-driven vehicles and other autonomous cars. How to combine the human values when they might be in conflict with the navigation system of autonomous cars? We need to think about this "robo-ethics" and make sure that these AI-vehicles take our human nature into account, so that they are well coordinated and well aligned with our desires and values system to increase our quality of life.

Moreover, as MIT professor Erik Brynjolfsson and research scientist Andrew McAfee argue about the paradox of robotics progress – known as the Moravec's paradox: contrary to traditional intuition, high level reasoning requires very little computation, but low-level sensorimotor skills require enormous computational resources. Robots and artificially intelligent computers are good at making precision welds on assembly lines, or at fast calculating the ideal distance in self-driving cars through its GPS system, but they still "can't tie their own shoes".

Robots and their AI behind are great at performing dirty, dull, monotonous and dangerous jobs that no one else wants to do. In terms of risk management, artificial intelligence out-maneuvers human intelligence in the field of *known knowns* such as fraud detection, medical diagnosis, bail decisions. In contrast to machines, humans are sometimes extremely good at prediction with little data. Cognitive superiority of humans, however, is still very valid in the area of ideation, large frame pattern recognition, and complex forms of communication. *Apple's Siri* and *Amazon's Alexa* can answer questions and can control devices around your home, but can they appreciate a joke? Not (yet) at this time.

As executives, making decisions, one needs to focus on the consequences (which one is able to know) rather than the probability (which one likely does not know). This is the idea of making executive decisions under uncertainty. AI deep learning machines may be able to assist (smart) decision-makers to provide some clue in terms of conditional probabilities and reduce this fundamental uncertainty.

Table 1. Comparison of AI and Humans (compiled by author)

	Little data available	*Big data available*
Known Knowns (Repetitive tasks)	Humans + AI (strong case for collaboration)	AI > Humans (better use AI = *Big Data Analytics and automation of repetitive tasks*)
Unknown Knowns *(incomplete information = randomness)*	Humans > AI (weaker case for collaboration, though *creativity of humans* may outsmart computers)	AI ≅ Humans (weaker case for collaboration though *computer power may augment human intelligence*)
Known Unknowns (Unique Decision)	Humans > AI (humans should take the lead, use *Heuristics*)	Humans + AI (strong case for collaboration where *AI augments the decision-power of humans*)
Unknown Unknowns *(Black Swans)*	Possibly Humans >AI ?? although too many unknown variables *(unclear what can be "expected")*	Possibly AI > Humans ?? *(unclear what can be predicted)*

Computers may be able to provide some lacking information (based on finding or revealing for humans hidden patterns) to improve decision-making. Unfortunately, with big data analytics the fundamental uncertainty may seem to vanish under (statistical) averaging, but randomness may therefore not have completely disappeared, despite the feeling that we are better informed through big data. However, in practice, this may be good enough (knowing how or practical technè versus the more elusive knowing that or episteme) to provide functioning AI driven tools.

In the face of *known unknowns* (rare events such as predicting earthquakes), humans make better decisions than machines. With *unknown knowns*, prediction machines appear to provide a very precise answer that could be very wrong. And in case of *unknown unknowns*, the black swans, Nassim Taleb convincingly argues that we cannot predict truly new events from past data, and likely both humans and machines fail. Nonetheless, in some instances, AI is able to uncover unknown unknowns as *GNS Healthcare* applies machine-learning AI to find overlooked relationships among data in patients' health records, enabling GNS to uncover a new drug interaction hidden in in unstructured patient notes.

However, we believe that machine learning and prediction can enhance the productivity of human decision-making by providing an initial prediction that humans can combine with their own assessments, such as checking the creditworthiness of loan applicants. Secondly, machine learning can provide a second opinion or facilitate monitoring (of patients in hospitals for instance). With a reliable diagnosis from an image, patients can forego an invasive biopsy. Advances in AI and machine learning mean less need to "satisficing" and more "ifs" and more "thens". In other words, AI allows for more complexity with less risk, transforming decision-making by expanding options. Machine-learning techniques are increasingly good at predicting missing information, including identification and recognition of items in images. This kind of pattern recognition to predict disease is what radiologists do. Prediction machines may be able to reduce uncertainty, but they won't always eliminate it.

Intelligent machines driven by AI use their specialized intelligence to solve parts of the problem; humans use their general intelligence to do the rest. In that sense, smart AI machines can help engage and coordinate large groups of people to become more effective and efficient.

Most likely, AI will shift human resources management toward the relational and away from the transactional. More crucially, the arrival of AI will lead to an increasing importance of human judgment (supported by AI-predictions). Prediction by AI and judgment by humans are complements: as the use of prediction increases, the value of judgment (or decision) rises. The (human) judgment uses (AI) predictions to make a smarter decision. Thinking about a network – as our brain functions – is analogous to thinking about entire ecosystems. How would you guide ecosystems to grow in a good direction? Artificial intelligence use methods to "learn" from large quantities of data where computers can recognize patterns and derive conclusions from these "insights". Big data is not use if one does not turn it into knowledge that can be applied in concrete cases. However, human learning and curiosity does not occur in isolation, but is always embedded in traditions and accumulated wisdom of past generations. Until scientists will have solved the basic paradox of learning, the best AI will be unable to compete with a four or five years old.

CONCLUSION

As long as we are aware of the potential threats from AI and take all possible measures to reduce those risks, including being aware of the dangers of complete dependency on technological digitization of our world view, we should be able to remain creative and innovate for a better and more fair world. The darker side of AI – be it the biases of weak AI, privacy violations, and overreliance on data of an AI driven Black Box, as well as the existential threats of a strong AI – cannot be ignored. We should be prepared for the danger of ideas, ideologies and institutions that allow information to feed collective decisions and understanding that may be contrary to an open and less dogmatic perspective of the world. If intelligence is the ability to deploy novel means to attain a goal, then we should allow some competitive forces to drive evolution. At this point, the progress of machine learning, particularly multilayered artificial neural networks, is not resulting yet in achieving general intelligence, but is mainly restricted to specific problems of mapping well-defined inputs to well-defined outputs. Likely the real danger lies not in the machine itself but in the way humans may use it. Instead of focusing on singularity, Berkeley scientist Ken Goldberg claims, we should embrace **multiplicity** – a hybrid view of how new technologies and humans might collaborate in partnership toward meaningful human solutions. Qualities like intuition, empathy, creativity remain crucial human qualities. Hence why a more holistic approach by humans could be blended with the precision that machines provide.

Artificial intelligence is becoming good at many human jobs such as diagnosing diseases, translating languages, providing customer service, and it is improving fast since 2013. Obviously, there is a fear that AI will ultimately replace human workers throughout the economy. But that does not need to be a necessity. Never before have digital devices and machine tools (Internet of Things is currently estimated to reach 20 billion devices) been so responsive to us. This kind of IoT technology may radically alter how works gets done and who does it. However, the impact may be even larger when AI technology will complement and augment human capabilities, not replacing them.

Admittedly, we do not understand yet the neural architecture of the human brain that through evolution was trained to run well. But evolution goes slow and we start to understand the constraints and limitations of our brain power. However, to achieve general intelligence, or human-level intelligence, learning machines need to ask normative questions that are guided by a kind of blueprint of reality, a model of society in which we aspire to live in. At this point, no learning machine is able yet to answer causal "what if" questions. The machine does not have a "purpose"; AI only aims to achieve some specific objectives, not the design of those – be objectives or purpose at this point in time. Data science only facilitates the interpretation of data and connect them with and to reality. No matter how big the data get and how skillfully they are manipulated by data scientists, such machine learning and AI remain quite opaque in their learning. AI research has so far focused on systems that are better and much faster at making decisions, but not necessarily at making better decisions (which would require a normative or value-laden stance). Machine's decisions may be ineffably stupid in the eyes of humans if the objective or utility function of the machine is not appropriately aligned with our human aspirations and values. Unless, an artificial general intelligence would emerge that has its own conscious to make their own related goals, utilities and values to be followed – almost completely independent of ours, which remains "science-fiction" today. However, if a weak or strong AI is meant to serve humankind, then we need to think about AI and its purpose in relationship to how we see a fairer and more just world, which is an ethical question. Addressing such enormous challenges will require top notch engineering, computer science, legislation and likely above all, moral and wise leadership to guide us through.

What makes us different from AI, is our unique history which gives us our notions of purpose and goals. There is no meaningful sense in which there is an abstract notion of purpose. It is likely embedded within our own history and traditions. Although there may not be a genuine demarcation line between intelligence and mere computation, we still see different kinds of intelligence beyond the brute force of rational computational logic thinking, including making sense and giving meaning on an experience. Finding a purposeful meaning – based on human values and human insights - to one's life or thinking while using working together with smart machines, is the best scenario we should strive for. Hence why wise beyond smart decision-making is not just a luxury but a necessity. Wisdom is breadth and a broader and often longer term framing.

At this point, deep learning machines are not achieving any form of general artificial intelligence, but have become good at predicting based on big data. The key question is not whether AI will bring benefits, but how those benefits will be distributed and how we can limit the dark side of AI. Will some companies and countries have a huge competitive advantage? And will this advantage be translated in a vicious or rather virtuous stream of decisions?

We have argued that [weak] AI may have contributed to better and decentralized matching processes but it has occasionally also created new forms of information asymmetries through centralized data in the hands of a few tech giants. Hence why some forms of transparency of the [use of] data and information [by algorithms] is necessary, but likely difficult to achieve. So, the alternative is specific regulations wanting to ensure competitive markets that mandate the [progressive] sharing of data. The future of our economy lies in the clever exploitation of our informational surplus which we can achieve in our data-rich markets. AI and big data can enable better human coordination in the market which makes us more sustainable. The old adage of "trust but verify" is still valid. However, we cannot and should not ignore the darker side of artificial intelligence that could easily undermine the trust in these new technology. The future lies in a beneficial collaboration between human general intelligence with artificial specific intelligence and deep learning machines. The human advantage lies in the ability to ask metaphysical (why) questions and address ethical concerns. Only humans can feel empathy and mindful compassion towards other beings – which seem to constitute ourselves as social beings (based on emotions inherent to most higher-level mammals). In addition, our neocortex allows us to think rationally or reasonable and make links between unexpected patterns that result in innovative and insightful improvements of tools.

And the use of intelligent artificial tools could improve organizations' products and services positively impacting our quality of life.

REFERENCES

Agrawal, A. (2018, Apr.). The economics of Artificial Intelligence. *McKinsey Quarterly*.

Agrawal, A., Gans, J., & Goldfarb, A. (2018). *Prediction Machines. The Simple Economics of Artificial Intelligence*. Boston, MA: Harvard Business Review Press.

Alexandre, L. (2017). *La Guerre des Intelligences: Intelligence Artificielle versus Intelligence Humaine*. Paris: JC Lattès.

Alpaydin, E. (2016). *Machine Learning. The new AI*. Cambridge, MA: The MIT Press.

Arbib, M. A. (Ed.). (2003). The Handbook of Brain Theory and Neural Networks. Cambridge, MA: The MIT Press.

Ariely, D. (2008). *Predicably Irrational. The Hidden Forces that Shape our Decisions*. New York: HarperCollins.

Baer, T. & Kamalnath, V. (2017). *Controlling machine-learning algorithms and their biases*. McKinsey & Company.

Barrat, J. (2013). *Our Final Invention. Artificial Intelligence and the end of the Human Area*. New York: Dunne Books.

Batra, G., Queirolo, A., & Santhanam, N. (2017). *Artificial Intelligence: The time to act is now*. McKinsey & Company.

Baxter-Kellman, R. (2015). *Het Membership Model. Wat je van Netflix, Spotify en Starbucks kunt leren*. Amsterdam: Business Contact.

Berns, G. (2008). *Iconoclast. A neuroscientist reveals how to think differently*. Academic Press.

Borison, A., & Hamm, G. (2010). Prediction Markets: A new tool for strategic decision making. *California Management Review*, *52*(4), 125–141.

Bostrom, N. (2014). *Superintelligence. Paths, Dangers, Strategies*. Oxford, UK: Oxford University Press.

Bourton, S., Lavoie, J., & Vogel, T. (2018). Will Artificial Intelligence make you a better leader? *The McKinsey Quarterly*.

Brafman, O., & Brafman, R. (2010). *Click. The Magic of Instant Connections*. New York: Random House.

Brockman, J. (Ed.). (2019). *Possible Minds. 25 Ways of Looking at AI*. London: Penguin.

Brynjolfsson, E., & McAfee, A. (2014). *The Second Machine Age. Work, Progress, and Prosperity in a Time of Brilliant Technologies*. New York: WW Norton Company.

Bughin, J., & van Zeebroeck, N. (2018, July). Artificial Intelligence: Why a Digital Base is critica. *McKinsey Quarterly*.

Burkhardt, R., Hohn, N. & Wigley, C. (2019). *Leading your organization to responsible AI.* McKinsey Analytics.

Chalmers, D. (1996). *The Conscious Mind. In search of a Fundamental Theory*. New York: Oxford University Press.

Christensen, C. M., Hall, T., Dillon, K., & Duncan, D. S. (2016). *Competing against Luck. The Story of Innovation and Customer Choice*. New York: HarperCollins Business Publ.

Davenport, T. H., & Ronanki, R. (2018, Jan.). Artificial Intelligence for the Real World. Don't start with moon shots. *Harvard Business Review*, 108–116.

Deheane, S. (2014). *Consciousness and the Brain: Deciphering How the Brain codes our Thoughts*. London: Penguin.

Domingos, P. (2015). *The Master Algorithm. How the quest for the ultimate learning machine will remake our world*. London: Penguin.

Erisman, P. (2015). *Alibaba's World. How a remarkable Chinese company is changing the face of global business*. London: Palgrave MacMillan.

Finger, Z. S. (2001). *Origins of Neuroscience: A history of explorations into Brain Function*. Oxford, UK: Oxford University Press.

Finkelstein, S., Whitehead, J., & Campbell, A. (2008). *Think Again. Why good leaders make bad decisions and how to keep it from happening to you*. Boston: Harvard Business Press.

Finlay, S. (2018). *Artificial Intelligence and Machine Learning for Business. A no-nonse guide to Data-driven Technologies*. London: Relativistic Publications.

Ford, M. (2018). *Architects of Intelligence. The truth about AI from the people building it*. Birmingham, UK: Packt Publishing.

Furr, N., & Shipilov, A. (2019, July). Digital doesn't have to be Disruptive. The best results can come from adaptation rather than revinvention. *Harvard Business Review*, 94–103.

Gazzaniga, M. (2011). *Who's in charge? Free will and the science of the brain*. New York: HarperCollins.

Gazzaniga, M. (2015). *Tales from both sides of the Brain. A life of neuroscience*. New York: HarperCollins.

Geissbauer, R.; Schrauf, S. & Pillsbury, S. (2018). Digital Champions. *Strategy + Business*.

Gigerenzer, B. (2014). *Risk Savvy. How to make good decisions*. Lane Books.

Gilovich, T., & Ross, L. (2016). *The Wisest One in the Room. How to harness Psychology's Most Powerful Insights*. London: OneWorld Publishing.

Gold, J. I., & Shadlen, M. N. (2007). The Neural Basis of Decision-Making. *Annual Review of Neuroscience*, *30*(1), 535–574. doi:10.1146/annurev.neuro.29.051605.113038 PMID:17600525

Grant Halverson, H. & Rock, D. (2015). Beyond Bias. *Strategy + Business*, (80).

Gratton, L. (2011). The Shift. The future of work is already here. London: William Collins (Harper Collins).

Gupta, S. (2018). *Driving Digital Strategy. A guide to reimagining your business*. Boston, MA: Harvard Business School Press.

Heath, C., & Heath, D. (2013). *Decisive. How to make better decisions*. London: Randomhouse.

Kahneman, D. (2011). *Thinking, Fast and Slow*. London: Penguin-Pearson.

Kahneman, D. (2011, Nov.). Beware the inside view. *McKinsey Quarterly*.

Kahneman, D. & Klein, G. (2010, Mar.). Strategic Decisions: When Can You Trust Your Gut? *McKinsey Quarterly*.

Kahneman, D., Lovallo, D., & Sibony, O. (2011, June). Before You Make That Big Decision. *HBR*, 50-60.

Kahneman, D., Rosenfield, A.M., Gandhi, L., & Blaser, T. (2016). Noise. Inconsistent Decision-making. *HBR*, 38-46.

Kanter, R. M. (2009). Supercorp. How Vanguard Companies Create Innovation, Profits, Growth, and Social Good. New York: Academic Press.

Kanter, R. M. (2011, Nov.). How Great Companies Think Differently. *Harvard Business Review*, 66–78.

Kevles, B. H. (1997). *Naked to the bone: Medical Imaging in the Twentieth Century*. New Brunswick, NJ: Rutgers University Press.

Kiel, F. (2015a). *Return on Character. The Real Reason Leaders and Their Companies Win*. Boston: Harvard Business Review Press.

Kiel, F. (2015b, Apr.). Measuring the Return On Character. *Harvard Business Review*, 20–21.

Kizza, J. M. (2017). *Ethical and Social Issues in the Information Age*. Cham: Springer. doi:10.1007/978-3-319-70712-9

Klein, G. (2013). *Seeing What Others Don't. The Remarkable Ways We Gain Insights*. London: Nicholas Brealey Publishing.

Kurzweil, R. (2006). *The Singularity is near. When humans transcend biology*. London: Penguin.

Kurzweil, R. (2012). *How to create a Mind. The secrets of human thoughts revealed*. London: Viking.

Lee, K.-F. (2018). *AI Superpowers China, Silicon Valley, and the New World Order*. New York: Houghton Mifflin Harcourt Publishing Company.

Libert, B., Beck, M., & Wind, J. (2016). *The Network Imperative. How to survive and grow in the Age of Digital Business Models*. Cambridge, MA: Harvard Business Review Press.

Lieberman, M. D. (2013). *Social. Why our brains are wired to connect*. New York: Penguin Randomn House.

Likens, S. & Kersey, K. (2019, May). Automating trust with new technologies. *Strategy + Business.*

Lindstrom, M. (2008). *Buyology: Truth and Lies about Why we Buy*. New York: Broadway Books.

Lohr, S. (2015). *Data-ism. The revolution transforming decision-making, consumer behavior, and almost everything else*. New York: HarperCollins.

London, S., Chui, M. & Whigley, C. (2019). *The ethics of Artificial Intelligence*. McKinsey & Company.

Lozano, J. M. (2010). *The Relational Company. Responsibility, Sustainability, Citizenship*. Bern: Peter Lang. doi:10.3726/978-3-0353-0326-1

Luca, M., Kleinberg, J., & Mullainanthan, S. (2016, Jan.). Algorithms need managers, too. Know how to get the most out of your predictive tools. *Harvard Business Review*, 96–101.

Luger, G. F., & Stubblefield, W. A. (1998). *Artificial Intelligence. Structures and Strategies for Complex Problem Solving*. Harlow, MA: Addison Wesley Longman.

Makridadis, S., Hogarth, R., & Gaba, A. (2010). *Dance with Chance. Making Luck Work For You.* London: Penguin.

Malone, T. W. (2018). How Human-Computer 'Superminds' are Redefining the Future of Work. *MIT Sloan Management Review*, 34–41.

Manyika, J., Chui, M., & Lund, S. (2017). *What's now and next in Analytics, AI and Automation*. McKinsey & Company.

Nanjok, N., Le Fleming, H. & Srivatsay, N. (2018). Digital Technology and Sustainability: Positive Mutual Enforcement. *Strategy + Business.*

Penrose, R. (2016). *The Emperor's Mind: Concerning Computers, Minds and the Laws of Physics*. Oxford, UK: Oxford University Press.

Pernick, R., & Wilder, C. (2008). *The Clean Tech Revolution. Discover the top trends, technologies, and companies to watch*. New York: HarperCollins.

Polson, N., & Scott, J. (2018). *AIQ. How Artificial Intelligence works and how we can harness its power for a better world*. London: Bantam Press-Penguin.

Priest, D., Krishnamurthy, & Blanter, A. (2018, Apr.). The New Automation is Smart, Fast and Small. Emerging digital tools and techniques are reinventing large-scale IT initiatives, one process at a time. *Strategy + Business.*

Rao, A. & Cameron, E. (2018, July 31). The future of Artificial Intelligence depends on Trust. *Strategy + Business.*

Rees, M. (2018). *On the Future. Prospects for Humanity*. Princeton, NJ: Princeton University Press.

Rifkin, J. (2014). *The Zero Marginal Cost Society. The internet of things, the collaborative commons, and the eclipse of capitalism*. New York: Palgrave MacMillan.

Satel, S., & Lilienfeld, S. O. (2013). *Brainwashed. The Seductive Appeal of Mindless Neuroscience.* New York: Perseus Books Books.

Schoemaker & Tetlock. (2017). Building more intelligent enterprises. *MIT Sloan Management Review, 58*(3), 27-37.

Schouteden, C., Sturges, D, Chow, E., Meloni, M., Engineer, N., Lange, A., … Saleh, T. (2018). *Artificial Intelligence and the Circular Economy. AI as a tool to accelerate the Transition.* Ellen MacArthur Foundation + Google + McKinsey & Company.

Schwartz, J.; Thomson, J. & Kleiner, A. (2016, Dec.). The Neuroscience of Strategic Leadership. Research shows how leaders can take the high road less traveled. *Strategy + Business.*

Schwarz, B., & Sharpe, K. (2010). *Practical Wisdom. The Right Way to Do the Right Thing.* London: Penguin Books.

Shermer, M. (2008). Five ways Brain Scans mislead us. *Scientific American, Novembner, 5,* 1412–1414.

Siegel, J. D. (2010). *Mindsight. Transform your brain with the new science of kindness.* London: One-World Publications.

Siegel, J. D. (2017). *Mind. A Journey to the Heart of Being Human.* New York: Norton & Company.

Silver, N. (2012). *The signal and the noise. Why so many predictions fail – but some don't.* New York: Penguin Group Publishing.

Sumpter, D. (2018). *Outnumbered. From Facebook and Google to fake news and filter-bubbles – the Algorithms that control our lives.* London: Bloomsbury Sigma.

Taleb, N. N. (2005). *Fooled by Randomness. The hidden role of Chance in Life and in the Markets.* New York: Random House Trade Paperbacks.

Taleb, N. N. (2007). *The Black Swan. The Impact of the Highly Improbable.* London: Allen Lane – Penguin.

Taleb, N. N. (2012). *The Antifragile.* Academic Press.

Taleb, N. N. (2018). *Skin in the Game. Hidden Asymmetries in daily life.* New York: Random House.

Tegmark, M. (2016). *Life 3.0. Being Human in the age of Artificial Intelligence.* London: Penguin.

Tenbrunsel, A. E., Diekmann, K. A., Wade-Benzoni, K. A., & Bazerman, M. H. (2010). The Ethical Mirage: A Temporal Explanation as to Why We Are Not As Ethical as We Think We Are. *Research in Organizational Behavior, 30,* 153–173. doi:10.1016/j.riob.2010.08.004

Tononi, G. (2012). *Phi. A Voyage from the Brain to the Soul.* New York: Pantheon Books.

Verhezen, P. (2013). Managerial Wisdom in Corporate Governance. In M. Thompson & D. Bevan (Eds.), *Wisdom and Complexity in Organizations.* London: CEIBS & Palgrave. doi:10.1057/9781137002655.0016

Wilson, J., & Daugherty, P. R. (2018, July). Collaborative Intelligence: Humans and AI are joining forces. *Harvard Business Review,* 114–123.

Zarkadakis, G. (2015). *In our Image. Savior or Destroyer? The History and Future of Artificial Intelligence*. New York: Pegasus Books.

Zhang, T., Gino, F., & Bazerman, M. H. (2014). Morality Rebooted: Exploring Simple Fixes to Our Moral Bugs. *Research in Organizational Behavior, 34*, 63–79. doi:10.1016/j.riob.2014.10.002

ENDNOTES

1 Reinforcement learning is "an area of machine learning concerned with how software agents ought to take actions in an environment so as to maximize some notion of cumulative reward. Reinforcement learning is one of three basic machine learning paradigms, alongside supervised learning and unsupervised learning. It differs from supervised learning in that labelled input/output pairs need not be presented, and sub-optimal actions need not be explicitly corrected. Instead the focus is finding a balance between exploration (of uncharted territory) and exploitation (of current knowledge). The environment is typically formulated as a Markov decision process (MDP), as many reinforcement learning algorithms for this context utilize dynamic programming techniques. The main difference between the classical dynamic programming methods and reinforcement learning algorithms is that the latter do not assume knowledge of an exact mathematical model of the MDP and they target large MDPs where exact methods become infeasible". Cf https://en.wikipedia.org/wiki/Reinforcement_learning

2 Even academic research itself is driven by citation indices and impact, because they were easy to calculate. In the process, they became the currency of science. In other words, an algorithm dictates in the academic career path who gets tenure track and who does not. Welcome to the tyranny of data that apparently drives the life of many.

3 Guilia Tononi argued to "quantify" consciousness, denoted by the Greek letter 'Phi', measuring how much different parts of a system know each other. The consciousness theory become known as the integrated information theory (IIT) which logically postulates that computers cannot have a real consciousness. This theory has been challenged by David Chalmers and AI expert Murray Shanahan.

Chapter 5
Ethical Values and Responsibilities of Directors in the Digital Era

Duane Windsor
https://orcid.org/0000-0003-0406-1030
Rice University, USA

ABSTRACT

This chapter addresses the ethical values and responsibilities of corporate directors in the unfolding digital era. Explanation for directors of private or public companies in the digital era involves three principal dimensions. The first concerns the ethical values and responsibilities of any director defined independently of the company or industry or era. The second concerns the additional ethical responsibilities of a director in the digital era, which imposes further conditions on directors. These conditions are heightened for directors of high technology, digital era-oriented businesses. The third dimension concerns whether ethical values and responsibilities of directors vary across countries and legal systems. This dimension separates into legal standards for directors and cultural variations in attitudes and behaviors of directors and managers. The chapter offers real company illustrations for these three dimensions. The chapter recommends four solutions: better and better prepared directors, sounder regulation, and a more unified theory of ethics and responsibility.

INTRODUCTION

This chapter addresses the ethical values and responsibilities of corporate directors in the unfolding digital era. There is an important difference between ethical values and responsibilities. Values are held by the individual director. The director should be a person of honor, honesty, professionalism, and competence. The director is a vital source of moral integrity and legal compliance for a business. The director also has responsibilities to stakeholders of the business. These responsibilities are more variable and subject to debate relative to moral integrity and legal compliance. Moral integrity may in certain limited circumstances require civil disobedience and thus is superior ultimately to legal compliance.

DOI: 10.4018/978-1-7998-2011-6.ch005

This chapter examines the increasing requirements for ethical values and responsibilities of directors in the digital era. The general perspective is that the digital era expands the scope of directors' ethical values and responsibilities. This expansion affects both private and public companies. In discussing this expansion, the author combines relevant aspects of corporate governance (CG), corporate social responsibility (CSR), and the stakeholder theory of business.

There are three principal dimensions in the study of ethical values of directors of private or public companies in the digital era involves. The first dimension concerns the ethical values and responsibilities of any director defined independently of the company or industry or era. The second dimension concerns the additional ethical responsibilities of a director in the digital era, which imposes further conditions on directors. These conditions are heightened for directors of high technology, digital era oriented businesses. The third dimension concerns whether ethical values and responsibilities of directors vary across countries and legal systems. Each dimension defines an objective for this chapter.

The first objective is to explain that minimum ethical values and responsibilities of any director have definition independently of the company or industry or era. Empirically, director and management conduct do not universally meet this minimum set of values and responsibilities.

The second objective is to explain the additional ethical responsibilities of a director in the digital era. That is, the digital era imposes further conditions of ethical values and responsibilities on directors of both private and public companies. These conditions increase directors of high technology, digital era oriented businesses. All businesses face increased scope of ethical responsibilities and certain businesses face added conditions in the digital era.

The third objective is to discuss whether ethical values and responsibilities of directors properly vary across countries. This variability separates into legal standards for directors and cultural variations in attitudes and behaviors. Both legal standards and cultures vary across countries. The vital question is whether those legal standards and cultural variations in attitudes and behaviors will tend to converge on a global model of CG, CSR, and stakeholder management practices. The previous two objectives undertake to establish the ethical values and responsibilities of that global model.

Additionally, the chapter proposes some solutions and recommendations for problems identified. The chapter also suggests future research directions for scholarship to help improve those solutions and recommendations. An important feature of the chapter is the set of references and recommended additional readings that in combination serve as a guide to the literature for the interested reader.

BACKGROUND

Businesses, and their stakeholders, have entered into an expanding and evolving digital era and knowledge economy (Ho, 2018; Sarrazin & Willmott, 2016; Swaminathan & Herzinger, 2018). The essential feature of the digital era is an accelerating shift in the 21st century from the industrial revolution of the 19th and 20th centuries to a new economic domination of information technology (IT). Broadly defined, IT includes artificial intelligence (AI) systems, communications modes, machine learning, and robotic systems. The digital era involves new business models, new interactions with stakeholders, and expanding access to private information that increase importance of and stress on ethical values and responsibilities of the directors of private and public companies. There will be increasing stress on proper CG principles and processes in this digital era.

An initial step here is to define CG. The important topic of CG has acquired both a broader general meaning and a narrower specific definition. Broadly, CG is the whole set or system of principles, codes, and relationships within which corporate management makes decisions and set policies. A principle is a standard for guiding conduct, and reflects some fundamental truth or established proposition. Maximize profit (in a competitive and innovative market economy) or maximize integrity (as a businessperson) are such principles. A code is a systematic statement of approved and prohibited actions to which a business should adhere. Codes affecting business actions may be legal and mandatory or private and voluntary. A legal code – such as domestic statutes and international treaties – is mandatory in the sense of authorizing governmental enforcement. A private code – such as an industry code or adherence to the UN Global Compact – is voluntary in the sense of not being enforced by governments. Both legal and private codes may include the narrower specific definition of CG.

Narrowly, CG typically means the structure of rights and responsibilities among the various stakeholders for control and operation of the business. This narrower definition addresses relationships, which typically separate into financial stakeholders and other kinds of stakeholders. The financial relationships emphasize the board of directors and the top management team, together with shareholders and creditors on the one hand, and auditors and regulators on the other hand. In theory, the directors, auditors (internal and external), and regulators safeguard the interests of the shareholders and creditors. Other kinds of stakeholders include but are not restricted to customers, employees, suppliers, media, communities, and governments.

There are two competing conceptions of relationships. The financial conception assumes conflicts of interest among stakeholders, including between management and shareholders. A web of contracts attempts to regulate these conflicts of interest. This financial conception views the manager as a fiduciary agent of the shareholders (Jensen & Meckling, 1976). The stakeholder conception assumes that cooperation among interested parties is feasible. The task of management is to foster such cooperation to mutual benefit (Freeman, 2017).

The methodology for the chapter involves combining three different approaches. First, the author provides the results and references obtained from direct study of relevant literatures and CG codes. The scope of study includes CSR, environmental, social, and governance (ESG), and stakeholder as well as CG literatures. These literatures include theoretical, quantitative empirical, and qualitative empirical perspectives. The author has selected those references and CG codes that seem most appropriate to the book's theme. Readers interested in a more detailed study of the qualitative CG perspective should see Yasin, Muhamad, and Sulaiman (2014) who provide a useful recent review. Second, the author formulates a statement of a proposed and globally valid model for the director and how that model extends into the digital era. Third, the author assesses global convergence on a model for the director and how that model extends into the digital era. The literature assessment, formulation of a director model, and assessment of global convergence provide the content of the next section.

THREE DIMENSIONS OF DIRECTOR ETHICS AND RESPONSIBILITIES

The introduction to this section emphasizes CG developments in the United Kingdom (UK). Other countries feature in the first sub-section below. The reason is straightforward. The modern conception of CG for publicly traded companies stems from the report of the Cadbury Committee (1992) on "The Financial Aspects of Corporate Governance" in the UK. The UK's Financial Reporting Council (FRC) continues to be active in supporting CG improvements. The Committee chaired by Sir Adrian Cadbury received appointment in May 1991 from the FRC, the London Stock Exchange, and the UK accountancy profession (Dahya, McConnell, & Travlos, 2002; McRitchie, 2013). The appointment of this committee reflected increasing concerns about financial reporting and auditing and was influenced while in course by the Bank of Credit and Commerce International (BCCI) and Robert Maxwell incidents. BCCI engaged in various financial crimes including money laundering. Authorities in several countries acted against BCCI (Bowers, 2012; Mufson & McGee, 1991). After Robert Maxwell, owner of Mirror Group, died in November 1991 there were revelations that he had improperly taken hundreds of millions of pounds from employee pension funds (Cohen, 1991).

The Cadbury report differentiated specific roles of the shareholders (to appoint directors and auditors) and the board (to set strategic aims, appoint and supervise top management, report to shareholders, and comply with relevant laws and regulations). This approach continues to define the now generally accepted understanding of good CG in the sense of financial performance on behalf of the shareholders (MSCI Inc., 2017; Stiles & Taylor, 1993). The report made various recommendations for strengthening CG practices.

The Cadbury report was the first proposal for adopting an "comply-or-explain" principle (Seidl, Sanderson, & Roberts, 2009, p. 3; Seidl, Sanderson, & Roberts, 2013) – arguably as a means of encouraging voluntary adherence to recommended practices (Arcot, Bruno, & Faure-Grimaud, 2010). If a company could not comply, it should explain why. This "comply-or-explain" approach is subject to criticism in permitting companies not to comply as long they can persuade regulators and concerned stakeholders to delay enforcement (Keay, 2014).

Today, the FRC maintains a UK Corporate Governance Code (Combined Code) which states practices for boards, director remuneration, shareholder relations, accountability, and audit. The latest version at time of writing in 2019 is July 2018 (Financial Reporting Council, 2018). The FRC also published a UK Stewardship Code for investors (Financial Reporting Council, 2012). At time of writing in 2019, the FRC was consulting on a revision of the Stewardship Code (Financial Reporting Council, 2019).

Baseline Ethical Values and Responsibilities of Directors

The baseline for consideration of the effects of a digital era is a model of the ethical values and responsibilities of directors defined independently of the company or industry or era (Aguilera & Cuervo-Cazurra, 2009; Aguilera & Jackson, 2010; Cuomo, Mallin, & Zattoni, 2016). A director has fiduciary, legal, and ethical duties. This section reviews the existing standards for directors. A fiduciary duty is to the owners of the business. However, fiduciary duty is not simply for profit maximization or shareholder wealth maximization. Rather fiduciary duty has a broader meaning of stewardship for a sustainable business (Minichilli, Zattoni, Nielsen, & Huse, 2012). Strict profit maximization comes into play only in conditions of merger-acquisition or bankruptcy when asset valuation must be as high as feasible. Legal duty is beyond fiduciary duty, in that directors are subject to compliance with a variety of statutes and regulations.

Ethical duty is broader still, in obliging a director to be honorable and honest, professional, and imbued with moral imagination and courage. These duties will be defined, explained, and related to examples of director codes of conduct as imposed by statutes, regulations, and stock exchange listing requirements.

Prescriptively, the critical attributes for a director – whether executive or non-executive – are independence, integrity, and competence (Zattoni & Cuomo, 2010). A director must be reasonably independent of the CEO and top management team. A director must be a person of moral integrity. A director must have reasonable competence to supervise a business and monitor management. In modern practice, a director is both a monitor of and an advisor to management (Ke, Li, & Zhang, 2019). The supervisory role of directors includes both these dimensions. Ke et al. (2019) find that the presence on a firm's board of more directors concurrently serving as directors or executives in related industries is associated with more accurate management forecasts, because such directors supply valuable information. This reported association increases with uncertainty facing the firm.

A way of combining these attributes is to say that a director should be reasonably professional. Herzog characterizes professional ethics in banking as including both duties toward stakeholders (to expand on Herzog) and the whole society (emphasizing "prevention of systemic harms"):

The paper develops a responsibility-based account of professional ethics in banking. From this perspective, bankers have duties not only toward clients—the traditional focus of professional ethics—but also regarding the prevention of systemic harms to whole societies. (Herzog, 2019, p. 531)

Directors have the duty to foster an ethical organization "from the bottom up and the outside in" (Hess & Broughton, 2014). As Hess and Broughton point out, corporate misconduct is widespread. Those authors draw on behavioral ethics to formulate a broader approach that moves beyond formal control systems to emphasize also informal practices.

... we illustrate how executives may strengthen organizational ethics through informal practices that work from the 'bottom up' and the 'outside in.' Our review includes practical recommendations regarding how to create shared responsibility for ethical leadership, how to empower employees to achieve both economic and ethical ends, how to enlist the aid of key stakeholders in identifying problems before they grow and spread, and how to redesign compliance practices to address the complex nature of corporate misconduct. (Hess & Broughton, 2014, p. 541)

A reasonable classification of countries relies on stage of economic development. There are advanced, emerging, and developing economies. A subset of emerging and developing categories comprises transition economies. Advanced economies are typically associated with democratic political regimes. Emerging economies (Jacoby, Liu, Wang, Wu, & Zhang, 2019) and developing economies may be associated with either democratic regimes (such as Singapore) or authoritarian regimes (such as Venezuela). An emerging economy is moving toward advanced status. A developing economy is not. Much of Africa and Latin America are developing economies (González & García-Meca, 2014). Transition economies are countries that have moved from communism and domination by the USSR toward more market oriented and independent conditions. Poland and Ukraine are examples. There are also communist one-party regimes that may be emerging (such as China and Vietnam) or remain developing (such as Cuba and North Korea). CG reasoning may not fit well with communist one-party regimes because of the strong influence of the government and party. Advanced economies separate into two basic models (Hall

Table 1. Composition of the Group of 20 (G20)

Type of Country	Geographic Location	Countries
advanced democratic economies	North America	Canada United States of America (USA)
	Western Europe	France Germany Italy United Kingdom (UK)
	Pacific Ocean Rim	Australia Japan
other democratic economies represented collectively by the European Union (EU)	Western Europe	EU members other than France, Germany, Italy, and UK
BRICS	Latin America	Brazil (B)
	Eastern Europe	Russia (R)
	South Asia	India (I)
	East Asia	China (C)
	Sub-Saharan Africa	South Africa (S)
other emerging economies	Latin America	Argentina Mexico
	East Asia	South Korea
	Southeast Asia	Indonesia
	Middle East	Saudi Arabia Turkey

Note: Author's classification of type of country and geographic location.

& Soskice, 2001): market capitalism (UK and USA being examples) and social democracy (Germany being an example).

The most important source of CG codes and practices is the set of advanced democratic economies within the Group of 20 (G20). This set includes the UK discussed in some detail earlier in this section. The G20 consists of 19 important economies plus the European Union (EU) representing collectively smaller European countries (Organisation for Economic Co-operation and Development, 2015). Table 1 provides a detailed classification of the G20 membership by type of country and geographic location around the globe. An advanced democratic economy is one that possesses both an advanced and important economy and a stable democratic political regime. In addition to the UK, the advanced democratic economies are Australia, Canada, France, Germany, Italy, Japan, and United States of America (USA). Australia, UK, and USA are the most important CG sources. Australia has a reputation for cutting-edge efforts at improving CG (Australian Government; 2010; Mees & Smith, 2019; Walters, 2015). A fundamental difference within the advanced democratic economies concerns the single board and dual board structures. The former is typical of the Anglo-American-Australian-Canadian CG approach; Germany illustrates the latter. The single board approach associates with shareholder emphasis. The dual board approach associates with a broader stakeholder arrangement. Japan also features a more stakeholder oriented CG framework. Table 1 separates the G20 between advanced and emerging economies. An emerging economy is one that has moved out of developing status toward advanced status. Table 1 does not distinguish within the EU collective representation between types of economies. Some smaller members of the EU are emerging rather than advanced economies. The other members of the G20 are all emerging economies. The emerging economies are Argentina, Brazil, China, India, Indonesia, Mexico, Russia, Saudi Arabia, South Africa, South Korea, and Turkey. Other than Saudi Arabia, China, and Russia the other emerging economies are presently more or less democratic regimes at least with respect to having regular, contested elections. China is a one-party communist state. Russia is best viewed as an authoritarian regime. Both China and Russia are transitional economies in the sense of having moved from communist central planning toward market economies. Some of the smaller EU members in Eastern Europe are also transitional economies in the same sense. A number of Eastern European countries were subject to domination by the communist Soviet Union until its disintegration. The G20 includes the set of five countries labeled the BRICS: Brazil, Russia, India, China, and South Africa.

The advanced democratic economies together with Mexico, South Korea, and Turkey and various smaller countries of the EU are members of the 36-country OECD (Organisation for Economic Co-operation and Development, n.d.). EU members show a diversity of national CG approaches (Cicon, Ferris, Kammel, & Noronha, 2012; Kubíček, Štamfestová, & Strouhal, 2016).

The USA is a federal republic, within which corporate chartering is by state and stock exchange listing requirements are important. Delaware is historically the most important state source of CG law, because many important public corporations are chartered there. Listing requirements for the important stock exchanges are standard sources: especially the New York Stock Exchange (NYSE) (2014) and also located in New York City the NASDAQ for the National Association of Securities Dealers (NASD) (2002) and the NYSE American (formerly the American Stock Exchange). Public company securities are subject to regulation by the U.S. Securities and Exchange Commission (SEC) under the Securities Act of 1933 and the Securities Exchange Act of 1934. The American Bar Association (ABA) provides guidance for directors (American Bar Association, 2011; Placenti, 2017). Stock exchanges in other countries perform a similar role. London Stock Exchange Group (2017) has issued guidance on environmental, social, and governance (ESG) reporting.

Like the UK, the USA is an important source of modern CG guidance. The USA has adopted two important statutes, amending securities laws, significantly affecting CG. The Sarbanes-Oxley (SOX) Act of 2002 followed a spate of notorious corporate scandals – especially Enron, Tyco International, and WorldCom (King & Case, 2014). This statute addressed financial reporting, conflicts of interest, corporate ethics, and accounting profession oversight. One provision established a Public Company Accounting Oversight Board (PCAOB) for supervising the accounting profession. SOX had broader effects on foreign shareholders and managers (Duarte, Kong, Siegel, & Young, 2014). The financial crisis of 2007 stimulated passage of the Dodd-Frank Act (the Wall Street Reform and Consumer Protection Act) of 2010 (Bainbridge, 2010). Among the significant CG provision of Dodd-Frank are: shareholder advisory voting on executive compensation ("say on pay"); independent compensation committees; disclosures concerning executive compensation; expansion of clawback rules in the SOX act; shareholder proxy access for nominating director candidates; disclosure of whether and why the CEO and Board Chair positions are combined or separated (Bainbridge, 2010; Jenson, Quinlivan, Radloff, Jenson, Cotter, & Weitz, 2010).

CG considerations partly overlap with CSR and ESG issues. CSR is generally equivalent to environment and social dimensions of ESG, which adds the governance dimension missing in CSR. Using data envelopment analysis (DES) one study estimates a nonlinear relationship between corporate efficiency and ESG disclosure (Xie, Nozawa, Yagi, Fujii, & Managi, 2019). The study reports moderate ESG transparency shows a positive association with corporate efficiency. The relationship is U-shaped, in that high or low disclosure levels are more inefficient. The positive association is strongest for CG disclosure, followed in order by social and then environmental information disclosures. The study also reports a nonnegative relationship between particular ESG activities and corporate financial performance (CFP).

An illustration is the Principles for Responsible Investment (PRI) promoted by the United Nations (Principles for Responsible Investment, n.d.). These six principles are, however, subject to the condition of consistency with fiduciary responsibilities. The first principle is to incorporate ESG issues into investment decisions. The second principle is that investors should encourage business owners to promote ESG issues. The third principle is that investors should seek appropriate disclosure of ESG information. The fourth principle is that participating investors should promote PRI within the investment industry. The fifth principle is that the investment industry should engage in collection action to support PRI implementation. The sixth principle is to engage in systematic reporting on PRI activities and progress.

The concept of profit maximization, translated as fiduciary responsibility in agency theory, is wrongly misinterpreted if understood to exclude all other considerations except strict legal compliance. Sanderson (2012) argues that viewing a manager as a "homo economicus" methodically and rationally maximizing profits (or utility) is "a straw-man characterization". As this chapter documents, directors have a much broader scope of responsibilities.

Empirical evidence supports taking a broader view of directing a business. A study of German firms listed on the Frankfurt Stock Exchange during 2006-2011 measures agency costs of external and internal CG mechanisms (Schäuble, 2019). An audit committee does not reduce agency costs. (A reason could be that audit committees are essentially widespread in German listed companies.) But an industry specialized audit firm, a large audit firm, abnormally high audit fees, management ownership, and variable management compensation do appear to reduce agency costs.

Barnett and Salomon (2012) report a U-shaped relationship between corporate social performance (CSP) and CFP measures for an unbalanced panel of about 1,214 firms during the period 1998-2006 for which Kinder, Lydenberg, Domini Research & Analytics (KLD) data measures were available. They conclude that firms with low CSP or high CSP have higher CFP than firms with moderate CSP; and that firms with high CSP have the highest CFP. In other words, firms can be profitable at either low or high CSP, and the latter is somewhat more profitable.

In the S&P Europe 350 – firms operating in 16 countries – a number of factors positively influence quality of CSR reporting. Those factors are ownership by directors, presence of a CSR committee, and firm size (Adel, Hussain, Mohamed, & Basuony, 2019). This study also tested independent variables on a number of CSR sub-categories: "community involvement, employees, environment, social product and service quality, supply chain sustainability and business ethics" (Abel et al., 2019). Only presence of a sustainability committee had a strong positive effect on disclosure of every CSR sub-category.

In general, modern boards of directors face a number of key responsibilities that go beyond monitoring of management and protection of the assets and reputation of the business on behalf of the shareholders. A recent illustration of the conventional conception of monitoring and protection is the collapse of Steinhoff of South Africa (Rossouw & Styan, 2019). Steinhoff's collapse is a classic case of management and supervision failure. It is less clear today that directors should focus on strategy and supervision.

Instead of purpose, there may be a few simple things to accomplish: take care of people and practice good citizenship while making profit (Kinni, 2019). Directors must safeguard the ethical values of the business, protect internal whistleblowers, monitor insider trading, forestall and correct corruption such as bribery and kickbacks, and ensure legal compliance including for antitrust and pollution regulation. Directors should also ensure CSR activities concerning sustainability and other responsibilities. The UN Global Compact's ten principles provide a reasonable working guide to those responsibilities. These principles cover human rights, labor rights, environmental protection, and anti-corruption.

Legal compliance by managers is not automatically assured. Abdelal, De Tella, and Schlefer (2008) document three forms of corruption in German companies. One instance is the practice of bribery globally by Siemens uncovered by German and USA authorities (Blanc, Cho, Sopt, & Branco, 2019). German law permitted tax deductions for overseas bribe payments until 1999, when the law changed in accord with new international accords. At VW, a senior executive corrupted union leaders with foreign travel and prostitutes in order to secure labor concessions. In the late 1980s, BASF and the Swiss firm Hoffmann-La Roche organized a decade-long global vitamin pricing cartel that significantly increased prices of many vitamins.

There are pressures on businesses to pursue profits while imposing negative externalities on stakeholders and evading government regulations. A recent example concerns DuPont, which evidently engaged in pollution over decades that violated environmental regulations and caused substantial negative externalities to stakeholders. The lawsuits imposed about $1 billion in compensation and legal expenses on the business. Shapira and Zingales (2017) studied DuPont documents disclosed during the lawsuits. They conclude that the pollution was financially a rational decision given certain estimates about likelihood of discovery (which was postponed for decades). They exclude alternative explanations, including bad governance. They conclude that the typically recommended control mechanisms of "legal liability, regulation, and reputation" were not effective. Some managers simply decided to pollute.

Taking into account the information summarized above, Bistrong (2019) argues that management and the board of directors can "own honesty or deceit" by choice. Cassin (2019) and Bistrong (2019) provide information on the corrupt situation at the German company Fresenius Medical Care. (The company is the world's largest supplier of dialysis equipment and services.) Fresenius managers engaged in bribery and cover up of bribery. At corporate headquarters, "legal, compliance, and internal audit functions failed to detect and prevent the bribery" (Bistrong, 2019). As early as 2009, corporate headquarters had received information that a general manager in Saudi Arabia was submitting phony reports disguising corruption as marketing and travel expenses. There were improper foreign corrupt payments occurring in 16 other countries including ten countries in Africa, Bosnia and Serbia in the Balkans, China, Mexico, Spain, and Turkey. Fresenius agreed to pay the US Department of Justice and the US Securities and Exchange Commission (SEC) $231 million. It appears that senior executives in Germany ordered field office employees to alter and destroy documents and delete computer files and emails. The SEC reported inadequate anti-corruption training and only minimal due diligence on third parties with which the business worked in various countries.

Further Conditions Imposed by the Digital Era

The digital era – with its attendant developments of artificial intelligence (AI) and robotic systems as well as information technology and knowledge management – is an expanding revolution in business activities (*Knowledge@Wharton*, 2019). Beyond the baseline model of the ethical, responsible, and professional director the digital era imposes further conditions on directors (Gouran, 2013; Walters, 2015). The most immediately obvious conditions are protection of the privacy of information of stakeholders (especially customers, employees, and investors) and cybersecurity of the business (Harris & Martin, 2019). The digital era is in a state of flux concerning these conditions. Additional conditions may arise or be identifiable as the digital era evolves. Business is entering a 5G world, which may be followed by increased emphasis on AI and robotic systems. The digital era will increasingly affect most if not all businesses. A business that operates partly or wholly cashlessly is already in the digital era, for example.

Digital era conditions are heightened for directors of high technology and knowledge-based businesses. Instances include Amazon, Facebook, Google, Microsoft, Twitter, Yahoo, and all major financial institutions. A question for consideration is whether the directorship practices at such businesses should and will serve as models for other businesses.

Business models for high technology businesses may be shifting (Vardi, 2019) and subjected to increasing governmental regulation (Satariano, 2019). Business practices may involve profound transformations (Bunyan & Sarkis, 2019). The EU General Data Protection Regulation (GDPR) became enforceable on May 25, 2018. GDPR provides stronger rules on personal data and tries to level the playing field for businesses (European Commission, n.d.). It is far from clear whether more governmental regulation is a useful approach (Bucci, 2019).

The structure of the economy may be shifting toward platforms (Fenwick, McCahery, & Vermeulen, 2019). A platform is a networking technology in some form that is required for or facilitates trading, information transfer, and interpersonal connections. Instances cited by Fenwick et al. include Amazon, Apple, Facebook, and Google (through Alphabet). The platform owner-operator earns profit through the role of intermediary. In April 2019, Facebook reserved $3 billion for potential costs of a U.S. Federal Trade Commission (FTC) investigation of the firm's privacy practices; a FTC fine might be between $3 and $5 billion (Facebook, 2019).

Satariano and Perlroth (2019) provide the following information on how cyberattacks on business may not be covered by insurance. The legal issue of exclusion as an alleged war risk is in courts through lawsuits for breach of contract. Mondelez International, a food brand company, suffered the "NotPetya" cyberattack of 2017 which struck some hundreds of companies. Mondelez's estimated costs amounted to more than $100 million. Zurich Insurance, the company's insurer, declined payment under an insurance policy explicitly covering cyberevents by invoking a "war exclusion" clause. The rationale for denial is that the U.S. government ascribed the "NotPetya" cyberattack to the Russian government.

In general, enterprise risk management (ERM) requirements are placing increasing stress on boards and board committees to safeguard business reputation (Pérez-Cornejo, de Quevedo-Puente, & Delgado-García, 2019). Osborne (2019) reports on security threats to US pipelines, as an example of risks facing infrastructure of various types.

It appears that knowledge-oriented businesses are especially susceptible to internal disputes by employees regarding both personnel treatment and policy stances. Google is a prime example, in which there are ongoing debates concerning sexual harassment and retaliation (Baron, 2019), privacy protection, and role of Google in China (Associated Press, 2019). The general problem for management and the board is the role of deliberative democracy in a firm of well-educated, politically active knowledge workers (Ferraro, 2019).

Cross-National Variations in Ethical Values and Responsibilities of Directors

The author argues that directors should adhere to a reasonably global standard for ethics and responsibilities. There is no cross-national variation in what is ethical business and some set of environmental and social responsibilities in operating a business. In practice, this standard must be stated by leading legislating bodies and stock exchanges and compared to national legislation and regulation. Empirically, given variances across countries, the issue is at what pace and in what ways convergence on a reasonably global standard for directors will occur.

Legislation and stock exchange listing requirements vary considerably by country and by state within the USA for instance (Haxhi & Van Ees, 2009). There is no agreed global or universal code of conduct for directors (Windsor, 2009). This circumstance raises the question of whether ethics and responsibilities can vary across countries or should there be a global or universal standard even in the absence of a unified legal system. This sub-section weighs the advantages and disadvantages of the global and decentralized approaches. The former approach emphasizes the global character of ethical values and responsibilities in business. The latter approach permits experimentation and variation in circumstances. In the longer run, the latter will tend in the author's opinion to converge toward the former (for empirical support of the convergence prediction see Martynova and Renneboog, 2011). The study of Areneke, Yusuf, and Kimani (2019) examines diffusion of Anglo-American CG practices to Cameroon, Kenya, and Pakistan.

Much of modern CG reasoning and research invokes agency theory (Filatotchev, Jackson, & Nakajima, 2013; Jensen & Meckling, 1976). The basic elements of agency theory are shareholder wealth maximization and financial incentives for managers to promote shareholder interests. The contrasting cross-national perspective is that variations in institutional contexts across countries greatly influence how agency will work. Filatotchev et al. (2013) argue that performance outcomes of specific CG mechanisms (such as boards, ownership, and incentives) vary on country institutional characteristics including legal system. Different CG practices may prove to be complements or substitutes depending on country institutions. Filatotchev et al. (2013, p. 965) argue that CG practices must be interpreted and analyzed within a "more holistic, institutionally embedded governance framework …"

A classic study of cross-country variation in CG focused on variations in how different legal systems provided investor protection (La Porta, Lopez-de-Silanes, Shleifer, & Vishny, 2000). In general, the stronger the investor protection is the higher the firm financial performance. That study distinguished among four legal systems: common law (18 countries), French civil law (21 countries), German civil law (6 countries), and Scandinavian civil law (4 countries). Common law means that judges determine legal precedents through case opinions. Common law is the Anglo-American system of Australia, Canada, New Zealand, UK, other members of the British Commonwealth, and USA. Civil law is the European system of governmental enactment of systematic legal codes. La Porta et al. identify three different civil law approaches: French, German, and Scandinavian. Modern Japan reflects a mixture of civil law (French and German) and American common law. The legal systems of modern China and Russia have communist one-party foundations. In theory post-USSR Russia has transitioned to a civil law system, but Russia is effectively a one-party state. Latin American and European countries generally are civil law systems.

The combination of financial structure and legal system is likely important. A study of 1,736 firms in 22 countries concludes that there is a joint effect of the country's financial structure and legal system on the relationship between firm financial performance and the level of CG. At the same level of CG, those firms that operate in the combination of market financing and common law have higher market valuations than firms that operate in the combination of bank financing and civil law (Anderson & Gupta, 2009).

A study of 41 countries finds that institutional ownership positively associated with environmental and social performance (Dyck, Lins, Roth, & Wagner, 2019). Dyck et al. (2019) argue that the relationship is causal: institutional ownership drives environmental and social performance outcomes. In those authors' view, institutional investors increase environmental and social performance after shocks that demonstrate benefits of environmental and social improvements. Additionally, institutional investors from countries with strong community belief in environmental and social performance transfer that expectation to other countries. Social norms concerning environmental and social issues may diffuse through shocks and investor beliefs.

A different study examines CG mechanisms in relationship to CSR reporting in the five BRICS emerging countries: Brazil, Russia, India, China, and South Africa (del Mar Miras-Rodríguez, Martínez-Martínez, & Escobar-Pérez, 2019). The sample included 281 companies. This study concludes that country institutions influence company CSR reporting.

South Africa has defined relatively advanced CG practices influenced by UK codes. The King Committee on Corporate Governance initiated the process in South Africa under the aegis of the Institute of Directors in Southern Africa (IoDSA). IoDSA has now issued four reports: 1994 (King I), 2002 (King II), 2009 (King III), and 2016 (King IV). Compliance with the King Code of Corporate Governance is a requirement for listing on the Johannesburg Stock Exchange and is now basically applicable to all entities. King is not a legislative enactment.

King III addressed fundamental principles of leadership, sustainability, and corporate citizenship. Sustainability was regarded as "the primary moral and economic imperative..." (PricewaterhouseCoopers Southern Africa, 2009, p. 2). King III defined governance in relationship to leadership as follows: "Good governance is essentially about effective leadership. Leaders need to define strategy, provide direction and establish the ethics and values that will influence and guide practices and behaviour with regard to sustainability performance" (PricewaterhouseCoopers Southern Africa, 2009, p. 2). "Responsible corporate citizenship implies an ethical relationship between the company and the society in which it operates" (PricewaterhouseCoopers Southern Africa, 2009, p. 5). An important feature of King IV is to extend governance principles and practices from listed companies to private companies, nonprofit organizations, and public sector entities (Institute of Directors in Southern Africa, 2016, p. 22). King IV intends a shift from a previous "apply or explain" regime to an "apply and explain" regime (Natesan & du Plessis, 2019).

A leading influence on CG practices around the world is the multinational corporation (MNC). A study of MNC board design finds a positive influence on CSR disclosure (Pham & Tran, 2019). The study defines board models in terms of two-tier and one-tier boards. The one-tier board is the USA approach. The two-tier approach is found in Germany. Board independence is measured as proportion of independent directors on the board. The study draws on a panel of 244 Fortune World's Most Admired corporations during 2005-2011. Over 20 countries, 117 firms used one-tier board model and 127 firms used two-tier board model. The study finds that two-tier model firms reveal more CSR information. There is a significant moderating effect of model on independence, having greater influence in the two-tier model. There is no influence of independence on CSR disclosure in general. Independence is significant in the two-tier model only.

Foreign institutional investors do have influence on voluntary disclosure practices in management forecasts (Tsang, Xie, & Xin, 2019). The study cited uses a sample of 32 countries, not including the USA. The influence of foreign institutional investors is greater than the influence of domestic institutional investors. The study finds stronger results for conditions in which foreign institutional investors are not familiar with the focal firm home country, have longer time horizons for investing, and come from countries that have more investor protection and disclosure requirements than the focal firm home country. If foreign institutional investors come from countries with weaker requirements or concentrated foreign institutional ownership, then voluntary disclosure becomes weaker.

Family enterprises make up the largest proportion of businesses in the world. Family directors are common in Malaysia and other Asian countries (Dinh & Calabrò, 2019). Al-Absy, Ismail, and Chandren (2019) study a three-year (2013-2014-2015) sample of Malaysian firms involving 864 firm-year observations. Those authors find that where a firm engages in aggressive earnings management (defined as income-increasing choices), family directors are associated with more discretionary accruals and abnormal real earnings management. When a firm engages in conservative earnings management (defined as income-decreasing choices), this association for family directors is mixed for discretionary accruals but significant for less conservative abnormal real earnings management. On the whole, family directors associate with more aggressive earnings management.

China, the world's largest population communist regime, involves a curious setting for study of CG issues (Allen & Rui, 2018; Mehta & Brett, 2017). Basically, the judiciary is not independent and the communist party leadership controls legislation which can change any policy rapidly. A comparison of Hong Kong, a special administrative unit of China, and Singapore, an independent country, can prove informative (Chen, 2019). Problems for Chinese businesses are corruption and political connections (Fu, 2019). Empirical studies are reporting useful evidence for Chinese conditions (Farag & Mallin, 2019; Jiang & Kim, 2015).

India, the world's largest population constitutional democracy, is an interesting setting for study of CG issues (Mehta, 2017). In 2013, India enacted a Companies Act including a requirement (Clause 135) for CSR spending. This act is the first legislation in the world to require compulsory corporate philanthropy. All companies – domestic and foreign – with annual turnover of at least \$161 million, or net worth of at least \$80 million, or net profit of at least \$800,000 (these figures are translated from Indian currency) must spend at least 2% of average net profit over the previous three years on CSR (Aggarwal & Jha, 2019). In January 2018, the Indian government adopted an amended Companies (Amendment) Act 2017. This amendment sought to reduce reported implementation difficulties and inconsistencies (Das, 2019). A study of 163 of the top 1,000 companies in India collected information on perceptions of CSR managers through a structured questionnaire and in-depth interviews (Bala & Verma, 2019). The final response set was 163 of a random sampling of 250 companies of the top 1,000. The study reports considerable diversity in managers' perceptions.

SOLUTIONS AND RECOMMENDATIONS

The author proposes four solutions for strengthening the ethical values and responsibilities of directors for the unfolding digital era.

The first solution involves the supply of directors. A director of any business must be a person of integrity, honor, and competence. In reality, selection of directors devolves to the focal business. Proposals for professional independent directors, sound as such, cannot conceivably fill the demand for directors of the many businesses in the world (Fram, 2005). Directors come from various sources, varying by country, industry, and kind of business (small, medium, large, family-owned, publicly traded, and so forth). Appointments occur for all kinds of reasons. The associated recommendation is that increasing standards for who becomes and remains a director moves in the correct direction. The vital distinction here is that any director can be a professional in conduct as distinct from being a professional independent director (Donaldson, 2000).

The second solution involves better preparation of the available directors, from whatever sources, for both the conventional responsibilities and the additional responsibilities occurring with the digital era and in high technology, knowledge intensive businesses in particular. There is no organized system for such preparation, which occurs ad hoc and by country at varying levels of attention. As noted in the text above and the references on sources on CG guidance, there are efforts at better preparation. The associated recommendation is that improving preparation of directors, especially for the digital era, moves in the correct direction.

The third solution involves sounder regulatory frameworks – governmental and private – moving toward some global convergence on a prescriptive model for the director of a business. Regulation of CG is highly fragmented across countries, industries, and stock exchanges. Sounder regulation involves both an intellectual process of better understanding and a political process of marshaling legislative and stock exchange concurrence. Sarbanes-Oxley and Dodd-Frank enactments were responses to scandal and crisis as distinct from careful ex ante inquiry. The associated recommendation is for further and systematic research into CG regulation and regulatory process.

The fourth solution concerns the need for a more unified theory of business ethics and CSR. The field of ethical values and responsibilities involves still unresolved debates. One fundamental tension is between (1) on the one hand a profit maximization, fiduciary responsibility, and agency theory of the firm operating in basically unregulated markets, and (2) on the other hand a CSR and stakeholder theory of the firm operating in much more strongly regulated economies. A business is typically caught in reality between these two views. Directors and managers are the individuals who in combination resolve the tension in practical policies and actions. The associated recommendation is for further and systematic research into how a theory of business ethics and CSR should and can interact with CG policies and practices. How convergence in values and practices can occur is an important research area associated with this solution (Paik, Lee, & Pak, 2019).

FUTURE RESEARCH DIRECTIONS

This book's theme addresses "Challenges and Opportunities of Corporate Governance Transformation in the Digital Era." This chapter's concern is with the ethical values and responsibilities of directors. The chapter's theme is that those ethical values and responsibilities will expand inevitably with the unfolding digital era. A central theme of the chapter is that ultimately a global model of ethical values and responsibilities for directors will be needed. Ultimately, managers are the decision makers for businesses. The basic role of a board of directors is to select and supervise the top executives. But the directors set the climate and tone for the ethical values and responsibilities of the business and the top executives. The directors must be topnotch. Otherwise the executives, however capable, will not be well selected or supervised. Within the domain of this chapter's topic, there are a number of future research directions that should be developed.

There is at best only weak empirical verification concerning whether the CG principles and practices prevalent in the democratic advanced economies function effectively and equivalently in emerging, developing, and transition economies (Chen, Li, & Shapiro, 2011). There are fundamental differences in institutional context and in the directors and managers of businesses operating in various countries.

Additionally, it is not empirically established that prescriptive CG principles and practices have a reliable relationship to earnings quality that is independent of institutional context (Giao & Raposo, 2014). The basic problem, as expressed in this chapter, is that the functioning of the board of directors rests in the final analysis on the integrity, honor, and competence of the individual directors. There is no real institutional or practice substitute for this necessary element of CG – in any country setting.

There is a broad scope of research that should be undertaken into the relationships among CG, CSR, and stakeholder conceptions (Gill, 2009). Windsor (2013) applies a distinction between CSR and corporate social irresponsibility (CSIR). Irresponsibility involves failures of either legal compliance or good business ethics. CSR, as a rubric term, thus involves three dimensions: good business ethics, legal compliance, and good citizenship. The board of directors should be able to readily define good business ethics and legal compliance. Good citizenship involves reputation, stakeholder relationships, and strategic considerations.

Broad social issues and sociopolitical activism are becoming more pressing. Two instances are environmental sustainability and economic inequality. Inequality is a rising concern even in the democratic advanced economies (Styhre & Bergström, 2019). But both environmental sustainability and economic inequality are subject to contest concerning meaning and importance in a business setting. Decisions in both dimensions are tough ones (Agarwal & Holmes, 2019; Smith & Soonieus, 2019). More broadly, directors will be drawn into an unavoidable world of triple bottom line performance: economic, environmental, and social.

How boards can effectively combat corruption and implement anti-corruption reforms in home and host countries is an important area of research. International Organization for Standardization (ISO) 37001 addresses anti-bribery management systems for implementation of the UN Global Compact's anti-corruption principle (International Organization for Standardization, n.d.). The ISO website cites an OECD source (CleanGovBiz, 2014, p. 2) estimating global bribery at over $1 trillion annually (International Organization for Standardization, n.d., para. 1). Windsor (2019) suggests a multiple-dimensioned approach for Asia Pacific region countries that might help increase influence on MNCs to undertake greater anti-corruption efforts. Among countries included in this region are China, Japan, and Singapore.

CONCLUSION

This chapter examines the increasing requirements for ethical values and responsibilities of directors of private and public companies in the digital era. The argument develops in three stages. First, there are baseline ethical and responsibility requirements for directors of all businesses. The author argues that this baseline is global in scope. Second, the digital era is increasing the scope and intensity of those requirements – and especially so for high technology, knowledge intensive businesses operating digitally. Third, there is erratic convergence toward a global standard model for directors of businesses. In reality, there is wide dispersion in attitudes, behaviors, and institutional contexts. These considerations suggest significant solutions and recommendations for improvement, and further research directions for improving understanding of CG policies and practices and the supply of desirable directors. The key source of CG guidance is the G20, identified earlier in Table 1. Within the G20, Australia, the UK, and the USA are leading sources of CG developments. There remains a fundamental difference between the shareholder-oriented CG perspective dominant in the UK and the USA on the one hand and the more stakeholder oriented CG perspective found in Germany and Japan.

ACKNOWLEDGMENT

This research received no specific grant from any funding agency in the public, commercial, or not-for-profit sectors.

REFERENCES

Abdelal, R., Di Tella, R., & Schlefer, J. (2008, July 30). *Corruption in Germany*. Harvard Business School case 709006. Retrieved from https://hbr.org/product/corruption-in-germany/709006-PDF-ENG

Adel, C., Hussain, M. M., Mohamed, E. K., & Basuony, M. A. (2019). Is corporate governance relevant to the quality of corporate social responsibility disclosure in large European companies? *International Journal of Accounting & Information Management*, *27*(2), 301–332. doi:10.1108/IJAIM-10-2017-0118

Agarwal, R., & Holmes, R. M. Jr. (2019). Dialogue: Let's not focus on income inequality. *Academy of Management Review*, *44*(2), 450–460. doi:10.5465/amr.2018.0128

Aggarwal, V. S., & Jha, A. (2019). Pressures of CSR in India: An institutional perspective. *Journal of Strategy and Management*, *12*(2), 227–242. doi:10.1108/JSMA-10-2018-0110

Aguilera, R. V., & Cuervo-Cazurra, A. (2009). Codes of good governance. *Corporate Governance*, *17*(3), 376–387. doi:10.1111/j.1467-8683.2009.00737.x

Aguilera, R. V., & Jackson, G. (2010). Comparative and international corporate governance. *The Academy of Management Annals*, *4*(1), 485–556. doi:10.5465/19416520.2010.495525

Al-Absy, M. S. M., Ismail, K. N. I. K., & Chandren, S. (2019). Corporate governance mechanisms and family directives: Aggressive or conservative in earnings management? *Academy of Accounting and Financial Studies Journal, 23*, 1-9. Retrieved from https://www.abacademies.org/articles/Corporate-Governance-Mechanisms-And-Family-Directives-1528-2635-23-1-335.pdf

Allen, J., & Rui, L. (2018, August 25). *Awakening governance: ACGA China corporate governance report 2018*. Asian Corporate Governance Association. Retrieved April 30, 2019, from https://corpgov.law.harvard.edu/2018/08/25/awakening-governance-acga-china-corporate-governance-report-2018/

American Bar Association. (2011). Corporate director's guidebook (6th ed.). Chicago, IL: American Bar Association (ABA), Business Law Section, Corporate Law Committee.

Anderson, A., & Gupta, P. P. (2009). A cross-country comparison of corporate governance and firm performance: Do financial structure and the legal system matter? *Journal of Contemporary Accounting & Economics*, *5*(2), 61–79. doi:10.1016/j.jcae.2009.06.002

Arcot, S., Bruno, V., & Faure-Grimaud, A. (2010). Corporate governance in the UK: Is the comply or explain approach working? *International Review of Law and Economics*, *30*(2), 193–201. doi:10.1016/j.irle.2010.03.002

Areneke, G., Yusuf, F., & Kimani, D. (2019). Anglo-American governance adoption in non-Anglo-American settings: Assessing practitioner perceptions of corporate governance across three emerging economies. *Managerial Auditing Journal*, *34*(4), 486–514. doi:10.1108/MAJ-12-2017-1733

Associated Press. (2019, March 28). Trump: Google will aid military, not China. *Houston Chronicle,* p. B2 (Business).

Australian Government, Department of Families, Housing, Community Services and Indigenous Affairs. (2010, June). *Corporate governance handbook for company directors and committee members: A reference guide to understanding the serious commitment of being a company director or committee member* (2nd ed.). Retrieved May 14, 2019, from https://www.dss.gov.au/sites/default/files/documents/05_2012/gov_handbook_2010.pdf

Bainbridge, S. M. (2010, October 27). *The corporate governance provisions of Dodd-Frank*. UCLA School of Law, Law-Econ Research Paper No. 10-14. Retrieved May 14, 2019, from https://ssrn.com/abstract=1698898

Bala, M., & Verma, D. (2019). An empirical investigation of managerial perceptions in Indian organizations regarding CSR after legislation of CSR in India. *International Journal of Research in Social Sciences*, *9*, 1098–1136. Retrieved from https://www.researchgate.net/profile/Deepak_Verma67/publication/332130202_AN_EMPIRICAL_INVESTIGATION_OF_MANAGERIAL_PERCEPTIONS_IN_INDIAN_ORGANISATIONS_REGARDING_CSR_AFTER_LEGISLATION_OF_CSR_IN_INDIA

Barnett, M. L., & Salomon, R. M. (2012). Does it pay to be really good? Addressing the shape of the relationship between social and financial performance. *Strategic Management Journal*, *33*(11), 1304–1320. doi:10.1002mj.1980

Baron, E. (2019, April 23). 2 [women] claim Google retaliation after organizing global walkout. *Houston Chronicle*, p. B5 (Business).

Bistrong, R. (2019, April 17). *Management can own honesty or deceit. So pick one*. Retrieved April 20, 2019, from http://www.fcpablog.com/blog/2019/4/17/management-can-own-honesty-or-deceit-so-pick-one.html

Blanc, R., Cho, C. H., Sopt, J., & Branco, M. C. (2019). Disclosure responses to a corruption scandal: The case of Siemens AG. *Journal of Business Ethics, 156*(2), 545–561. doi:10.100710551-017-3602-7

Bowers, S. (2012, May 17). *Files close on BCCI banking scandal: Liquidators and lawyers acting for creditors to BCCI hold final meeting with victims of bank's collapse*. Retrieved May 14, 2019, from https://www.theguardian.com/business/2012/may/17/files-close-bcci-banking-scandal

Bucci, S. (2019, April 26). More regulation isn't answer to pipeline cyberattacks. *Houston Chronicle*, p. A15.

Bunyan, D., & Sarkis, K. (2019, May 6). *Making connections with the new digital consumer: To thrive in a world of apps, platforms, and privacy concerns, marketers have to become multitaskers*. Retrieved from https://www.strategy-business.com/feature/Making-connections-with-the-new-digital-consumer?

Cadbury Committee. (1992). *Report of the committee on the financial aspects of corporate governance (Cadbury Report)*. London, UK: Gee. Retrieved May 14, 2019, from http://www.ecgi.org/codes/documents/cadbury.pdf

Cassin, R. L. (2019, April 4). *At Fresenius, management owned the graft*. Retrieved April 20, 2019, from http://www.fcpablog.com/blog/2019/4/4/at-fresenius-management-owned-the-graft.html

Chen, C. C. (2019). A one-size-fits-all approach to corporate governance codes and compliance by smaller listed firms: An examination of companies listed in Hong Kong and Singapore. *Berkeley Business Law Journal, 15*(2), 337-364. Retrieved May 14, 2019, from https://ssrn.com/abstract=3339668

Chen, V. Z., Li, J., & Shapiro, D. M. (2011). Are OECD-prescribed "good corporate governance practices" really good in an emerging economy? *Asia Pacific Journal of Management, 28*(1), 115–138. doi:10.100710490-010-9206-8

Cicon, J. E., Ferris, S. P., Kammel, A. J., & Noronha, G. (2012). European corporate governance: A thematic analysis of national codes of governance. *European Financial Management, 18*(4), 620–648. doi:10.1111/j.1468-036X.2010.00542.x

CleanGovBiz. (2014). *The rationale for fighting corruption*. Retrieved May 13, 2019, from http://www.oecd.org/cleangovbiz/49693613.pdf

Cohen, R. (1991, December 20). *Maxwell's empire: How it grew, how it fell – A special report; Charming the big bankers out of billions*. Retrieved May 14, 2019, from https://www.nytimes.com/1991/12/20/business/maxwell-s-empire-it-grew-it-fell-special-report-charming-big-bankers-billions.html

Cuomo, F., Mallin, C., & Zattoni, A. (2016). Corporate governance codes: A review and research agenda. *Corporate Governance, 24*(3), 222–241. doi:10.1111/corg.12148

Dahya, J., McConnell, J. J., & Travlos, N. G. (2002). The Cadbury Committee, corporate performance, and top management turnover. *The Journal of Finance, 57*(1), 461–483. doi:10.1111/1540-6261.00428

Das, S. C. (2019). Indian company law on corporate governance–A critical analysis. *The Management Accountant Journal*, *54*(2), 61–64. doi:10.33516/maj.v54i2.61-64p

del Mar Miras-Rodríguez, M., Martínez-Martínez, D., & Escobar-Pérez, B. (2019). Which corporate governance mechanisms drive CSR disclosure practices in emerging countries? *Sustainability*, *11*(1), 61–80. doi:10.3390u11010061

Dinh, T. Q., & Calabrò, A. (2019). Asian family firms through corporate governance and institutions: A systematic review of the literature and agenda for future research. *International Journal of Management Reviews*, *21*(1), 50–75. doi:10.1111/ijmr.12176

Donaldson, T. (2000). Are business managers "professionals?" *Business Ethics Quarterly*, *10*(1), 83–93. doi:10.2307/3857697

Duarte, J., Kong, K., Siegel, S., & Young, L. (2014). The impact of the Sarbanes–Oxley Act on shareholders and managers of foreign firms. *Review of Finance*, *18*(1), 417–455. doi:10.1093/rof/rft008

Dyck, A., Lins, K. V., Roth, L., & Wagner, H. F. (2019). Do institutional investors drive corporate social responsibility? International evidence. *Journal of Financial Economics*, *131*(3), 693–714. doi:10.1016/j.jfineco.2018.08.013

European Commission. (n.d.). *2018 reform of EU data protection rules: Stronger rules on data protection mean people have more control over their personal data and businesses benefit from a level playing field*. Retrieved May 14, 2019, from https://ec.europa.eu/commission/priorities/justice-and-fundamental-rights/data-protection/2018-reform-eu-data-protection-rules_en

Facebook will reserve $3 billion in probe. (2019, April 25). *Houston Chronicle*, p. B2 (Business).

Farag, H., & Mallin, C. (2019). Monitoring corporate boards: Evidence from China. *European Journal of Finance*, *25*(6), 524–549. doi:10.1080/1351847X.2017.1369138

Fenwick, M., McCahery, J. A., & Vermeulen, E. P. (2019). The end of "corporate" governance: Hello "platform" governance. *European Business Organization Law Review*, *20*(1), 171–199. doi:10.100740804-019-00137-z

Ferraro, F. (2019). Going political? Towards deliberative corporate governance. *The Journal of Management and Governance*, *23*(1), 3–20. doi:10.100710997-018-9433-9

Filatotchev, I., Jackson, G., & Nakajima, C. (2013). Corporate governance and national institutions: A review and emerging research agenda. *Asia Pacific Journal of Management*, *30*(4), 965–986. doi:10.100710490-012-9293-9

Financial Reporting Council. (2012, September). *The UK Stewardship Code*. London: FRC. Retrieved May 14, 2019, from https://www.frc.org.uk/getattachment/d67933f9-ca38-4233-b603-3d24b2f62c5f/UK-Stewardship-Code-(September-2012).pdf

Financial Reporting Council. (2018, July). *The UK Corporate Governance Code*. London: FRC. Retrieved May 14, 2019, from https://www.frc.org.uk/getattachment/88bd8c45-50ea-4841-95b0-d2f4f48069a2/2018-UK-Corporate-Governance-Code-FINAL.PDF

Financial Reporting Council. (2019, January 30). *Consulting on a revised UK Stewardship Code*. Retrieved May 14, 2019, from https://www.frc.org.uk/consultation-list/2019/consulting-on-a-revised-uk-stewardship-code

Fram, E. (2005, Winter). *Are professional board directors the answer?* Retrieved May 13, 2019, from https://sloanreview.mit.edu/article/are-professional-board-directors-the-answer/

Freeman, R. E. (2017). The new story of business: Towards a more responsible capitalism. *Business and Society Review*, *122*(3), 449–465. doi:10.1111/basr.12123

Fu, Y. (2019). The value of corporate governance: Evidence from the Chinese anti-corruption campaign. *The North American Journal of Economics and Finance*, *47*, 461–476. doi:10.1016/j.najef.2018.06.001

Giao, C., & Raposo, C. C. (2014). Corporate governance and earnings quality: International evidence. *Journal of Accounting and Finance*, *14*, 52–74. Retrieved from http://www.na-businesspress.com/JAF/RaposoCC_Web14_3_.pdf

Gill, A. (2009). Corporate governance as social responsibility: A research agenda. *Berkeley Journal of International Law*, *26*, 5. doi:10.15779/Z38MS9P

González, J. S., & García-Meca, E. (2014). Does corporate governance influence earnings management in Latin American markets? *Journal of Business Ethics*, *121*(3), 419–440. doi:10.100710551-013-1700-8

Gouran, M. (2013, February 13). Corporate governance 2.0: The boardroom collides with the digital age. *Korn Ferry Institute Briefing Magazine*. Retrieved April 20, 2019, from https://www.kornferry.com/institute/579-corporate-governance-2-0-the-boardroom-collides-with-the-digital-age

Hall, P. A., & Soskice, D. (Eds.). (2001). *Varieties of capitalism: The institutional foundations of comparative advantage*. Oxford, UK: Oxford University Press. doi:10.1093/0199247757.001.0001

Harris, M. A., & Martin, R. (2019). Promoting cybersecurity compliance. In I. Vasileiou & S. Furnell (Eds.), *Cybersecurity education for awareness and compliance* (pp. 54–71). Hershey, PA: IGI Global. doi:10.4018/978-1-5225-7847-5.ch004

Haxhi, I., & Van Ees, H. (2009). Explaining diversity in the worldwide diffusion of codes of good governance. *Journal of International Business Studies*, *41*(4), 710–726. doi:10.1057/jibs.2009.39

Herzog, L. (2019). Professional ethics in banking and the logic of "integrated situations": Aligning responsibilities, recognition, and incentives. *Journal of Business Ethics*, *156*(2), 531–543. doi:10.100710551-017-3562-y

Hess, M. F., & Broughton, E. (2014). Fostering an ethical organization from the bottom up and the outside in. *Business Horizons*, *57*(4), 541–549. doi:10.1016/j.bushor.2014.02.004

Ho, J. (2018, May 3). *Governance in the digital age*. Retrieved October 15, 2019, from https://home.kpmg/sg/en/home/media/press-contributions/2018/05/governance-in-the-digital-age.html

Institute of Directors in Southern Africa. (2016). *King IV: Report on corporate governance for South Africa 2016*. Retrieved October 15, 2019, from https://cdn.ymaws.com/www.iodsa.co.za/resource/collection/684B68A7-B768-465C-8214-E3A007F15A5A/IoDSA_King_IV_Report_-_WebVersion.pdf

International Organization for Standardization. (n.d.). *ISO 37001 – Anti-bribery management systems.* Retrieved May 13, 2019, from https://www.iso.org/iso-37001-anti-bribery-management.html

Jacoby, G., Liu, M., Wang, Y., Wu, Z., & Zhang, Y. (2019). Corporate governance, external control, and environmental information transparency: Evidence from emerging markets. *Journal of International Financial Markets, Institutions and Money*, *58*, 269–283. doi:10.1016/j.intfin.2018.11.015

Jensen, M. C., & Meckling, W. H. (1976). Theory of the firm: Managerial behavior, agency costs and ownership structure. *Journal of Financial Economics*, *3*(4), 305–360. doi:10.1016/0304-405X(76)90026-X

Jenson, D., Quinlivan, S., Radloff, J., Jensen, T., Cotter, A., & Weitz, M. (2010, August 15). *Summary of corporate governance provisions in the Dodd-Frank Act*. Stinson LLP. Retrieved April 30, 2019, from http://dodd-frank.com/summary-of-corporate-governance-provisions-in-the-dodd-frank-act/

Jiang, F., & Kim, K. A. (2015). Corporate governance in China: A modern perspective. *Journal of Corporate Finance*, *32*, 190–216. doi:10.1016/j.jcorpfin.2014.10.010

Ke, R., Li, M., & Zhang, Y. (2019, March 15). Directors' informational role in corporate voluntary disclosure: An analysis of directors from related industries. SMU Cox School of Business Research Paper No.19-4. Retrieved April 20, 2019, from doi:10.2139srn.3353395

Keay, A. (2014). Comply or explain in corporate governance codes: In need of greater regulatory oversight? *Legal Studies*, *34*(2), 279–304. doi:10.1111/lest.12014

King, D. L., & Case, C. J. (2014). Sarbanes-Oxley Act and the Public Company Accounting Oversight Board's first eleven years. *Journal of Business and Accounting*, *7*, 11–23.

Kinni, T. (2019, April 18). *In praise of the purposeless company: No purpose? No problem. Create customers, care for employees, be a good citizen, and make money instead.* Retrieved April 30, 2019, from https://www.strategy-business.com/blog/In-praise-of-the-purposeless-company?gko=5c476&utm

Knowledge@Wharton. (2019, April 17). *Don't panic: The digital revolution isn't as unusual as you think* [interview with Tom Wheeler, author of From Gutenberg to Google: The history of our future, 2019]. Retrieved April 20, 2019, from https://knowledge.wharton.upenn.edu/article/tom-wheeler-fcc-book/

Kubíček, A., Štamfestová, P., & Strouhal, J. (2016). Cross-country analysis of corporate governance codes in the European Union. *Economia e Sociologia (Evora, Portugal)*, *9*, 319–337. doi:10.14254/2071-789X.2016/9-2/22

La Porta, R., Lopez-de-Silanes, F., Shleifer, A., & Vishny, R. (2000). Investor protection and corporate governance. *Journal of Financial Economics*, *58*(1-2), 3–27. doi:10.1016/S0304-405X(00)00065-9

London Stock Exchange Group. (2017, September 2). *London Stock Exchange Group launches guidance for ESG reporting*. Retrieved May 14, 2019, from https://www.lseg.com/resources/media-centre/press-releases/london-stock-exchange-group-launches-guidance-esg-reporting

Martynova, M., & Renneboog, L. (2011). Evidence on the international evolution and convergence of corporate governance regulations. *Journal of Corporate Finance*, *17*(5), 1531–1557. doi:10.1016/j.jcorpfin.2011.08.006

McRitchie, J. (2013, November 20). *Review & reflections: The Cadbury Committee*. Review of L. F. Spira and J. Slinn, *The Cadbury Committee: A History*. Oxford, UK: Oxford University Press. Retrieved May 14, 2019, from https://www.corpgov.net/2013/11/review-reflections-the-cadbury-committee/

Mees, B., & Smith, S. A. (2019). Corporate governance reform in Australia: A new institutional approach. *British Journal of Management*, *30*(1), 75–89. doi:10.1111/1467-8551.12298

Mehta, J. (2017, December 19). *MSCI corporate governance country report – India*. Retrieved May 14, 2019, from https://www.arx.cfa/post/MSCI-Corporate-Governance-Country-Report-India-3861.html

Mehta, J., & Brett, A. (2017, July 4). *MSCI's China governance country report*. Retrieved May 14, 2019, from https://www.arx.cfa/post/MSCI-39-s-China-Governance-Country-Report-4818.html

Minichilli, A., Zattoni, A., Nielsen, S., & Huse, M. (2012). Board task performance: An exploration of micro- and macro-level determinants of board effectiveness. *Journal of Organizational Behavior*, *33*(2), 193–215. doi:10.1002/job.743 PMID:23365485

MSCI Inc. (2017, September). *Corporate governance in China: Scores for Chinese companies cluster around the median relative to global peers, VIEs and SOEs have distinct governance risks*. Retrieved April 30, 2019, from https://www.msci.com/documents/10199/1d443a3d-0437-4af7-aa27-ada3a2655f6d

Mufson, S., & McGee, J. (1991, July 28). *BCCI scandal: Behind the 'Bank of Crooks and Criminals.'* Retrieved May 14, 2019, from https://www.washingtonpost.com/archive/politics/1991/07/28/bcci-scandal-behind-the-bank-of-crooks-and-criminals/563f2216-1180-4094-a13d-fd4955d59435/?utm_term=.dc9193c4c686

Natesan, P., & du Plessis, P. (2019, February 20). *Why King IV's "apply and explain" is so important*. Retrieved October 15, 2019, from https://www.iodsa.co.za/news/438882/Why-King-IVs-apply-and-explain-is-so-important.htm

National Association of Corporate Directors. (2002). *Corporate director's ethics and compliance handbook*. Arlington, VA: NACD.

New York Stock Exchange. (2014). *NYSE: Corporate governance guide*. Retrieved May 14, 2019, from https://www.nyse.com/publicdocs/nyse/listing/NYSE_Corporate_Governance_Guide.pdf

Organisation for Economic Co-operation and Development. (2015, November 30). *G20/OECD principles of corporate governance*. Retrieved May 14, 2019, from https://www.oecd-ilibrary.org/governance/g20-oecd-principles-of-corporate-governance-2015_9789264236882-en

Organisation for Economic Co-operation and Development. (n.d.). *List of OECD member countries - Ratification of the Convention on the OECD*. Retrieved May 14, 2019, from http://www.oecd.org/about/membersandpartners/list-oecd-member-countries.htm

Osborne, J. (2019, May 12). Who will protect U.S. pipelines? Understaffed TSA under scrutiny over security failures as hacking threats mount for vulnerable, critical network. *Houston Chronicle*, pp. B1, B7 (Business).

Paik, Y., Lee, J. M., & Pak, Y. S. (2019). Convergence in international business ethics? A comparative study of ethical philosophies, thinking style, and ethical decision-making between US and Korean managers. *Journal of Business Ethics, 156*(3), 839–855. doi:10.100710551-017-3629-9

Pérez-Cornejo, C., de Quevedo-Puente, E., & Delgado-García, J. B. (2019). How to manage corporate reputation? The effect of enterprise risk management systems and audit committees on corporate reputation. *European Management Journal, 37*(4), 505–515. doi:10.1016/j.emj.2019.01.005

Pham, H. T. S., & Tran, H. T. (2019). Board and corporate social responsibility disclosure of multinational corporations. *Multinational Business Review, 27*(1), 77–98. doi:10.1108/MBR-11-2017-0084

Placenti, F. M. (Ed.). (2017). *Director's handbook: A field guide to situations commonly encountered in the boardroom*. Chicago, IL: American Bar Association, Business Law Section, Corporate Law Committee.

PricewaterhouseCoopers Southern Africa. (2009, September 2). *Executive guide to King III*. Retrieved May 14, 2019, from https://www.pwc.co.za/en/assets/pdf/executive-guide-to-kingiii.pdf

Principles for Responsible Investment. (n.d.). *What are the Principles for Responsible Investment?* Retrieved April 30, 2019, from https://www.unpri.org/pri/what-are-the-principles-for-responsible-investment

Rossouw, J., & Styan, J. (2019). Steinhoff collapse: A failure of corporate governance. *International Review of Applied Economics, 33*(1), 163–170. doi:10.1080/02692171.2019.1524043

Sanderson, A. R. (2012). *Schlefer, Jonathan. The assumptions economists make. Harvard, 2012*. Retrieved May 14, 2019, from http://home.uchicago.edu/arsx/br/Schlefer.pdf

Sarrazin, H., & Willmott, P. (2016, July). *Adapting your board to the digital age*. Retrieved October 15, 2019, from https://www.mckinsey.com/business-functions/mckinsey-digital/our-insights/adapting-your-board-to-the-digital-age

Satariano, A. (2019, May 12). Europe is reining in tech giants, but some say it's going too far: Clampdown online on violent content, hate speech and misinformation brings accusations of government censorship. *Houston Chronicle*, p. B3 (Business).

Satariano, A., & Perlroth, N. (2019, April 22). Conflict arises between insurers, businesses over cyberattacks. *Houston Chronicle,* pp. B26-27.

Schäuble, J. (2019). The impact of external and internal corporate governance mechanisms on agency costs. *Corporate Governance: The International Journal of Business in Society, 19*(1), 1–22. doi:10.1108/CG-02-2018-0053

Seidl, D., Sanderson, P., & Roberts, J. (2009, June). *Applying 'comply-or-explain': Conformance with codes of corporate governance in the UK and Germany*. Centre for Business Research, University of Cambridge Working Paper No. 389. Retrieved May 21, 2019, from https://www.cbr.cam.ac.uk/fileadmin/user_upload/centre-for-business-research/downloads/working-papers/wp389.pdf

Seidl, D., Sanderson, P., & Roberts, J. (2013). Applying the 'comply-or-explain' principle: Discursive legitimacy tactics with regard to codes of corporate governance. *The Journal of Management and Governance, 17*(3), 791–826. doi:10.100710997-011-9209-y

Shapira, R., & Zingales, L. (2017, September 1). *Is pollution value-maximizing? The DuPont case.* Retrieved May 14, 2019, from http://www.law.northwestern.edu/research-faculty/colloquium/law-economics/documents/Spring18Zingales.pdf

Smith, N. C., & Soonieus, R. (2019). *What's stopping boards from taking action on sustainability? Boards need to look past the low-hanging fruit and start making tough decisions.* Retrieved May 13, 2019, from https://knowledge.insead.edu/responsibility/whats-stopping-boards-from-taking-action-on-sustainability-11436

Stiles, P., & Taylor, B. (1993). Benchmarking corporate governance: The impact of the Cadbury Code. *Long Range Planning, 26*(5), 61–71. doi:10.1016/0024-6301(93)90078-T

Styhre, A., & Bergström, O. (2019). The benefit of market-based governance devices: Reflections on the issue of growing economic inequality as a corporate concern. *European Management Journal, 37*(4), 413–420. doi:10.1016/j.emj.2019.01.002

Swaminathan, A., & Herzinger, K. (2018). *Directors and the digital age.* Retrieved October 15, 2019, from https://s3.amazonaws.com/cdn.orrick.com/files/EB-Spring2018-Orrick.pdf

Tsang, A., Xie, F., & Xin, X. (2019). Foreign institutional investors and corporate voluntary disclosure around the world. *The Accounting Review, 94*(5), 319–348. doi:10.2308/accr-52353

Vardi, M. Y. (2019, April 19). Facebook's problem lies in business model. *Houston Chronicle*, p. A19.

Walters, K. (2015, December 1). *Corporate governance in the digital age.* Australian Institute of Company Directors. Retrieved April 20, 2019, from http://www.companydirectors.com.au/director-resource-centre/publications/company-director-magazine/2015-back-editions/december/walters-corporate-governance-in-the-digital-age

Windsor, D. (2009). Tightening corporate governance. *Journal of International Management, 15*(3), 306–316. doi:10.1016/j.intman.2009.02.003

Windsor, D. (2013). Corporate social responsibility and irresponsibility: A positive theory approach. *Journal of Business Research, 66*(10), 1937–1944. doi:10.1016/j.jbusres.2013.02.016

Windsor, D. (2019). Influencing MNC strategies for managing corruption and favoritism in Pacific Asia countries: A multiple-theory configurational perspective. *Asia Pacific Business Review, 25*(4), 501–533. doi:10.1080/13602381.2019.1589769

Xie, J., Nozawa, W., Yagi, M., Fujii, H., & Managi, S. (2019). Do environmental, social, and governance activities improve corporate financial performance? *Business Strategy and the Environment, 28*(2), 286–300. doi:10.1002/bse.2224

Yasin, F. M., Muhamad, R., & Sulaiman, N. A. (2014). *Corporate governance research: A review of qualitative literature.* International Conference on Technology and Business Management, University of Malaya. Retrieved May 14, 2019, from http://eprints.um.edu.my/13413/1/D4145-Final.pdf

Zattoni, A., & Cuomo, F. (2010). How independent, competent and incentivized should non- executive directors be? An empirical investigation of good governance codes. *British Journal of Management, 21*(1), 63–79. doi:10.1111/j.1467-8551.2009.00669.x

ADDITIONAL READING

American Law Institute. (1993). *Principles of corporate governance: Analysis and recommendations* (Vols. 1–2). Philadelphia, PA: American Law Institute.

Arena, M., Arnaboldi, M., & Azzone, G. (2010). The organizational dynamics of Enterprise Risk Management. *Accounting, Organizations and Society*, *35*(7), 659–675. doi:10.1016/j.aos.2010.07.003

Calder, A. (2019). *Duty of care: An executive's guide for corporate boards in the digital era*. New York: John Wiley & Sons.

Eisenberg, M. A. (1993). An overview of the Principles of Corporate Governance. *Business Lawyer*, *48*, 1271–1296. Retrieved from https://www.jstor.org/stable/40687423

Flyverbom, M., Deibert, R., & Matten, D. (2019). The governance of digital technology, big data, and the Internet: New roles and responsibilities for business. *Business & Society*, *58*(1), 3–19. doi:10.1177/0007650317727540

Gentile, M. C. (2010). *Giving voice to values: How to speak your mind when you know what's right.* New Haven, CT: Yale University Press.

Goh, C. F., Rasli, A., & Khan, S.-U.-R. (2014, May 15). Corporate governance: A literature review with a focus on the technology firms. In *Procedia - Social and Behavioral Sciences* (vol. 129, pp. 39-45). 2nd International Conference on Innovation, Management and Technology Research, R. S. R. Kasim & F. Emdad (Eds.). 10.1016/j.sbspro.2014.03.645

Ribas-Ferrer, V. (2016). Corporate governance in European listed companies and financial institutions. *Athens Journal of Law*, *2*(1), 49–60. doi:10.30958/ajl.2-1-4

Schwartz, M. S. (2011). *Corporate social responsibility: An ethical approach.* Peterborough, ON: Broadview Press.

Stafford, B., & Schindlinger, D. (2019). *Governance in the digital age: A guide for the modern corporate board director*. Hoboken, NJ: John Wiley & Sons.

Suzor, N. P. (2019). *Lawless: The secret rules that govern our digital lives.* Cambridge, UK: Cambridge University Press. doi:10.1017/9781108666428

KEY TERMS AND DEFINITIONS

Corporate Governance (CG): The set of principles, codes, and relationships within which corporate management makes decisions and set policies. Codes may be legal and mandatory or private and voluntary.

Cybersecurity: Security measures against various forms of cyberattacks on the business.

Digital Era: The 21st century shift from the industrial revolution to a new economic domination of information technology.

Enterprise Risk Management (ERM): Preparation for identifying and handling any potential dangers or hazards to the business and communication, and communication of action plans to stakeholders.

Ethical Values: Assign degree of importance to anything or anyone according to morally based principles, rules, or norms that define virtuous behavior.

Professionalism: Adherence to a code of conduct appropriate to a profession and defining virtuous behavior of a professional in terms of what to do and what not to do. One might define a profession in terms of required governmental licensing (e.g., accounting, law, or medicine) or higher education (e.g., MBA or non-medical doctorate).

Responsibilities: Directors' and managers' legal and ethical obligations or duties to various stakeholders of the business.

Shareholder Wealth Maximization: A doctrine or theory that the primary (but not sole) responsibility of directors and managers is to seek increased wealth for the shareholders.

Stakeholder Theory of Management: An alternative to shareholder wealth maximization that emphasizes instead the responsibility of directors and managers to seek increased welfare for as many stakeholders as feasible.

Chapter 6
The Cultural Clash:
Traditional Automakers vs. Digital Companies – Can They Work Together? Transformation of Business Culture in the Digital Age

Mikhail Bakunin
Moscow State University, Russia

Mikhail Y. Kuznetsov
https://orcid.org/0000-0001-5657-8184
Moscow State University, Russia

ABSTRACT

Until recently, traditional automakers and digital companies have been working separately at their own pace, preserving their cultures and ways of doing business and driving innovation. In the early 2010s, younger generations of customers were spoilt by seamless ecosystems in digital and started wondering why they are still operating knobs while seated behind steering wheel. From this point, the process of interpenetration of two industries started, provoking transformation and cultural shifts in the traditional automakers industry. How far will it go? What are the main challenges of this transformation? What forms and principles of corporate culture will appear and dominate in the industry in the future?

INTRODUCTION

Until recently traditional automakers and digital companies have been working separately at their own pace, preserving their cultures and ways of doing business and driving innovation. In early 2010s younger generations of customers were spoilt by seamless eco-systems in digital and started wondering why they are still operating knobs while seated behind steering wheel. From this point the process of interpenetration of two industries started, provoking transformation and cultural shifts in the traditional

DOI: 10.4018/978-1-7998-2011-6.ch006

automakers industry. How far will it go? What are the main challenges of this transformation? What forms and principles of corporate culture will appear and dominate in the industry in the future?

BACKGROUND

Corporate culture is one of the keystones of strategic development of any organization. As Yuval Noah Harari states, «Huge masses of people unfamiliar with each other are capable to cooperate successfully if they are united by a myth. A limited liability company is separated from the people who founded it, and from those who invested in it or who manage it. Over the past centuries, it was these companies that became leaders in the economy, we got used to them and began to forget that they exist only in our imagination» (Yuval Noah Harari, Sapiens: A Brief History of Humankind, 2014). A famous phrase, attributed to Peter Druker and often quoted, states that "Culture eats strategy for breakfast." And in practice we often see, that a company's culture, based on common values and behavioral patterns of employees normally can thwart any attempts to implement a strategy that is contradictory to it's culture.

The topic of corporate culture influence on strategy execution has been investigated from different dimensions. Hofstede's Cultural Dimensions Theory (Culture's Consequences: International Differences in Work-Related Values. Geert Hofstede, SAGE Publications, 1980.) long ago has suggested a framework for cultural assessment, and proved, that human beings think, feel and act from their own cultural perspective, and cultural differences could become significant barriers to change.

Five sorts (dimensions) of differences/value perspectives between cultures by Hofstede include Power distance (the degree of inequality among people which the population of a country considers as normal), Individualism versus collectivism (the extent to which people feel they are supposed to take care for, or to be cared for by themselves, their families or organizations they belong to), masculinity versus femininity (the extent to which a culture is conducive to dominance, assertiveness and acquisition of things. Versus a culture which is more conducive to people, feelings and the quality of life), uncertainty avoidance (the degree to which people in a country prefer structured over unstructured situations), long-term versus short-term orientation.

The phenomenon of corporate culture influence on strategy implementation has been investigated by Henry Minztberg (Strategy Safari: A Guided Tour Through The Wilds of Strategic Management. Henry Mintzberg, Bruce Ahlstrand, Joseph Lampel, 1998.). He looks at the strategic process as fundamentally collective and cooperative. Strategic process is viewed as very much influenced by the power of culture. Common interests and integration are the main important drivers of the process.

The influence of culture is widely acknowledged as one of the main factors, important for the success of the company. In the Deloitte research (Global human capital trends 2016. The new organization: different by design. Deloitte university press.) (figure 1), culture, leadership and organizational design were named the main human capital trends.

The acknowledgement of corporate culture influence on strategy and long-term success of the organization has been also reflected in the amendments to corporate governance codes.

For example, the UK CG Code suggests, that a company's culture should promote integrity and openness, value diversity and be responsive to the views of shareholders and wider stakeholders. One of the Code principles states, that "The board should establish the company's purpose, values and strategy, and satisfy itself that these and its culture are aligned. All directors must act with integrity, lead by example and promote the desired culture"(The UK Corporate Governance Code. July, 2018, p.1.). This statement

Figure 1. The 10 trends ranked in order of importance (compiled by authors)

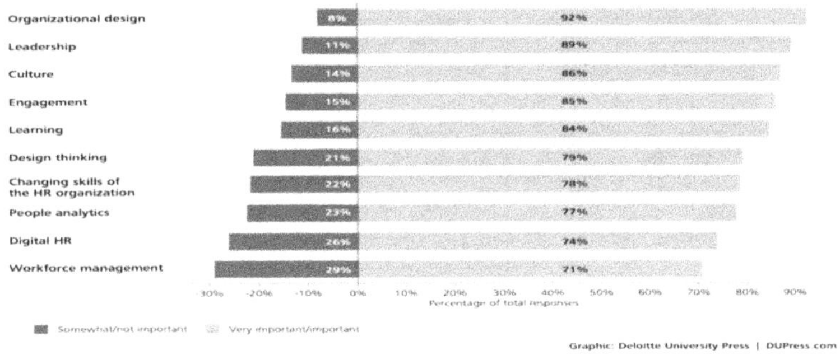

Figure 2. How boards influence culture in business (compiled by authors)

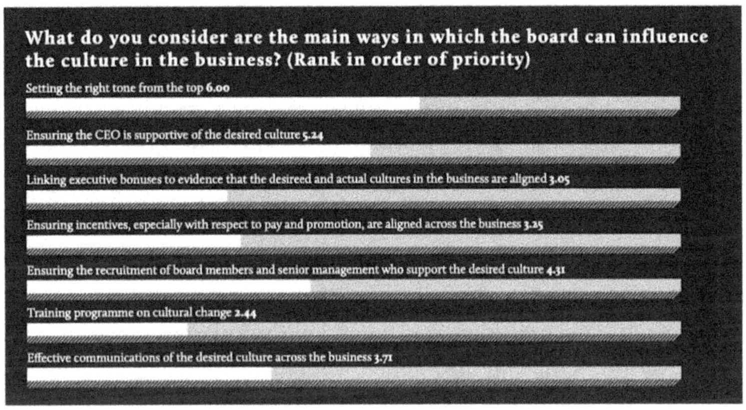

has some supportive rules, which state, that "The board should assess and monitor culture. Where it is not satisfied that policy, practices or behaviour throughout the business are aligned with the company's purpose, values and strategy, it should seek assurance that management has taken corrective action. The annual report should explain the board's activities and any action taken. In addition, it should include an explanation of the company's approach to investing in and rewarding its workforce".

This approach presumes, that the boards of directors should not only monitor the culture of the company, it's integrity and alliance with the strategy, but should themselves "lead by example", setting the "tone from the top" approach.

However, the research from survey by tax and accountancy firm Mazars, the INSEAD business school in Paris and Board Agenda magazine, held among European company board directors reveals that this belief is not being reinforced by action on how their businesses behaves.

While believing that the culture of business can be influenced from the top, particularly through the role of the CEO, only one in five board directors believe they are spending the right amount of time addressing cultural issues (Research report on board leadership of corporate culture in Europe, Mazars, 2019.).

Table 1. Comparative analysis of digital hires (compiled by authors)

Automaker	Digital Executive	Former Employer	Arrival to OEM	Departure from OEM
VW Group	Johann Jungwirth	Apple	2015	2019
BMW	Jens Monsees	Google	2016	2019
BMW	Dieter May	Nokia	2014	2019
Porsche	Thilo Koslowski	Gartner (CA)	2016	2019
Renault-Nissan Alliance	Ogi Redzic	Nokia, Here	2016	2018
PSA Group	Brigitte Cantaloube	Yahoo	2016	2018

The study (Research report on board leadership of corporate culture in Europe, Mazars, 2019.) shows, that culture has been ranked among the top three priorities for company boards, but only 20% of 450 London-based directors reported spending the time required to manage and improve it.

Around 62% of survey respondents felt that they were primarily responsible for setting culture from the top of an organization, however, a similar proportion (63%) either did not consider culture as part of their formal risk assessment or failed to routinely consider the risk associated with their corporate culture.

At the same time, the influence of culture becomes even more evident, if we have a close look at the technological trends, and first of all digitalization, as a transformational force, which provides both new opportunities and risks to most of businesses all over the world. The strategic implications of these changes have wide effects on organizations, industry ecosystems and society. All projects of digital transformation are in fact based on deep cultural transformation of companies. Here we would like to investigate this process based on digital vs automotive companies.

The interactions between the two worlds – digital and automotive companies - started slowly – from radios and CD players to digital maps and digital eco-systems. It became obvious that automakers lack talent and capabilities in digital. Key OEMs such as VW, BMW, Porsche and PSA started hiring digital executives in an attempt to close the gap. In many cases the solution didn't work out. The recent departure of the Volkswagen Group CDO Johann Jungwirth reconfirmed the trend started in 2018 of external digital hires exodus from OEMs.

What could be the reasons for these short-lasting relationships? We can suggest that it's hard for digital newcomers to adjust to the slow speed, bureaucracy and inertia of automakers. In addition to that, tech companies are more used to uncertainty and higher risks associated with it. In digital world decisions would be data driven, but in case of lack of information tech companies are ready to take risks, whereas car-makers would tend to avoid decision making at all. The long cycles industries executive decisions are by nature all about avoidance of significant mistakes.

Table 2. Comparative analysis of traditional car makers and digital companies (compiled by authors)

	Traditional car makers	Digital
Planning horizon	5+ years	1-2 years
Planning flexibility	Low *processes driven culture*	High *agile culture*
Decision making speed	Low	High
Generation	Baby boomers / Generation X	Millenials
Gender mix	Dominated by men *especially, in Japan*	More balanced
Employment cycle	Long	Short

Figure 3. Autonomous vehicle market forecast (compiled by authors)

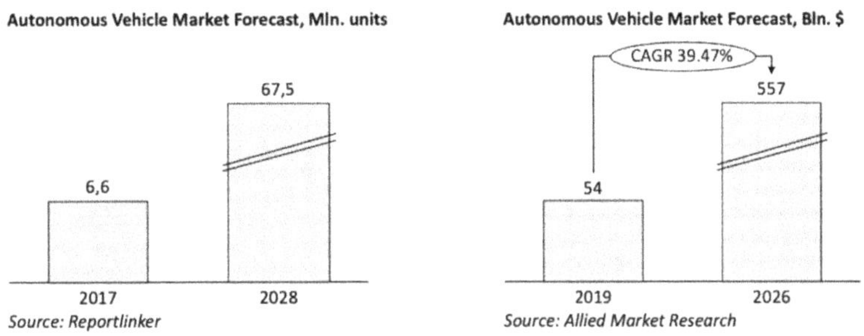

THE MAIN CHALLENGES FOR CULTURAL TRANSFORMATION

The "Fail fast" concept originated in digital and startup world, is totally alien to carmakers. At the same time, relatively rapid departures could also be attributed to employment patterns borrowed from digital. The average tenure of a tech worker in Silicon Valley would be between 2 and 3 years for such companies as Airbnb, Facebook and Dropbox.

No matter what the reasons are, OEMs are pedaling back and choosing company insiders and veterans to replace external hires. Is that a sign that automakers are not ready for a change? Phase 1 of closing the cultural gap between traditional car-markers and tech companies can hardly be seen as a success story.

Connectivity became a trigger for automakers to explore digital, however, it's been always difficult to justify the investment and needs for OEMs to adjust their processes and culture. Carmakers have been always struggling with the connected car monetization leaving themselves an excuse and hope that they could still manage digital in-house by following the milestones and processes put in place in the 20th century. This approach may not stand against the new challenge approaching traditional carmakers.

Transition to autonomous driving seems inevitable. According to Morgan Stanley, the self-driving technology can save just the US economy a total of $1.3 trillion per year. Luckily, this time there is a consensus around the business model. Robotaxis could be the first economically viable application. Frost & Sullivan suggests that introduction of autonomous technology in ride-hailing can eliminate driver wages, ultimately reduce wait time to 36 seconds and the cost to $.50 per mile.

Table 3. Self-driving technology partnerships (compiled by authors)

Automaker	Self-driving Technology Partner	Self-driving Technology Partner's Nature	Self-driving Technology Partner's HQ Location
Toyota	Uber ATG	Digital	San Francisco, CA Pittsburgh, PA
VW group	Apple Nvidia	Digital	Cupertino, CA Santa Clara, CA
Renault-Nissan-Mitsubishi Alliance	Waymo	Digital	Mountain View, CA
Ford	Argo AI	Digital	Pittsburgh, PA
General Motors Honda	Cruise Automation	Digital	San Francisco, CA
BMW	Magna (sensors) Intel	Nondigital Digital	Aurora, Canada Tencent, China
Daimler	Bosch	Nondigital	Gerlingen, Germany
Fiat Chrysler	Aurora Waymo	Digital	Palo Alto, CA Mountain View, CA
Hyundai	Aurora Yandex	Digital	Palo Alto, CA Moscow, Russia
Jaguar	Waymo	Digital	Mountain View, CA

We'd need to acknowledge the fact that there are debates around the time when self-driving market is going to take off. The earlier predictions were too optimistic. The accident happened with Volvo XC90 equipped with the Uber self-driving stack in March 2018 in Arizona cooled down the expectations. No matter what the timeline is, commercial introduction of self-driving vehicles will go hand in hand with connectivity and electrification and will disrupt a number of industries and produce massive secondary effects. Transportation, energy sector and car industry will be among the most impacted.

T. Comparative Analysis of Digital Hires

Autonomous drive technology is hard to master and finance. Artificial intelligence, cloud computing, test miles driven in simulation and physically on the roads are pushing the check into the multi-billion-dollar category. At the same time, automakers are heavily committing to electrification, which leaves themselves less space for maneuver in terms of resources.

A few tech companies such as Waymo, Apple and Zoox originally have anced intentions or even tried to build their own vehicles with self-driving capabilities, but the majority are focusing on the areas of their core expertise: machine learning, artificial intelligence, cloud computing, mapping, chips, sensors etc. Eventually, Waymo, the globally recognized leader in self-driving technology with almost unlimited resources of their shareholder Alphabet, has declared that they are "building a safer driver for everyone", not a car.

An obvious choice for the two worlds would be to partner; and we see partnerships are being formed for all major automakers. They are choosing to create alliances with digital companies headquartered in California, acknowledging the fact that the self-driving technology is coming from outside of the traditional automakers' eco-system. Phase 2 has started.

Theoretically, the potential size of the pie should be attractive enough for both sides to become more flexible and accommodating. Waymo was among the first tech companies to realize this need. The former president and CEO of Hyundai Motor America John Krafcik was hired in 2015 to help Google become a world leader in driverless transportation. Since then, the Google's spinoff Waymo has struck two vehicle supply deals with FCA and Jaguar, but somehow missed opportunities with VW Group and Honda. Recently, VW Group has also terminated the partnership with Aurora.

The reasons for such failures normally are not public and it's not hard to imagine that there would be a combination of factors, including business and cultural disconnects. As an example, the "Winner takes it all" strategy may incentivize both sides to bring up exclusivity requests and by doing this create additional tension. Industrial behemoths and "we are changing the world" Silicon Valley companies both have strong ambitions and may think that they deserve an exclusive relationship. Lack of transparency, also typical for both sides, can only worsen the situation. The Uber – Waymo autonomous driving technology scandal made public a lot of conspiracy behind digital companies' scenes. What if a similar strategy is applied towards OEMs? How this could help close cultural gaps and create an atmosphere of trust and mutual respect?

The extended timeline of self-driving systems commercialization could have released some pressure at OEMs. Imagine a five to ten years payback for a product planned for launch in 2026. How many automotive world C-level executives will remain in their seats between now and then? Some of them, especially those close to retirement, may decide to limit investment amounts and make less efforts to make any risky partnership work.

The road to driverless future looks quite bumpy, but, apparently, traditional car-makers and digital companies have no choice, but to find a way to work together efficiently. The fear of becoming Kodak must be strong enough for automotive not to give it a try. Ford and General Motors have decided a different approach: not to host work on driverless transportation in-house. GM's Cruise is based in San Francisco and Ford's Argo AI in Pittsburgh close to Carnegie Mellon University and far enough from automotive HQs. Cruise is run by Dan Ammann, the former president of GM. While both start-ups are hosting former car industry professionals, it would be a stretch to say that they are inheriting automotive mentality. On the contrary, Cruise and Argo AI must preserve speed and flexibility to remain competitive in the field. By looking at Automated Driving Vehicles Leaderboard by Navigant Research we could conclude that GM's and Ford's approach to externalize driverless transportation development is showing promising results and allowing the respective OEMs stay in a small group of Leaders.

FUTUTRE RESEARCH DIRECTIONS

The topic of cultural transformation has many directions. Further research could be done as for the role of the Boards of directors in the cultural transformation of business. Further investigation is needed in the topic of cultural transformation under the pressure of digital transformation in other "traditional" industries: metallurgy, energy sector, e.t.c. The evolution of "digital" companies' cultures is also a matter of discussion and further research.

Figure 4. Partnership strategies (compiled by authors)

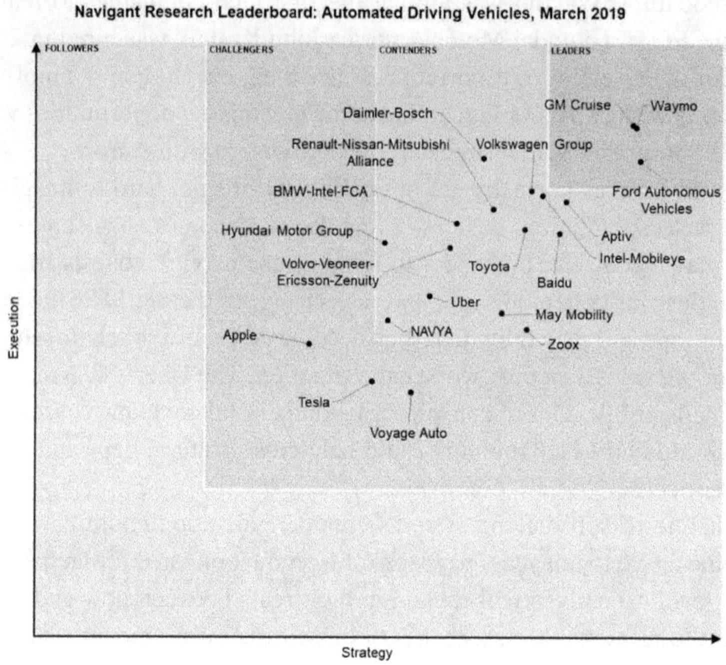

CONCLUSION

In this chapter, we have tried to investigate the cultural transformation, which takes place in the automakers' industry under the pressure of technological revolution. We made comparative cultural analysis of traditional car makers vs digital companies on a range of features, including planning horizon, planning flexibility, decision making speed, generation, gender mix, employment cycle, e.t.c. We can make a general conclusion, that the cultural gaps will remain, but with strong executive support, cross-industry hiring and willingness of automotive companies to release the grip and let self-driving technology mature outside of traditional car engineering and manufacturing circles, it may be possible to develop successful partnerships. The future leaders are tech and traditional companies ready for a change and willing to commit to a painful process of cultural transformation.

REFERENCES

Artificial Intelligence (AI) as a key factor in the digitalization of the global economy. (2017). CRN/RE. Retrieved from https://www.crn.ru/news/detail.php? ID=117544

Athanasopoulou, A., Bouwman, H., & Nikayin, F. (n.d.). *The disruptive impact of digitalization on the automotive ecosystem: a research agenda on business models, platforms and consumer issues*. Retrieved from https://pdfs.semanticscholar.org/181c/f4663467b69658aff1c6171813d518c26662.pdf

BCG (Flexible Cell Manufacturing). (n.d.). Retrieved from https://www.bcg.com/publications/2018/flexible-cell-manufacturing-revolutionize-carmaking.aspx

By 2075 the thought processes of the robot will be indistinguishable from human. (2017). Astera. Retrieved from http://www.astera.ru/news/?id=118667

CNBC.com. (n.d.). Retrieved from https://www.cnbc.com/2018/09/10/is-fast-fast-enough-for-vinfast-vietnams-first-automaker.html

Culture's Consequences. (1980). *International Differences in Work-Related Values. Geert Hofstede*. SAGE Publications.

DARPA SyNAPSE Program. (2013). *Artificial Brains*. Retrieved from www.artificialbrains.com/darpasynapse-program

Deep Learning for Enterprise Applications. (2016). *Tractica*. Retrieved from https://www.tractica.com/research/deeplearning-for-enterprise-applications

Deep Learning Market by Application (Image Recognition, Signal Recognition, Data Mining), Offering (Hardware (Von Neumann and Neuromorphic Chip), and Software), End-User Industry, and Geography – Global Forecasts to 2022. (2016). *Markets and Markets*. Retrieved from http://www.marketsandmarkets.com/Market-Reports/deeplearning-market-107369271.html

Deep learning: opportunities, prospects and abit of history. (2016). *Habrahabr*. Retrieved from https://habrahabr.ru/company/it-grad/blog/309024

Digital transformation in the automotive industry. (n.d.). Retrieved from https://www.ibm.com/downloads/cas/LVDZDXOA

Digital Transformation of Industries. Automotive Industry. (2016). *Word Economic Forum*. Retrieved from http://reports.weforum.org/digital-transformation/wp-content/blogs.dir/94/mp/files/pages/files/wef-dti-automotivewhitepaper-final-january-2016.v1.pdf

Forbes.com. (n.d.). Retrieved from https://www.forbes.com/sites/maryjosephs/2017/03/15/u-s-manufacturing-labor-shortage-how-to-make-your-company-a-happy-exception/#190cfda17e13

Global Automotive Executive Survey, KPMG. (2018). Retrieved from https://home.kpmg/uk/en/home/insights/2018/01/2018-global-automotive-executive-survey.html

Global digital operations research. (2018). Retrieved from https://www.pwc.com/gx/en/industries/industry-4-0.html

Hanelt, A., Piccinini, E., Gregory, R., Hildebrandt, B., & Kolbe, L. (2015). Digital Transformation of preliminary Industries. Exploring the impact of Digital trends on business Models of Automobile Manufacturers. *Proceedings of the 12th Internationalen Tagung Wirtschaftsinformatik*, 1313-1327.

Hinton, G. E., & Salakhutdinov, R. R. (2006). Reducing the Dimensionality of Data with Neural Networks. *Science, 313*. Retrieved from http://www.cs.toronto.edu/~hinton/science.pdf

IBM Institute for business value. (2015). *Automotive 2025: Industry without borders, Executive Report*. IBM Corporation.

IBM. (n.d.). Retrieved from https://www.ibm.com/blogs/internet-of-things/iot-data-that-keeps-your-workers-safe/

Kavis, M. (2015). How connected cars will transform industries. *Forbes*. Available at: http://www.forbes.com/sites/mikekavis/2015/02/20/how-connected-cars-will-transformindustries/

Kote, T. (2015). How Silicon Valley will reinvent the auto industry. *Forbes*. Available at: http://www.forbes.com/sites/thejokote/2015/05/05/how-silicon-valley-will-reinvent-the-autoindustry/

Koushanfar, F., Sadeghi, A.-R., & Seudi, H. (2012). *EDA for Secure and Dependable Cyber-cars: Challenges and Opportunities*. Paper presented at DAC 2012, San Francisco, CA.

KPMG. (2014). *Me, my car, my life the ultra-connected age*. KPMG International report.

Manyika, J., Chui, M., Bughin, J., Dobbs, R., Bisson, P., & Marrs, A. (2013). *Disruptive technologies: Advances that will transform life, business, and the global economy*. McKinsey Global Institute. Retrieved from http://www. mckinsey.com/business-functions/digital-mckinsey/our-insights/disruptive-technologies

Mikusz, M., Jud, C., & Schäfer, T. (2015). Business Model patterns for the Connected Car and the Example of data orchestrator. In *ICSOB 2015, LNBIP* (pp. 167–173). doi:10.1007/978-3-319-19593-3_14

Miorandi, D., Sicari, S., De Pellegrini, F., & Chlamtac, I. (2012). Internet of things: Vision, applications and research challenges. *Ad Hoc Networks*, *10*(7), 1497–1516. doi:10.1016/j.adhoc.2012.02.016

Mohaghegzadeh, A. & Svahn F. (2015). *Resource Transformation in Platform Envelopment*. ECSI 2015 Research in Progress papers.

Nottingham Business School. (n.d.). Retrieved from https://www4.ntu.ac.uk/nbs/document_uploads/73575.pdf

PwC. (2018a). *Глобальное исследование цифровых операций в* 2018 *г*. Retrieved from https://www.pwc.ru/ru/iot/digital-champions.pdf

PWC. (2018b). *Завтрашний день автомобильной отрасли*. 2018. Retrieved from https://www.pwc.ru/ru/publications/autotech-survey-2018.html

Roberts, J. (2016). Thinking Machines: The Search for Artificial Intelligence Distillations. *Chemical Heritage Foundation*. Retrieved from https://www.chemheritage.org/distillations/magazine/thinking-machines-the-search-forartificial-intelligence

State of The Advanced Mobility Industry. (2019). *The Drive Towards an Electric and Autonomous Future by GS Capital*. Academic Press.

Strategy Safari. (1998). *A Guided Tour Through The Wilds of Strategic Management*. Author.

The Deep Learning Market Map. 60+ Startups Working Across E-Commerce, Cybersecurity,Sales, And More. (2016). *CB Insights*. Retrieved from https://www.cbinsights.com/blog/deep-learning-aistartups-market-map-company-list

The Digitalisation of the UK Automotive Industry. (n.d.). Retrieved from https://assets.kpmg/content/dam/kpmg/br/pdf/2016/12/smmt-digitalisation-automotive-industry-report.pdf

Thomas insights. (n.d.). Retrieved from https://news.thomasnet.com/companystory/downtime-costs-auto-industry-22k-minute-survey-481017

Trends in der Transportlogistik. (2017). *Das Logistik-magazin*, 11—12. Retrieved from https://www.verkehrsrundschau.de/fm/3576/WIW_2018.pdf

Ustinov, P. (2017). Are you going to treat us? Robots in white coats. *Forbes*. Retrieved from http://www.forbes.ru/tehnologii/338785-vy-za-nas-eshche-ilechit-budete-roboty-v-belyh-halatah

Warranty Week. (n.d.). Retrieved from https://www.warrantyweek.com/archive/ww20180405.html

What is the difference between artificial intelligence, machine learning and deep learning? (2016). *Nvidia*. Retrieved from http://www.nvidia.ru/object/whatsdifference-ai-machine-learning-deep-learning-blogru.html

World Economic Forum Annual Meeting 2016: Mastering the Fourth Industrial Revolution. (2016). *World Economic Forum*. Retrieved from https://www.weforum.org/reports/world-economicforum-annual-meeting-2016-mastering-the-fourthindustrial-revolution

KEY TERMS AND DEFINITIONS

Acknowledgment or Acknowledgement: The act of admitting the truth or existence of.

Artificial: Created by human beings.

Automate (Automate, Automated): To convert to a mechanical or electronic system of operation.

Automated: Able to operate without the help or work of a human.

Autonomous: Free and independent, as a state or an organism; self-governing.

Behavioral: Of or concerning the actions and reactions of a group, person, animal, or thing.

Behemoth: A huge beast, perhaps a hippopotamus, mentioned in the Book of Job in the Old Testament.

Boom1 (Boomer): To make a prolonged, deep, resounding noise.

Capability: The characteristic of being qualified or able; capacity.

Carmaker: An automobile manufacturing company.

Collectivism: The doctrine or practice of centralized economic control, especially of the means of production.

Compute (Computing): To calculate by mathematical operations.

Computing: The use and operation of computers.

Conducive: Tending to produce or cause (usually followed by "to").

Connective (Connectivity): Serving or tending to connect.

Corporate: Of or relating to a corporation.

Cultural: Of or pertaining to culture.

Culture: The sum of the language, customs, beliefs, and art considered characteristic of a particular group of people.

Cycle: A circle of events that repeats in a regular pattern.

Dimension: Size as measured in a particular direction such as height, width, or depth.

Dominate: To control or govern by the use of power or influence; rule.

Ecosystem: A community of living things, together with their environment.

Exodus: A departure, usually of a great number of people.

Externalize: To manifest or make external.

Humankind: Humans collectively; the human race or species.

Implement (Implementation): Something used in order to accomplish a particular thing, especially a tool, device, or instrument to perform a task.

Implementation: The act, process, or way of carrying (something) out or putting (something) into effect.

Industrial: Of or pertaining to the production of goods and services by industry.

Intelligence: The capacity to learn, reason, and understand.

Interpenetrate (Interpenetration): To penetrate throughout; permeate.

Investigate: To systematically examine or search into.

Liability: The condition of or potential for being held responsible.

Limit (Limited): The line or point at which something ends.

Pay Back: To return what is owed or borrowed; repay.

Revolution: The internal, usually forcible, overthrow of a political system or legitimate government.

Shareholder: A person who owns stock in a business organization.

Silicon: A chemical element that has fourteen protons in each nucleus, that is found naturally only in compounds such as silica, that composes one fourth of the earth's crust, and that is used in many industrial applications (symbol: Si).

Simulation: The act or process of pretending or imitating.

Stakeholder: Someone who holds the money that is bet by one or more persons and who pays it to the winner of the bet.

Strategy: A plan, method, or series of actions designed to achieve a specific goal or effect.

Technology: A field of knowledge concerned with the use of industrial arts and applied science to achieve practical objectives, or the various inventions and means of solving problems that result from research in this field.

Transformation: A significant change in the form, structure, character, or nature of something or someone.

Transportation: The act or process of transporting.

University: An educational institution devoted to learning and research and authorized to award degrees on both the graduate and undergraduate levels.

Unstructured: Lacking strict regulation or planning.

Valley: A long area of relatively low elevation, often having a stream bed at the bottom, surrounded by mountains or hills.

Vehicle: A device used to transport people or things.

Chapter 7
Agency Cost Management in the Digital Economy

Dmitriy A. Zhdanov
https://orcid.org/0000-0001-9372-2931
Central Economics and Mathematics Institute, Russian Academy of Sciences, Russia

ABSTRACT

The purpose of the present study was to find the answer to the following questions: How the growing digitalization will affect agency relations, an important element of corporate governance, and what preventive measures should be taken in this situation? Therefore, the impact of digitalization on opportunistic behavior and agency costs was reviewed. The analysis revealed that digitalization provokes reduction of information asymmetry, leads to a decrease in the initiative of top managers, thereby changing the preconditions of opportunistic behavior. On the basis of the ordinal approach, an original toolkit was developed, which made it possible to model the identified dependencies, transformation of the agents' utility in case the principals' demands altering, and to demonstrate ways to reduce agency costs by proper selection of candidates for top manager positions. In conclusion, by means of the developed toolkit, the methodological recommendations were suggested for selecting the agents during the process of recruitment, taking into account the impact of digitalization.

INTRODUCTION

Digital technologies are more and more actively and universally invading the economy and the corporate governance in particular. They expand the capabilities of the existing management tools, update them, new approaches and mechanisms are created on their basis. At the same time, the digitalization of business sets additional managerial tasks, the solution of which will require an adequate methodological tools and algorithmic support. The level and status of corporate management in many respects determine the efficiency of corporations and the perspective for their development. The successful operation of such entities, as a rule these are the largest enterprises, determines the condition of the country's economy in general.

DOI: 10.4018/978-1-7998-2011-6.ch007

One of the essential elements of corporate governance is agency relations. By this concept, we understand the relations that arise between the owners of companies (principals) and the top managers (agents) they hire, who are delegated the rights of managing the assets owned by shareholders.

The relationship between the owners of companies and agents hired by them is traditionally characterized by a whole bunch of contradictions. In literature, such contradictions are traditionally called 'agency problems'. Problems and conflicts of agency relations derive from objectively existing circumstances. First of all, that involves the information asymmetry of the principal and the agent, and the problem of incomplete contracts, as it's impossible to take into account all the essential job requirements in the contract concluded with the agent. These features of relationships create preconditions for the hired manager to take unilateral egoistic actions, including actions related to behavior called managerial opportunism, i.e. manifestation of the "behavioral" uncertainty of the agent (Williamson, 1985). The owners' costs for compensation, rectification and insurance against emerging agency problems, compensation for the consequences of such conflicts are called agency costs.

Due to the speedy digitization of the economy, there arises a necessity of studying the way these processes influence corporate governance. Thus, the purpose of this study is to analyze the changes emerging in corporate governance, primarily in the sphere of agency relations; to review the specific features of managing the agency costs in the digital age; and, if such features are found, to assess possible ways to transform corporate governance practices. The object of this paper is agency relations, and the subject is - the peculiarities of implementing such relations in the digital age.

At the beginning of the study, let us briefly outline the features inherent in the digitalization of production and the economy in general. Discussing in this regard the digitalization, it should be noted that this topic is closely intertwined with the concepts of the Fourth Industrial Revolution (or Industry 4.0) and Industrial Internet of Things (Industrial Internet of Things - IIoT). This technology provides transfer to digital platforms, obtaining and transmission of information in any form and volume from anywhere in the company. It consolidates all equipment and workplaces of the enterprise into an information network; integrates powerful intellectual systems of interpreting the received information, making and implementing decisions into a unified software environment; synchronizes work of all departments; adapts chains of business processes to reach a single goal; visualizes information, etc.

Digitalization ensures obtaining information promptly, in real time mode. It reduces time and increases the quality of decision-making, accelerates implementation of the decisions, speeds up changes. The growing information awareness opens up new opportunities as well as creates business risks.

From the point of view of corporate governance, this technology helps to reduce the problem of information asymmetry, thereby helping to alleviate the agency problems and reduce agency costs. Nowadays, a large amount of internal or external data, which was previously difficult to retrieve and / or not stored in the digitized form, becomes available to interested parties, in particular the shareholders of the company. Owing to new methods and tools of data processing, e.g., Big Data technology, such information can now be promptly processed in order for the principal to monitor the activity of the agent, assess the quality of his performances, coordinate actions and decisions.

At the same time, the tendency to increase the availability of data does not completely eliminate the problem of information asymmetry and the associated prerequisites for opportunistic behavior. For example, it is often difficult to formalize and record data based on experience, intuition, and implicit knowledge of managers. The increase in the amount of available information partially reduces the preconditions for opportunistic behavior, however other dangerous tendencies arise, such as the agents' evading from fulfillment of their obligations.

Further, in this study there will be highlighted two aspects of agency relations, which will be used for analyzing the changes introduced by digital technologies in this area. As the first research field, we will consider the effect of digitalization on opportunistic behavior. The second research field is agency relations, mechanisms for selecting and hiring top managers by the company's principals. Finally, there will be methodological recommendations formulated, which enable to reduce agency costs and improve the company effectiveness.

TRANSFORMATION OF OPPORTUNISTIC BEHAVIOR

Initial Preconditions

The intensive use of modern digital technologies allows to substantially increase the information transparency of the business. The availability of information increases the tendency to shift from rigidly centralized management of business processes to a decentralized model for collecting, processing information and making decisions. At the same time, the availability of diversified digital information permits to strengthen the centralization of management. Now at the head office any information is available on the activities of various structural elements of the company, which was previously hard to attain due to the high costs and difficulties in generating, collecting, processing and storing distributed data.

Since the problem of information asymmetry is of an informational nature, it is logical to assume that now, as part of total digitalization, business owners and the corporate head offices can quickly receive a wide variety of information about the company's activities and thereby alleviate the asymmetry problem and the problem of opportunistic behavior of agents.

It should also be emphasized that the asymmetry of information is not the only reason for opportunistic behavior. Among other reasons are the imperfect mechanisms for coordinating the economic interests of the parties, lack of necessary incentives, which does not at all motivate top managers to high-performance actions.

The concept of opportunism was introduced to economics by Oliver E.Williamson. He identified three variants of egoistic behavior (Williamson, 1985. p. 47): strong form — opportunism, semi-strong form — self-interest seeking (used in the classical economic approach) and weak form — obedience (neglecting one's interests). It is believed that the agents that adhere to a strong form of egoistic behavior, opportunism, have "behavioral" uncertainty, can provide the principal with incomplete or distorted information, can pursue their interests notwithstanding formal and conventional norms, and make profit to the detriment of the owner's interests.

From the point of view of the contractual process, Williamson identified two types of opportunist agent:

- pre-contract opportunism, before the conclusion of the transaction (ex ante), expressed in unfavorable selection and change of plans (adverse selection);
- post-contract opportunism, after the conclusion of the transaction (ex post), manifested in shirking, negligence, the threat of dishonest behavior (moral hazard).

Later there were proposed other features and variants of opportunism classification. For example, the work (Wathne & Heide, 2000. p. 36-37) identifies active opportunism (this includes lies, theft and fraud) and passive (lack of commitment to achieve the best results); in the article (Jap et al., 2013), opportunism with high (high-stake) and low (low-stake) benefits is highlighted; The work (Wathne & Heide, 2000. p. 41) deals with opportunism in a steady and changing situations. A theoretical analysis of agent problems (peculiarities of agent behavior), which are a precondition of opportunistic behavior, and information asymmetry is presented in the works (Jensen & Mecking, 1976; Aghion et al., 2014).

The practice of opportunistic behavior, when agents use the existing rules and procedures to achieve their goals, to which such norms were not originally oriented, is called «gaming». A theoretical study of this phenomenon is presented in (Pearce & Perry, 1983; Lowe & Wilson, 2015). Z. Radnor showed the influence of the organization's culture on gaming (Radnor, 2008), S. Kerr (Kerr, 1975. p.780) showed that the reason for gaming is the fact that it is easier for the principal to give the agent easy-to-measure reference points than the hard-to-measure ones, which, however, reflect the necessary requirements. The most common form of gaming is goal displacement (Bohte & Meier, 2000) and tunnel vision (Smith, 1995).

Developing further the noted views, A. Jackson (Jackson, 2002) identified three types of organizational gaming:

- determinative (incorrect choice of control criteria, performance indicators);
- digital (insufficient quantitative fixation of target parameters);
- behavioral (inactive behavior of employees).

As we can see, digital gaming is associated with the lack of a full-fledged and accessible information environment, which could allow the principal to timely receive the quantitative data required to control the agent's performance. This circumstance does not let to correctly set the numerical values of the performance indicators, which leads to a shift in goals and makes it possible for the agent to choose those aspects of work that provide him with the most benefit.

Digitalization and the industrial Internet of Things reduce the role of this factor in opportunistic behavior. The task of the correct digital measurement of target (planned) criteria is being solved within Industry 4.0, quantification and data consolidation on all key aspects of the company's activities. Therefore, the preconditions of opportunistic behavior associated with the complexity of the digital measurement of the parameters that define the targets for agents, are eliminated.

At the same time, another kind of organizational gaming, called «behavioral» by Jackson, may, on the contrary, increase due to total control. Informational pressure will inadvertently lead to further decrease in top manager's initiative, an increase in apathy, which will entail exacerbation of this prerequisite for opportunistic behavior.

Let's look at another example related to the features of opportunistic behavior. Consolidating the variants of relations arising between the owners of the company and the hired top managers. the following types of agent behavior can be identified:

- obvious opportunism. This behavior involves illegal alienation or misuse of corporate property; misappropriation of the corporation assets, as well as implementation of discretionary projects in order to strengthen one's position or to obtain additional privileges.
- soft opportunism. It lies in the fact of concealing and distorting information about opportunities and reserves in order to create more comfortable conditions for their work (understating output, overestimating costs, concealing information about reserves, development perspectives, etc.). The consequence of mild opportunism is loss of potential opportunities, loss of earnings due to business decline in comparison with the possible level;
- hidden opportunism (apathy, lack of initiative). In this option, the motivation of the agents to the efficient performance of their duties is significantly reduced. As in the case of mild opportunism, there are also missed opportunities, inefficient use of the agent's abilities and competencies, passivity, lack of action, unwillingness to be proactive, etc. According to the terminology introduced by H. Leibenstein (Leibenstein, 1966), we can say that these circumstances prevent the agent from increasing X-efficiency.

The introduction of digital solutions, Industry 4.0, Big Data technology, as mentioned above, can reduce the problem of information asymmetry. Now the principals and the head corporate office in real time mode are able to track and process information about the current state of the corporation, existing stocks, expenditure of resources, equipment loading, divisions' efficiency, fulfillment of assignments, etc.. In other words, digitalization makes it possible to accomplish the tasks of planning, managing and controlling the usage of various factors of production with minimal human participation.

This circumstance creates opportunities for improving the efficiency of the corporation, moving to new markets, and in the meantime, it forms the illusion of expediency of transition to more rigid, centralized forms of governance. This misconception is based on a simplified interpretation of the principal–agent problem, as well as on the idea that the only factor causing this problem is information asymmetry. Meanwhile, the opportunistic behavior of agents can be caused not only by the information asymmetry, but also by low incentives, which result from the inability to adequately measure the contribution and remuneration of top managers in terms of functional division of labor, and is also attributed to the reduction of the agent's ability to make independent decisions.

Solutions and Recommendations

The analysis makes it possible to conclude that first two types of the opportunistic behavior discussed above, explicit and soft opportunism, can be minimized by applying digitalization capabilities, when prompt provision of diverse management information prevents attempts of unlawful expropriation or unauthorized use of corporate assets.

Moreover, it results in an increase of preconditions for displaying of the third type of opportunistic behavior - apathy (lack of initiative). The more regulated and controlled the agent's operational environment is getting and the less autonomy he has, the more inert he becomes, less focused on self-realization, on disclosure of his creative abilities and, in the long run, on efficient work in the interests of the entire corporation. Excessive management centralization and bureaucracy lead to ossification of the routine, a decrease of incentives for effective work, and growth of monitoring elements, though digitalization creates a necessity for top managers to work in conditions of uncertainty, accomplishing complicated analytical tasks that require improvisation and creativity[1].

Exclusion of the executive's proactive creativity from the company's resource potential complicates its development. Up-to-date software tools and all-knowing automatic controllers can find, process, measure and evaluate mostly explicit information, assist in accomplishing routine tasks, while comprehensive assessment of problematic situations, long-term management decisions are based, to a significant extent, on implicit knowledge and on top manager's intuition and initiative.

That brings up another interconnected problem - to what extent the evaluation criteria, built into software algorithms, correlate with the arising nonstandard situations, for example, an ability to correctly predict the consequences of the events that have taken place, to assess the trend of their changes.

Thus, the use of digital technologies provides possibilities to substantially increase the informational transparency of business, which leads to alleviation of information asymmetry. This circumstance affects the peculiar features of the agent's opportunistic behavior. Nowadays there are various approaches for classifying the types of opportunistic behavior. In particular, with the framework of gaming (situations when the agent, adhering to the established rules, seeks self-interest rather than the interests of the principal) the following classification of opportunistic behavior is distinguished: determinative gaming; digital gaming; behavioral gaming.. In regards of another grouping option considered in this review, the following types of such rejecting behavior are noted: obvious opportunism (property misappropriation and implementation of discretionary projects), hidden opportunism (shirking and concealing information) and soft opportunism (apathy).

As the analysis showed, there are the following possible reasons for various types of opportunistic behavior: firstly, the principal's lack of required quantitative data about the situation in the company and, secondly, the inactive behavior of the agent. Digitalization, by reducing the acuity of the information asymmetry, makes it possible to weaken the first group of the identified preconditions (as they are related to the lack of the required quantitative data) and thereby cut down one of the reasons for opportunistic behavior.

Simultaneously, the same process enhances the second group of preconditions; it provokes a decrease in initiative and growth of inaction of the agents. Digitalization, providing extensive informational monitoring, makes principals to increase a comprehensive control over the agents, which leads to a weakening of their initiative and increases the apathy that is the cause of such deviant behavior.

This circumstance should be taken into consideration when analyzing the effects of digitalization. All possible measures should be taken for preserving reasonable freedom for the agents in managerial actions, there should be created opportunities for showing initiative. Moreover, overcoming of the mentioned above negative preconditions will be facilitated by introduction of special incentives for implementing independent actions, or any other additional payments if the agent is proactive in the new digital working conditions.

AGENCY COSTS MANAGEMENT

Initial Preconditions

In this section, we will review another aspect of the digitalization's impact on corporate governance. Let us dwell on the impact of this technology on agency relations and agency costs, and determine how to manage such costs and reduce losses from eliminating the effects of agency conflicts.

There are two main approaches to solving agency problems. The first, most common and studied approach is to set up an organizational tool for monitoring the activities of the agents in order to identify cases of opportunistic behavior. Various methods and tools for controlling the decisions made by agents and evaluating their actions have been formed to achieve this goal. However, the control tools, as well as measures to compensate and remedy the consequences of the violations committed, mean for the company additional agency costs.

The second way to mitigate agency problems, less studied although widespread, is the selection of executives who can be trusted with asset management. That means to attract the agents who are initially loyal to the dominant owner[2], which will make it possible not to spend money on control over such executives in the future.

As it was noted in the previous section, digitalization allows to provide informational transparency of the company and makes it easier to monitor the agent's activities. It facilitates agency cost reduction providing access to various operational data which the owner uses to control activities of the top-executives. However, it is not possible to set up a comprehensive control over the agents as there always be some information above the corporate control or that cannot be formulated, and this fact does not let to eliminate agency contradictions.

Therefore, in this section we will examine the second of the above mentioned methods for reducing agency costs. The method consists in hiring adequate managers, whose personal features initially allow mitigating agency contradictions rather than setting up various control mechanisms.

Thus, we will formulate the purpose of this section as follows: how to select an agent (candidate) that requires the minimum agency costs and how does digitalization affect this process?

In order to find an answer to this question, the following initial research task has been defined by the author — to establish personal qualities that, from the position of the owner, an "ideal" top executive should possess, i.e. to identify the features on the basis of which the selection of agents takes place in practice. As a result of the conducted research, it was found that when selecting the top executives of Russian corporations, the potential candidate needs to have two of the following main groups of specific features (sets of qualities):

1. Qualifications (knowledge, experience, communication skills, etc.). The requirement for having this quality is quite predictable;
2. Loyalty (reputation, ability to take responsibility, etc.). The requirement of this quality is not announced, but in practice it is widely used.

Under the two marked generalized characteristics we will understand the following set of personal qualities of the applicant. *Qualification* is the manager's certain specific knowledge and skills, professional efficiency, experience in similar area (industry), the presence of high managerial competencies and business skills. Of course, in assessing the professionalism of executives, such factors as initiative in decision-making, readiness to take responsibility for the consequences of such decisions, leadership qualities, ability to organize work, communication skills, and entrepreneurship are essential. Digitalization highlights the ability to learn, digital literacy, the ability to integrate solutions, proficiency in Agile technologies. As a result, qualification reveals a possibility of the agent to ensure high productivity of the business.

The concept of *loyalty* also includes several aspects, such as experience of liaising, the relationship of trust between the manager and the dominant owner, reputation, honesty, responsibility, membership in the same team, and as an option - "clan" affinity, which is typical, for example, for a family business or a company built on a national basis (community). In other words, everything that allows the principal to believe that the agent will not pursue his interests behind the owner's back. In addition, the readiness to pursue commercial interests is significant, as well as being guided by the owner's opinion, being committed to his goals, in certain cases despite his own understanding of economic expediency, and even with possible damage to personal professional image. Loyalty implies the possibility of reducing agency costs and conflicts due to proven, trusting, "personal" relationships.

Now, having defined the basic requirements for the agent by the owners, we will articulate the goals, which the specified qualities of the top manager help to achieve, answer the question - why are they so important for the principal? Each of the two selected qualities of an agent is focused on achieving the most suitable goal for successful implementation. It can be stated that the usefulness of a top manager for the owner is determined by the ability to fulfill the following categories of tasks:

- increasing the effectiveness of the company, which can be ensured by a high level of the agent's qualification (1st group of qualities);
- reduction of agency problems due to the relationship of trust (2nd group of qualities).

The owner is faced with a permanent task - to ensure that the hired top manager follows not so much the letter (including incomplete contracts), but the spirit of the relationship. This problem is especially relevant in a situation where the value of specific intangible assets (business, lobbying, corruption ties) is increasing - as in countries with emerging economies, including Russia. Therefore, so often there are hired executive officers that are "close" to the owner, including acquaintances with whom a positive work experience has already been formed; relatives; friends; executives recommended by trusted people. At the same time, such restrictions significantly reduce the possibility of hiring highly qualified, but outside specialists who know the specific production.

Research Tools

We will use the ordinal approach as a methodological basis for further research on the relationship of professional qualifications and loyalty of top managers, on the one hand, and the effectiveness of their work, on the other hand. The notion of the potential "*utility*" of a top manager for a company will be introduced. It (utility) characterizes such personal features of the agent, that allow to ensure high management efficiency, reduce potential agency problems and increase the value of the business.

Figure 1. The behavior of the isoline of utility, depending on the "loyalty" and "qualifications" of top managers
Source: prepared by the author

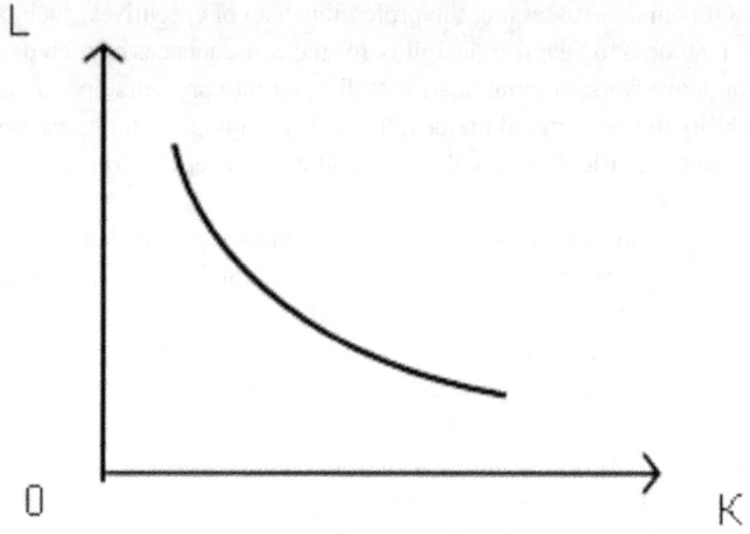

Suppose hiring an agent by a principal as a consumer choice (in our case, the dominant owner or top management of a corporation) of a certain product (a top manager in this capacity) with two specified "benefits" - complementary qualities, which determine the agent's "utility".

This case can be represented by the *function of utility* of the executive office for a particular company (for its owner). Such utility (U) will depend on two main groups of variables: "qualifications" (K) and "loyalty" (L), as well as other factors (p). In turn, each of the groups is formed by a number of components. The components in the "qualification" group are denoted as: $k_1, k_2, ..., k_N$, and the "loyalty" group as - $l_1, l_2, ..., l_M$, where M and N is the maximum number of elements included in each of the groups. Thus, the function of utility can be represented as follows:

$$U = U [K (k_n), L (l_m), p]$$

Each agent possesses individual combination of these properties, but with different combinations of them, the total "utility" of certain executives can be approximately equal. Hence, a multiplicity of potentially suitable for hiring managers can be reviewed as a set of groups of people distinguished by their "utility". Thus, within the same group the managers with similar "utility" but with a different combination of certain features will integrate.

Since the manager's "utility" for the principal depends on two basic complementary and interchangeable qualities ("benefits"), its behavior can be plotted by an isoline in the coordinates of the indicated qualities. At each point of this isometric line the "utility" of top-managers will have the same value. This approach allows to draw a conditional parallel with such a well-known plotting as an *indifference curve*. The line precisely shows a combination of two benefits, provided that their total consumer utility is maintained for the buyer, in our case, the agent's utility for the principal. The indicated dependence is shown in Figure 1.

Presented in Figure 1 curve is downward. It will have a concave shape based on the reduction of the marginal rate of substitution, the slope of the curve and the level of its concavity depend on the level of interchangeability of the two parameters under consideration. The marginal rate of substitution demonstrates how one "quality" of a top manager can be replaced by another, and will depend on the location of the point on the chart.

The more the requirements for the top-manager's "utility" are tightening, the less number of potential employees will meet these requirements, the more difficult it will be to find an appropriate candidate in the market. And on the contrary: if the requirements are not too high, the more applicants can meet these requirements. Hence, the *supply function* of such employees, that is, the change in the number of potential candidates with an increase in the requirements for their "utility," will have a diminishing character. With a decrease in the "utility" requirements, the number of applicants that meet this not so stringent requirement will grow, and the search for the necessary candidate will be made easier.

It is also worth noting that personal "loyalty" refers to the category of special human capital that is claimed by the owner inside a particular company. In this way, it differs from the "qualification", which includes both general (versatile) and special human capital demanded in a particular business.

Solutions and Recommendations

The contribution of each of the two indicated "benefits" to the utility of a top manager (comparing their significance) will be assessed further, and based on that assessment there will be recommendations made on the use of the introduced tools for increasing top manager's efficiency. In order to do this, we will consider the parameters that determine the requirements for the indicated components that make up the "utility" of a top manager, which is reflected in the form of the "utility" isoline. It is influenced by the following groups of factors:

1. principal's demands to the agent (top manager);
2. specific requirements for the functional position occupied by the agent;
3. level of the company's digitalization.

Requirements of the principal to the agent (top manager). Depending on the importance of a particular quality of the hired agent to the dominant shareholders, the following group of shareholders can be distinguished:

Group A - includes the dominant owners, who foremost value the qualification of the candidate, as he will manage the technologically sophisticated productions, reach challenging objectives, etc. In this case the traditional professional selection takes place, and the loyalty factor is considered to a slight level;

Group B - this type of owner takes into account both the qualification and the loyalty of the top manager;

Group C - the importance of loyalty for these type of shareholders is relatively high, and the requirements for the qualification are in second place. Close attention is paid to loyalty, since trust is important, belonging to a team, strict adherence to agreements, procedures, a "can-do" attitude (it mostly concerns a family business or a commercial business with involvement of local personnel), or in case when a comprehensive control of the top manager is hampered.

Figure 2. Employer's requirements to the proportion of factors composing top manager's "utility" (indifference curve)
Source: prepared by the author

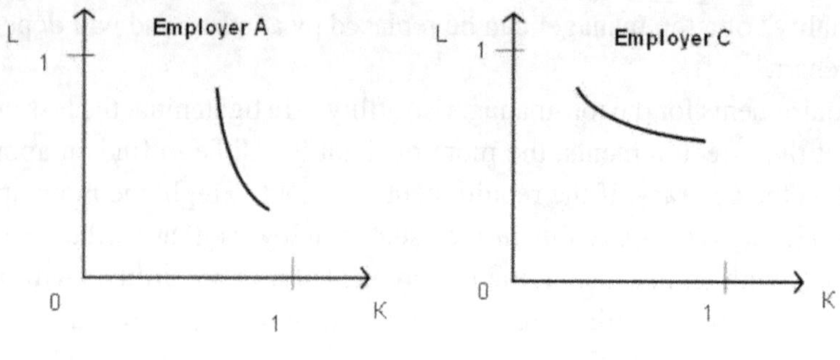

Different groups of employers (different business situations) have a different level of flexibility to the considered qualities - i.e. the possibility of replacing one quality with the other one, the limits of such a substitution. Accordingly, the graphs characterizing the required "utility" of the hired top manager will differ.

Charts (a) and (b) Figure 2 show the relation of such difference to the limits of substitution for two categories of employers: "A" and "C". On Figure 2 both of the analyzed parameters vary in the range from 0 to 1, where 0 corresponds to the minimum value and 1 to the maximum. The expectations of the owner of category "B" correspond to the isoline of utility, shown earlier in Figure 1.

As it can be seen, the graph (a) describing the requirements of employer "A" will have a steeper slope. This is due to the dominance of professional requirements, which in this case must be at a high level. The requirements of employer "C" corresponds to the graph (b), which has a more gentle appearance, which corresponds to the prevalence of the "loyalty" factor.

The categorization of an owner to a certain group depends both on objective and subjective reasons. The first (objective) requirements include the specifics of the company's activities, the level of its digitalization, business conditions, including the prevailing aspects of the director's work, the kind of decisions made, the particular business or administrative situation, the company profile, the stage of business development, etc.

The subjective, individual factors include personal preferences of the dominant owner, the importance for him of certain managerial qualities. Thus, for the principal of category "A" the qualifications of the agent (professionalism, competence) are most important. Owners of category "B" and especially "C" pay special attention to mental, ethical and psychological needs, to comfortable operating conditions, the temper of the hired top manager. The increase in the importance of these factors for the principal enhances attention of the owner to the qualities that make up the loyalty of the agent (his moral, psychological, behavioral characteristics). And, on the contrary, with their decrease, attention to traditional professional criteria grows.

Special requirements for the position occupied by the agent. Various demands to the ratio of these properties of the agent that form the utility may also arise when hiring directors responsible for managing certain functional divisions of the company, for example, financial, commercial, or production. In this case, in the same corporation there may be different demands to the indifference curve of the utility of managers occupying such positions. This fact is illustrated in Figure 3, which depicts the requirements for managers who are in charge of various functional divisions of the company.

Figure 3. The "utility" isoline of different top managers in the same company
Source: prepared by the author

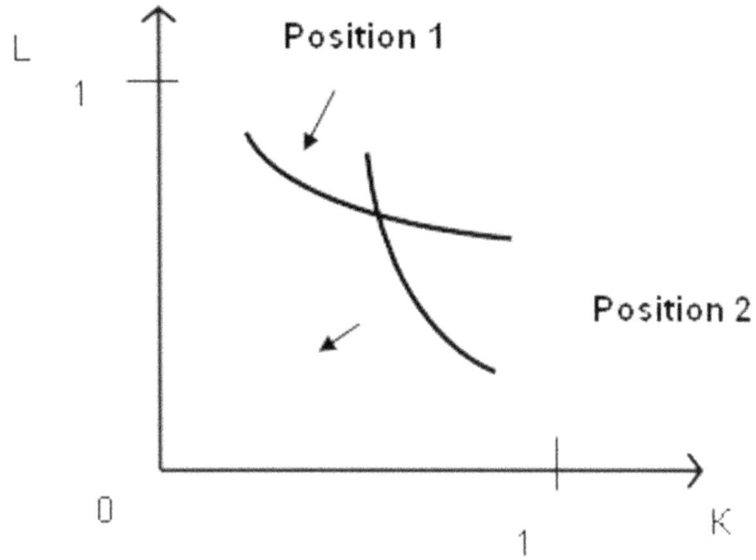

The "Position 1" graph is more likely to meet the requirements for a commercial and/or financial director who controls commercial transactions or cashl flows, relationships with stakeholders, where traditionally much attention is paid to loyalty. It could also be relations with the agent, who are required to be promptitude in obeying, rather than proactive, which often takes place in rigidly administrative structures. "Position 2" more relates to the position of technical director, production director or chief engineer, for whom professional competence and personal autonomy are more significant than trustworthy relations with the owner or the first person.

The level of digitalization of the company. Digitalization, as mentioned above, significantly modernizes the company's activities, the organization of its business processes, the technologies used, the requirements for managers, etc. On the one hand it results in increased demands for the qualifications of top managers, especially for competencies related to the category of "Knowledge" (the ability to work in conditions of vagueness, to perform complicated analytical tasks that require improvisation and creativity). On the other hand, it facilitates monitoring of the top manager though hindering his initiative, and makes it easier to detect the signs of his opportunistic behavior. These circumstances lead to the fact that the agent's loyalty factor is receding into the background, and more attention is paid to his qualifications.

Digitization also affects two other factors noted above that determine a requirement for the agent's utility: 1) the preferences of principals and 2) special requirements for the agent's functional position. The need for the company's activities to comply with the conditions of a rapidly changing digital environment reinforces the principal's attention to the agent's proper qualifications and the presence of cognitive, socio-psychological and digital competences. The same situation is with the special requirements for the position of the top manager. This is due to the fact that the areas of activity where the loyalty factor is particularly important, i.e. finance, commerce, public relations, are primarily affected by digitalization, which makes it necessary to improve digital competencies of the appropriate functional manager. These

Figure 4. Transformation of the "utility" isoline as a result of the influence of digitalization factors
Source: prepared by the author

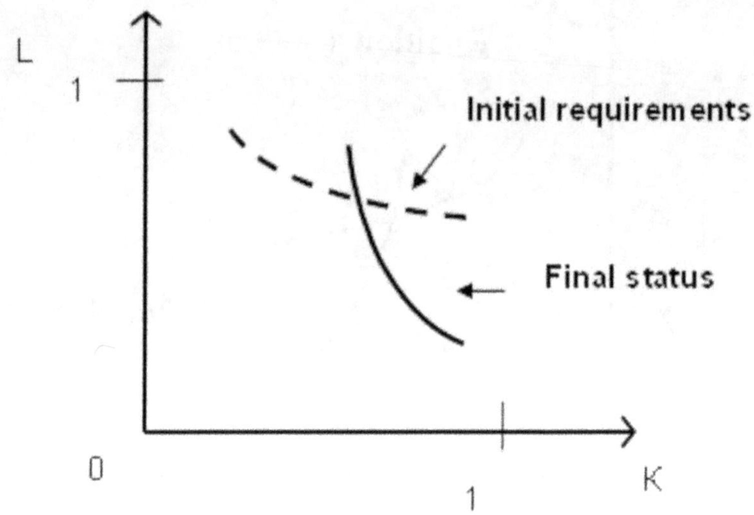

circumstances suggest that the importance of the "qualification" component in the "utility" of the agent in terms of increasing digitalization.

As a result, the "utility" isoline of the hired top manager becomes more sensitive to their qualifications and less to loyalty. Figure 4 illustrates this trend for the case when the principal initially sets the highest standard for the agent's loyalty.

It is also worth noting that due to digitalization, the number of potential applicants for a vacant position increases, since recruitment services have access to extensive information from various, previously unavailable sources: social networks, various specialized analytical reports, databases.

METHODICAL RECOMMENDATIONS FOR THE SELECTION OF AGENTS

Suggested Algorithm of Actions

In conclusion, there will be formulated the guidelines for selection by principals of candidates for a vacant position of top manager, thereby demonstrating the possibilities of practical use of the proposed approach to assessing the effectiveness of senior managers. The task under review arises whenever the owner needs to rank the possible candidates (agents) in order to select the most suitable one for the vacant managerial position. The proposed guidelines do not replace the traditional methods of professional selection, but complement them by including the loyalty factor in the mechanism of such selection and take into account its importance for certain shareholders, kinds of businesses and positions.

The descriptive view used above made it possible to describe the regularities of the selection of the agents by principals, the factors that determine such a choice and its goals. In this section, a practical mechanism for implementing the identified relationships is reviewed. In this regard, we will use not the ordinalist, as before, but the cardinal approach, will introduce the numerical indicators of the dependencies used.

The procedure of achieving this objective is proposed to divide into the following integrated steps:

Stage 1: Pre-selection of candidates in compliance with the general basic requirements for the vacancy.
Stage 2: Adjustment of job description and Personal Specification by formulating the requirements for the vacant position, the definition of acceptable limits of qualifications and loyalty.
Stage 3: Determine the relative importance of the two parameters under consideration, that is, the form of the utility isoline for the vacant position.
Stage 4: Assessment of the qualifications and loyalty of each of the applicants.
Stage 5: Definition of the "utility" of candidates and their final ranking.

Suppose it is necessary to select applicants for a vacant position, the requirements for "utility" which are described by isolines in Figure 5. Let us outline the actions that should be taken at each of these stages.

Stage 1. Pre-selection of candidates.

If certain requirements are initially claimed to applicants, such as, previous work experience, additional training, age, gender, etc., a preliminary screening of relevant candidates is carried out at this stage.

Suppose, as a result of the preliminary selection, l number of candidates were chosen with the necessary work experience, i is the candidate number, i = 1. . . I.

Stage 2. "Position Profile" development

At the second stage, the requirements for the vacant position are finalized, and first of all, the required "qualifications" and "loyalty" are determined. In order to do this, there can be introduced the measurement scale for each of the parameters, for example, assign the maximum possible value to N, and the minimum to 0, and specify the desired interval for changing the indicated criteria within the introduced scale. If a single scale is used for several managerial positions in the company, then within this scale there can be requirements set for certain managerial vacancies, indicating for each them their own unique range of desired parameters (acceptable minimum and maximum values).

Let's assume that the profile of the offered job is described by the following requirements:

- Parameter L must be in the range from L_1 to L max, where L_1 is the minimum acceptable loyalty level; L max - the maximum allowable.
- Parameter K - in the range from K_1 to K max, K_1 - the minimum acceptable skill level; K max - the maximum allowable.

In order to facilitate the formation of the scale of parameters, in addition to numerical indicators there can be used verbal (qualitative) gradation of possible values to assess "qualifications" and "loyalty". For example, in case of a five-level classification, these will be the following levels: the indicator can be of any value; or its value should start at a level below average; at the average; at above average; or just the highest.

Figure 5. An example of an indifference curve map of a "job profile"
Source: prepared by the author

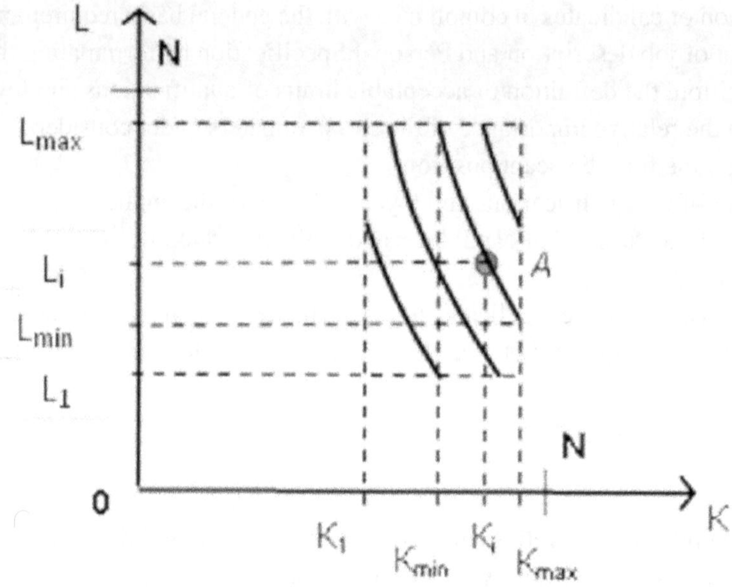

Stage 3. Determine the relative importance of the parameters, that is, the form of the utility isoline for the vacant position.

Then it is necessary to determine the interdependence of the considered parameters, their comparative weights, or the marginal rate of substitution of one parameter by another. This sets the shape of the indifference curve, i.e. how one of the criteria will change with the dynamics of the other, while preserving the utility of the manager. The variants of the utility isolines are shown in Figure 3. Since the requirements for the isolines' form for different executive positions in the company may differ, this procedure should be carried out for each vacant position.

The set of utility isolines within the two selected coordinates can be represented as a kind of "indifference map" of the utility of managers applying for the vacant position within the allowable interval of parameters' change, which is reflected in Figure 5. The more distant from the origin of coordinates the considered curve is, the more significant its utility. Moreover, as noted before, the higher is the level of loyalty and qualifications that the manager must possess, the fewer people initially meet this requirement (and, accordingly, this contour line).

The form of indifference curves (angle of inclination) are determined by the priority for the position of one or another criterion. For example, Figure 5 presents a map of indifference curves of an imagined technical director.

In our case, the utility isoline (indifference curve) for the offered position is close to linear dependence, i.e. it can be approximated by a linear function without any damage to content, the marginal rate of substitution of one parameter by another one will be constant at any point of such a graph. Let us introduce parameter P, the correlation coefficient between L and K for our indifference curve. It can be calculated as the ratio of the range of "qualification" changes to the range of "loyalty" changes of a single isoline of utility. For the situation shown in Figure 4, the eligible qualifications range from Kmin to Kmax, and loyalty ranges from Lmin to Lmax, then:

$$P = (Lmax - Lmin) / (Kmax - Kmin) \quad (1)$$

Stage 4. Assessment of the qualifications and loyalty for each of the applicants.

Considering the introduced scale of measurements, each of the potential candidates is assigned numerical values of his qualifications and loyalty. This procedure can be carried out in various ways. For example, a qualification assessment is usually carried out with the help of special professional tests or personal interviews. The level of the candidate's loyalty can be described in the same way, by testing for "truthfulness", liaise experience at the previous job, evaluating colleagues, etc.). An alternative option of assessment – expert assessment, is used when it's difficult to apply formal criteria.

After that, knowing the requirements for the position, the minimum allowable values of "qualification" and "loyalty" in particular, it is possible to further screen out candidates who do not have these qualities at the required level (who did not get the necessary points).

Let the "qualification" and "loyalty" of applicant i be evaluated by experts as Ki and Li and exceed the minimum required level of "qualification" and "loyalty". The place of this applicant is indicated as point A on the map of indifference curves of utility.

Stage 5. Determination of the candidates' utility and their final ranking.

At the last stage, the potential utility (efficiency) of managers is calculated. To do this, the points scored by candidates for each of the criteria are summed up taking into account their significance (weight). In conclusion, applicants are ranked based on the accumulated total "points", and the most suitable candidate is determined.

Below is the calculation of Qi - the final assessment of the applicant. It is defined as the sum of the individual "loyalty" and "qualifications", adjusted for the significance (weight) of indicators. Then, taking into account the introduced form of the isoline of utility, it can be defined as follows:

$$Qi = P * Ki + Li \quad (2)$$

Using formula (1), the final grade can be presented as follows:

$$Qi = ((Lmax - Lmin) / (Kmax - Kmin)) * Ki + Li \quad (3)$$

At the end, the applicants are ranked by the received grades (Qi), and the winner who received the highest rating is selected.

Table 1. Qualifications and loyalty of candidates

Candidate Number	Candidate's loyalty (%)	Candidate 's qualification (%)
A	60	90
B	80	80
C	90	50
Criteria "weight"	0,66	0,34

Source: prepared by the author

Table 2. Final assessment of candidates

Candidate's number	Final grade of the candidate	Candidate's rating
A	69,9	3
B	79,9	1
C	76,6	2

Source: prepared by the author

Example of Estimation

Below is an example of utilizing the proposed toolkit. A number of assumptions have been made, designed to alleviate the practical situation under consideration, while retaining the main points of the introduced approach. It is assumed that there is a possibility to establish the level of competence and loyalty of the agents, in any case, to compare different candidates. The second assumption is that the shape of the isoline of utility can be described using a linear dependence, i.e. the marginal rate of substitution of the two factors considered is constant.

Therefore, suppose that in company X a vacancy of a management position is announced. Requirements for a potential candidate are described by the following parameters: age from 35 to 50, an MBA level, leadership experience in similar positions for at least 10 years. The "qualification" of the applicant should be in the range of 60% to 90% of the maximum possible value, and "loyalty" in the range from 50% to 90%. So, we need o find the most suitable candidate on the market within a limited period of time.

Let the form of the indifference curve of utility for the desired position have the form of a uniformly decreasing linear dependence. The coefficient of interrelation of parameters equals to two, based on the requirements of the shareholder, is equal to two, that means that the applicant, first of all, is required to be highly qualified and such competence will be twice valuable than the importance of loyalty.

Suppose that for this executive position, after the initial dropout, three candidates have applied, whose personal qualities can be described by the parameters given in Table 1. The values of loyalty and qualification are estimated as a percentage of the maximum possible value of the parameter.

All three candidates meet the requirements for the position and can be considered further. With the help of the introduced algorithm, the score of each of the applicants were calculated, the candidates have been rated on this basis, and the results are summarized in Table 2.

As can be seen from the table, the most useful of the candidates currently on the market is candidate "B". Although he is slightly less qualified than candidate "A", his behavior is more predictable for the principal, which allowed him to win this competition. Candidate "C" takes the second place, despite his maximum loyalty, his qualification is significantly lower than the previous candidate's. Candidate "A" is on the last place. Although he is the most qualified of all, his loyalty to the principal, from the point of view of the latter, is low, while the vacant position requires a certain level of trust.

Since the analysis is made of the activities of top managers who have a free hand in disposing the assigned assets, a certain level of trust in such an agent from the shareholder is required. If, in a particular situation, while selection of the top manager, the question of his loyalty fades into the background, and only professional competencies are important, the situation is simplified and its resolution takes place within the framework of traditional qualification selection, which corresponds to the analysis of only one of the noted factors.

CONCLUSION

The transition to business digitalization sets the task of assessing the impact of these processes on corporate governance, which requires the use of adequate methodological tools and algorithmic support. In this regard, the purpose of the study was to analyze changes in corporate governance and, above all, in the area of agency relations; as well as examination of the piculiarities of agency costs management in the digital age and an assessment of possible ways to adjust corporate governance practices.

The use of modern digital technologies makes it possible to enhance the information transparency of business, which leads to an alleviation of the information asymmetry problem. This circumstance affects the preconditions of opportunistic behavior, helps to mitigate the typical agency problems and reduce agency costs. However, the increase in data does not completely eliminate the problem of information asymmetry and related reasons for opportunistic behavior.

In the presented study, two aspects of agency relations have been highlighted in order to examine the changes introduced by digital technologies in this area. The first one - the influence of digitalization on solving the problem of opportunistic behavior, the second aspect disposes the agency relations, selection and hiring mechanisms of top managers by principals.

As the first example, the preconditions for the manifestation of opportunistic behavior were analyzed and two permanently present groups of reasons were identified. This is, firstly, the principal's lack of necessary information about the situation in the company and, secondly, inert behavior of agents. When analyzing the impact of digitalization on these causes, it is noted that reducing the severity of information asymmetry allows to weaken the first group of the indicated preconditions (related to the lack of necessary data) and thereby reduce the manifestation of opportunistic behavior.

In the meantime, the same process enhances the second group of preconditions; it contributes to an increase in the lack of initiative and the passivity of agents. Digitalization, providing ubiquitous information monitoring, provokes principals to increase total control over the agents, which leads to a weakening of their initiative and reinforces apathy, which is the cause of such deviant behavior.

It is shown that in order to remedy this situation, it is necessary to take various measures to preserve the agents' reasonable freedom of management actions, a possibility of taking the initiative. The introduction of special incentives for self-directed actions by the manager, additional payments in case they are proactive in the new digital working conditions, will help to overcome these negative preconditions.

Within the second case, the possibility of reducing agency costs through the correct selection of top managers was investigated, which is an obvious and traditional way of reducing such costs. It was noted that the solution of this task is influenced both by objective circumstances, requirements related to the company's activities, as well as subjective ones - preferences of the dominant owners in selecting the top manager most appropriate to their behavioral and psychological needs.

As a result, it was stated that when hiring top managers, the principal actually considers two collective properties of the agent: "qualification" (knowledge, experience, professional competencies) and "loyalty" (proximity to the owner, personal responsibility to him, reputation, belonging to the "team") . At the same time, the importance (weights) of these factors may differ for different operational situations, for example, attention to loyalty is enhanced in companies for which specific intangible assets are important (political, business, lobbyist, and corrupt ties of business owners).

There was introduced the concept of agent's (top manager's) utility for the principal (company), which describes the ability to ensure high efficiency of management, reduce potential agency problems and increase the value of the business due to certain personal qualities of the agent. Based on the ordinal approach, a model toolkit was formed, allowing to evaluate candidates for top positions. The potential effectiveness of managers is presented as a utility function of an agent for a principal, depending on the two key qualities ("benefits") of the top manager, his level of qualification and loyalty.

A multitude of managers suitable for hiring has been presented as a set of groups of employees distinguished by their utility. The consumer utility of each of these groups is interpreted in the coordinates of "loyalty" and "qualification" as an indifference curve for the utility of managers (an isoline), at each point of which the utility will be the same, with a different combination of these qualities ("benefits"). The requirements for the desired manager determine the necessary composition of his qualities, and, accordingly, the type of the isoline of utility, the elasticity of the two properties under consideration (the marginal rate of replacement of one quality by another).

It is shown that the contribution of each of the two marked "benefits" to the utility of a top manager depends on the following groups of factors: 1) the principal's demands to the agent; 2) special requirements for the position occupied by the agent; 3) the level of digitalization of the company.

With the increase in the "*level of digitalization*", the requirements for the "qualification" component in the manager's utility grow, especially in the presence of special digital knowledge, the ability to work under uncertainty, to fulfill complicated analytical tasks that require improvisation and creativity, the presence of cognitive and socio-psychological competencies. Digitalization also affects two other factors noted above that determine a demand for the agents utility: 1) *preferences of principals*, and 2) *special requirements for the functional position*. In this case the demand for digital competencies is also strengthened. In addition, digitalization facilitates control over the top manager, it becomes easier to detect manifestations of his disloyal behavior.

Thus, during the process of digitizing, the agent's "loyalty" factor increasingly fades into the background, and more attention is paid to the "qualification" component of the manager's utility, i.e. the isoline of the utility of the hired top manager becomes more sensitive to his qualifications and less to loyalty.

In conclusion of the current study there were proposed the guidelines for selecting the candidates by the principal for the vacant position of a top manager, based on the introduced theoretical approach. This task arises when the owner needs to rank the possible candidates in order to select the most suitable candidate for the vacant managerial position. The recommendations do not replace traditional methods of professional selection, but complement them, taking into account the loyalty factor, which is important for certain types of business and positions, as well as for addressing the behavioral preferences of owners.

FUTURE RESEARCH DIRECTIONS

The present study demonstrates possibilities to reduce agency costs and reduce the preconditions of opportunistic behavior in view of digitalization. At the same time, the considered problems of opportunistic behavior, in our opinion, cannot be completely solved with the help of digital technologies, even taking into account the fact that such technologies are developing rapidly and, probably, will soon open up new managerial opportunities based, for example, on artificial intelligence or a multiple increase in computational capabilities.

This conclusion is based on several causes. Thus, with the help of digital technologies it is rather difficult to completely remove the problem of information asymmetry, since it is almost impossible to ensure full control of the agent, and not all the required information is submitted to formalizing and can be collected and recorded. At the same time, there are deep-seated contradictions between the principal and the agent due to the difference of their economic interests, which are not eliminated by digitalization, and the fundamental solution of this problem lies in the area of property relations, convergence of interests of the parties within such relations.

The use of the proposed tool for selecting top managers based on the representation of their utility as a function of qualifications and loyalty may be primarily in demand in companies where the factor of loyalty of the manager is initially significant, and where this parameter will be weakened due to digitalization processes . The developed model approach can also be in demand in the case of the emergence of other, besides qualification and loyalty, key features of the agent's utility considered while selecting candidates in digitalization conditions. For example, it is possible to replace the loyalty factor with such a requirement as the presence of digital competencies. However, it will be possible to fully appreciate this opportunity, as well as other indicated trends, when there is enough statistics characterizing the activities of companies in the digital environment.

REFERENCES

Aghion, P., Bloom, N., & Van Reenen, J. (2014). Incomplete Contracts and Internal Organization of Firms. *Journal of Law Economics and Organization, 30*(suppl 1), i37–i63. doi:10.1093/jleo/ewt003

Bohte, J., & Meier, K. J. (2000). Goal displacement: Assessing the motivation for organizational cheating. *Public Administration Review, 60*(2), 173–182. doi:10.1111/0033-3352.00075

Jackson, A. (2002). Gaming of performance indicators: A classification related to impact. In A. Neely & A. Walters (Eds.), *Performance Management Association 2002 conference proceedings*. Boston: PMA.

Jap, S. D., Robertson, D. C., Rindfleisch, A., & Hamilton, R. (2013). Low-stakes opportunism. *JMR, Journal of Marketing Research, 50*(2), 216–227. doi:10.1509/jmr.10.0121

Jensen, M. C., & Meckling, W. H. (1976). Theory of the firm: Managerial behavior, agency costs and ownership structure. *Journal of Financial Economics, No., 3*(4), 303–360. doi:10.1016/0304-405X(76)90025-8

Kerr, S. (1975). On the folly of rewarding A, while hoping for B. *Academy of Management Journal, 18*(4), 769–783. PMID:1235930

Leibenstein, H. (1966). Allocative Efficiency VS. "X-Efficiency. *The American Economic Review, 56*(3).

Lowe T., Wilson R. (2015). Playing the game of outcomes-based performance management. Is gamesmanship inevitable? Evidence from theory and practice. *Social Policy and Administration*. doi:10.1111pol.12205

Pearce, J. L., & Perry, J. L. (1983). Federal merit pay: A longitudinal analysis. *Public Administration Review, 43*(4), 315–325. doi:10.2307/975834

Radnor, Z. (2008). Muddled, massaging, manoeuvring or manipulated? A typology of organizational gaming. *International Journal of Productivity and Performance Management, 57*(4), 316–328. doi:10.1108/17410400810867526

Russia 2025: Resetting the Talent Balance. (n.d.). *The Boston Consulting Group*. Retrieved from http://d-russia.ru/wp-content/uploads/2017/11/Skills_Outline_web_tcm26-175469.pdf

Smith, P. (1995). On the unintended consequences of publishing performance data in the public sector. *International Journal of Public Administration, 18*(2/3), 277–310. doi:10.1080/01900699508525011

Wathne, K. H., & Heide, J. B. (2000). Opportunism in interfirm relationships: Forms, outcomes, and solutions. *Journal of Marketing, 64*(4), 36–51. doi:10.1509/jmkg.64.4.36.18070

Williamson, O. E. (1985). The Economic Institutions of Capitalism. Firms, Markets, Relational Contracting. The Free Press.

KEY TERMS AND DEFINITIONS

Agency Costs: The owners' costs for compensation, rectification, and insurance against emerging agency problems, compensation for the consequences of such conflicts are called agency costs.

Agency Relations: Relations that arise between the owners of the companies (principals) and the top managers (agents) they hire, and who are delegated the rights to manage the assets owned by shareholders.

Agent's Loyalty: The relationship of trust between the manager and the dominant owner, based on experience working together, being the same team players, clan affinity.

Agent's Utility: Personal qualities of the agent, that allow to ensure high management efficiency, reduce potential agency problems and increase the value of the business.

Gaming: Practice of opportunistic behavior when the agent uses the established regularities and procedures for seeking self-interest, though initially such norms were not meant for this.

Incomplete Contract: Contract, executed between the principal and the agent, which cannot specify all the essential job requirements to assigned work.

Opportunistic Behavior: The behavior when the agent can provide the principal with incomplete or distorted information, can pursue self-interests notwithstanding formal and conventional norms, and make profit regardless the owner's interests.

ENDNOTES

1 The Boston Consulting Group conducted an assessment of the requirements to personnel in conditions of digitalization (Russia-2015, 2017). The company stated a necessity to replace the top managers with such skills as "Ability" and "Rule" by the top managers with the skill "Knowledge" as this skill implies analytical work, improvisation, creativity, ability to work in situations of uncertainty, autonomy in decision-making.

2 Research of the shareholding in Russian corporations shows that, as a rule, there is only one or at the most two dominant shareholders in domestic companies. Therefore, speaking about the principals, we will mean the dominant owners.

Chapter 8
Corporate Governance Efficiency:
Automation of Corporate Governance Procedures

Sergey Nikolaevich Endutkin
Kutafin Moscow State Law University (MSAL), Russia

ABSTRACT

Since the time of the first corporations, shareholders have expected boards to manage corporate governance processes in the best way. At the same time, the era of digital technology can significantly increase the effectiveness of corporate governance procedures through automation of corporate governance procedures as business processes. The board of directors and the corporate secretary can rely on performance indicators and manage the effectiveness of corporate governance processes. This chapter discusses opportunities for improving the business processes, including automation and analytics. The author considers approaches to project management of corporate governance procedures automation and its limitations.

INTRODUCTION

Advanced technologies of the 21st century allow companies to work more efficiently with data and optimize business processes. However, some areas in companies exploit the insufficient capacity of available data. One of these areas is corporate governance procedures.

Corporate information systems, which record business transactions and fiscal liabilities, have amassed material data that may be of interest to investors and decision-makers. Top managers need such data to make their day-to-day decisions and justify their strategic vision, and the board of directors and shareholders need data to see that the executive decisions are justified, and the underlying information is complete and valid.

DOI: 10.4018/978-1-7998-2011-6.ch008

Moreover, the development of automation project requirements simplifies business processes, automates routine, and accelerates business processes.

Thus, it is reasonable to set at least two goals for automation projects:

- manage information recording and storage and stakeholders' access to information systems,
- develop algorithms for corporate governance decision-making, and
- visualize digital data related to corporate business.

BACKGROUND

While boards are quite conservative due to their sensitivity and overregulation, the possibilities of automation in corporate governance draw attention of researchers and corporations.

Emerging research suggests serious consequences for boards that continue to ignore or delegate enterprise-level technology governance (Valentine, 2014).

There are two trends affecting the use of accumulated information and its disclosure to investors. The core OECD public markets suffer from a saturation of disclosure requirements —there is too much, not too little of it. The number of pages in the annual reports of UK FTSE 300 companies have on average more than trebled in the last 20 years. Investors have probably more information than they can use, and often the forest is lost to the trees. Here is no indication that they will use boards less or in significantly different ways than their predecessors. The only thing that has probably changed is the funding of it all—the "food chain" works differently: it is now less about public equity markets and more about private flows of capital (Nestor, 2018).

The technology must offer users and participants 'connectivity', 'choice', and 'convenience'. Nevertheless, it should also enable monetization, as well as analytical (including artificial intelligence) activities (Fenwick, McCahery, & Vermeulen, 2019).

METHODOLOGY

Prerequisites

Between 2010 and 2015, the author researched the various aspects of corporate governance from the inside and viewed corporate governance as a combination of business processes. The author worked as a corporate secretary, corporate governance director, HR director, and board member for engineering plants and distribution networks in car manufacturing.

The scope of corporate governance covered up to 100 joint-stock companies and limited liability companies simultaneously. Shareholders within the author's responsibility area were global automotive manufacturers, and more than 5,000 professional investors and non-professional private shareholders.

The author's task was to develop and implement the standards and processes for corporate governance. Shareholders expected to improve the manageability of disparate companies and the transparency and validity of reporting and protect their investments in technology development and upgrading.

Table 1. The average performance of one corporate secretary

	2010	2014	2017
Companies in the area of responsibility, per year	8	15	10
Procedures per year across all companies	50	850	600
Procedures per year per company	6.3	56.7	60

Approach to Research and Methodology

In 2016-2018, the author researched corporate governance processes to identify the possibilities for automation and system design and fit them into corporate processes.

The author researched twelve quantitative and qualitative metrics of corporate governance, in particular, the information and organizational support of more than 70 boards at the same time. The author used the following methods to investigate this area and formulate his proposals:

- researching the relevant corporate policies and procedures and legal documents,
- conducting the survey of shareholders, board members, and other stakeholders in the form of questionnaires and interviews,
- identifying and studying the best corporate governance practice used by top international players in the motor industry,
- describing 'as is' business processes in corporate governance, including the quantitative assessment of corporate processes and specifying the scope and duration of business milestones, the role of persons involved, and their subordination structure,
- assessing and identifying backup steps and roles,
- identifying a mismatch between responsibility for milestone results and the scope of authority,
- a quantitative assessment of the performance, efficiency, and effectiveness of employees involved in a business process, including corporate secretaries,
- modeling target business processes for corporate governance and their approval with shareholders and boards, in particular, calculating the target indicators of performance, efficiency, and effectiveness,
- reviewing the intermediate and final results of implementing the target business processes of corporate governance, and
- consistently collecting data and calculating the qualitative and quantitative metrics of corporate processes.

Practical Results

The above research and measures applied allowed achieving the shareholders' objectives. Importantly, the preparation and automation have improved the performance of the corporate secretary's office as follows:

Due to this performance improvement, the number of corporate secretaries eventually went down from 6 in 2010 to 3 in 2014 to 2 in 2017.

Due to this performance improvement, the number of corporate secretaries eventually went down from 6 in 2010 to 3 in 2014 to 2 in 2017.

The research of McKinsey Global Institute found that despite the evident positive effect of automation, it will cause occupational changes and even opposition from workers whose jobs could be lost to automation (McKinsey Global Institute, 2017).

Regarding the automation of corporate secretary's operations, the author envisaged additional motivation for employees to use a new information system and possibilities to transfer the holding company's employees whose jobs are automated to other positions in the company

CORPORATE SECRETARY: BASIC FUNCTIONS

The corporate service responsible for corporate governance must ensure a continuous operation of the management and supervisory bodies. This is one of the key goals, which consists of many repetitive operations based on law, regulatory requirements, and by-laws.

Corporate governance functions with the highest level of routine operations include:

- holding corporate events and keeping a corporate calendar; holding the Board of directors meetings, and general meetings of shareholders or members
- processing the applications of subsidiaries and affiliates to the board of directors, and
- monitoring and analysis of business process performance

All of these functions can be automated. This chapter discusses possibilities, challenges, limitations and approaches related to automation. The author also considers what actions need to be taken before automating business processes and what internal resources to improve efficiency a company can find in the field of corporate governance.

CORPORATE PROCEDURE LANDSCAPE

The author assumes that his proposed approach to automation will be sought after by companies with non-linear team management models, which are typical for matrix and 'parent company – subsidiary' models.

Matrix Management Model

According to the matrix model, the unit head on the subsidiary level reports to her direct executive under their employment contract. At the same time, the subsidiary unit manager reports to the relevant functional manager at the parent company or corporate center.

The matrix management model as an approach to building and developing the corporate governance system faces occasional highs and lows. The authors believe this model to be in crisis as it is inconsistent with one of the key business principles, i.e. mobility and fast decision-making. Fast decision-making is required to roll out and test products and monitor the market's response.

Still, the matrix model remains a powerful tool to set up holding companies. A vertical direct connection within the same role can enable consistent decision-making without engaging the subsidiary CEO or managing director for approval or task-setting.

Parent Company Management Models

A parent company that plays the role of an operating and holding company at the same time is a common business scenario. The top-management team at such parent company is focused on supporting and developing the company's operations. For example, if the parent company is a large-size manufacturer, an individual unit director will focus on managing its functional operations related to the company's core business. With this approach to management, such director will leave the subsidiary as a secondary priority. Such director will focus on managing their own specific operations at best and delegate all other functions to the top management of the subsidiary or affiliate.

APPROVAL AS A BUSINESS PROCESS

Approval Process as a Service

The following issues arise when the parent company combines the operating management of its holding company and the governance of its subsidiary.

Every time when the corporate center makes any management decision related to its managed company, it will give such company a secondary priority compared with the parent company. This may be a threat, which can tip the balance in favor of the management company, and managers hired to manage the company, or the board of directors can infringe shareholder rights.

Besides, top managers in a large parent company will have conflicts among themselves. Such conflicts also pose a threat if the top management team confront each other in the subsidiary or the board of directors or over the need to approve their subsidiary decisions as part of the matrix management model. The authors believe that the matrix management model takes conflicts down to the level of subsidiaries whenever they arise at the parent company.

How can the corporate center handle such conflicts while being the operating company at the same time? The most obvious way is to assign the functions of the corporate center to a separate unit in the parent company and grant it the relevant powers. Such a unit will be usually referred to as the "corporate governance service" or "corporate center". It will manage all units and matters, such as the corporate secretary, legal service, planning and analysis, asset safety and security, etc.

Assigning corporate governance functions to a separate unit can be beneficial but also can become an intermediate stage in building the management structure. The next step will be to hire a management company to manage the subsidiary. Then the parent company will act as the asset owner only and may nominate members to the board of directors.

If a more deep-going separation between corporate and operating functions is needed at the level of the parent company, the company can establish a separate legal entity to transfer the ownership of subsidiaries. Then corporate governance will be carried out on behalf of such new holding company.

The authors discuss corporate governance models because they determine the business process owner.

Corporate Secretary

It is important to determine the position of the process service vendor - the corporate secretary - within the holding company. When a company improves its business processes and performance, whether or not by using automation, it must keep in mind that such improvement is made for the benefit of business and shareholders rather than for the sake of an individual corporate secretary. Replacing the customer's interest with the corporate secretary's personal needs is unlikely to attend to customer satisfaction with changes.

If the company wishes to automate its routine operations and simplify submission and approval processes, its goal will be not to make it easier for the secretary to prepare a document package but to accelerate and improve approval processes at all stages:

- from identifying the need for approval to obtaining an approval decision,
- from approval to compliance, and
- from compliance to reviewing compliance reports.

Based on such automation goal, the authors will generate their expectations and view the possibilities of automation.

Corporate Secretary Functions

The authors recommend looking at the corporate secretary's role in more detail to define areas for automation.

The corporate secretary is responsible for checking draft decisions for compliance with law and by-laws, whether or not statutory. By checking the validity and compliance of any project with internal standards and any other applicable documents (e.g. strategy, budget, policies, and procedures), the corporate secretary affects the balance of company's and shareholders' interests.

The corporate secretary office develops and implements procedure rules and keeps the corporate calendar.

It is important to include corporate events in the calendar not only for compliance with law and by-laws as may be required. The corporate secretary must take care of other units, such as financial and production, which may need to make some extraordinary transactions subject to the approval of the board or the meeting of shareholders or members during the year. The corporate secretary can include approval processes related to such transactions in the corporate calendar and plan her workload.

Our experience in corporate governance projects showed that the corporate secretary often fails to ensure a regular control of compliance with decisions. The authors recommend that the corporate secretary takes due care of such function as long as such control is the only way to oversee compliance. For example, such control identifies whether or not any transaction complies with the approved terms and conditions.

The corporate secretary provides advisory services and discloses complete and valid information to the board. While some members of the board may not be the company employees, the corporate secretary can become their reliable source of complete and valid company information. Automation will set up a good communication channel and interface between the board and the corporate secretary.

Approval Process

The subsidiary (managed company) submits a request for approval to the management company through the corporate secretary. It is a good practice to have such a request made in a standard approved form with an attached standard document package and have it approved under the rule known to and approved by the board. This request will be approved by the corporate center and then registered with the CEO and sent for approval to the board of directors.

It is no easy task to automate even such a simple process because it involves many actors:

- the subsidiary or managed company,
- the management company, and
- the board, shareholders, or members.

The task gets even more complicated if the board includes shareholders' employees nominated to the board of directors. In fact, any process actor - from a subsidiary to shareholders whose employees are nominated to the board - can use different systems for document and business process management and different rules for submissions and approvals.

The automation challenge is to bring together such separate document management systems and their management rules. This issue must be addressed before automation starts. The authors address this and other challenges to be dealt with during automation.

CORPORATE PROCEDURE ISSUES AND SOLUTIONS

Compliance

The same documents and matters put to the vote usually contain the finite set of risks to be assessed by the corporate secretary. Similar risks require similar assessment processes.

The company management may expect that once a loan agreement has been agreed upon and approved by the board under the charter, the next request related to any similar loan agreement will be successfully agreed upon and approved in the same procedure, other conditions being equal.

A standard procedure and formalized policy related to risk management will enable the company to estimate whether or not the next loan agreement will be agreed and approved. The formalization will enable the company to automate a) the estimates of such process success and b) the selection of approval process pathways.

While an authorized approver is appointed by the charter or law, such choice can be automated at the step when the subsidiary or managed company completes its submission.

Besides, the authors recommend automating the selection and launching of the approval pathway depending on the type of submission and approvers. For example, the board approval pathway for a transaction will include certain board committees as approval units. To submit such transaction to the meeting of shareholders or members, the pathway may add some more approvers and consultants to obtain the relevant reports and opinions.

Such software functionality will eliminate errors related to the incorrect selection of authority and approvers. This will reduce the requirements for employees responsible for launching submissions for approval.

Amending Submissions

Another challenge related to the approval process with the board is to deal with too many changes in submissions made by the authorized units of the corporate center.

For example, a subsidiary asks for prior approval of a two-year loan at 3 percent per annum. Additionally, this subsidiary asks to approve a guarantee to the lender from the parent company. As a potential lender, the subsidiary mentions one member of the holding company and an independent company, which is not controlled by the parent company or the subsidiary.

As part of the approval process, the parent company reviews the transaction and proposes its own terms. For example,

- the financial unit confirmed the loan term but proposed a two-percent rate instead of 3%;
- the legal unit refused to approve the parent company's guarantee with a view to restrictions imposed by the board but said it would not object to a bank guarantee;
- the compliance unit refused to approve such a loan from an independent company but approved a loan from a holding company member.

As part of a default document management process, every unit mentioned above refused to approve and sent the submission for updating to include their proposals. The corporate secretary will face the following risks:

- in-house incoherence or misalignment.

The risk here is that every unit makes its proposals and changes to the initial submission without thinking of the consequences to other services.

- data loss.

Any approver can use some other communication channels along with the document management system, which processed the submission. There is a threat of data loss due to multiple communication channels used and the corporate secretary or submitter is unable to identify the submission status and changes made.

- overlapping submission processing operations.

The risk is when the subsidiary must provide the same information and documents upon the parent company's request more than once due to data loss.

- the violation of regulations.

The risk is missing preclusive terms imposed by law or regulations and any other deadlines related to the company's obligations.

To avoid such risks, the authors recommend the company to have approved a special card stating the terms to be approved rather than use the full document for this purpose. Technologically speaking, the approval of such a card can be compared to a document wizard:

- the corporate secretary at the parent company will generate templates for each type of matters reserved for the board or the parent company;
- such templates will consist of logical units with embedded links in the form of a decision-tree;
- a questionnaire for submitters will be developed based on such decision chain. Answers to questions will determine any further questions. For example, the answer to the question related to the loan term - two years - in the above case will exclude questions that can arise if no definite loan term is stated. The submission card is generated based on such questionnaire;
- the subsidiary submitter will generate a request by completing such a questionnaire in the document wizard;
- when such submission is generated, the software program will create a document card with the main terms and conditions to be approved. Any additional materials are attached to such card;
- as mentioned earlier, the program will automatically create a text file with the full submission text based on such card. The process participants can use the card to open its full text and attachments;
- the software uses completed submission card fields to define a) the need for corporate approval, b) authorized approvers, and c) the preconfigured approval pathway with the parent company;
- the parent company approvers will be assigned to approve the submission in the document management system. But they do not have to open long text files and attached documents because the program will offer them the full summary card.

Approvers can change any authorized card fields. For example, the financial unit will change 3% per annum to 2%. The system will store the updated file with a new figure of 2% automatically. Besides, it will store the log indicating who has made changes and when and both the initial and updated term. The process can be set so as to authorize every unit to change only the fields that are referred to their powers. Any approver can review all text submissions and attached documents, including the draft loan agreement, which is amended by the financial service from 3% to 2%.

The authors believe that such approval settings together with the submission wizard will lower requirements for the qualification of an employee responsible for creating such approval task in the system and reduce the workload on approvers and submitters and accelerate the approval process. This will enable the corporate secretary to manage the performance of all process participants.

CORPORATE PROCESS PERFORMANCE: SOLUTIONS AND RECOMMENDATIONS

The corporate secretary is responsible for accepting and processing submissions and organizing the meetings of shareholders and the board. This performance can be measured by reviewing the performance of all actors involved.

If submissions are processed by more than one employee at each approval step, such metrics will allow comparing their performance to reveal any deviations and understand their reasons.

Efficiency can be assessed by using performance metrics. The most common metrics include the following.

1. **Submission acceptance and processing time.** Measured in minutes or hours per request. This metric defines how fast the submission is accepted.

The authors suggest setting the limit of time to accept the task and sending alerts to executives if the submission is not accepted within the set limit of time or shortly before expiry.

2. **The number of processes completed over a period of time.** Measured in the number of procedures per calendar month, quarter, half-year or year. Authors believe there is no point in setting a period shorter than one month as the monthly load varies and loads may become irregular. As our experience shows, the workload is balanced out within a one-month time horizon.

Monthly metric shows peak values and determine seasonal workloads. For example, an IT company, where authors audited business processes for automation purposes, found out that it has mistakenly assumed that the load of the corporate secretary office peaked at the turn of each financial year. The analysis showed that the real peak occurred three months later. The company was launching many new projects at the beginning of each financial year after their plans and budgets for the next year had been approved. Such data allowed the company to improve the planning of their corporate service workload and reschedule vacations to ensure continuous operations during peak months.

3. **The average time per process by process type.** This metric shows the timing of each process from submission to the final decision. The authors recommend introducing gradation by the type of process depending on the approver's authority, its definition by the charter or law, and the complexity of draft decisions to be approved. This metric is measured in minutes or hours per process.

Metric can be used to consider which process takes reasonable time and which deviates from standards. How to deal with the different levels of the task complexity to assess this metric reasonably?

The degree of complexity can depend on the type of issue to be addressed, the participants in the deal to be approved, the jurisdiction of the counterparty to the approved transaction, and the law governing such a transaction. This list is not final and can be continued.

The authors recommend identifying the dependence of the process average time on the approver who is in charge of the matter. This metric helped us to identify company units, which submissions take more time to approve compared with other submissions of the same degree of complexity. Such units showed less care about generating their submissions and collecting data required for their review.

If the company identifies units, which approval processes are less successful, it can understand the reasons for such poor statistics and take remedial actions.

4. **No delays in process timelines set by law and in-house regulations.** This is a quantitative metric, which is measured easily - the fact of delay is either there or not.

The authors recommend the company not only to rank actors by this metric but also look for connections between data related to submitters and those related to the type and conditions of their submissions. This will help us to establish what factors influence the delay. The authors' experience shows that delays are often caused by incomprehensible documents, delayed submissions, technical errors in requests and attached documents, the absence of documents required for approval, such as the reports of advisors and compliance officers and legal opinions, and the need to clarify certain aspects of the approved matter.

5. **Approval iterations.** This is an important quantitative metric that shows how many attempts a company has made to have its submission approved. The unreasonable number of iterations (e.g. more than two) can signal both individual and critical issues. For example, if the number of iterations exceeds the reasonable level, this can mean that the submitter's employee is not qualified for making submissions. This issue can be solved easily by educating such an employee about communication problems. If such poor statistics becomes wide-spread, it can indicate some systemic issues, such as the lack of communications among units or the failure by a subsidiary to understand management standards adopted by the parent company or unreasonable formalism in relations.

How to Use These Metrics?

The above metrics alone have no meaning other than showing delays. For them to become a meaningful foundation of data-driven management, the authors recommend to do the following:

- at the very minimum, compare metrics for the current and the relevant previous period. This can be done in terms of employees, units or business process types. It seems reasonable to make adjustments for any changes incorporated from the previous period. For example, there may be changes related to submission rules, approvers and their roles, management authorities, etc.

- at the maximum, use comprehensive statistical tools for a more detailed data review. With no big data, a business analyst can do with expert opinions and minimal data verifications, such as employee interviews.

How to Obtain Data for Analysis?

Today, business is managed by a wide range of information systems. They integrate with varying degrees of success, can run independently, and automate most business processes. The software supports document management, business processes, finance, accounting, HR, knowledge, contracts, and electronic voting. Employees communicate through chat rooms or emails.

Information systems have gathered huge arrays of data related to company's business and processes, and its employees' habits and performance. Why not use such data to enhance performance and management?

Still, the business faces significant challenges in implementing this idea as it poses the following questions:

- where do we get such data?
- where do we process it and which algorithms to use?
- who needs the analysis outcomes?
- how do we visualize this analysis?
- what do we do with the deliverables and what decisions shall we make?

Data Analysis Potential

If a company runs electronic document management and business process systems, analysis data can be downloaded from any available electronic spreadsheets.

Unfortunately, document management systems have limited functionality to analyze workloads and tasks. Companies still have to use electronic spreadsheets or dedicated professional software. For example, business intelligence software visualizes spreadsheet data as dashboards to make it easier to compare data by different criteria at different time. This seems not enough as companies want the software to answer their question "what will happen next?" based on the accumulated employee and process data. Predictive analytics software can answer this question. It is focused on HR and finance management at any level. Its advantages include the user-friendly and customized visualization of individual workload, project completion status, resources used, workload drivers (services and counterparties), and employee ranking. Predictive analytics software functions can include conflict forecasting, current conflict deepening, employee layoff and default risks.

But the business expects even more and along with questions "what is going on?" and "what will happen next?" it wants to know "what needs to be done for timely and high-quality completion?".

If the corporate secretary finds the relationship between business process speed and performance factors that are contained in such information systems, she can manage performance at all levels, from submitters to approvers to the board of directors. In terms of business process performance, the board members are the same employees as the corporate secretary and other approval actors. Their performance can be measured by the same rules.

Consider this example.

Selecting an Employee for Submission Approval

The corporate secretary office prepares documents to have a loan agreement approved by the board of directors. The corporate secretary must select one of its three reports to assign the task of having the request prepared and approved by date X. The authors deliberately simplify the task for clarity and assume that the task will be deemed to have been completed if the application is approved or rejected by date X.

The corporate secretary is aware that Andy will need more approval iterations for this submission than Mary or Alex.

Mary is known to have any submission approved by only one iteration.

Alex will need more than one iteration but fewer than Andy usually needs.

The corporate secretary also knows that Mary needs more time to process submissions than Andy or Alex. Alex is the fastest of all but spends much more time than Andy or Maria out of the office at meetings.

Maria spends more time in the office than all other employees. At work, Maria spends more time to complete a task similar to the one that needs to be done by date X. Alex spends less time on a similar task at the workplace than Maria or Andy.

The corporate secretary knows that all three have an equal workload by date X with Maria's being slightly less than the others.

Maria is the slowest at doing such job but it takes her only one iteration. The above means that Maria will cope with the task some time or other, regardless of the initial submission quality. Maria will focus only on this task judging by the metrics of time in the office and time spent on such task.

Maria is very well-liked. Whatever the task, she will cope. Even with improper submissions and missing documents, Maria will improve them and find the required documents. Colleagues praise Maria to her executives.

Alex is the fastest to do this job but she needs several iterations. She still has time to do a lot of additional work, both in the office and outside. This means that Alex will review improper submissions and return them to the submitter marking any follow-up issues. Still, it is not unlikely that the submitter of such improper request will fail to remedy issues pointed out by Alex and she will have to follow up with issues once again. In real life, colleagues complain about Alex to her executives and ask to give all their submissions to Maria.

Andy's metrics look worse than Alex's or Maria's. He is not so good at work as Maria or Alex.

Who will the corporate secretary select to assign the job to be completed by date X? The authors suggest assigning the job to Alex and here's why.

With equal workload but higher performance, Alex is more likely to do the job on time. Alex is fast at communicating her issues and always have enough time to remedy them and have the documents approved one more time. With Maria, there is a risk of missing the deadline because Maria remedies all submitters' defects doing their job for them but has no direct access to their documents.

Andy is the least likely to complete the task by the deadline, judging by his metrics, so he is out of the question.

With Maria, the company pays twice for having the same job done - first time, when submitters prepare their documents and the second time when Maria corrects their mistakes.

In this real example, the authors recommended the corporate secretary to do the following:

- educate submitters about preparing high-quality submissions;
- simplify submission forms;
- standardize the required documents depending on the issue;
- explain to Maria that by not saying "no" to submitters she fails to enhance the process performance and she has to change her attitude and stop doing other people's job.

This case with Maria, Andy and Alex is a good example that automation of the business process without a prior audit and simplifying is considered by the authors to be ineffective. Most likely, automation would speed up the entry of tasks into the corporate secretariat, but it would not lead to a shortening of the deadlines for the implementation of incoming tasks from colleagues by employees of the corporate secretariat. In this case, as the authors believe, the corporate secretariat would become a "bottleneck" of the business process.

Coming Up with the Best Business Process

Let's assume that it takes the management company one month to approve the submission for a loan agreement. Both, the approver and the submitter, wish to make the process "better".

What does it mean "better"? In figures, such as the number of steps in a time period, "better" will mean cutting steps and time spent on such a process.

This is the best option. If the company is not sure how many steps or how much time to cut for the process to make it "better", it is recommended to indicate any fewer steps to develop the target business process and then think how the company can use fewer steps to complete the procedure.

For example, if the procedure has ten steps, the company can seek to reduce them to five. If the company realizes that it is unable to complete the process in five steps, it can use six steps, to begin with, which will be still better than ten.

This approach brings about a natural constraint. When the owners of the "better" target process work for one company for a long time, they limit their access to the best practice of other companies unless they keep sharing their experience with peers. If they do, they can ask questions to understand how other companies implement the same process and how long it takes. You can expect your peers to have better performance and use their practice.

Approval Process Automation at the Board Level

As mentioned above, the board members can have no document management system in place or run any other system, which is different from the one used by the management company.

Besides, the board members can be employed by some other parent organization, which has its own rules, e.g. those requiring the board members to negotiate all of their decision with the company.

Moreover, the board member can be a member of any other boards in the companies, of which the secretary is unaware. Granting such board member access to the company's document management system through an account can be unreasonable because such a board member may have too many accounts in other document management systems proportionately to the boards where they sit. Such a board member may decide against using corporate accounts. She may propose that company secretaries in all companies where she is a board member use her personal email or refer them to her personal assistant's email.

Corporate secretaries have to deal with the same issue. They need a single system account and access to all directors with whom they have to deal with.

Such solutions are available, and they enable the corporate secretary and the board members to use one software product and keep the corporate calendar, generate meeting agendas, call meetings, distribute materials to the board, and vote on the agenda items.

Onboarding New Board Members

Let's assume the company holds the annual meeting of shareholders or members and elects the new board of directors.

The new board needs to be oriented to be aware of which important issues have been addressed by their peers and which items have been or must be included in the agenda. This is similar to the orientation of a new employee where they get to know their new job and become acquainted with the work environment. They go through the adaptation process. New board members also need such adaptation.

The authors recommend setting a requirement for automation products where any new board member will have easy access to all previous decisions and their supporting documents, such as reports and opinions, and the corporate event calendar.

Besides, any new or existing board member may wish to have access to information related to compliance and implementation. The corporate calendar automation solution, therefore, must have such a function.

Any new board member should be aware of the rules established for corporate processes outside and inside the board of directors and submitters and approvers before their request is reviewed by the board meeting. Thus, automation software should embed pathways for approval and bringing to the vote of any submissions, both inside and outside the board of directors, and the need to have a submission reviewed by the board committee.

Such software should also involve the corporate secretary who continues to monitor approval processes inside the board and refer them to the relevant units if there are any issues.

The Board Response to Automation

Is the board of directors operating or formal?

The operating board of directors can include independent directors and employees and members of a management company, direct shareholder, beneficiary or a key director. Such a board would like to accelerate its proceedings.

The automation software will improve the transparency of communications involving the company, corporate secretary, and board members. The board operations become more transparent.

Surprisingly, more transparency can invite the board's objections to automation because they will have no reason to delay their decisions on a pretext of the need to review submissions and obtain more information. Once the company has its business processes described and regulated and automated, no board members will be able to avoid their duties without a reason.

While automation may not improve performance in the short term, it will identify inactive board members who have lost interest in their job after their election.

Automation of Submissions

After establishing a reliable information space, the authors suggest making the following requirements for automation:

- generating requests to the board based on data contained in the accounting systems of subsidiaries and affiliates.

This means that the corporate secretary will use a document management template or document wizard to generate submissions and complete only those fields that are related to such a request. All other fields, such as board member and company details, approval criteria, transaction cost calculation, and interest, may be filled out automatically based on the system data;

- the resulting submission package, including questionnaires, voting ballots, the resolution on the board meeting call, and board minutes, will be generated automatically by completing a request for calling a board meeting.

The rationale is as follows: the request fields overlap with those in the resulting documents. For example, "Please approve the transaction on such-and-such conditions, on such-and-such legal grounds according to xxx section of the charter or law" set out in a submission overlaps with the board minutes, ballot, questionnaire or the chair's resolution to call the board meeting;

- if changes are made in the course of approval by the management company, such changes will be automatically shown in the resulting document package.

This approach allows the corporate secretary to obtain requests together with final draft documents, cut routine tasks and errors in generating draft minutes and focus on having submissions approved by the relevant directors of the management company.

It will be a good practice to incorporate automatic notification of the subsidiary trying to change the approved and agreed transactions after prior approval. This will relieve the corporate secretary of the need to check compliance manually and the subsidiary of the need to prepare reports.

AUTOMATION SOLUTIONS

Business Processes Subject to Automation

The automation software market survey shows that the following operations can be automated:

- the corporate secretary's office management, task setting, supervision, and escalation;
- document management, including correspondence processing and tasks from in-house and outside customers;
- signing and approval;
- compliance and implementation control;
- organizing the meetings of management bodies, including preparing materials, communicating with the board members, and compliance control;
- voting;
- generating documents;
- Know Your Client;
- knowledge management;
- corporate calendar.

Every product has limitations and advantages, with new functions and features being developed consistently. It makes sense to review the market and make informed decisions if the board is willing to automate.

The authors suggest considering the following reasonable functions at the level of *subsidiary - parent company* and managed company - managing company:

- preparing requests, minutes, and supporting documents by using the document wizard and templates in document management and business process systems;
- HR and task management.

Electronic document management and business process systems will become a good channel for setting tasks and generating reports; office management software will help the company to manage workload and generate employee performance reports.

To automate processes at the level of *corporate center - board of directors*, the authors recommend the following automation process:

- incorporate document wizards and templates into document management and business process systems.

They are used to generate submissions to management bodies and get their feedback;

- dedicated software to manage tasks and affairs for the corporate secretary.

This will bring together the corporate secretary and board members into one landscape and help them to keep the corporate calendar and send documents, organize and hold meetings and remote electronic voting.

The authors recommend using dedicated compliance and KYC automation software at all levels.

It is also recommended to integrate the corporate secretary management solutions into the HR management system to expand analysis and decision-making and improve employee performance and relieve the corporate secretary of manual operations related to metrics and employee performance analysis.

Limitations of Automation

Consider the following limitations in selecting software:

- there is no universal solution;
- the company may have a document management system in place; therefore, new products must seamlessly integrate with their existing system;
- if the company chooses more than one automation product, decide whether or not they need integration and who will be in charge of such integration and automation processes.

Along with specifications and product selection, the key automation challenge is to select a company in charge of implementation and integration. If you contact an individual vendor, you will most likely get a solution to address just one challenge on your approval pathway.

System integrators will help you to match your automation needs with real software functionality and their customization potential. The system integrator competence is no less important than the basic functionality of software.

SOLUTIONS AND RECOMMENDATIONS: AUTOMATION PROJECT

Project-Based Approach

As a rule, corporate governance units have no significant experience in automating their operations. For mother of them, it is limited to implementing document management systems and integrated individual dedicated solutions. This may be due to the following:

- their automation experience is limited to the installation of retail software related to specific functions, e.g. verifying counterparties;
- corporate governance automation requires the cross-functional engagement of many company units;
- there is no demand for change from the board of directors;
- they have found software tested by corporate secretaries nonfunctional, inconvenient, and too expensive;
- legal education and professional training include no skills required for automation, such as project management, business analysis, organizational development, etc.

Process automation involves all approvers of the holding company, in-house customers who send submissions, business advisors, and analysts.

It is reasonable to create an automation project team focused on the development and approval of the automation statement of work. While developing the statement of work, the team will shape the vision of the future approval process, target timeline, and describe documents to be created during the approval process.

The most advanced ideas related to corporate process improvement will be most valued. The statement of work together with vendor consultations will help the team to understand current and future automation options, which can satisfy your needs.

Automation may meet only some of your expectations, but it will help you to achieve more results through organizational measures.

Some automation options offered by vendors will show you alternative pathways. The authors recommend considering the limitations of automation to avoid cost and time overrun.

Automation Priorities

While it is impossible to automate the whole system and there is no universal solution, it is advisable to look at the automation sequence.

Firstly, you need to upgrade or start using the maximal functions of the existing document management or business process system. Consult with your IT department to understand which functions are not used by the corporate secretary and how to improve your existing system to meet your expectations. They will make some interesting proposals.

Secondly, simplify and standardize your corporate process documents. Standardize such documents as process requests, executive summary, voting ballots, and board meeting minutes. Standard documents can be created by using templates in the document management or business process systems or document wizards. This will eliminate errors in final documents.

Thirdly, review the lists, roles, and number of approvers. If any approver fails to give feedback, which can terminate approval and lead to rejection, it makes no sense to grant them full approval authority. Limit it to notifications to keep them informed of the process.

Finally, you can proceed with the board automation after your business process has been improved, documents simplified, and technical errors eliminated.

Consider how to transfer current tasks to your new system. Implementation is accompanied by developing new regulatory documents (rules, policies, and new documents) and the training of personnel involved in the operating of a new system.

The authors recommend reviewing employee incentives for those who will transfer to running such a new system.

Key Automation Project Stages

The authors recommend that companies describe the current business process specifying its steps and timeline before planning the target business process, including its launch from the managed company, approval by the corporate center, and preparing the required document package. This will make it easier to cut steps and time in the target project. Otherwise, seeking to improve and give a detailed description of the process, the company risks involving more steps and participants in a new process.

Such reduced new numbers of steps and timing will become the basis for the project's KPIs.

You will need to make effective your legal and electronic documents, amend regulations, including those related to the board of directors, if the board elects to use electronic voting, and determine, which decisions the board will make by electronic voting.

It is important to select the approval pathway - umbrella or sequential - and define whether or not to use the default approval procedure, i.e. whether or not approval is deemed to have been given if there is no response from the approver.

You need to take care of your data safety, including data processing by the board and hired advisors and experts.

Benefits of Automation

The high-quality automation of corporate governance will bring significant benefits:

No routine:

- Automated information download from the accounting system and open online sources;
- Task completion status is available in real time;
- Electronic document management.

Efficient HR management:

- Time management by unit, company, project, and employee;
- Task status and workload analysis;
- Project task history in one place;
- Distributed team management;
- Event notification;
- KPI measurement;

Legal operations quality:

- Personal account and available legal services
- Chat rooms in lieu of emails and internal memos
- Accelerated task acceptance
- Standard solutions to standard tasks

Customer relations:

- Access to tasks
- Standard tasks and standards solutions
- Manageable timelines

Outlook for Automation

The author assumes there are ample opportunities to improve corporate processes by using predictive and prescriptive analytics as part of automation functional requirements.

The idea is as follows. The analysis of current corporate procedures and their participants in combination with predictive analytics allows describing the mathematical model of a business process and identifying connections between the process results and any factors that directly impact corporate processes but are non-evident to a corporate secretary. Besides, the model allows assessing the impact of such factors on performance and efficiency. Such connections are shown in the case of Maria, Andy, and Alex.

Thus, a corporate secretary will have the automation tool to handle three functions at once:

- enumerate possibilities for completing a job by taking into account the ability of employees and other persons involved to perform their tasks on time and with proper quality,
- assess the probability of completing a job based on a certain combination of individuals involved, and
- advise an option for the best completion with the highest probability or even the automated launch of the best route to perform a task in the information system.

Taking the case of Maria, Andy, and Alex as an example, the information system, which operates as described above, will select Alex for this job and save the corporate secretary the time needed to:

- review the job and select the best employees to complete it,
- assess the probability of completion by employees available,
- redistribute the workload among employees, and
- select one employee and assign the job to her.

Hypothesis Testing

The author tested this idea on corporate processes and analyzed data related to 80,000 operations completed by a business with a similar logic over three years. The process was related to the approval of agreements by a holding company based on a matrix system. The corporate center must have new and additional agreements approved upon request of their subsidiaries.

The author chose to review this approval process because it carries out many more processes over the same period than the corporate process, and this increases the reliability of the mathematical model underlying such a business process.

The mathematical model was developed to predict task completion probability by the corporate center and subsidiary employees. In a first approximation, the model showed a 65% predicting power of the task completion by an individual employee. After upgrading, the author expects this figure to reach 75%.

After training corporate secretaries in specific corporate data, the model will allow them to automatically identify and report any factors that can affect the completion of various milestones in a corporate process. A corporate secretary will be able to remedy any reasons for possible delays proactively.

CONCLUSION

The efficiency of automating corporate procedures and using data is a critical condition for company survival in the digital age. Corporate governance procedures automation as part of corporate governance is driven by the use of algorithms, on the one hand, and data about corporations, their stakeholders, and business affairs, on the other hand, to improve the performance and quality of corporate governance.

However, corporate secretaries with legal degrees, who are involved in automation projects, have no skills required for such job, and errors may be too costly. At the same time, the corporate secretary is responsible for doing their job. Companies and boards of directors require high performance and efficiency from their corporate secretaries and other top managers, which means they should do more with improved quality for less money.

The author believes that corporate governance configured as a business process, including the automation or routine tasks related to preparing and delivering information and documents to be approved by the board, will enhance the performance of employees involved in corporate processes, in particular, the board members. Besides, this will also drive stakeholders' satisfaction with the quality of corporate governance.

REFERENCES

Bankewitz, Aberg, & Teuchert. (2016). *Digitalization and Boards of Directors: A New Era of Corporate Governance?* doi:10.5430/bmr.v5n2p58

Brynjolfsson, E., & McAfee, A. (2014). *The second machine age: work, progress and prosperity in a time of brilliant technologies*. New York: W.W Norton and Company.

Fenwick, M., & McCahery, J.A., & Vermeulen. (2019). The End of 'Corporate' Governance: Hello 'Platform' Governance. *European Business Organization Law Review*, *1*(20), 171. doi:10.100740804-019-00137-z

George, G., Haas, M. R., & Pentland, A. (2014). Big data and management. *Academy of Management Journal*, *57*(2), 321–326. doi:10.5465/amj.2014.4002

Huse, M. (2007). *Boards, governance and value creation: The human side of corporate governance*. Cambridge, UK: Cambridge University Press; doi:10.1017/CBO9780511611070

Manyika, J., Lund, S., Chui, M., Bughin, J., Woetzel, J., Batra, P., . . . Sanghvi, S. (2017). *Jobs lost, jobs gained: What the future of work will mean for jobs, skills, and wages*. Retrieved from https://www.mckinsey.com/featured-insights/future-of-work/jobs-lost-jobs-gained-what-the-future-of-work-will-mean-for-jobs-skills-and-wages#part4

Minichilli, A., Zattoni, A., Nielsen, S., & Huse, M. (2012). Board task performance: An exploration of micro- and macro-level determinants of board effectiveness. *Journal of Organizational Behavior*, *33*(2), 193–215. doi:10.1002/job.743 PMID:23365485

Newell, S., & Marabelli, M. (2015). Strategic opportunities (and challenges) of algorithmic decision-making: A call for action on the long-term societal effects of "datification." *The Journal of Strategic Information Systems*, *24*(1), 3–14. doi:10.1016/j.jsis.2015.02.001

Stilpon Nestor. (2018). *Corporate Governance 2030: Thoughts on the Future of Corporate Governance.* Retrieved from https://corpgov.law.harvard.edu/2018/12/26/corporate-governance-2030-thoughts-on-the-future-of-corporate-governance

Valentine. (2014). *Are Boards Flying Blind When it Comes to Enterprise Technology Governance?* doi:10.1080/07366981.2014.881163

Valentine, E., & Stewart, G. (2013, Apr.). The emerging role of the board of directors in enterprise business technology governance. *International Journal of Disclosure and Governance*, 1–17.

Chapter 9
Benford's Law for Fraud Detection:
A Case Study of Portuguese Companies

Adriana Nunes
ISCA, University of Aveiro, Portugal

Helena Inácio
https://orcid.org/0000-0003-1281-2156
University of Aveiro, Portugal

Rui Pedro Marques
https://orcid.org/0000-0001-8449-0526
University of Aveiro, Portugal

ABSTRACT

In order to detect evidence of fraud effectively, it is essential for the auditor to be aware of new and differentiated methods. Thus, the auditor can identify and assess the risks of material misstatement so that auditing is as reliable as possible. In this sense, the relevance of the application of the Benford's Law arises in order to demonstrate that the identification of situations of greater risk of fraud is appropriate in auditing. The objective of this study is to analyze the behavior of 27,058 Portuguese companies.

INTRODUCTION

Corporate governance introduces management and supervisory measures for organizations improving their management. The number of public scandals has put the theme fraud on the agenda, discussing the effectiveness of corporate governance and auditing. As referred by Birol (2019) the basic corporate governance principles are applied for establishing more reliable financial reporting of firms even if in his study he did not proof that the corporate governance measures had reduce de fraud risk in Turkey. It is known that corporate governance and auditing contribute to the prevention and detection of fraud,

DOI: 10.4018/978-1-7998-2011-6.ch009

being that corporate governance is more focused on fraud committed by top management which is usually reflected in the manipulation of financial statements. But it is precisely this type of fraud that worries external auditors because it is the one that affects the reliability of financial statements.

According to Rigaud (1980) the success of an organization depends on timely decisions made right. This requires companies to invest in preventing and detecting evidence of fraud, as it can be committed by anyone and can have serious economic repercussions.

The auditor has a very important role in this field, because although the audit is not specifically aimed at finding fraud, errors or irregularities it is important to detect them in a timely manner. Thus, specific work methodologies should be adopted so that the existing resources are directed to the areas that present more risks in order to detect possible fraud.

The occurrence of fraud in addition to financial losses also entails large losses that cannot be measured, for example, the negative image that the company must face later and the consequent loss of confidence of employees, suppliers, customers and other stakeholders. In addition, the information contained in the financial statements should be as correct and real as possible since failure to detect material misstatements could influence the decision-making of several stakeholders.

Fraud can result from corruption, misappropriation of assets or fraudulent financial reporting. According to the Association of Certified Fraud Examiners (ACFE, 2018) in 2018, similarly to what happened in previous years, fraudulent financial reporting is the type of fraud, compared to misappropriation of assets and corruption, which has a higher percentage decrease of occurrence (10%) but is the one that causes higher losses (800,000 USD).

For Franceschetti and Koschtial (2013), fraud in financial statements is defined as the intentional misrepresentation of a company's financial conditions, through intentional distortion or omission of values or disclosures to deceive its users. On the one hand, there are companies that intend to present a better financial situation than the real, in order to deceive a potential investor, show results to partners, reassure creditors or influence stock prices. On the other hand, some companies intend to show inferior results to the real ones for fiscal reasons (de Almeida, 2015).

Detection of fraud in the financial statements requires more advanced procedures than just standard audit procedures (Asllani & Naco, 2014). It is in this sense that the Benford's Law can be an advantage, since it allows the analysis of large amounts of data in a simple, fast and efficient manner determining the expected proportion for the distribution of the data. The comparison between the observed and expected probability can indicate the occurrence of fraud and errors when significant deviations are detected.

The main purpose of using this law is to improve the effectiveness of identifying fraudulent data. Thus, the main objective of this study is to verify the conformity of the records of the turnover item (which includes sales and services) with this law and consequently to evaluate the quality of the financial information of the Portuguese companies under analysis.

In addition to this introduction, this study contemplates a theoretical framework on the Benford's Law and its importance and use for audit. This is followed by the case study, where the research methodology is presented, as well as the analysis and interpretation of the results. The study ends with the conclusion and respective solutions and recommendations, as well as future research directions.

Figure 1. Probability of occurrence of each digit according to Benford's Law (compiled by the authors)

Digit / Position	0	1	2	3	4	5	6	7	8	9
1st	0,00%	30,10%	17,61%	12,49%	9,69%	7,92%	6,70%	5,80%	5,12%	4,58%
2nd	11,97%	11,39%	10,88%	10,43%	10,03%	9,67%	9,34%	9,04%	8,76%	8,50%
3rd	10,18%	10,14%	10,10%	10,06%	10,02%	9,98%	9,99%	9,90%	9,86%	9,83%
4th	10,02%	10,01%	10,01%	10,01%	10,00%	10,00%	9,99%	9,99%	9,99%	9,98%

BACKGROUND

Benford's Law

The Benford's Law was discovered in 1881 by Newcomb and later reinforced by Frank Benford in 1938 which found that the first pages of the logarithms were more worn than the last. Thus, he concluded that the numbers do not occur with the same probability. That is, people more often looked for numbers that started with low digits than those that started with the remaining digits.

Thus Benford's Law can be expressed in a set of data where the probability of occurrence as the first digit on the left is different for each of the digits 1, 2, 3 ... where numbers starting with 1 occur more frequently than those starting with 2, which are in turn more frequent than those starting with 3, and so on, so the numbers starting with 9 are the least frequent (Hindls & Hronová, 2015). It is possible to verify this distribution through Figure 1.

This law presents itself as a simple and efficient analytical tool for analyzing accounting numbers. Moreover, it presents invariance of scale, that is, if a certain element fits into Benford's Law, then it will follow the law, regardless of the measure unit in which it is expressed. For example, if the law applies to the total annual turnover of companies, the law will be followed regardless of the currency in which it is expressed. However, it should be noted that the Benford's Law does not confirm whether there is fraud or error since it only identifies data that does not conform to the expected behavior, giving evidence to the auditor to investigate certain suspect points. Likewise, even if no deviations have been verified, the possibility of fraud and error is not extinct (Nunes, Inácio, & Marques, 2019).

Before carrying out an analysis based on the Benford's Law it is necessary to examine the type of data to be analyzed in order to obtain an effective analysis as there is data that does not follow Benford's distribution. Shi, Ausloos and Zhu (2018) analyzed 10 industry sectors in 6 emerging countries over 15 years and concluded that the results of Benford's Law must be complemented with accounting techniques tests before deciding whether some data is manipulated. Moreover, the results indicate that data reliability is a mandatory aspect to be observed before the application of the law. Indeed, some practical information must be necessarily outlined before and after some scientific analysis.

Therefore, we must consider the following points:

1. The sample size - should be large enough so that the digit pattern can appear. Thus, although an adequate size is not defined, Collins (2017) argues that Benford's Law works best with larger data sets;
2. Data may not be uniformly distributed;
3. The numbers cannot be limited to a minimum and a maximum - for example, only registering an asset if it exceeds a certain value (if it does not exceed this value in expenses);
4. Numbers must occur naturally - that is, they should not contain assigned numbers such as phone numbers, checks, postal codes, bank account numbers, car registrations, and so on;
5. The data must be random, that is, the digits distributed between 0 and 9 must have the same probability of occurrence as the first or second digits (Raimi, 1976).

In this sense, and since this law is applicable only when numbers occur naturally (not applying to invented numbers) it can be extremely useful in detecting fraudulent financial data since they are not invented by nature, so when manipulated they will not obey to Benford's Law, thus increasing the possibility of its detection.

Application to Audit

In order to meet the requirements of auditing standards for fraud prevention and detection, Drake and Nigrini (2000) suggests that auditors use Benford's Law as a tool to be included in analytical procedures. Nigrini (Nigrini, 2017) adds that Benford's Law can be applied in auditing to identify red flags, that is, non-compliance with the law can be an alert to identify intentional or unintentional material distortions.

It is true that auditors play a key role in supporting and certifying the information contained in the financial statements. However, more and more it is necessary that the audit be carried out to a greater number of accounting records to guarantee it reliability, increasing for this the sample to analyze, consuming time and resources

It is in this sense that the Benford's Law can be a contribution, since it allows the analysis of large amounts of data in a simple, fast and efficient way, with the help of the up-to-date computer resources.

This type of test, according to Nigrini and Miller (2009), helps to protect auditors regarding the risk of not detecting material errors arising from the use of sampling, since Benford's Law allows the analysis of large datasets. Also Durtschi, Hillison and Pacini (2004) argue that Benford's Law allows to signal the accounts with evidence of fraud and thus auditing them in greater depth. According to the same authors, before using the Benford's Law in an attempt to detect fraud, there are several issues that should be considered by the auditors. First, it is important to seek to know in what type of accounts the law can be used, that is, on which accounts it is foreseeable that its records follow the behavior indicated by the law. Although most of the accounting-related data sets conform to the Benford distribution, as noted earlier, there are some exceptions.

Another issue to consider is about the tests to be performed and how the results of these tests should be interpreted. As there are high costs associated with false positives (identifying fraud when it did not actually occur), as well as false negatives (not identifying a fraud condition when it exists), an acceptable level of significance should be considered in order to minimize these errors. Finally, it must be verified whether there are categories of fraud that cannot be signaled through digital analysis (Durtschi et al., 2004).

In addition to the above issues, Durtschi et al. (2004) add that an auditor when deciding to use digital analysis, namely the Benford's Law, in order to detect the existence of fraud, should know:

- Select accounts that are effectively susceptible to follow the expected frequency according to Benford's Law;
- Select the statistical tests that must be performed to determine deviations;
- Interpret adequately the results of statistical tests.

Although Benford's analysis alone may not be a surefire way to detect fraud, it can be a useful tool to help identify some accounts with deviations in order to perform additional testing.

Thus, auditors should use digital analysis to assess the probability of fraud by identifying data whose digits do not follow the expected frequency and can thus direct their efforts to areas with higher risks (Drake & Nigrini, 2000; Nigrini, 2012). However, this approach cannot replace the professional, comprehensive and extensive work performed by the auditors.

Therefore, to complement Benford's analysis, auditors should also check the physical existence of assets, be aware of the company performance, comparing them with other companies in the same industry and they should maintain professional skepticism regarding explanations of deviations in the records.

Although the comparison of current account balances with previous years may show large deviations (e.g. large company growth), these deviations do not mean that fraud or material errors have occurred. In this case, carrying out a test of the accounting balances is very important because, even in abnormal circumstances, the standards of the digits must follow Benford's Law (Drake & Nigrini, 2000; Nigrini, 2012).

Busta and Weinberg (1998) point out that traditional analytical procedures establish comparisons that generally detect high magnitude distortions and that when the magnitude is reduced there is less likelihood of being detected. For example, the high number of fraudulent sales can be detected through traditional analysis procedures, comparing sales with the cost of goods sold. On the other hand, when the value of fraudulent sales is reduced but numerous, it may not be detected by traditional analytical methods.

However, the use of Benford's Law may find potential manipulation, since this law is not sensitive to the magnitude of the error and does not require relationships between accounts. Thus, it can be particularly useful to detect frauds that are still in the beginning and have not yet reached high magnitudes.

In the context of detecting financial fraud, the more a set of observed data deviate from the Benford's Law standard, the greater is the probability that the data has been manipulated, and therefore the more suspected is data set.

According to Nigrini (2012), the deviations verified under the Benford's Law should cause the validity, accuracy and completeness of the numbers to be questioned since a small deviation can lead to later cases of large-scale financial statement fraud.

However, a simple breach of Benford's Law does not necessarily imply that we are dealing with a fraud case. It merely provides some statistical evidence that the data may have been manipulated, but it does not reveal whether such manipulation is fraudulent.

In order to obtain a more effective analysis, the positive numbers should also be analyzed separately from the negative numbers since the incentives to manipulate them are contrary. For example, managers tend to manipulate earnings when they are positive, but strive to keep them close to zero when earnings are negative (Nigrini, 2012).

A more complex analysis applying Benford's Law to a set of transactions can identify situations of fraud (Hess & Cottrell, 2016). While this review alone is not a "safe" way to detect fraud, it can be a useful tool to assist in identifying some items for re-testing and therefore should assist auditors in financial statements (Durtschi et al., 2004).

The application of this law can be of significant added value as it provides a solid and effective basis for analysis to enable the whole population to be tested quickly, which helps to protect auditors about the risk of non-detecting material errors arising from the use of sampling.

In the opinion of Durtschi et al. (2004) Benford's analysis is useful when it results from two distinct distributions, such as accounts receivable and payables, which result from the quantity sold and the quantity purchased, multiplied by the price. The same applies to the turnover as by virtue of its characteristics (resulting from the multiplication between the selling price and the quantities sold) satisfies the requirements to comply with Benford's Law.

However, this law also has some limitations, namely that it does not detect the omission or duplication of transactions and registrations. Therefore, when a fraud involves transactions that were not recorded as happens in the case of bribes or theft of assets, it cannot be expected that digital analysis will detect these. For this reason, its use must be complemented with additional tests, for example the verification of the company's behavior in relation to the sector and in relation to previous years (Durtschi et al., 2004).

Related Work

The first application of Benford's Law in accounting is due to Charles Carslaw. Carslaw (1988) analyzed the occurrence frequency of the second digit of the profits of 220 New Zealand companies for 5 years in order to see if the occurrence of the numbers is in accordance with the expected random distribution. However, this compliance was not verified, because for the second digit there was an excess of 0's and a lack of 9's. That is, managers to present a more positive company's situation rounded up their profits by improving their image to stakeholders. For example, a company with a result of 6,97 million euros changed that result to 7.0 million euros.

Thomas (1988) replicated the Carslaw's study using digital analysis in US publicly traded companies and examined companies with positive results as well as those with negative results. The results showed that, on average, managers of US companies rounded up the positive results numbers (such as the managers of New Zealand companies reported by Carslaw), that is, obtained an excess of 0's and a shortage of 9's to the second digit. In the same way, the author obtained an excess of 9's and a shortage of 0's in the second digit in the companies that presented negative results, which showed that companies with negative results tended to decrease the value of those same results.

Jordan, Clark, and Hames (2011) looked at the largest 1,002 companies in the United States to see if sales and assets follow Benford's Law for the second digit. Through the Z-Value, P-level tests and comparing the expected frequency with the frequency observed for each of the digits, it was found that for the second digit, the values of the assets followed the Benford distribution. This method was replicated for sales analysis, however, it was concluded that the results were manipulated in order to achieve a higher result, since the use of 0's in the second digit was more frequently than expected and

Figure 2. Summary of data analyzed (compiled by the authors)

	Total of Companies	Companies with positive sales turnover	Companies with Net Loss	Companies with Net Profit
Lodging	7 280	5 216	1 831	3 385
Restoration	25 024	21 842	9 323	12 519
Total	**32 304**	**27 058**	**11 154**	**15 904**

7's in second position less than expected, which showed that there were rounding of the second digit 7's to 0's thus increasing the first digit. Therefore there is a clear pattern of manipulation in order to reach a higher first digit of sales and showing sales values higher than the real ones, as verified in the study carried out by Carslaw (1988)(1988).

In Portugal, Ferreira (2013) carried out a study with the objective of identifying the deviations occurring in the frequencies of the turnover digits of the Portuguese Manufacturing Industry. The results showed that the sectors of the Apparel and Leather Products Industry show more significant deviations. It has also been found that the most recent and the smallest companies have more deviations.

An analysis of a Portuguese a medium entity that receive a clean audit report in the years 2010 and 2011, using the Benford's Law in the expenses and income accounts of these years verified that both distributions is not in conformity to the distribution of Benford's Law, which leads one to suspect that there are some deviations in the analyzed accounts. The most significant variances occurred in the last two-digit test in the profit accounts and in the subcontract's accounts. The author suggested the comparison of these results with the documents that originated the records in order to prove whether the roundings are legitimate (Santos, 2014).

MAIN FOCUS OF THE CHAPTER

Issues, Controversies, Problems

The main objective of this study is to verify if the Portuguese companies belonging to the Restoration and Lodging sectors follow the Benford's Law, using the data referring to the turnover of 2017. According to the National Statistical Institute (Instituto Nacional de Estatística, 2018) companies of the Restoration and Lodging sectors stood out as those that presented the most significant growth in 2017 in most of the economic indicators, evidencing that the turnover increased 16.5%. Given this significant increase it is interesting to analyze the turnover of this group of companies in order to verify if this increase hides significant deviations which may result from the existence of fraud.

Accordingly, the financial information of the companies available on the SABI basis was analyzed, establishing, for this purpose, certain criteria, namely: all companies are Portuguese with known values in 2017, carrying out activities in the Restoration and Lodging sectors and the value of sales and services rendering is greater than 0, so that all observations have a first digit. Figure 2 summarizes the number of companies in the study by the different sectors.

Figure 3. Critical values of the Chi-square test at a significance level of 5% (compiled by the authors)

Significance Level	Degrees of Freedom		
	8	9	89
5%	15,507	16,919	112,022

Figure 2 shows that there are approximately 32,000 companies with information related to the period of 2017. Of these companies, only 27,058 were analyzed, since companies whose turnover was not known were excluded. If we analyze the information by sector we can verify that 5,216 companies belong to the Lodging sector and 21,842 companies belong to the Restoration sector

From the sample of companies selected, turnover ranges from € 1,000 to € 143,797,512.58. The lowest net result is € -21,305,803.30 and the highest € 32,010,947.50, which shows a great diversity of companies under study.

In order to respond to the proposed objectives, three main questions are raised, as follows:

- Do the companies under analysis follow the Benford's Law?
- Do companies with negative net profit or loss show more deviations from the distribution of the Benford's Law?
- How do companies with a net profit or loss of the period close to zero behave in relation to the distribution of the Benford's Law?

To address the research questions and in order to analyze the differences between the observed frequencies and the expected frequencies, the following hypotheses were tested:

H0: There is no statistically significant difference between the observed distributions and the Benford's distribution

H1: There is a statistically significant difference between the observed distributions and the Benford's distribution

If we reject H0, that is, we reject the hypothesis that the values obtained in each result follow the expected values according to the Benford's Law, for each digit, if the observed values are higher than the critical values.

Thus, statistical tests were carried out, namely, the Z-test for all individual digits and the Chi-Square and MAD (Mean Absolute Deviation) statistics for the overall analysis. These tests were performed on all groups of study samples for the first digit, second digit and first two digits.

For the analysis of the results, we considered a 5% significance level (95% confidence) established a priori, so as not to reject a true hypothesis or to accept a false hypothesis. Thus, the null hypothesis H0 will be rejected when the value of Z-test, Chi-Square or MAD is higher than the critical value for the defined level of significance. It should be noted that the higher the level of significance used the lower the critical point value, that is, the greater its accuracy and consequently the fewer deviations are tolerated.

Figure 4. Intervals of conformity for MAD test. Adapted from Ferreira (2013)

	Total Conformity	Acceptable Conformity	Marginally Accepted Conformity	Nonconformity
First Digit	0,000 - 0,006	0,006 - 0,012	0,012 - 0,015	> 0,015
Second Digit	0,000 - 0,008	0,008 - 0,010	0,010 - 0,012	> 0,012
First Two Digits	0,000 - 0,012	0,012 - 0,018	0,018 - 0,022	> 0,022

The Z-test allows us to verify if a given digit appears more or less frequently at a particular position compared to the Benford distribution, thus determining whether the proportion of a specific digit is suspect (Durtschi et al., 2004). The critical value of the Z-test at a significance level of 5% is 1.96, that is, we reject H0 whenever the value of the Z-test obtained is greater than 1.96.

The Chi-Square are used to verify that all digits comply with Benford's Law or whether the deviations between the sample and the Benford distribution are statistically significant. Figure 3 shows the critical values of this test for a significance level of 5%. While the Z-test identifies deviations in the digits individually, the Chi-Square is a test that evidences the deviations in all digits of the sample.

The number of degrees of freedom to which Figure 3 refers is given by (k - 1), that is, for the first digit we have k = 9 (nine possible digits as the first digit) so the number of degrees of freedom is 8. Consequently, for the second digit are 9 degrees of freedom and for the first two digits the test is evaluated using 89 degrees of freedom (Nigrini, 2012).

Finally, the MAD is an average deviation between the frequencies observed and the frequencies provided by the Benford's Law, calculated by the sum of the absolute deviations and divided by the number of digits in each test. The advantage of calculating the MAD in relation to Z-test and Chi-Square is that it does not consider the number of data in the sample (Nigrini, 2012).

The MAD has no limits or intervals, such as the Z-test and Chi-Square, on which the auditors can base their assertions on whether a deviation is significant. In this way, Nigrini (2012) has developed compliance intervals for this statistic for the first, second and first two digits. Thus, the MAD value should be compared with the critical values shown in Figure 4 developed by Ferreira (2013), in order to determine if the hypothesis H0 is rejected or if there is no statistically significant difference between the two distributions.

Therefore, in order to verify the differences between the frequencies observed and the expected frequencies, the MAD statistic and the Chi-square test were applied. Finally, for each of the digits 1 to 9, the value of Z-test was determined individually, comparing this value with the critical value of Z-test.

This procedure was performed for the first digit, for the second digit and for the first two digits of all companies in the sample, companies with net profit, companies with net loss and companies with net profit or loss close to zero.

Figure 5. Results of the first digit test of the turnover of the total of companies (compiled by the authors)

First Digit	Observed Frequency	Expected Frequency	Observed Proportion	Expected Proportion	Deviation	Value of the Z-Test
1	8 365	8 145	30,92%	30,10%	0,81%	2,9121
2	4 677	4 765	17,29%	17,61%	-0,32%	1,3994
3	3 241	3 381	11,98%	12,49%	-0,52%	2,5665
4	2 565	2 622	9,48%	9,69%	-0,21%	1,1752
5	2 064	2 142	7,63%	7,92%	-0,29%	1,7671
6	1 884	1 811	6,96%	6,69%	0,27%	1,7647
7	1 610	1 569	5,95%	5,80%	0,15%	1,0625
8	1 377	1 384	5,09%	5,12%	-0,03%	0,1954
9	1 275	1 238	4,71%	4,58%	0,14%	1,0732
Total:	**27 058**	**27 058**	**100%**	**100%**		

Z-Test		Chi-Squared		MAD	
Critical Value	1,96	Critical Value	15,507	Critical Value	0,015
		Obtained Value	22,532	Obtained Value	0,00304

Figure 6. Results of the second digit test of the turnover of the total of companies (compiled by the authors)

Second Digit	Observed Frequency	Expected Frequency	Observed Proportion	Expected Proportion	Deviation	Value of the Z-Test
0	3 192	3 238	11,80%	11,97%	-0,17%	0,87
1	3 089	3 082	11,42%	11,39%	0,03%	0,14
2	2 900	2 944	10,72%	10,88%	-0,16%	0,87
3	2 844	2 832	10,51%	10,43%	0,08%	0,42
4	2 729	2 714	10,09%	10,03%	0,05%	0,30
5	2 633	2 616	9,73%	9,67%	0,05%	0,35
6	2 581	2 527	9,54%	9,34%	0,20%	1,14
7	2 406	2 445	8,89%	9,04%	-0,14%	0,82
8	2 373	2 369	8,77%	8,76%	0,01%	0,08
9	2 311	2 300	8,54%	8,50%	0,04%	0,24
Total:	**27 058**	**27 058**	**100%**	**100%**		

Z-Test		Chi-Squared		MAD	
Critical Value	1,96	Critical Value	16,919	Critical Value	0,012
		Obtained Value	3,549	Obtained Value	0,00096

PRESENTATION AND RESULTS DISCUSSION

Analysis of Turnover of All Companies

First Digit Test

For the first digit of the turnover of the total of companies under study and analyzing the results obtained in Figure 5, we verified that the MAD value is lower than its critical value. However, the Chi-Square value is higher than its critical value showing the existence of a nonconformity for the significance level of 5%. Thus, by the Chi-Square, we reject H0, that is, we reject the hypothesis of data compliance with Benford's Law. Once this hypothesis is rejected, it is advisable for the auditor to analyze digit by digit using the Z-test. From this analysis it turns out that the values of Z-test for the first digit 1 and 3 are higher than their critical value, showing that there is a shortage of digit 3 and an excess of digit 1.

Figure 7. Results of the two first digits test of the turnover of the total of companies (compiled by the authors)

Two First Digits	Observed Frequency	Expected Frequency	Observed Proportion	Expected Proportion	Deviation	Value of the Z-Test
15	**819**	**758**	**3,03%**	**2,80%**	**0,22%**	**2,23**
16	**795**	**712**	**2,94%**	**2,63%**	**0,31%**	**3,14**
19	**654**	**603**	**2,42%**	**2,23%**	**0,19%**	**2,11**
23	468	500	1,73%	1,85%	-0,12%	1,45
27	391	427	1,45%	1,58%	-0,13%	1,77
36	**284**	**322**	**1,05%**	**1,19%**	**-0,14%**	**2,13**
38	**269**	**305**	**0,99%**	**1,13%**	**-0,13%**	**2,09**
45	**210**	**258**	**0,78%**	**0,95%**	**-0,18%**	**3,02**
52	196	224	0,72%	0,83%	-0,10%	1,87
55	**177**	**212**	**0,65%**	**0,78%**	**-0,13%**	**2,40**
59	174	198	0,64%	0,73%	-0,09%	1,68
65	204	179	0,75%	0,66%	0,09%	1,84
73	178	160	0,66%	0,59%	0,07%	1,44
89	**105**	**131**	**0,39%**	**0,49%**	**-0,10%**	**2,30**
93	144	126	0,53%	0,46%	0,07%	1,64
...	...	...	...	...	...	...
Total:	**27 058**	**27 058**	**100%**	**100%**		

Z-Test		Chi-Squared		MAD	
Critical Value	1,96	Critical Value	112,022	Critical Value	0,022
		Obtained Value	0,000	Obtained Value	0,00052

Second Digit Test

Analyzing the results of Figure 6, we can see that the MAD value is close to the total conformity with the Benford's Law, according to the limits established by Nigrini (2012), so that H0 is not rejected.

The same is true for the Chi-square test with a value of 3.549, which is much lower than its critical value (16,919). Thus, we can conclude that for both global statistics there are no statistically significant deviations between the observed distributions and the Benford distribution.

The values of the Z-test for all digits are less than their critical value for the significance level of 5%, which means that none of the frequency deviations for the first digit in individual terms is significant. Thus, we can say that for a significance level of 5% we do not reject H0, that is, we do not exclude the hypothesis that the data are compatible with the Benford's Law.

Two First Digits Test

Figure 7 shows only the digits whose value of Z-test is higher than the critical value as well as the digits that show the greatest deviations since the figure would be very large to represent all digits.

From the analysis on the first two digits, we find that for the global statistical tests (Chi-Square and MAD) the values obtained are lower than the critical values which means that the sample as a whole follows the Benford's Law.

Although for the global tests there is no significant difference between the results obtained and the expected results according to the Benford's Law, it is important to analyze the first two digits individually with the Z-test. In this analysis we find that the digits 15, 16, 19, 36, 38, 45, 55 and 89 show Z-test value above its critical value, which may indicate the occurrence of rounding and possible deviations that may be the result of fraud or error. In this case, it would be relevant for the auditor to analyze the companies whose turnover starts with those digits in order to verify in greater detail the transactions carried out.

Thus, we reject the H0 hypothesis since the digits present statistically significant differences with respect to the Benford's Law.

Considering the results obtained in each performed analysis we verified that the analysis to the first two digits is the one that presents more significant deviations when analyzed by the Z-test. However, most of the deviations are not significant, and there is a satisfactory global compliance of the data. In order to verify if this behavior is verified for both companies with net profit and net loss will be analyzed in the following sections.

Analysis of the Turnover of Companies with Net Profit

First Digit Test

For the analysis of the first digit we performed the tests Qui-Square, MAD and Z-test similarly to procedures performed for the total of companies in the previous section. From the analysis of these tests we verified that for the global tests (Chi-Square and MAD), only the Chi-Square test fails the conformity once the value obtained (54,205) is higher than the critical value. Thus, we reject the hypothesis H0 that the data follow the Benford distribution.

Furthermore, the Z-test shows that, as in the case of the global sample, only the deviations in digits 1, 3 and 5 are significant, and the digit 1 appears as the first digit more times than would be expected instead of the digits 3 and 5.

Second Digit Test

For the second digit test of companies with net profit we found that there is compliance for all test statistics, so there is no statistically sufficient evidence to state that there are significant errors or that the data is not accurately portraying reality. Therefore, we can say that, for a significance level of 5%, we do not reject the null hypothesis (H0) since there is no statistically significant difference between the observed distributions and the Benford distribution.

Two First Digits Test

Testing the first two digits with the global tests (Chi-Square and MAD) we found that only the Chi-Square test failed, since the value obtained (138,438) is greater than its critical value. Thus, we reject the H0 hypothesis since the data present statistically significant differences with respect to the Benford distribution.

In order to check which digits have deviations from the Benford distribution, a digit-by-digit analysis is required. Thus, for the Z-test, the observed frequency of digits 13, 15, 16, 17 and 19 is higher than the expected frequency according to the Benford distribution. On the other hand, the higher digits, namely 36, 38, 45, 52, 55 and 59 occur less often than would be expected. Evidence that the highest digits occur less often may mean that rounding has been done in order to change the companies' result.

Analysis of the Turnover of Companies with Net Loss

First Digit Test

The application of the global tests allows to conclude that the MAD value shows a total conformity with the Benford's Law, according to the limits established by Nigrini (2012). However, the Chi-square test fails since the value obtained (43.822) is greater than the critical value. Thus, we reject H0 and exclude the hypothesis that the data follow the Benford distribution since there are significant differences between the observed frequencies and the expected frequencies.

For a significance level of 5%, it is observed that the frequency of digits 1 and 2 is lower than the frequency expected according to the Benford's Law. The opposite is for digits 5, 6 and 7 whose observed frequency is higher than expected, which allows us to conclude that there is a possibility that companies with lower results are rounding up their turnover to higher values.

Thus, we can conclude that the behavior of companies with net loss, for the first digit, is quite different from the companies with positive results. For companies with positive results, we can see that the turnover value shows more digits 1 and less 3 and 5, however, the opposite is true for companies with negative results, with digit 1 being one of the least observed being the digits 5, 6 and 7 those that have an observed value higher than expected according to Benford's Law.

Second Digit Test

The application of the tests to the second digit of turnover for companies with net loss allows us to conclude that there are no relevant deviations since, for all statistical tests, the values obtained are lower than the respective critical values, so we can conclude that the analyzed data follow the Benford distribution for the second digit.

Thus, we do not reject the H0 hypothesis since the data do not present statistically significant differences. As noted earlier, the fact that there are no significant differences does not guarantee the absence of errors or failures.

Two First Digits Test

From the analysis performed on the first two digits we find that the MAD value is lower than its critical value, although the Chi-square obtained is higher (129,069), which means that there is a statistically significant difference between the observed distributions and the Benford distribution.

In order to make a more detailed analysis it is important to verify the value of the Z-test for every two first digits. From this analysis we find that the lowest digits, namely 13, 14, 20, 21 and 25 have an observed frequency lower than expected. On the contrary, the higher digits, 54, 60, 65, 93 have an observed frequency higher than would be expected. This trend is contrary to what happens for companies with net profit in which the larger digits present lower observed frequency than expected.

Analysis of the Turnover of Companies with Net Profit or Loss Close to Zero

First Digit Test

Since companies often aim to minimize the tax payable, it becomes important to analyze companies whose net profit or loss is close to zero in order to see if companies have manipulated their results. However, it can not be said that the ultimate goal of companies is to present negative results, but they tend to present results close to zero in order to minimize the tax payable.

On the other hand, it is natural that companies with negative results should aim to achieve more favorable results and close to zero since the probability that companies obtain financing at a reasonable cost is intertwined with the quality of their accounting results. In this way, managers may tend to manipulate their results in order to present more favorable results and ratios, hence the importance of the analysis of this group of companies.

Thus, for companies with net profit or loss close to zero, the MAD value is quite similar to its critical value, being within the marginally acceptable limit as proposed by Nigrini (2012). This trend is accentuated by analyzing the result of the Chi-Square test for the first digit, which is higher than its critical value (47,481). Thus, the hypothesis H0 is rejected, since there are significant deviations between the Benford's Law and the results observed.

Since there are statistically significant differences for the overall analysis of the digits it is important for the auditor to analyze the deviations verified digit by digit. Thus, the Z-test reinforce the existence of significant deviations, at a significance level of 5%, in digits 2, 3, 7, 8 and 9, with digits 2 and 3 being less than expected and digits 7, 8 and 9 more times than would be expected according to the distribution of Benford's Law. Therefore, we can conclude that the lower digits occur less often than the higher digits. Since deviations are found in much of the digits, a more detailed analysis of this group of companies should be made in order to conclude whether the existing deviations are due to accounting errors, lack of controls or actually existed intent to commit fraud.

Second Digit Test

For the second digit we found that, considering Chi-Square and MAD, the values obtained are lower than the critical values and, through this analysis, it could be concluded that the second digits may be in accordance with the Benford's Law, at the level of global tests.

However, by doing a more detailed analysis, digit by digit, through the Z-test, we can verify that the second digit 6 occurs more times than expected according to the Benford distribution so the value of Z-test for this digit is higher than critical value.

Thus, we can conclude that the H0 hypothesis is rejected since there are statistically significant differences for the second digit of companies with net profit or loss close to zero.

Two First Digits Test

The results of the application of the Benford's Law to the first two digits show that the global statistical tests Qui-Square and MAD present values higher than the critical ones and, therefore, we can affirm that for a significance level of 5%, we reject the hypothesis null (H0), thus excluding the hypothesis that the data are in accordance with the Benford distribution.

From the analysis carried out in the first two digits of the sample under study, we find that two first digits 16, 23, 24, 31, 71, 73, 74 and 79 have values of Z-test higher than their critical value and these groups of companies should be analyzed later.

CONCLUSION

The ability to detect fraud and irregularities is one of the main concerns of the auditors. In order to complement the literature on this topic with one more case study to prove, this chapter pedagogically presents the advantages of applying the Benford's Law as a significant tool and method to identify accounts with deviations as well as to reduce the sample to be audited by identifying the data whose digits do not follow the expected frequency thus allowing more effective and efficient audits.

In this work, the Benford's Law was applied to the item turnover of companies in the Lodging and Restoration sectors with different financial situations in order to signal the accounts with indications of fraud and thus audit them in greater depth. We can verify that, after applying the statistical tests (Z-test, Chi-Square and MAD), several digits have been found that deviate from the Benford's Law, however, the deviations are different depending on the financial situation of the company.

For companies with net profit, for the first digit, we find that the lowest digits occur more often than would be expected according to Benford distribution. On the contrary, for companies with net loss the lower digits occur less times than expected. The differences obtained may be related to the manipulation of the data that would have been in opposite directions considering the financial situation of the company. These digits should be further analyzed in greater detail since the application of Benford's Law indicates that turnover values may have been manipulated to generate a certain desirable result.

The application of the tests to the second digit of the turnover for companies with net profit and loss allows to conclude that there is no sufficient statistically evidence to affirm that there are significant errors or that the data is not correctly portraying reality. For all statistical tests, the value obtained from Z-test, Chi-Square and MAD are lower than their critical values, so we can conclude that this data group follows the Benford distribution. However, the fact that there are no significant differences does not guarantee the absence of errors or failures.

From the analysis done to companies with net profit or loss close to zero, for the first digit, we conclude that there are statistically significant differences for both the Chi-Square statistic and the Z-test, with the lowest digits occurring less than the highest digits high. This trend also applies to companies with net loss which may indicate that companies are manipulating their results by rounding from the lowest digits to the highest digits in order to obtain better results.

Thus, we can conclude that after applying the statistical tests were found several digits with deviations from the Law, however, deviations are different depending on the financial situation of the company.

In order to verify the true causes of the digits not complying with the Benford's Law, it is necessary to carry out an analysis at the level of the transactions and registrations of the item turnover, or to compare the amounts with the accounting documents. With this analysis it may be possible to determine whether the differences between the observed frequencies and the expected frequencies resulted from rounding, duplication of records, errors in accounting or fraud. It would also be interesting to apply the same analysis to another variable, for example the net result or the accounts receivable and payable.

REFERENCES

ACFE. (2018). *Report to the Nations 2018 - Global Study on Occupational Fraud and Abuse Asia-Pacific Edition*. Retrieved from https://www.acfe.com/uploadedFiles/ACFE_Website/Content/rttn/2018/RTTN-Asia-Pacific-Edition.pdf

Asllani, A., & Naco, M. (2014). Using Benford's Law for Fraud Detection in Accounting Practices. *Journal of Social Science Studies*, *2*(1), 129. doi:10.5296/jsss.v2i1.6395

Birol, B. (2019). Corporate Governance and Fraud Detection: A Study From Borsa Instanbul. *Eurasian Journal of Business and Management*, *7*(1), 44–64. doi:10.15604/ejbm.2019.07.01.005

Carslaw, C. A. P. N. (1988). Anomalies in Income Numbers: Evidence of Goal Oriented Behavior. *The Accounting Review*, *63*(2), 321–327. doi:10.2307/248109

Collins, J. C. (2017). Using Excel and Benford ' s Law to detect fraud. *Journal of Accountancy*. Retrieved from https://www.journalofaccountancy.com/issues/2017/apr/excel-and-benfords-law-to-detect-fraud

de Almeida, M. L. F. (2015). *A fraude de relato financeiro e a indepenência dos auditores*. Universidade Autónoma de Lisboa. Retrieved from http://repositorio.ual.pt/handle/11144/2400

dos Santos, C. C. (2014). *Aplicação da Lei de Benford na auditoria : estudo de caso*. Instituto Politécnico de Leiria. Retrieved from https://iconline.ipleiria.pt/handle/10400.8/1114

Drake, P. D., & Nigrini, M. J. (2000). Computer assisted analytical procedures using Benford's Law. *Journal of Accounting Education*, *18*(2), 127–146. doi:10.1016/S0748-5751(00)00008-7

Durtschi, C., Hillison, W., & Pacini, C. (2004). The Effective Use of Benford ' s Law to Assist in Detecting Fraud in Accounting Data. *Journal of Forensic Accounting*, *9*(99), 17–34.

Ferreira, M. J. M. (2013). *Lei de Benford e detecção de fraude contabilística : aplicação à indústria transformadora em Portugal*. Instituto Superior de Economia e Gestão. Retrieved from https://www.repository.utl.pt/handle/10400.5/6134

Franceschetti, B. M., & Koschtial, C. (2013). Do bankrupt companies manipulate earnings more than the non-bankrupt ones? *Journal of Finance & Accountancy*, *12*, 4–24.

Hess, M. F., & Cottrell, J. H. Jr. (2016). Fraud risk management: A small business perspective. *Business Horizons*, *59*(1), 13–18. doi:10.1016/j.bushor.2015.09.005

Hindls, R., & Hronová, S. (2015). Benford's Law and Possibilities for Its Use in Governmental Statistics. *Statistika: Statistics and Economy Journal*, *95*(2), 54–64.

Jordan, C. E., Clark, S. J., & Hames, C. (2011). Manipulating Sales Revenue To Achieve Cognitive Reference Points: An Examination Of Large U.S. Public Companies. *Journal of Applied Business Research*, *25*(2). doi:10.19030/jabr.v25i2.1039

Nigrini, M. J. (2012). *Benford's Law - applications for forensic accounting, auditing, and fraud detection*. Hoboken, NJ: John Wiley & Sons, Inc. doi:10.1002/9781119203094

Nigrini, M. J. (2017). Audit Sampling Using Benford's Law: A Review of the Literature with Some New Perspectives. *Journal of Emerging Technologies in Accounting*, *14*(2), 29–46. doi:10.2308/jeta-51783

Nigrini, M. J., & Miller, S. J. (2009). Data Diagnostics Using Second-Order Tests of Benford's Law. *Auditing*, *28*(2), 305–324. doi:10.2308/aud.2009.28.2.305

Nunes, A., Inácio, H., & Marques, R. P. (2019). A Lei de Benford e a deteção de fraude em auditoria nas empresas portuguesas. In *Iberian Conference on Information Systems and Technologies, CISTI*. Coimbra, Portugal: IEEE.

Raimi, R. A. (1976). The First Digit Problem. *The American Mathematical Monthly*, *83*(7), 521–538. doi:10.1080/00029890.1976.11994162

Rigaud, L. (1980). *Os Sistemas de Informação na empresa*. Porto: Rés-Editor.

Shi, J., Ausloos, M., & Zhu, T. (2018). Benford's law first significant digit and distribution distances for testing the reliability of financial reports in developing countries. *Physica A*, *492*, 878–888. doi:10.1016/j.physa.2017.11.017

Thomas, J. K. (1988). Unusual Patterns In Reported Earnings. *The Accounting Review*, *64*(4), 773. Retrieved from https://ideas.repec.org/p/fth/colubu/fb-_88-34.html

Chapter 10
Sovereign Bureaucrats vs. Global Tech Companies: Ethical and Regulatory Challenges

Alexander A. Filatov
GenezisTechCapital, Russia

ABSTRACT

We live in a changing world. Disruptive technologies and digital platforms particularly are reshaping the world, making it more open and accessible on the one hand, but more fragile and uncertain on the other, rising risks of cybersecurity, personal data security. Do markets really need any kind of regulatory interventions under these circumstances? We see many cases where "state bureaucrats" impose restrictions on global companies based on digital platforms – technology champions. Are those actions effective, do they make sense in terms of global security, or it is only political game?

INTRODUCTION

Do we want technology to keep giving more people a voice, or will traditional gatekeepers control what ideas can be expressed?

(Mark Zuckerberg, 2019)

Mother, do you think they'll drop the bomb?

Mother, do you think they'll like the song?

Mother, do you think they'll try to break my balls?

Mother, should I build the wall?

DOI: 10.4018/978-1-7998-2011-6.ch010

Mother, should I run for president?

Mother, should I trust the government?

Mother, will they put me in the firing line?

Is it just a waste of time?

(Roger Waters - Pink Floyd The Wall, 1979)

...10 minutes before the strike I stopped it...I am in no hurry, our Military is rebuilt, new, and ready to go, by far the best in the world. Sanctions are biting & more added last night.

(Donald J. Trump, 2019)

BACKGROUND

Will the US government and lawmakers follow tactics similar to deterrence of Iran in confronting the launch by Facebook its cryptocurrency? Or it'll make a strike to kill it at an early stage? Facebook recently revealed the details of its cryptocurrency, Libra (libra.org), which will let you buy things or send money to people with nearly zero fees. You'll pseudonymously buy or cash out your Libra online or at local exchange points like grocery stores, and spend it using interoperable third-party wallet apps or Facebook's own Calibra wallet that will be built into WhatsApp, Messenger and its own app. Regulators are already bristling. Democrat Senator Sherrod Brown tweeted that "We cannot allow Facebook to run a risky new cryptocurrency out of a Swiss bank account without oversight" (Brown, 2019).

In July 2018 the European Commission fined Google $5 billion for favoring its own applications on Android devices over those of its competitors. While Google's fine is the largest to date, it isn't the first time the European Union has sanctioned a company for this sort of abuse. Nor is it the first time that a fine has been handed to Google — which had already set a record last year — but other companies such as Microsoft and Telefonica have also received hefty punishments. Back in 2016, the EU forced Apple to pay $16 billion in back taxes to Ireland, which the company just finished paying.

Amazon is already under pressure in the US over its market dominance. At the end of August 2018, US President Donald Trump hinted that he thought Amazon, among other tech companies, could be a "very antitrust situation," and news emerged in September that US Attorney General Jeff Sessions was open to investigating Silicon Valley giants.

President Trump has finally succeeded in building his wall: not the one he keeps demanding on the southwestern border, but a far more complex barrier meant to block China's national telecommunications champion, Huawei, from operating in the United States and starve it of American technology as it builds networks around the globe.

All these cases deal with state bureaucrats imposing restrictions on global companies based on digital platforms - technology champions. Officials confront them in order to demonstrate that bureaucrats fulfill their duty to regulate markets. But do markets really need this kind of regulatory interventions? Isn't it simply that bureaucrats and politicians are trying to justify their salaries and to demonstrate their own importance in the face of general public - their voters?

Let's depict what corporate digital ecosystems are, how they are reshaping the world, what arguments global bureaucrats are using to impose restrictions, and if these restrictions are effective, finally.

DIGITAL PLATFORMS ARE IN FACT RESHAPING THE WORLD

Amazon digital platform open for third party sellers grabs US e-commerce markets. Amazon is set to clear $258.22 billion in US retail sales in 2018, according to eMarketer's figures, which will work out to 49.1 percent of all online retail spending in the country, and 5 percent of all retail sales. It started as an online bookstore, but today Amazon is a behemoth in all areas of e-commerce, fueled by a strong Marketplace network of third-party sellers, an ever-expanding range of goods from groceries to fashion, and a very popular loyalty program in the form of Prime.

Later the figure was downgraded based on Amazon 2019 second quarter report, but still with about 38 percent of the market the e-commerce giant still holds a commanding lead over rivals. EBay ranked second with a 6.1 percent share of U.S. e-commerce sales, followed by Walmart at 4.7 percent and Apple at 3.8 percent. "Third-party sales have grown from $0.1 billion to $160 billion – a compound annual growth rate of 52%. To provide an external benchmark, eBay's gross merchandise sales in that period have grown at a compound rate of 20%, from $2.8 billion to $95 billion," Bezos wrote in the letter, adding that "third-party sellers are kicking our first-party butt." (Bezos, 2018) Amazon generated net sales of $232.9 billion in fiscal 2018.

WeChat as digital way of living embraces more than a billion of customers and businesses combined in one universal ecosystem. WeChat was launched in 2011 as Weixin – Mandarin for 'micro-message'. As the name suggests, it originally functioned as a simple messenger app – a Chinese equivalent to WhatsApp in essence. Like WhatsApp, the WeChat app has evolved considerably since those early days. Video clips and functionality to find other users followed, then voice and video calls, as well as Facebook-like Moments feed. WeChat's development would grow more innovative after this. Leveraging Tencent's involvement in gaming (which would get deeper in years to come), it added games integration, and presciently, it also moved into the digital payments field – an area in which WhatsApp is trying to follow in the Indian market. Add shopping, the ability to hail taxis (through Didi Chuxing), and mini brand apps run entirely within WeChat. In short, WeChat's range of services give it the functionality of a whole suite of apps for its huge user base. Tencent, the parent company of WeChat, announced in early 2019 that daily active users of the app had climbed to over one billion. Only Facebook, YouTube, WhatsApp, and Facebook Messenger can claim a greater share of global usage.

Speaking to the FT, Matthew Brennan, the founder of consultancy ChinaChannel (which focuses on WeChat), posited that much of the growth that we've seen over the past couple of years came from international markets – chiefly in Southeast Asia, Europe, and the US. Much is likely to be from the Chinese diaspora aiming to stay in touch with those back home. WeChat has become as much a place to do business as a social media app. Mini programs are one of the key channels through which brands can reach prospective customers through WeChat – marrying the benefit of a ready-made audience with the streamlined cost and process of these versus a full-blown app. According to mini program developer, Jisu App, WeChat mini programs number over one million, with 600 million users – or 170 million per day. The average user opens four mini programs daily. The highest levels of WeChat mini program traffic are reported by lifestyle services, at 264 million (over July 2018). This is followed closely by 252 million for e-commerce, and 234 million for travel.

The mobile payments market has taken off in a big way in China. According to Business Insider, no fewer than 900 million people use WeChat Pay on a monthly-basis. This compares to a relatively paltry 127 million users of Apple Pay. The iResearch Consulting Group estimates that WeChat commands 40% of the market, compared to 54% for Alipay.

A later survey conducted by Ipsos and pertaining to the third quarter of 2018, shows Tenpay edging out into the lead in terms of penetration at least (Tenpay also incorporates payment apps incorporated into other Tencent-owned media – most notably, QQ). By this measure, Tenpay is comfortably in the lead over its chief rival. The top-two payments apps are leagues ahead of anyone else, with the next highest penetration standing at 11.6% (China Unionpay Quick Pass), compared to Alipay's 63.6% and Tenpay's 84.3%.

Google is a monopoly in a way: android platform is used by over 75% of mobile devices. In April 2019, online search engine Bing accounted for 3.13 percent of the global search market. During the same month, Chinese search engine Baidu had a market share of 0.66 percent. Ever since the introduction of Google Search in 1997, the worldwide market share of all search engines has been rather lopsided. Google has dominated the search engine market, maintaining an 88.47 percent market share as of April 2019. Google handles 1.2 trillion search queries per year and has partnered with over 2 million websites which have a reach to over 90% of people on the internet. Imagine advertising to such a huge market. The majority of Google revenues are generated through advertising. The company has also expanded its services to mail, productivity tools, enterprise products, mobile devices and other ventures. As a result, Google earned one of the highest tech company revenues in 2018 with roughly 136.22 billion U.S. dollars (Worldwide desktop market share of leading search engines from January 2010 to July 2019)

. In 2018, advertising revenue from Google sites amounted to 70.9% of the company's revenues and advertising revenue from Google network sites amounted to 16%.

The current eight largest Internet leaders — Apple, Amazon, Microsoft, Google, Alibaba, Tencent, and Netflix — represent almost $5 trillion dollars in net worth, and all have dominating positions in their respective markets. They've also all achieved that success very differently. Apple, Microsoft, and Netflix are primarily direct sales. Facebook and Google have mastered ad supported everything. And Amazon (power shoppers), Alibaba (power marketplace buyers and sellers), and Tencent (power gamers) are leading the pack at shared-value transactions, with their deep ecommerce expertise. The core idea of shared-value transactions is to take your engaging consumer platform and allow the best users on those platforms to generate 1,000 times (and sometimes 10,000) more revenue than the average user.

Morgan Stanley estimates that the average Amazon Prime user spends 4.5 times as much each year as the average non-Prime user (Louis Columbu, 2018). There are plenty of examples of big Amazon spenders purchasing $5,000, $10,000, $30,000 or more each year, or greater than 10 times the average Prime user. Google might follow this business model and add buy button on Instagram and YouTube, which are its best properties that are already filled with incredibly popular product content that already drives purchase decisions. This will definitely diversify its current ad supported model and generate much revenue from its best users.

MYTHS ABOUT DIGITALIZATION CREATING MONSTROUS BUSINESS EMPIRES

Does exponential growth of disruptive digital technologies cover customers globally and create monopolies? Assisting smaller third-party producers to joining platforms those digital giants create new markets and provide better choice for end customers.

Do those digital giants create ecosystems that limit access of competing technologies? One could never stop technological progress, next new technologies will disrupt established companies and replace their ecosystems.

Do digital giants buy out new tech companies before they grow to become competitors? Yes they do, providing revolving turnover of venture capital that is invested into new start ups.

Is the world moving to oligopolistic competition of digital ecosystems rather than a competition among single advanced technology companies? Yes, it is, so what's wrong with this? Big 3 competing consulting companies enlist McKinsey, BCG and Bain, Big 4 global auditors are harshly competing with each other, there are 3-5 competing telecom operators in each national market, and few leading messengers globally.

Questions arise from this:

- is this competition fair and ethical?
- does this oligopoly competition limits or accelerates progress?
- as digital ecosystems become global and transnational, should national governments and nations interfere to regulate the process to protect their companies?
- should governing bodies of economic and political unions regulate digital ecosystems' competition?
- does economic and political bureaucracy has conflict of interest in regulating digital markets?
- bureaucracy vs. business: who is going to win?

We already noticed above that current eight largest Internet leaders — Apple, Amazon, Microsoft, Google, Alibaba, Tencent, and Netflix are diversifying their business models and compete with each other in all markets. Alibaba and Ant Financials ecosystem incorporates e-commerce, deliveries and payments. Apple enters into financial sector and video streaming production confronting Netflix and Amazon.

The management teams running Facebook, Google, Amazon, Microsoft, etc. are all unquestionably brilliant. And none of them actually run a business with bad economics. In fact, their businesses have some of the best economics in the history of business. Perhaps the only thing greater than what these businesses have already accomplished is what they aspire to accomplish going forward. There seems to be nothing off limits for these industry giants, which means more competition is inevitable particularly with each other. As the fight continues for control of our phones, our homes, our cars, our wallets, our food, our health, our time, a key weapon on the battlefield will be what business model they wield.

Amazon reshapes business and consumer sectors hosting convenient digital platform open for third-party sellers. This is sometimes the only opportunity for those smaller companies to enter the market. So Amazon as a platform enables third-party businesses to operate, providing access to clients, charging feasible commission for this. At the other hand, third-party sellers are an important part of Amazon's income, up 40% year-on-year. So it looks like a win-win deal, not restricting competition, but actually establishing new markets. EU's competition commissioner, MargretheVestager, confirmed that her team had launched a preliminary investigation into how Jeff Bezos' company was using data from third-party sellers on its platform.

"The question here is about the data, because if you as Amazon get the data from the smaller merchants that you host -- which can be of course completely legitimate because you can improve your service to these smaller merchants -- well, do you then also use this data to do your own calculations? What is the new big thing, what is it that people want, what kind of offers do they like to receive, what makes them buy things". In my view, using big data analysis is completely legitimate, and if advantages in business result from technology, which the company acquired through its R&D and investments, not from artificially constructed barriers, why would regulators bother to interfere?

Facebook with its Libra wants to bring its family of apps' 2.7 billion users into the world of cryptocurrency. Today's money doesn't work for everyone. Those of us living comfortably in developed nations likely don't see the hardships that befall migrant workers or the unbanked abroad. Preyed on by greedy payday lenders and high-fee remittance services, targeted by muggers and left out of traditional financial services, the poor get poorer. Facebook CEO Mark Zuckerberg explained some of the philosophy behind Libra and Calibra. "Facebook is coming together with 27 organizations around the world to start the non-profit Libra Association and create a new currency called Libra (Zuckerberg, 2019). Libra's mission is to create a simple global financial infrastructure that empowers billions of people around the world. It's powered by blockchain technology and the plan is to launch it in 2020. Being able to use mobile money can have an important positive impact on people's lives because you don't have to always carry cash, which can be insecure, or pay extra fees for transfers. This is especially important for people who don't have access to traditional banks or financial services. Right now, there are around a billion people who don't have a bank account but do have a mobile phone. It's decentralized — meaning it's run by many different organizations instead of just one, making the system fairer overall. It's available to anyone with an internet connection and has low fees and costs. And it's secured by cryptography which helps keep your money safe. This is an important part of our vision for a privacy-focused social platform — where you can interact in all the ways you'd want privately, from messaging to secure payments."

That's deeply worrisome to some experts and officials. Experts claim it arises the issue of security. They remind that allowing anyone to build on the Facebook app platform and its low barriers to "innovation" are exactly what opened the door for Cambridge Analytica to hijack 87 million people's personal data and use it for political ad targeting. Facebook naturally has a huge target on its back for hackers. A shady developer could build a wallet that just cleans out a user's account or funnels their coins to the wrong recipient, mines their purchase history for marketing data or uses them to launder money. Digital risks become a lot less abstract when real-world assets are at stake. $1.7 billion in cryptocurrency was stolen last year alone, according to CypherTrace via CNBC. Calibra's head of product Kevin Weil says: "The minute that you start limiting it is the minute you start walking back to the system you have today with a closed ecosystem and a smaller number of competitors, and you start to see fees rise." "As with anything, there's fraud and there are scams in the existing financial ecosystem today . . . that's going to be true of Libra too. There's nothing special or magical that prevents that," says Weil, who concluded, "I think those pros massively outweigh the cons."(Weil, 2019).

"We should assume that there is a chance that this could have systemic risk and design it in a way that it cannot become a systemic risk," David Marcus, the head of new Facebook subsidiary Calibra, told on October 15th, 2019. He mentioned that Facebook's massive user base of about 2.7 billion people could make Libra so large that disruption could risk system-wide financial instability. Nevertheless, Facebook users will not instantly become Libra users on day one. Those wanting to have a "Calibra" wallet for the currency will have to upload their government ID and identify themselves before they can buy, sell, and pay for things using Libra. In his view, it's going to take a long time for Libra to actually on-board a lot of people for this to come even close to a systemic risk. In this case, it is obvious, that government should track the developments and gradually regulate the process, instead of banning it.

GLOBAL BUREACRATS AS NEW COMMUNISTS

French Finance Minister Bruno Le Maire told Europe 1 radio that Libra can't be allowed to "become a sovereign currency." Why are officials so anxious? Steve Forbes, Editor-in-Chief of Forbes magazine, in his open letter to Mark Zuckerberg writes: "...if you play your cards right with the Libra, you could be to money and finance what Henry Ford was to automobiles. Your new currency could take its place alongside the inventions of coins and paper money many centuries ago. It could replace the U.S. dollar as the global currency" (Forbes, 2019).

Bureaucrats are afraid they are losing control over monetary circulation that takes national currencies emission centers out of business. And bureaucrats out of job. Strict anti-laundering, anti-terrorist and KYC regulation imposed on banks globally did not make the world neither more honest nor safer, but laid excessive burden upon financial institutions and their clients, piling up their costs related to performing formal regulatory procedures. And vastly extending bureaucratic staff numbers within institutions. Bureaucrats have won this game, now they are looking at how to put their hands on still unregulated crypto world.

The US government has taken extreme and unprecedented steps against Huawei, cutting it off from every US partner at the risk of a long-term rupture in trade between the US and China. American intelligence officials and telecommunications executives and experts have begun to concede that the United States will be operating in a world where Huawei and other Chinese telecom companies most likely control 40 to 60 percent of the networks over which businesses, diplomats, spies and citizens do business. Official position of the US government on primary source of the controversy is the long-held belief from lawmakers and the US intelligence community that Huawei acts on behalf of the Chinese government, undermining US national security and posing cybersecurity and privacy risks for American and UK customers.

Real explanation of measures taken can be found in Donald Trump's words: "Huawei is something that's very dangerous. You look at what they've done from a security standpoint, from a military standpoint, it's very dangerous. So, it's possible that Huawei even would be included in some kind of a trade deal. If we made a deal, I could imagine Huawei being possibly included in some form, some part of a trade deal".

CONCLUSION

This case demonstrates that big American boss easily uses administrative pressure as instrument in global trade war among nations (against China with its Huawei, and Russia with its Nord Stream gas pipeline), at the same time intending to strengthen the position of his national corporations. Global technological disruption affects the world economy boosting markets volatility and political instability. It frightens sovereign bureaucrats making them fight back and impose regulations to freeze changes. Donald Trump's election and Brexit demonstrated reaction of population to bureaucrats' claims to regulate each and every one from the top. Trump was seen as an opponent to bureaucratic establishment. Nevertheless, after becoming US President, Trump is eager to use administrative instruments to regulate markets in favor of his nation. This is what all bureaucrats do in their countries to demonstrate their importance to the public. Will these setbacks stop globalization that goes through global tech platforms? Not necessarily. Even if the US administration stops Facebook from launching its Libra, there is Pavel Durov's GRAM under way.

REFERENCES

Barrabi, Y. (2018). *Amazon's online market share may be smaller than previously thought*. Retrieved from https://www.foxbusiness.com/retail/amazon-market-share-ecommerce-sales

Brandom, R. (2019). *Trump's latest explanation for the Huawei ban is unacceptably bad*. Retrieved from https://www.theverge.com/2019/5/23/18637836/trump-huawei-ban-explanation-trade-deal-national-security-risk

Columbus, L. (2018). *10 Charts That Will Change Your Perspective of Amazon Prime's Growth*. Retrieved from https://www.forbes.com/sites/louiscolumbus/2018/03/04/10-charts-that-will-change-your-perspective-of-amazon-primes-growth/#7af3d41f3fee

Constine, J. (2019). *The real risk of Facebook's Libra coin is crooked developers. They'll steal your money, not just your data*. Retrieved from https://techcrunch.com/2019/06/18/libra-analytica/?guccounter=1&guce_referrer_us=aHR0cHM6Ly9tLmhpZ2h0ZWNoLnBsdXMvMjAxOS8wNi8xOS92bGFzdGktc3NoYS1wb3p2YWxpLWN1a2VyYmVyZ2EtbmEta292ZXItemEtbGlicmEtZHVyb3Ytc2xlZHV5dXNoaWk&guce_referrer_cs=WsUh01_2aY0HYUPOmILv8A

Cheung, B. (2019). *Libra's co-founder: 'There is a chance' the cryptocurrency could present systemic risk*. Retrieved from https://finance.yahoo.com/news/libra-david-marcus-cofounder-on-systemic-risk-facebook-cryptocurrency-112940839.html

Feng, E. (2018). *Who Has The Best Business Model (And It's Not Google Or Facebook)*. Retrieved from https://medium.com/@efeng/who-has-the-best-business-model-and-its-not-google-or-facebook-ca36f967bbd1

Forbes, S. (2019). *Open Letter To Mark Zuckerberg*. Retrieved from https://www.forbes.com/sites/steveforbes/2019/06/25/open-letter-to-mark-zuckerberg/#265a15ca2614

Hamilton, I. A. (2018). *After Slapping Google and Apple With Major Fines, the EU Is Now Investigating Amazon.* Retrieved from https://www.inc.com/business-insider/eu-investigating-amazon-data-use-after-google-apple.html

Hamilton, I. A. (2018). *Trump says Google, Amazon, and Facebook may be 'very antitrust' but stops short of calling for a breakup of the firms.* Retrieved from https://www.businessinsider.com/donald-trump-says-google-amazon-and-facebook-may-be-very-antitrust-2018-8?r=UK

Harrison, J. (2018). *One photo shows that China is already in a cashless future.* Retrieved from https://www.businessinsider.com/alipay-wechat-pay-china-mobile-payments-street-vendors-musicians-2018-5?r=US&IR=T

Iqbal, M. (2019). *WeChat Revenue and Usage Statistics (2019).* Retrieved from https://www.businessofapps.com/data/wechat-statistics/

Lecher, C. (2019). *European regulators are already pressing Facebook about its cryptocurrency.* Retrieved from https://www.google.com/amp/s/www.theverge.com/platform/amp/2019/6/18/18683574/facebook-libra-cryptocurrency-regulation-europe-france-germany

Lunden, I. (2018). *Amazon's share of the US e-commerce market is now 49%, or 5% of all retail spend.* Retrieved from https://techcrunch.com/2018/07/13/amazons-share-of-the-us-e-commerce-market-is-now-49-or-5-of-all-retail-spend/?guccounter=1&guce_referrer_us=aHR0cHM6Ly90ZWNoY3J1bmNoLWNvbS5jZG4uYW1wcHJvamVjdC5vcmcv&guce_referrer_cs=ezIDg2mi5Ro6jfkFq37XJg

Sanger, D. (2019). *Trump Wants to Wall Off Huawei, but the Digital World Bridles at Barriers.* Retrieved from https://www.nytimes.com/2019/05/27/us/politics/us-huawei-berlin-wall.html

Worldwide desktop market share of leading search engines from January 2010 to July 2019. (2019). Retrieved from https://www.statista.com/statistics/216573/worldwide-market-share-of-search-engines/

Yang, Y. (2018). *China's WeChat hits 1bn user accounts worldwide.* Retrieved from https://www.ft.com/content/8940f2d0-2059-11e8-a895-1ba1f72c2c11

Yoo, E. (2018). *WeChat mini programs 1 year on: Key figures and trends.* Retrieved from https://technode.com/2018/01/18/wechat-mini-programs-2017/

YutingF. (2018). Retrieved from http://chinafilminsider.com/the-secret-to-wechat-mini-games-success-interview-with-li-qing-director-of-mini-games-department/

A. (2018). *The 7 biggest fines the EU have ever imposed against giant companies.* Retrieved from https://www.businessinsider.com/the-7-biggest-fines-the-eu-has-ever-imposed-against-giant-corporations-2018-7#4-qualcomm-fined-12-billion-in-2018-4

ZuckerbergM. (2019). Retrieved from https://m.facebook.com/story.php?story_fbid=10107693323579671&id=4&_rdr

Kelly, M. (2019). *Top Democrat calls for strict oversight on Facebook's new cryptocurrency.* Retrieved from https://www.theverge.com/2019/6/18/18683996/facebook-cryptocurrency-democrat-sherrod-brown-oversight-libra

KEY TERMS AND DEFINITIONS

Amazon: An American multinational technology company based in Seattle, Washington, that focuses on e-commerce, cloud computing, digital streaming, and artificial intelligence. It is considered one of the Big Four technology companies along with Google, Apple, and Facebook.

Anti-Laundering Regulation: A set of laws, regulations, and procedures intended to prevent criminals from disguising illegally obtained funds as legitimate income. Though anti-money-laundering (AML) laws cover a relatively limited range of transactions and criminal behaviors, their implications are far-reaching.

Anti-Terrorist Regulation: Laws with the purpose of fighting terrorism. They usually, if not always, follow specific bombings or assassinations. Anti-terrorism legislation usually includes specific amendments allowing the state to bypass its own legislation when fighting terrorism-related crimes, under the grounds of necessity.

Calibra: Wallet app is built on blockchain technology to enable people to move Libra, a borderless cryptocurrency, freely, securely and affordably.

Cybersecurity: Is the protection of internet-connected systems, including hardware, software and data, from cyberattacks. In a computing context, security comprises cybersecurity and physical security -- both are used by enterprises to protect against unauthorized access to data centers and other computerized systems.

Digital Platform: Any web-based platform for presenting content (things like Facebook, Twitter, Blogs, Websites, and sometimes SMS).

Digital Risks: Cyber risks and traditional risks with a digital component.

E-Commerce: Is the activity of electronically buying or selling of products on online services or over the internet. electronic commerce draws on technologies such as mobile commerce, electronic funds transfer, supply chain management, internet marketing, online transaction processing, electronic data interchange (edi), inventory management systems, and automated data collection systems. e-commerce is in turn driven by the technological advances of the semiconductor industry, and is the largest sector of the electronics industry.

Facebook: An American online social media and social networking service company based in Menlo Park, California.

Google: An American multinational technology company that specializes in Internet-related services and products, which include online advertising technologies, search engine, cloud computing, software, and hardware. It is considered one of the Big Four technology companies, alongside Amazon, Apple, and Facebook.

Huawei: A Chinese multinational technology company that provides telecommunications equipment and sells consumer electronics, including smartphones and is headquartered in Shenzhen, Guangdong province.

KYC Regulation: Is the process of a business verifying the identity of its clients and assessing their suitability, along with the potential risks of illegal intentions towards the business relationship. The term is also used to refer to the bank regulations and anti-money laundering regulations which govern these activities. Know your customer processes are also employed by companies of all sizes for the purpose of ensuring their proposed customers, agents, consultants, or distributors are anti-bribery compliant. Banks, insurers, export creditors and other financial institutions are increasingly demanding that customers provide detailed due diligence information.

Libra: A global cryptocurrency built on blockchain to promote financial inclusion.

Microsoft: An American multinational technology company with headquarters in Redmond, Washington. It develops, manufactures, licenses, supports, and sells computer software, consumer electronics, personal computers, and related services.

Pavel Durov: Is a Russian entrepreneur who is best known for being the founder of the social networking site VK, and later the Telegram Messenger.

Pavel Durov's GRAM: Cryptocurrency based on the TON blockchain platform created by Pavel Durov.

R&D: Is the process by which a company works to obtain new knowledge that it might use to create new technology, products, services, or systems that it will either use or sell.

Silicon Valley: A region in the southern part of the San Francisco Bay Area in Northern California that serves as a global center for high technology, innovation, and social media.

Telefonica: A Spanish multinational telecommunications company headquartered in Madrid, Spain. It is one of the largest telephone operators and mobile network providers in the world. It provides fixed and mobile telephony, broadband and subscription television, operating in Europe and the Americas.

Compilation of References

A. (2018). *The 7 biggest fines the EU have ever imposed against giant companies*. Retrieved from https://www.businessinsider.com/the-7-biggest-fines-the-eu-has-ever-imposed-against-giant-corporations-2018-7#4-qualcomm-fined-12-billion-in-2018-4

Abdelal, R., Di Tella, R., & Schlefer, J. (2008, July 30). *Corruption in Germany*. Harvard Business School case 709006. Retrieved from https://hbr.org/product/corruption-in-germany/709006-PDF-ENG

Accountability. (2005). *Stakeholder Engagement. The practical guide to organizing*. Retrieved from http://www.urban-economics.ru/sites/default/files/2528_import.pdf

ACFE. (2018). *Report to the Nations 2018 - Global Study on Occupational Fraud and Abuse Asia-Pacific Edition*. Retrieved from https://www.acfe.com/uploadedFiles/ACFE_Website/Content/rttn/2018/RTTN-Asia-Pacific-Edition.pdf

Adel, C., Hussain, M. M., Mohamed, E. K., & Basuony, M. A. (2019). Is corporate governance relevant to the quality of corporate social responsibility disclosure in large European companies? *International Journal of Accounting & Information Management*, *27*(2), 301–332. doi:10.1108/IJAIM-10-2017-0118

Agarwal, R., & Holmes, R. M. Jr. (2019). Dialogue: Let's not focus on income inequality. *Academy of Management Review*, *44*(2), 450–460. doi:10.5465/amr.2018.0128

Aggarwal, V. S., & Jha, A. (2019). Pressures of CSR in India: An institutional perspective. *Journal of Strategy and Management*, *12*(2), 227–242. doi:10.1108/JSMA-10-2018-0110

Aghion, P., Bloom, N., & Van Reenen, J. (2014). Incomplete Contracts and Internal Organization of Firms. *Journal of Law Economics and Organization*, *30*(suppl 1), i37–i63. doi:10.1093/jleo/ewt003

Agrawal, A. (2018, Apr.). The economics of Artificial Intelligence. *McKinsey Quarterly*.

Agrawal, A., Gans, J., & Goldfarb, A. (2018). *Prediction Machines. The Simple Economics of Artificial Intelligence*. Boston, MA: Harvard Business Review Press.

Aguilera, R. V., & Cuervo-Cazurra, A. (2009). Codes of good governance. *Corporate Governance*, *17*(3), 376–387. doi:10.1111/j.1467-8683.2009.00737.x

Aguilera, R. V., & Jackson, G. (2010). Comparative and international corporate governance. *The Academy of Management Annals*, *4*(1), 485–556. doi:10.5465/19416520.2010.495525

Al-Absy, M. S. M., Ismail, K. N. I. K., & Chandren, S. (2019). Corporate governance mechanisms and family directives: Aggressive or conservative in earnings management? *Academy of Accounting and Financial Studies Journal*, *23*, 1-9. Retrieved from https://www.abacademies.org/articles/Corporate-Governance-Mechanisms-And-Family-Directives-1528-2635-23-1-335.pdf

Alexandre, L. (2017). *La Guerre des Intelligences: Intelligence Artificielle versus Intelligence Humaine*. Paris: JC Lattès.

Allen, J., & Rui, L. (2018, August 25). *Awakening governance: ACGA China corporate governance report 2018*. Asian Corporate Governance Association. Retrieved April 30, 2019, from https://corpgov.law.harvard.edu/2018/08/25/awakening-governance-acga-china-corporate-governance-report-2018/

Alpaydin, E. (2016). *Machine Learning. The new AI*. Cambridge, MA: The MIT Press.

American Bar Association. (2011). Corporate director's guidebook (6th ed.). Chicago, IL: American Bar Association (ABA), Business Law Section, Corporate Law Committee.

Anderson, A., & Gupta, P. P. (2009). A cross-country comparison of corporate governance and firm performance: Do financial structure and the legal system matter? *Journal of Contemporary Accounting & Economics*, *5*(2), 61–79. doi:10.1016/j.jcae.2009.06.002

Arbib, M. A. (Ed.). (2003). The Handbook of Brain Theory and Neural Networks. Cambridge, MA: The MIT Press.

Arcot, S., Bruno, V., & Faure-Grimaud, A. (2010). Corporate governance in the UK: Is the comply or explain approach working? *International Review of Law and Economics*, *30*(2), 193–201. doi:10.1016/j.irle.2010.03.002

Areneke, G., Yusuf, F., & Kimani, D. (2019). Anglo-American governance adoption in non-Anglo-American settings: Assessing practitioner perceptions of corporate governance across three emerging economies. *Managerial Auditing Journal*, *34*(4), 486–514. doi:10.1108/MAJ-12-2017-1733

Ariely, D. (2008). *Predicably Irrational. The Hidden Forces that Shape our Decisions*. New York: HarperCollins.

Artificial Intelligence (AI) as a key factor in the digitalization of the global economy. (2017). CRN/RE. Retrieved from https://www.crn.ru/news/detail.php? ID=117544

Asllani, A., & Naco, M. (2014). Using Benford's Law for Fraud Detection in Accounting Practices. *Journal of Social Science Studies*, *2*(1), 129. doi:10.5296/jsss.v2i1.6395

Associated Press. (2019, March 28). Trump: Google will aid military, not China. *Houston Chronicle,* p. B2 (Business).

Athanasopoulou, A., Bouwman, H., & Nikayin, F. (n.d.). *The disruptive impact of digitalization on the automotive ecosystem: a research agenda on business models, platforms and consumer issues*. Retrieved from https://pdfs.semanticscholar.org/181c/f4663467b69658aff1c6171813d518c26662.pdf

Australian Government, Department of Families, Housing, Community Services and Indigenous Affairs. (2010, June). *Corporate governance handbook for company directors and committee members: A reference guide to understanding the serious commitment of being a company director or committee member* (2nd ed.). Retrieved May 14, 2019, from https://www.dss.gov.au/sites/default/files/documents/05_2012/gov_handbook_2010.pdf

Baer, T. & Kamalnath, V. (2017). *Controlling machine-learning algorithms and their biases*. McKinsey & Company.

Bainbridge, S. M. (2010, October 27). *The corporate governance provisions of Dodd-Frank*. UCLA School of Law, Law-Econ Research Paper No. 10-14. Retrieved May 14, 2019, from https://ssrn.com/abstract=1698898

Bainbridge, S. M. (2008). *The new corporate governance in theory & practice*. Oxford University Press.

Bakan, J. (2001). *The corporation*. Free Press.

Bala, M., & Verma, D. (2019). An empirical investigation of managerial perceptions in Indian organizations regarding CSR after legislation of CSR in India. *International Journal of Research in Social Sciences*, *9*, 1098–1136. Retrieved from https://www.researchgate.net/profile/Deepak_Verma67/publication/332130202_AN_EMPIRICAL_INVESTIGATION_OF_MANAGERIAL_PERCEPTIONS_IN_INDIAN_ORGANISATIONS_REGARDING_CSR_AFTER_LEGISLATION_OF_CSR_IN_INDIA

Bank of Russia. (2003). *Polozhenie Banka Rossii ot 16 dekabrya 2003 g. N° 242-P «Ob organizacii vnutrennego kontrolya v kreditny`x organizaciyax i bankovskix gruppax»* (in Russian). Retrieved from http://base.garant.ru/584330

Bank of Russia. (2005). *Pis`mo Banka Rossii N° 92-T «Ob organizacii upravleniya pravovy`m riskom i riskom poteri delovoj reputacii v kreditny`x organizaciyax i bankovskix gruppax»* (in Russian). Retrieved from http://base.garant.ru/585600

Bank of Russia. (2018). *Polozhenie o raskry`tii informacii e`mitentami e`missionny`x cenny`x bumag* (N 454-P, approved on 30.12.2014 by the Bank of Russia) (Zaregistrirovano v Minyuste Rossii 12.02.2015 N 35989) (in Russian). Retrieved from http://www.consultant.ru/document/cons_doc_LAW_175536/

Bankewitz, Aberg, & Teuchert. (2016). *Digitalization and Boards of Directors: A New Era of Corporate Governance?* doi:10.5430/bmr.v5n2p58

Barnett, M. L., & Salomon, R. M. (2012). Does it pay to be really good? Addressing the shape of the relationship between social and financial performance. *Strategic Management Journal*, *33*(11), 1304–1320. doi:10.1002mj.1980

Baron, E. (2019, April 23). 2 [women] claim Google retaliation after organizing global walkout. *Houston Chronicle*, p. B5 (Business).

Barrabi, Y. (2018). *Amazon's online market share may be smaller than previously thought.* Retrieved from https://www.foxbusiness.com/retail/amazon-market-share-ecommerce-sales

Barrat, J. (2013). *Our Final Invention. Artificial Intelligence and the end of the Human Area.* New York: Dunne Books.

Basel Committee on Banking Supervision. (2009). *Consultative Document. Proposed Enhancements to the Basel II Framework.* Retrieved from http://www.bis.org/publ/bcbs150.pdf

Basel Committee on Banking Supervision. (2011). *Basel III: A Global Regulatory Framework for More Resilient Banks and Banking Systems.* Retrieved from http://www.bis.org/publ/bcbs189.pdf

Batra, G., Queirolo, A., & Santhanam, N. (2017). *Artificial Intelligence: The time to act is now.* McKinsey & Company.

Baxter-Kellman, R. (2015). *Het Membership Model. Wat je van Netflix, Spotify en Starbucks kunt leren.* Amsterdam: Business Contact.

BCG (Flexible Cell Manufacturing). (n.d.). Retrieved from https://www.bcg.com/publications/2018/flexible-cell-manufacturing-revolutionize-carmaking.aspx

Berle, A., & Means, G. (1932). *The modern corporation & private property.* Transaction Press.

Berns, G. (2008). *Iconoclast. A neuroscientist reveals how to think differently.* Academic Press.

Birol, B. (2019). Corporate Governance and Fraud Detection: A Study From Borsa Instanbul. *Eurasian Journal of Business and Management*, *7*(1), 44–64. doi:10.15604/ejbm.2019.07.01.005

Bistrong, R. (2019, April 17). *Management can own honesty or deceit. So pick one.* Retrieved April 20, 2019, from http://www.fcpablog.com/blog/2019/4/17/management-can-own-honesty-or-deceit-so-pick-one.html

Blanc, R., Cho, C. H., Sopt, J., & Branco, M. C. (2019). Disclosure responses to a corruption scandal: The case of Siemens AG. *Journal of Business Ethics*, *156*(2), 545–561. doi:10.100710551-017-3602-7

Bohte, J., & Meier, K. J. (2000). Goal displacement: Assessing the motivation for organizational cheating. *Public Administration Review*, *60*(2), 173–182. doi:10.1111/0033-3352.00075

Borison, A., & Hamm, G. (2010). Prediction Markets: A new tool for strategic decision making. *California Management Review*, *52*(4), 125–141.

Bostrom, N. (2014). *Superintelligence. Paths, Dangers, Strategies*. Oxford, UK: Oxford University Press.

Bourton, S., Lavoie, J., & Vogel, T. (2018). Will Artificial Intelligence make you a better leader? *The McKinsey Quarterly*.

Bowers, S. (2012, May 17). *Files close on BCCI banking scandal: Liquidators and lawyers acting for creditors to BCCI hold final meeting with victims of bank's collapse*. Retrieved May 14, 2019, from https://www.theguardian.com/business/2012/may/17/files-close-bcci-banking-scandal

Brafman, O., & Brafman, R. (2010). *Click. The Magic of Instant Connections*. New York: Random House.

Brandom, R. (2019). *Trump's latest explanation for the Huawei ban is unacceptably bad*. Retrieved from https://www.theverge.com/2019/5/23/18637836/trump-huawei-ban-explanation-trade-deal-national-security-risk

Brockman, J. (Ed.). (2019). *Possible Minds. 25 Ways of Looking at AI*. London: Penguin.

Brown, S. R. (2010). *Merchant kings: When companies ruled the world, 1600–1900*. Macmillan.

Brynjolfsson, E., & McAfee, A. (2014). *The Second Machine Age. Work, Progress, and Prosperity in a Time of Brilliant Technologies*. New York: WW Norton Company.

Brynjolfsson, E., & McAfee, A. (2014). *The second machine age: work, progress and prosperity in a time of brilliant technologies*. New York: W.W Norton and Company.

Bucci, S. (2019, April 26). More regulation isn't answer to pipeline cyberattacks. *Houston Chronicle*, p. A15.

Bughin, J., & van Zeebroeck, N. (2018, July). Artificial Intelligence: Why a Digital Base is critica. *McKinsey Quarterly*.

Bunyan, D., & Sarkis, K. (2019, May 6). *Making connections with the new digital consumer: To thrive in a world of apps, platforms, and privacy concerns, marketers have to become multitaskers*. Retrieved from https://www.strategy-business.com/feature/Making-connections-with-the-new-digital-consumer?

Burkhardt, R., Hohn, N. & Wigley, C. (2019). *Leading your organization to responsible AI*. McKinsey Analytics.

By 2075 the thought processes of the robot will be indistinguishable from human. (2017). Astera. Retrieved from http://www.astera.ru/news/?id=118667

Cadbury Committee. (1992). *Report of the committee on the financial aspects of corporate governance (Cadbury Report)*. London, UK: Gee. Retrieved May 14, 2019, from http://www.ecgi.org/codes/documents/cadbury.pdf

Campbell, D., Meyer, M., Xin, L., & Stack, K. (2015). *Haier: Zero distance to the customer*. Harvard Business School Case Study 115-006. Retrieved from https://www.hbs.edu/faculty/Pages/item.aspx?num=49076

Carslaw, C. A. P. N. (1988). Anomalies in Income Numbers: Evidence of Goal Oriented Behavior. *The Accounting Review*, *63*(2), 321–327. doi:10.2307/248109

Cassin, R. L. (2019, April 4). *At Fresenius, management owned the graft*. Retrieved April 20, 2019, from http://www.fcpablog.com/blog/2019/4/4/at-fresenius-management-owned-the-graft.html

Chalmers, D. (1996). *The Conscious Mind. In search of a Fundamental Theory*. New York: Oxford University Press.

Chen, C. C. (2019). A one-size-fits-all approach to corporate governance codes and compliance by smaller listed firms: An examination of companies listed in Hong Kong and Singapore. *Berkeley Business Law Journal, 15*(2), 337-364. Retrieved May 14, 2019, from https://ssrn.com/abstract=3339668

Chen, V. Z., Li, J., & Shapiro, D. M. (2011). Are OECD-prescribed "good corporate governance practices" really good in an emerging economy? *Asia Pacific Journal of Management, 28*(1), 115–138. doi:10.100710490-010-9206-8

Cheung, B. (2019). *Libra's co-founder: 'There is a chance' the cryptocurrency could present systemic risk*. Retrieved from https://finance.yahoo.com/news/libra-david-marcus-cofounder-on-systemic-risk-facebook-cryptocurrency-112940839.html

Christensen, C. M., Hall, T., Dillon, K., & Duncan, D. S. (2016). *Competing against Luck. The Story of Innovation and Customer Choice*. New York: HarperCollins Business Publ.

Christie, A. (1930). The Murder at the Vicarage. Academic Press.

Cicon, J. E., Ferris, S. P., Kammel, A. J., & Noronha, G. (2012). European corporate governance: A thematic analysis of national codes of governance. *European Financial Management, 18*(4), 620–648. doi:10.1111/j.1468-036X.2010.00542.x

CleanGovBiz. (2014). *The rationale for fighting corruption*. Retrieved May 13, 2019, from http://www.oecd.org/cleangovbiz/49693613.pdf

CNBC.com. (n.d.). Retrieved from https://www.cnbc.com/2018/09/10/is-fast-fast-enough-for-vinfast-vietnams-first-automaker.html

Cohen, R. (1991, December 20). *Maxwell's empire: How it grew, how it fell – A special report; Charming the big bankers out of billions*. Retrieved May 14, 2019, from https://www.nytimes.com/1991/12/20/business/maxwell-s-empire-it-grew-it-fell-special-report-charming-big-bankers-billions.html

Collins, J. C. (2017). Using Excel and Benford ' s Law to detect fraud. *Journal of Accountancy*. Retrieved from https://www.journalofaccountancy.com/issues/2017/apr/excel-and-benfords-law-to-detect-fraud

Columbus, L. (2018). *10 Charts That Will Change Your Perspective of Amazon Prime's Growth*. Retrieved from https://www.forbes.com/sites/louiscolumbus/2018/03/04/10-charts-that-will-change-your-perspective-of-amazon-primes-growth/#7af3d41f3fee

Constine, J. (2019). *The real risk of Facebook's Libra coin is crooked developers. They'll steal your money, not just your data*. Retrieved from https://techcrunch.com/2019/06/18/libra-analytica/?guccounter=1&guce_referrer_us=aHR0cHM6Ly9tLmhpZ2h0ZWNoLnBsdXMvMjAxOS8wNi8xOS92bGFzdGktc3NoYS1wb3p2YWxpLWN1a2VyYmVyZ2EtbmEta292ZXItemEtbGlicmEtZHVyb3Ytc2xlZHV5dXNoaWk&guce_referrer_cs=WsUh01_2aY0HYUPOmlLv8A

Cooke, C. A. (1950). *Corporation, trust, and company: An essay in legal history*. Manchester University Press.

Coolhaas, W. Ph. (Ed.). (1960). *Generate Missiven van Gouverneurs-Generaal en Raden aan Heren XVII der Verenigde Oostindische Compagnie*. Gelderblom.

Corrales, M., Fenwick, M., & Haapio, H. (Eds.). (2019). *Legal Tech, Smart Contracts & Blockchain*. Springer.

Culture's Consequences. (1980). *International Differences in Work-Related Values. Geert Hofstede*. SAGE Publications.

Cuomo, F., Mallin, C., & Zattoni, A. (2016). Corporate governance codes: A review and research agenda. *Corporate Governance, 24*(3), 222–241. doi:10.1111/corg.12148

Dahya, J., McConnell, J. J., & Travlos, N. G. (2002). The Cadbury Committee, corporate performance, and top management turnover. *The Journal of Finance*, *57*(1), 461–483. doi:10.1111/1540-6261.00428

DARPA SyNAPSE Program. (2013). *Artificial Brains*. Retrieved from www.artificialbrains.com/darpasynapse-program

Das, S. C. (2019). Indian company law on corporate governance–A critical analysis. *The Management Accountant Journal*, *54*(2), 61–64. doi:10.33516/maj.v54i2.61-64p

Davenport, T. H., & Ronanki, R. (2018, Jan.). Artificial Intelligence for the Real World. Don't start with moon shots. *Harvard Business Review*, 108–116.

de Almeida, M. L. F. (2015). *A fraude de relato financeiro e a indepenência dos auditores*. Universidade Autónoma de Lisboa. Retrieved from http://repositorio.ual.pt/handle/11144/2400

Deep Learning for Enterprise Applications. (2016). *Tractica*. Retrieved from https://www.tractica.com/research/deeplearning-for-enterprise-applications

Deep Learning Market by Application (Image Recognition, Signal Recognition, Data Mining), Offering (Hardware (Von Neumann and Neuromorphic Chip), and Software), End-User Industry, and Geography – Global Forecasts to 2022. (2016). *Markets and Markets*. Retrieved from http://www.marketsandmarkets.com/Market-Reports/deeplearning-market-107369271.html

Deep learning: opportunities, prospects and abit of history. (2016). *Habrahabr*. Retrieved from https://habrahabr.ru/company/it-grad/blog/309024

Deheane, S. (2014). *Consciousness and the Brain: Deciphering How the Brain codes our Thoughts*. London: Penguin.

del Mar Miras-Rodríguez, M., Martínez-Martínez, D., & Escobar-Pérez, B. (2019). Which corporate governance mechanisms drive CSR disclosure practices in emerging countries? *Sustainability*, *11*(1), 61–80. doi:10.3390u11010061

Deloitte. (2017). *Researching Advanced Management Tools and Practices*. Retrieved from https://www2.deloitte.com/content/dam/Deloitte/ru/Documents/financial-services/russian/issledovanie-peredovyh-upravlencheskih-instrumentov-i-praktik.pdf

Digital transformation in the automotive industry. (n.d.). Retrieved from https://www.ibm.com/downloads/cas/LVDZDXOA

Digital Transformation of Industries. Automotive Industry. (2016). *Word Economic Forum*. Retrieved from http://reports.weforum.org/digital-transformation/wp-content/blogs.dir/94/mp/files/pages/files/wef-dti-automotivewhitepaper-final-january-2016.v1.pdf

Dinh, T. Q., & Calabrò, A. (2019). Asian family firms through corporate governance and institutions: A systematic review of the literature and agenda for future research. *International Journal of Management Reviews*, *21*(1), 50–75. doi:10.1111/ijmr.12176

Domingos, P. (2015). *The Master Algorithm. How the quest for the ultimate learning machine will remake our world.* London: Penguin.

Donaldson, T. (2000). Are business managers "professionals?" *Business Ethics Quarterly*, *10*(1), 83–93. doi:10.2307/3857697

dos Santos, C. C. (2014). *Aplicação da Lei de Benford na auditoria : estudo de caso*. Instituto Politécnico de Leiria. Retrieved from https://iconline.ipleiria.pt/handle/10400.8/1114

Drake, P. D., & Nigrini, M. J. (2000). Computer assisted analytical procedures using Benford's Law. *Journal of Accounting Education*, *18*(2), 127–146. doi:10.1016/S0748-5751(00)00008-7

Drucker, P. (1946). *The concept of the corporation*. Academic Press.

Duarte, J., Kong, K., Siegel, S., & Young, L. (2014). The impact of the Sarbanes–Oxley Act on shareholders and managers of foreign firms. *Review of Finance*, *18*(1), 417–455. doi:10.1093/rof/rft008

Durtschi, C., Hillison, W., & Pacini, C. (2004). The Effective Use of Benford ' s Law to Assist in Detecting Fraud in Accounting Data. *Journal of Forensic Accounting*, *9*(99), 17–34.

Dyck, A., Lins, K. V., Roth, L., & Wagner, H. F. (2019). Do institutional investors drive corporate social responsibility? International evidence. *Journal of Financial Economics*, *131*(3), 693–714. doi:10.1016/j.jfineco.2018.08.013

Economist Intelligence Unit. (2005). *Reputation: Risk of Risks*. Retrieved from http://www.acegroup.com/eu-en/assets/risk-reputation-report.pdf

Erisman, P. (2015). *Alibaba's World. How a remarkable Chinese company is changing the face of global business*. London: Palgrave MacMillan.

European Commission. (n.d.). *2018 reform of EU data protection rules: Stronger rules on data protection mean people have more control over their personal data and businesses benefit from a level playing field*. Retrieved May 14, 2019, from https://ec.europa.eu/commission/priorities/justice-and-fundamental-rights/data-protection/2018-reform-eu-data-protection-rules_en

Evseeva, S.A. (2012). Stakeholder theory as the basis of the concept of sustainable development of an organization. *Science and Business: Development Paths, 10*(16).

Facebook will reserve $3 billion in probe. (2019, April 25). *Houston Chronicle*, p. B2 (Business).

Farag, H., & Mallin, C. (2019). Monitoring corporate boards: Evidence from China. *European Journal of Finance*, *25*(6), 524–549. doi:10.1080/1351847X.2017.1369138

Feng, E. (2018). *Who Has The Best Business Model (And It's Not Google Or Facebook)*. Retrieved from https://medium.com/@efeng/who-has-the-best-business-model-and-its-not-google-or-facebook-ca36f967bbd1

Fenwick, M., & Vermeulen, E. P. M. (2016). *Seven corporate venturing strategies to foster innovation*. TILEC Discussion Paper No. 2016/23. Retrieved from https://papers.ssrn.com/sol3/papers.cfm?abstract_id=2823008

Fenwick, M., & Vermeulen, E. P. M. (2018). Evaluating the board of directors. *European Corporate Governance Institute Law*. Working Paper No. 425/2018.

Fenwick, M., Vermeulen, E. P. M. (2019). Technology & corporate governance. *The Texas Journal of Business Law, 48*(1).

Fenwick, M. (2016). The new corporate criminal law & transnational legal risk. In M. Fenwick, & S. Wrbka (Eds.), *Flexibility in modern business law: a comparative assessment*. (p. 149). Springer. doi:10.1007/978-4-431-55787-6_8

Fenwick, M., McCahery, J. A., & Vermeuelen, E. P. M. (2019). The end of 'corporate' governance: hello platform governance. *European Business Organization Law Review*, *20*(1), 171–199. doi:10.100740804-019-00137-z

Fenwick, M., & Vermeulen, E. P. M. (2015). The New Firm: Staying Relevant, Unique, & Competitive. *European Business Organization Law Review*, *16*(4), 595–623. doi:10.100740804-016-0040-4

Fenwick, M., & Vermeulen, E. P. M. (2020). *The unmediated and technology-driven corporate governance of today's winning companies*. New York University Journal of Law and Business.

Ferraro, F. (2019). Going political? Towards deliberative corporate governance. *The Journal of Management and Governance*, *23*(1), 3–20. doi:10.100710997-018-9433-9

Ferreira, M. J. M. (2013). *Lei de Benford e detecção de fraude contabilística : aplicação à indústria transformadora em Portugal.* Instituto Superior de Economia e Gestão. Retrieved from https://www.repository.utl.pt/handle/10400.5/6134

Filatotchev, I., Jackson, G., & Nakajima, C. (2013). Corporate governance and national institutions: A review and emerging research agenda. *Asia Pacific Journal of Management, 30*(4), 965–986. doi:10.100710490-012-9293-9

Financial Reporting Council. (2012, September). *The UK Stewardship Code.* London: FRC. Retrieved May 14, 2019, from https://www.frc.org.uk/getattachment/d67933f9-ca38-4233-b603-3d24b2f62c5f/UK-Stewardship-Code-(September-2012).pdf

Financial Reporting Council. (2018, July). *The UK Corporate Governance Code.* London: FRC. Retrieved May 14, 2019, from https://www.frc.org.uk/getattachment/88bd8c45-50ea-4841-95b0-d2f4f48069a2/2018-UK-Corporate-Governance-Code-FINAL.PDF

Financial Reporting Council. (2019, January 30). *Consulting on a revised UK Stewardship Code.* Retrieved May 14, 2019, from https://www.frc.org.uk/consultation-list/2019/consulting-on-a-revised-uk-stewardship-code

Finger, Z. S. (2001). *Origins of Neuroscience: A history of explorations into Brain Function.* Oxford, UK: Oxford University Press.

Finkelstein, S., Whitehead, J., & Campbell, A. (2008). *Think Again. Why good leaders make bad decisions and how to keep it from happening to you.* Boston: Harvard Business Press.

Finlay, S. (2018). *Artificial Intelligence and Machine Learning for Business. A no-nonse guide to Data-driven Technologies.* London: Relativistic Publications.

Forbes, S. (2019). *Open Letter To Mark Zuckerberg.* Retrieved from https://www.forbes.com/sites/steveforbes/2019/06/25/open-letter-to-mark-zuckerberg/#265a15ca2614

Forbes.com. (n.d.). Retrieved from https://www.forbes.com/sites/maryjosephs/2017/03/15/u-s-manufacturing-labor-shortage-how-to-make-your-company-a-happy-exception/#190cfda17e13

Ford, M. (2018). *Architects of Intelligence. The truth about AI from the people building it.* Birmingham, UK: Packt Publishing.

Fram, E. (2005, Winter). *Are professional board directors the answer?* Retrieved May 13, 2019, from https://sloanreview.mit.edu/article/are-professional-board-directors-the-answer/

Franceschetti, B. M., & Koschtial, C. (2013). Do bankrupt companies manipulate earnings more than the non-bankrupt ones? *Journal of Finance & Accountancy, 12*, 4–24.

Freeman, R. E. (1984). *Strategic Management: A Stakeholder Approach.* Boston: Harpercollins College Div.

Freeman, R. E. (2017). The new story of business: Towards a more responsible capitalism. *Business and Society Review, 122*(3), 449–465. doi:10.1111/basr.12123

Fronin, V. (2018). *Vladislav Fronin: V CzK o publikacii ne znali!* (in Russian). Retrieved from https://www.kp.ru/daily/26918/3965399/

Furr, N., & Shipilov, A. (2019, July). Digital doesn't have to be Disruptive. The best results can come from adaptation rather than revinvention. *Harvard Business Review*, 94–103.

Furta, S.D., & Solomatina, T.B. (2010). *Stakeholder map - a tool for analyzing the business environment.* Academic Press.

Future 500. (2018). *Top 10 Stakeholder Engagement Trends of 2018*. Retrieved from https://www.future500.org/blog/top-10-stakeholder-engagement-trends-2018

Fu, Y. (2019). The value of corporate governance: Evidence from the Chinese anti-corruption campaign. *The North American Journal of Economics and Finance*, *47*, 461–476. doi:10.1016/j.najef.2018.06.001

Galbraith, J. K. (1967). *The new industrial state*. Houghton Mifflin.

Galloway, S. (2017). *The four: The hidden DNA of Amazon, Apple, Facebook, & Google*. Random House.

Gazzaniga, M. (2011). *Who's in charge? Free will and the science of the brain*. New York: HarperCollins.

Gazzaniga, M. (2015). *Tales from both sides of the Brain. A life of neuroscience*. New York: HarperCollins.

Geissbauer, R.; Schrauf, S. & Pillsbury, S. (2018). Digital Champions. *Strategy + Business*.

Gelderblom, O. (2013). *Cities of commerce: The institutional foundations of international trade in the low countries, 1250–1650*. Princeton University Press.

George, G., Haas, M. R., & Pentland, A. (2014). Big data and management. *Academy of Management Journal*, *57*(2), 321–326. doi:10.5465/amj.2014.4002

Giao, C., & Raposo, C. C. (2014). Corporate governance and earnings quality: International evidence. *Journal of Accounting and Finance*, *14*, 52–74. Retrieved from http://www.na-businesspress.com/JAF/RaposoCC_Web14_3_.pdf

Gigerenzer, B. (2014). *Risk Savvy. How to make good decisions*. Lane Books.

Gill, A. (2009). Corporate governance as social responsibility: A research agenda. *Berkeley Journal of International Law*, *26*, 5. doi:10.15779/Z38MS9P

Gilovich, T., & Ross, L. (2016). *The Wisest One in the Room. How to harness Psychology's Most Powerful Insights*. London: OneWorld Publishing.

Global Automotive Executive Survey, KPMG. (2018). Retrieved from https://home.kpmg/uk/en/home/insights/2018/01/2018-global-automotive-executive-survey.html

Global digital operations research. (2018). Retrieved from https://www.pwc.com/gx/en/industries/industry-4-0.html

Gold, J. I., & Shadlen, M. N. (2007). The Neural Basis of Decision-Making. *Annual Review of Neuroscience*, *30*(1), 535–574. doi:10.1146/annurev.neuro.29.051605.113038 PMID:17600525

González, J. S., & García-Meca, E. (2014). Does corporate governance influence earnings management in Latin American markets? *Journal of Business Ethics*, *121*(3), 419–440. doi:10.100710551-013-1700-8

Gordeeva, M.V., & Petrova, I.A. (2018). Project quality management in the context of the digitalization of the economy. *Step into the future: artificial intelligence and the digital economy. A revolution in management: a new digital economy or a new world of machines*, 33-35.

Gouran, M. (2013, February 13). Corporate governance 2.0: The boardroom collides with the digital age. *Korn Ferry Institute Briefing Magazine*. Retrieved April 20, 2019, from https://www.kornferry.com/institute/579-corporate-governance-2-0-the-boardroom-collides-with-the-digital-age

Grant Halverson, H. & Rock, D. (2015). Beyond Bias. *Strategy + Business*, (80).

Gratton, L. (2011). The Shift. The future of work is already here. London: William Collins (Harper Collins).

GRI. (n.d.). Retrieved from http://database.globalreporting.org/search/

Gupta, S. (2018). *Driving Digital Strategy: A Guide to Reimaging Your Business*. Harvard Business Review Press. Retrieved from http://en.wikipedia.org/wiki/Intangible_asset

Gupta, S. (2018). *Driving Digital Strategy. A guide to reimagining your business*. Boston, MA: Harvard Business School Press.

Guthry, J. (2019). *The woman who saved John McAfee from an epically bad deal*. Retrieved from https://www.wired.com/story/the-woman-who-saved-john-mcafees-biscuits/?fbclid=IwAR0HXX0093NMMXco4mz41zvsmoCy33SH7bFxGhp6HLk8lyApquTze1x_tgM&mbid=social_fb&utm_brand=wired&utm_campaign=wired&utm_medium=social&utm_social-type=owned&utm_source=facebook

Hadden, T. (1972). *Company law and capitalism*. Weidenfeld & Nicolson.

Hagel, J. (2016). The big shift in business models. *The Marketing Journal*. Retrieved from http://www.marketingjournal.org/the-big-shift-in-business-models-john-hagel/

Hall, P. A., & Soskice, D. (Eds.). (2001). *Varieties of capitalism: The institutional foundations of comparative advantage*. Oxford, UK: Oxford University Press. doi:10.1093/0199247757.001.0001

Hamel, G., & Zanini, M. (2018). The end of bureaucracy. *Harvard Business Review*. Retrieved from https://hbr.org/2018/11/the-end-of-bureaucracy

Hamilton, I. A. (2018). *After Slapping Google and Apple With Major Fines, the EU Is Now Investigating Amazon*. Retrieved from https://www.inc.com/business-insider/eu-investigating-amazon-data-use-after-google-apple.html

Hamilton, I. A. (2018). *Trump says Google, Amazon, and Facebook may be 'very antitrust' but stops short of calling for a breakup of the firms*. Retrieved from https://www.businessinsider.com/donald-trump-says-google-amazon-and-facebook-may-be-very-antitrust-2018-8?r=UK

Hanelt, A., Piccinini, E., Gregory, R., Hildebrandt, B., & Kolbe, L. (2015). Digital Transformation of preliminary Industries. Exploring the impact of Digital trends on business Models of Automobile Manufacturers. *Proceedings of the 12th Internationalen Tagung Wirtschaftsinformatik*, 1313-1327.

Harris, M. A., & Martin, R. (2019). Promoting cybersecurity compliance. In I. Vasileiou & S. Furnell (Eds.), *Cybersecurity education for awareness and compliance* (pp. 54–71). Hershey, PA: IGI Global. doi:10.4018/978-1-5225-7847-5.ch004

Harrison, J. (2018). *One photo shows that China is already in a cashless future*. Retrieved from https://www.businessinsider.com/alipay-wechat-pay-china-mobile-payments-street-vendors-musicians-2018-5?r=US&IR=T

Harwell, W. (2018). *Research handbook on the history of corporate and company law*. Edward Elgar.

Haxhi, I., & Van Ees, H. (2009). Explaining diversity in the worldwide diffusion of codes of good governance. *Journal of International Business Studies*, *41*(4), 710–726. doi:10.1057/jibs.2009.39

Heath, C., & Heath, D. (2013). *Decisive. How to make better decisions*. London: Randomhouse.

Heather, A. (2017). Is this Netflix presentation Silicon Valley's most important document? *Mindtools*. Retrieved from https://www.mindtools.com/blog/netflix-presentation/

Herzog, L. (2019). Professional ethics in banking and the logic of "integrated situations": Aligning responsibilities, recognition, and incentives. *Journal of Business Ethics*, *156*(2), 531–543. doi:10.100710551-017-3562-y

Hess, M. F., & Broughton, E. (2014). Fostering an ethical organization from the bottom up and the outside in. *Business Horizons*, *57*(4), 541–549. doi:10.1016/j.bushor.2014.02.004

Hess, M. F., & Cottrell, J. H. Jr. (2016). Fraud risk management: A small business perspective. *Business Horizons*, *59*(1), 13–18. doi:10.1016/j.bushor.2015.09.005

Hindls, R., & Hronová, S. (2015). Benford's Law and Possibilities for Its Use in Governmental Statistics. *Statistika: Statistics and Economy Journal*, *95*(2), 54–64.

Hinton, G. E., & Salakhutdinov, R. R. (2006). Reducing the Dimensionality of Data with Neural Networks. *Science*, *313*. Retrieved from http://www.cs.toronto.edu/~hinton/science.pdf

Ho, J. (2018, May 3). *Governance in the digital age*. Retrieved October 15, 2019, from https://home.kpmg/sg/en/home/media/press-contributions/2018/05/governance-in-the-digital-age.html

Hoffman, R., Casnocha, B., & Yeh, C. (2014). The Alliance: Managing Talent in a Networked Age. *Harvard Business Review*.

Huse, M. (2007). *Boards, governance and value creation: The human side of corporate governance*. Cambridge, UK: Cambridge University Press; doi:10.1017/CBO9780511611070

Hwang, V. W., & Horowitt, G. (2012). *The Rainforest: The Secret to Building the Next Silicon Valley*. Regenweld.

IBM Institute for business value. (2015). *Automotive 2025: Industry without borders, Executive Report*. IBM Corporation.

IBM. (n.d.). Retrieved from https://www.ibm.com/blogs/internet-of-things/iot-data-that-keeps-your-workers-safe/

Institute of Directors in Southern Africa. (2016). *King IV: Report on corporate governance for South Africa 2016*. Retrieved October 15, 2019, from https://cdn.ymaws.com/www.iodsa.co.za/resource/collection/684B68A7-B768-465C-8214-E3A007F15A5A/IoDSA_King_IV_Report_-_WebVersion.pdf

International Organization for Standardization. (n.d.). *ISO 37001 – Anti-bribery management systems*. Retrieved May 13, 2019, from https://www.iso.org/iso-37001-anti-bribery-management.html

International Regulatory Framework for Banks (Basel III). (n.d.). Retrieved from http://www.bis.org/bcbs/basel3.htm

Iqbal, M. (2019). *WeChat Revenue and Usage Statistics (2019)*. Retrieved from https://www.businessofapps.com/data/wechat-statistics/

Jackson, A. (2002). Gaming of performance indicators: A classification related to impact. In A. Neely & A. Walters (Eds.), *Performance Management Association 2002 conference proceedings*. Boston: PMA.

Jacoby, G., Liu, M., Wang, Y., Wu, Z., & Zhang, Y. (2019). Corporate governance, external control, and environmental information transparency: Evidence from emerging markets. *Journal of International Financial Markets, Institutions and Money*, *58*, 269–283. doi:10.1016/j.intfin.2018.11.015

Jap, S. D., Robertson, D. C., Rindfleisch, A., & Hamilton, R. (2013). Low-stakes opportunism. *JMR, Journal of Marketing Research*, *50*(2), 216–227. doi:10.1509/jmr.10.0121

Jensen, M. C., & Meckling, W. H. (1976). Theory of the firm: Managerial behavior, agency costs and ownership structure. *Journal of Financial Economics*, *3*(4), 305–360. doi:10.1016/0304-405X(76)90026-X

Jensen, M. C., & Meckling, W. H. (1976). Theory of the firm: Managerial behavior, agency costs and ownership structure. *Journal of Financial Economics, No.*, *3*(4), 303–360. doi:10.1016/0304-405X(76)90025-8

Jenson, D., Quinlivan, S., Radloff, J., Jensen, T., Cotter, A., & Weitz, M. (2010, August 15). *Summary of corporate governance provisions in the Dodd-Frank Act.* Stinson LLP. Retrieved April 30, 2019, from http://dodd-frank.com/summary-of-corporate-governance-provisions-in-the-dodd-frank-act/

Jenson, M. C., & Meckling, W.H. (1976). Theory of the Firm: Managerial Behavior, Agency Costs and Ownership Structure. *Journal of Finance & Economics, 3*(305).

Jiang, F., & Kim, K. A. (2015). Corporate governance in China: A modern perspective. *Journal of Corporate Finance, 32*, 190–216. doi:10.1016/j.jcorpfin.2014.10.010

Jordan, C. E., Clark, S. J., & Hames, C. (2011). Manipulating Sales Revenue To Achieve Cognitive Reference Points: An Examination Of Large U.S. Public Companies. *Journal of Applied Business Research, 25*(2). doi:10.19030/jabr.v25i2.1039

Kahneman, D. & Klein, G. (2010, Mar.). Strategic Decisions: When Can You Trust Your Gut? *McKinsey Quarterly.*

Kahneman, D. (2011). *Thinking, Fast and Slow*. London: Penguin-Pearson.

Kahneman, D. (2011, Nov.). Beware the inside view. *McKinsey Quarterly.*

Kahneman, D., Lovallo, D., & Sibony, O. (2011, June). Before You Make That Big Decision. *HBR*, 50-60.

Kahneman, D., Rosenfield, A.M., Gandhi, L., & Blaser, T. (2016). Noise. Inconsistent Decision-making. *HBR*, 38-46.

Kanter, R. M. (2009). Supercorp. How Vanguard Companies Create Innovation, Profits, Growth, and Social Good. New York: Academic Press.

Kanter, R. M. (2011, Nov.). How Great Companies Think Differently. *Harvard Business Review*, 66–78.

Kavis, M. (2015). How connected cars will transform industries. *Forbes*. Available at: http://www.forbes.com/sites/mikekavis/2015/02/20/how-connected-cars-will-transformindustries/

Kay, J. (2019). The Concept of the Corporation' (2019). *Business History, 61*(7), 1129–1143. Accessed 20 August2019. doi:10.1080/00076791.2018.1509956

Ke, R., Li, M., & Zhang, Y. (2019, March 15). Directors' informational role in corporate voluntary disclosure: An analysis of directors from related industries. SMU Cox School of Business Research Paper No.19-4. Retrieved April 20, 2019, from doi:10.2139srn.3353395

Keay, A. (2014). Comply or explain in corporate governance codes: In need of greater regulatory oversight? *Legal Studies, 34*(2), 279–304. doi:10.1111/lest.12014

Kelly, M. (2019). *Top Democrat calls for strict oversight on Facebook's new cryptocurrency.* Retrieved from https://www.theverge.com/2019/6/18/18683996/facebook-cryptocurrency-democrat-sherrod-brown-oversight-libra

Kerr, S. (1975). On the folly of rewarding A, while hoping for B. *Academy of Management Journal, 18*(4), 769–783. PMID:1235930

Kevles, B. H. (1997). *Naked to the bone: Medical Imaging in the Twentieth Century.* New Brunswick, NJ: Rutgers University Press.

Khalin, V.G., & Chernova, G.V. (2018). Digitalization and its impact on the Russian economy and society: advantages, challenges, threats and risks. *Management Consulting, 10*, 46-63.

Kiel, F. (2015a). *Return on Character. The Real Reason Leaders and Their Companies Win.* Boston: Harvard Business Review Press.

Kiel, F. (2015b, Apr.). Measuring the Return On Character. *Harvard Business Review*, 20–21.

King, D. L., & Case, C. J. (2014). Sarbanes-Oxley Act and the Public Company Accounting Oversight Board's first eleven years. *Journal of Business and Accounting*, *7*, 11–23.

Kinni, T. (2019, April 18). *In praise of the purposeless company: No purpose? No problem. Create customers, care for employees, be a good citizen, and make money instead.* Retrieved April 30, 2019, from https://www.strategy-business.com/blog/In-praise-of-the-purposeless-company?gko=5c476&utm

Kizza, J. M. (2017). *Ethical and Social Issues in the Information Age*. Cham: Springer. doi:10.1007/978-3-319-70712-9

Klein, G. (2013). *Seeing What Others Don't. The Remarkable Ways We Gain Insights.* London: Nicholas Brealey Publishing.

Knowledge@Wharton. (2019, April 17). *Don't panic: The digital revolution isn't as unusual as you think* [interview with Tom Wheeler, author of From Gutenberg to Google: The history of our future, 2019]. Retrieved April 20, 2019, from https://knowledge.wharton.upenn.edu/article/tom-wheeler-fcc-book/

Kote, T. (2015). How Silicon Valley will reinvent the auto industry. *Forbes*. Available at: http://www.forbes.com/sites/thejokote/2015/05/05/how-silicon-valley-will-reinvent-the-autoindustry/

Koushanfar, F., Sadeghi, A.-R., & Seudi, H. (2012). *EDA for Secure and Dependable Cyber-cars: Challenges and Opportunities*. Paper presented at DAC 2012, San Francisco, CA.

KPMG. (2014). *Me, my car, my life the ultra-connected age*. KPMG International report.

Kubíček, A., Štamfestová, P., & Strouhal, J. (2016). Cross-country analysis of corporate governance codes in the European Union. *Economia e Sociologia (Evora, Portugal)*, *9*, 319–337. doi:10.14254/2071-789X.2016/9-2/22

Kurzweil, R. (2006). *The Singularity is near. When humans transcend biology*. London: Penguin.

Kurzweil, R. (2012). *How to create a Mind. The secrets of human thoughts revealed*. London: Viking.

La Porta, R., Lopez-de-Silanes, F., Shleifer, A., & Vishny, R. (2000). Investor protection and corporate governance. *Journal of Financial Economics*, *58*(1-2), 3–27. doi:10.1016/S0304-405X(00)00065-9

Lawrence, M. A. (2017). Financialism: A (Very) Brief History. In *Understanding the 12 Technological Forces that Will Shape Our Future*. Academic Press.

Lecher, C. (2019). *European regulators are already pressing Facebook about its cryptocurrency*. Retrieved from https://www.google.com/amp/s/www.theverge.com/platform/amp/2019/6/18/18683574/facebook-libra-cryptocurrency-regulation-europe-france-germany

Lee, K.-F. (2018). *AI Superpowers China, Silicon Valley, and the New World Order*. New York: Houghton Mifflin Harcourt Publishing Company.

Leibenstein, H. (1966). Allocative Efficiency VS. "X-Efficiency. *The American Economic Review*, *56*(3), •••.

Libert, B., Beck, M., & Wind, J. (2016). *The Network Imperative. How to survive and grow in the Age of Digital Business Models*. Cambridge, MA: Harvard Business Review Press.

Lieberman, M. D. (2013). *Social. Why our brains are wired to connect*. New York: Penguin Randomn House.

Likens, S. & Kersey, K. (2019, May). Automating trust with new technologies. *Strategy + Business*.

Lindstrom, M. (2008). *Buyology: Truth and Lies about Why we Buy*. New York: Broadway Books.

Lohr, S. (2015). *Data-ism. The revolution transforming decision-making, consumer behavior, and almost everything else*. New York: HarperCollins.

London Stock Exchange Group. (2017, September 2). *London Stock Exchange Group launches guidance for ESG reporting*. Retrieved May 14, 2019, from https://www.lseg.com/resources/media-centre/press-releases/london-stock-exchange-group-launches-guidance-esg-reporting

London, S., Chui, M. & Whigley, C. (2019). *The ethics of Artificial Intelligence.* McKinsey & Company.

Lowe T., Wilson R. (2015). Playing the game of outcomes-based performance management. Is gamesmanship inevitable? Evidence from theory and practice. *Social Policy and Administration*. doi:10.1111pol.12205

Lozano, J. M. (2010). *The Relational Company. Responsibility, Sustainability, Citizenship*. Bern: Peter Lang. doi:10.3726/978-3-0353-0326-1

Luca, M., Kleinberg, J., & Mullainanthan, S. (2016, Jan.). Algorithms need managers, too. Know how to get the most out of your predictive tools. *Harvard Business Review*, 96–101.

Luger, G. F., & Stubblefield, W. A. (1998). *Artificial Intelligence. Structures and Strategies for Complex Problem Solving*. Harlow, MA: Addison Wesley Longman.

Lunden, I. (2018). *Amazon's share of the US e-commerce market is now 49%, or 5% of all retail spend.* Retrieved from https://techcrunch.com/2018/07/13/amazons-share-of-the-us-e-commerce-market-is-now-49-or-5-of-all-retail-spend/?guccounter=1&guce_referrer_us=aHR0cHM6Ly90ZWNoY3J1bmNoLWNvbS5jZG4uYW1wcHJvamVjdC5vcmcv&guce_referrer_cs=ezIDg2mi5Ro6jfkFq37XJg

Makridadis, S., Hogarth, R., & Gaba, A. (2010). *Dance with Chance. Making Luck Work For You.* London: Penguin.

Malone, T. W. (2018). How Human-Computer 'Superminds' are Redefining the Future of Work. *MIT Sloan Management Review*, 34–41.

Manyika, J., Chui, M., Bughin, J., Dobbs, R., Bisson, P., & Marrs, A. (2013). *Disruptive technologies: Advances that will transform life, business, and the global economy*. McKinsey Global Institute. Retrieved from http://www. mckinsey.com/business-functions/digital-mckinsey/our-insights/disruptive-technologies

Manyika, J., Lund, S., Chui, M., Bughin, J., Woetzel, J., Batra, P., . . . Sanghvi, S. (2017). *Jobs lost, jobs gained: What the future of work will mean for jobs, skills, and wages*. Retrieved from https://www.mckinsey.com/featured-insights/future-of-work/jobs-lost-jobs-gained-what-the-future-of-work-will-mean-for-jobs-skills-and-wages#part4

Manyika, J., Chui, M., & Lund, S. (2017). *What's now and next in Analytics, AI and Automation*. McKinsey & Company.

Martynova, M., & Renneboog, L. (2011). Evidence on the international evolution and convergence of corporate governance regulations. *Journal of Corporate Finance*, *17*(5), 1531–1557. doi:10.1016/j.jcorpfin.2011.08.006

McCahery, J. A., & Vermeulen, E. P. M. (2009). Corporate Governance of Non-Listed Companies Oxford University Press.

McKinsey Global Institute. (2017). *Artificial Intelligence: The Next Digital Frontier?* Retrieved from: https://www.mckinsey.com/~/media/McKinsey/Industries/Advanced%20Electronics/Our%20Insights/How%20artificial%20intelligence%20can%20deliver%20real%20value%20to%20companies/MGI-Artificial-Intelligence-Discussion-paper.ashx

McRitchie, J. (2013, November 20). *Review & reflections: The Cadbury Committee*. Review of L. F. Spira and J. Slinn, *The Cadbury Committee: A History*. Oxford, UK: Oxford University Press. Retrieved May 14, 2019, from https://www.corpgov.net/2013/11/review-reflections-the-cadbury-committee/

Mediascope. (2019). *Mediascope Webindex as of March 2019* (in Russian). Retrieved from https://webindex.mediascope.net/report/general-statistics?byGeo=1&byDevice=3&byDevice=1&byDevice=2&byMonth=201903&id=88155&id=16571&id=12285

Mees, B., & Smith, S. A. (2019). Corporate governance reform in Australia: A new institutional approach. *British Journal of Management*, *30*(1), 75–89. doi:10.1111/1467-8551.12298

Mehta, J. (2017, December 19). *MSCI corporate governance country report – India*. Retrieved May 14, 2019, from https://www.arx.cfa/post/MSCI-Corporate-Governance-Country-Report-India-3861.html

Mehta, J., & Brett, A. (2017, July 4). *MSCI's China governance country report*. Retrieved May 14, 2019, from https://www.arx.cfa/post/MSCI-39-s-China-Governance-Country-Report-4818.html

Micklethwait, J., & Wooldridge, A. (2005). *The Company: A Short History of a Revolutionary Idea*. Weidenfeld.

Mikusz, M., Jud, C., & Schäfer, T. (2015). Business Model patterns for the Connected Car and the Example of data orchestrator. In *ICSOB 2015, LNBIP* (pp. 167–173). doi:10.1007/978-3-319-19593-3_14

Milovidov, V.D. (2017). Corporate Governance 2.0: Evolution of the Corporate Relations System in the Information Society. *Problems of National Strategy, 4*(43).

Minichilli, A., Zattoni, A., Nielsen, S., & Huse, M. (2012). Board task performance: An exploration of micro- and macro-level determinants of board effectiveness. *Journal of Organizational Behavior*, *33*(2), 193–215. doi:10.1002/job.743 PMID:23365485

Miorandi, D., Sicari, S., De Pellegrini, F., & Chlamtac, I. (2012). Internet of things: Vision, applications and research challenges. *Ad Hoc Networks*, *10*(7), 1497–1516. doi:10.1016/j.adhoc.2012.02.016

MIT Media Lab. (2012). Retrieved from http://blog.media.mit.edu/2012/07/compasses-over-maps.html

Mitchell, R. K., Agle, B. R., & Wood, D. J. (1997). Toward a Theory of Stakeholder Identification and Salience: Defining the Principle of Who and What Really Counts. *Academy of Management Review*, *22*(4), 853–886. doi:10.5465/amr.1997.9711022105

Moazed, A., & Johnson, N. J. (2016). *Modern Monopolies: What it Takes to Dominate the Twenty First Century Economy*. St. Martin's Press.

Mohaghegzadeh, A. & Svahn F. (2015). *Resource Transformation in Platform Envelopment*. ECSI 2015 Research in Progress papers.

MSCI Inc. (2017, September). *Corporate governance in China: Scores for Chinese companies cluster around the median relative to global peers, VIEs and SOEs have distinct governance risks*. Retrieved April 30, 2019, from https://www.msci.com/documents/10199/1d443a3d-0437-4af7-aa27-ada3a2655f6d

Mufson, S., & McGee, J. (1991, July 28). *BCCI scandal: Behind the 'Bank of Crooks and Criminals.'* Retrieved May 14, 2019, from https://www.washingtonpost.com/archive/politics/1991/07/28/bcci-scandal-behind-the-bank-of-crooks-and-criminals/563f2216-1180-4094-a13d-fd4955d59435/?utm_term=.dc9193c4c686

Nanjok, N., Le Fleming, H. & Srivatsay, N. (2018). Digital Technology and Sustainability: Positive Mutual Enforcement. *Strategy + Business.*

Natesan, P., & du Plessis, P. (2019, February 20). *Why King IV's "apply and explain" is so important*. Retrieved October 15, 2019, from https://www.iodsa.co.za/news/438882/Why-King-IVs-apply-and-explain-is-so-important.htm

National Association of Corporate Directors. (2002). *Corporate director's ethics and compliance handbook*. Arlington, VA: NACD.

New York Stock Exchange. (2014). *NYSE: Corporate governance guide*. Retrieved May 14, 2019, from https://www.nyse.com/publicdocs/nyse/listing/NYSE_Corporate_Governance_Guide.pdf

Newell, S., & Marabelli, M. (2015). Strategic opportunities (and challenges) of algorithmic decision-making: A call for action on the long-term societal effects of "datification." *The Journal of Strategic Information Systems*, *24*(1), 3–14. doi:10.1016/j.jsis.2015.02.001

Nigrini, M. J. (2012). *Benford's Law - applications for forensic accounting, auditing, and fraud detection*. Hoboken, NJ: John Wiley & Sons, Inc. doi:10.1002/9781119203094

Nigrini, M. J. (2017). Audit Sampling Using Benford's Law: A Review of the Literature with Some New Perspectives. *Journal of Emerging Technologies in Accounting*, *14*(2), 29–46. doi:10.2308/jeta-51783

Nigrini, M. J., & Miller, S. J. (2009). Data Diagnostics Using Second-Order Tests of Benford's Law. *Auditing*, *28*(2), 305–324. doi:10.2308/aud.2009.28.2.305

Norris, F. (2010). *Demystify the Lehman shell game*. Retrieved from http://www.nytimes.com/2010/04/02/business/02norris.html?_r=0

Nottingham Business School. (n.d.). Retrieved from https://www4.ntu.ac.uk/nbs/document_uploads/73575.pdf

Novozhilova, Y.V. (2017). Information and analytical support of integrated reporting: assessment of the influence of stakeholders on the change in created value. *Statistics and Economics, 1*, 43-50.

NSD. (2018). *NSD and Interfax Launch New Product – the Single Disclosure Window Service*. Retrieved from https://www.nsd.ru/en/press/ndcnews/index.php?id36=634082

Nunes, A., Inácio, H., & Marques, R. P. (2019). A Lei de Benford e a deteção de fraude em auditoria nas empresas portuguesas. In *Iberian Conference on Information Systems and Technologies, CISTI*. Coimbra, Portugal: IEEE.

O'Neill, R. (2018). *Common Threads: Designing Impactful Engagement*. Retrieved from https://sustainability.com/wp-content/uploads/2018/11/sa-common-threads-full-report.pdf

OECD. (2015). *G20/OECD Principles of Corporate Governance*. Paris: OECD Publishing. Retrieved from https://onekindplanet.org/animal/seagull/

Organisation for Economic Co-operation and Development. (2015, November 30). *G20/OECD principles of corporate governance*. Retrieved May 14, 2019, from https://www.oecd-ilibrary.org/governance/g20-oecd-principles-of-corporate-governance-2015_9789264236882-en

Organisation for Economic Co-operation and Development. (n.d.). *List of OECD member countries - Ratification of the Convention on the OECD*. Retrieved May 14, 2019, from http://www.oecd.org/about/membersandpartners/list-oecd-member-countries.htm

Osborne, J. (2019, May 12). Who will protect U.S. pipelines? Understaffed TSA under scrutiny over security failures as hacking threats mount for vulnerable, critical network. *Houston Chronicle*, pp. B1, B7 (Business).

Paik, Y., Lee, J. M., & Pak, Y. S. (2019). Convergence in international business ethics? A comparative study of ethical philosophies, thinking style, and ethical decision-making between US and Korean managers. *Journal of Business Ethics*, *156*(3), 839–855. doi:10.100710551-017-3629-9

Parker, G. G., Van Alstyne, M. W.,, ., & Shandgeet, P. C. (2016). *Platform Revolution: How Networked Markets are Transforming the Economy and How to Make them Work for You*. Penguin.

Pearce, J. L., & Perry, J. L. (1983). Federal merit pay: A longitudinal analysis. *Public Administration Review*, *43*(4), 315–325. doi:10.2307/975834

Penrose, R. (2016). *The Emperor's Mind: Concerning Computers, Minds and the Laws of Physics*. Oxford, UK: Oxford University Press.

Pérez-Cornejo, C., de Quevedo-Puente, E., & Delgado-García, J. B. (2019). How to manage corporate reputation? The effect of enterprise risk management systems and audit committees on corporate reputation. *European Management Journal*, *37*(4), 505–515. doi:10.1016/j.emj.2019.01.005

Pernick, R., & Wilder, C. (2008). *The Clean Tech Revolution. Discover the top trends, technologies, and companies to watch*. New York: HarperCollins.

Pham, H. T. S., & Tran, H. T. (2019). Board and corporate social responsibility disclosure of multinational corporations. *Multinational Business Review*, *27*(1), 77–98. doi:10.1108/MBR-11-2017-0084

Placenti, F. M. (Ed.). (2017). *Director's handbook: A field guide to situations commonly encountered in the boardroom*. Chicago, IL: American Bar Association, Business Law Section, Corporate Law Committee.

Polson, N., & Scott, J. (2018). *AIQ. How Artificial Intelligence works and how we can harness its power for a better world*. London: Bantam Press-Penguin.

PricewaterhouseCoopers Southern Africa. (2009, September 2). *Executive guide to King III*. Retrieved May 14, 2019, from https://www.pwc.co.za/en/assets/pdf/executive-guide-to-kingiii.pdf

Priest, D., Krishnamurthy, & Blanter, A. (2018, Apr.). The New Automation is Smart, Fast and Small. Emerging digital tools and techniques are reinventing large-scale IT initiatives, one process at a time. *Strategy + Business*.

Primavera, D. F., & Wright, A. (2018). *Blockchain & the Law*. Harvard University Press.

Principles for Responsible Investment. (n.d.). *What are the Principles for Responsible Investment?* Retrieved April 30, 2019, from https://www.unpri.org/pri/what-are-the-principles-for-responsible-investment

Pro-appraisal. (n.d.). *Ocenka delovoj reputacii* (in Russian). Retrieved from http://pro-appraisal.ru/drugie-vidyi-otsenki/otsenka-delovoy-reputatsii-goodwill

PWC. (2013). *Stabilization Course*. 16th Annual Survey of the Leaders of the World's Largest Companies. Retrieved from https://www.pwc.ru/en/ceo-survey/assets/16th-ceo-survey-russia-rus.pdf

PWC. (2014). *Growth without acceleration*. 17th Annual Survey of the Leaders of the World's Largest Companies. Retrieved from https://www.pwc.ru/en/ceo-survey/assets/17th-ceo-survey-russia-rus.pdf

PWC. (2017). *Peering hopefully into the distance*. 20 Annual Survey of the Leaders of the World's Largest Companies. Retrieved from https://www.pwc.ru/ru/ceo-survey/20th-ceo-survey.pdf

PwC. (2018). *Achieving perfection*. Retrieved from https://www.pwc.ru/ru/publications/achieving-excellence3.html

PwC. (2018a). *Глобальное исследование цифровых операций в* 2018 *г*. Retrieved from https://www.pwc.ru/ru/iot/digital-champions.pdf

PWC. (2018b). *Завтрашний день автомобильной отрасли*. 2018. Retrieved from https://www.pwc.ru/ru/publications/autotech-survey-2018.html

Radnor, Z. (2008). Muddled, massaging, manoeuvring or manipulated? A typology of organizational gaming. *International Journal of Productivity and Performance Management*, *57*(4), 316–328. doi:10.1108/17410400810867526

Raimi, R. A. (1976). The First Digit Problem. *The American Mathematical Monthly*, *83*(7), 521–538. doi:10.1080/00029890.1976.11994162

Randolph, M. (2019). *That Will Never Work: The Birth of Netflix and the Amazing Life of an Idea*. Little, Brown and Company.

Rao, A. & Cameron, E. (2018, July 31). The future of Artificial Intelligence depends on Trust. *Strategy + Business*.

RBC. (2019). *Kompaniyam i bankam razreshili zakretit` 18 vidov danny`x iz-za sankcij* (in Russian). Retrieved from https://www.rbc.ru/economics/11/04/2019/5cae1ee29a7947722c3e75bd?fbclid=IwAR23Jd9pw0GSZ8oU0jR_YrdJC1nt-kX4q745w96eNxnbonS31COKnMbG9MYw

Rees, M. (2018). *On the Future. Prospects for Humanity*. Princeton, NJ: Princeton University Press.

Regan L. (2008). A framework for intergrating reputation risk into the enterprise risk management process. *Journal of Financial Transformation*, *22*, 187–194.

Regulation of the digital economy in France and Europe. (2017). Retrieved from https://www.gouvernement.fr/en/regulation-of-the-digital-economy-in-france-and-europe

Rifkin, J. (2014). *The Zero Marginal Cost Society. The internet of things, the collaborative commons, and the eclipse of capitalism*. New York: Palgrave MacMillan.

Rigaud, L. (1980). *Os Sistemas de Informação na empresa*. Porto: Rés-Editor.

Rink, O. (2005). *Technologies and Innovations. Criteria for Investment Appraisal* (Unpublished MBA dissertation). Kingston Business School.

Rink, O. (2013). *Reputation Management and a Corporate Identity*. Theses of a speech at the ComFest 2013 conference "Communication Unlimited", Mumbai, India. Retrieved from https://www.slideshare.net/olgarink/2013-10-17-arfi-reputation-management-short-32437868

Rink, O. L. (2014). Upravlenie reputacionny`mi riskami: uravnenie s neskol`kimi neizvestny`mi (in Russian). *Moskva: Upravlenie finansovy`mi riskami*, *4*(40), 242-248. Retrieved from https://www.slideshare.net/olgarink/ufr-4-20141

Rink, O., Martyushev, S., Matovnikov, M., & ... (2010). *Organizaciya svyazej s investorami. Rossijskaya i zarubezhnaya praktika*. Moskva: Al`pina. (in Russian)

River, C. (2017). *The Dutch East India Company: The History of the World's First Multinational Corporation*. Createspace.

Roberts, J. (2016). Thinking Machines: The Search for Artificial Intelligence Distillations. *Chemical Heritage Foundation*. Retrieved from https://www.chemheritage.org/distillations/magazine/thinking-machines-the-search-forartificial-intelligence

Rossouw, J., & Styan, J. (2019). Steinhoff collapse: A failure of corporate governance. *International Review of Applied Economics*, *33*(1), 163–170. doi:10.1080/02692171.2019.1524043

Russia 2025: Resetting the Talent Balance. (n.d.). *The Boston Consulting Group*. Retrieved from http://d-russia.ru/wp-content/uploads/2017/11/Skills_Outline_web_tcm26-175469.pdf

Russian Customs Academy. (n.d.). *Digitalization of foreign economic activity*. Report of the expert of the Institutional Development Committee. Retrieved from http://rta.customs.ru/nrta/attachments/4628_Tsifrovizatsia_VED.pdf

Sanderson, A. R. (2012). *Schlefer, Jonathan. The assumptions economists make. Harvard, 2012*. Retrieved May 14, 2019, from http://home.uchicago.edu/arsx/br/Schlefer.pdf

Sanger, D. (2019). *Trump Wants to Wall Off Huawei, but the Digital World Bridles at Barriers*. Retrieved from https://www.nytimes.com/2019/05/27/us/politics/us-huawei-berlin-wall.html

Sarrazin, H., & Willmott, P. (2016, July). *Adapting your board to the digital age*. Retrieved October 15, 2019, from https://www.mckinsey.com/business-functions/mckinsey-digital/our-insights/adapting-your-board-to-the-digital-age

Satariano, A. (2019, May 12). Europe is reining in tech giants, but some say it's going too far: Clampdown online on violent content, hate speech and misinformation brings accusations of government censorship. *Houston Chronicle*, p. B3 (Business).

Satariano, A., & Perlroth, N. (2019, April 22). Conflict arises between insurers, businesses over cyberattacks. *Houston Chronicle,* pp. B26-27.

Satel, S., & Lilienfeld, S. O. (2013). *Brainwashed. The Seductive Appeal of Mindless Neuroscience*. New York: Perseus Books Books.

Schäuble, J. (2019). The impact of external and internal corporate governance mechanisms on agency costs. *Corporate Governance: The International Journal of Business in Society*, *19*(1), 1–22. doi:10.1108/CG-02-2018-0053

Scherbachenko, P. S. (2018). *Management of interaction with stakeholders in Russian companies*. Retrieved from https://cyberleninka.ru/article/n/upravlenie-vzaimodeystviem-so-steykholderami-v-rossiyskih-kompaniyah

Schoemaker & Tetlock. (2017). Building more intelligent enterprises. *MIT Sloan Management Review*, *58*(3), 27-37.

Schouteden, C., Sturges, D, Chow, E., Meloni, M., Engineer, N., Lange, A., … Saleh, T. (2018). *Artificial Intelligence and the Circular Economy. AI as a tool to accelerate the Transition*. Ellen MacArthur Foundation + Google + McKinsey & Company.

Schwartz, J.; Thomson, J. & Kleiner, A. (2016, Dec.). The Neuroscience of Strategic Leadership. Research shows how leaders can take the high road less traveled. *Strategy + Business*.

Schwarz, B., & Sharpe, K. (2010). *Practical Wisdom. The Right Way to Do the Right Thing*. London: Penguin Books.

Seidl, D., Sanderson, P., & Roberts, J. (2009, June). *Applying 'comply-or-explain': Conformance with codes of corporate governance in the UK and Germany*. Centre for Business Research, University of Cambridge Working Paper No. 389. Retrieved May 21, 2019, from https://www.cbr.cam.ac.uk/fileadmin/user_upload/centre-for-business-research/downloads/working-papers/wp389.pdf

Seidl, D., Sanderson, P., & Roberts, J. (2013). Applying the 'comply-or-explain' principle: Discursive legitimacy tactics with regard to codes of corporate governance. *The Journal of Management and Governance*, *17*(3), 791–826. doi:10.100710997-011-9209-y

Shapira, R., & Zingales, L. (2017, September 1). *Is pollution value-maximizing? The DuPont case*. Retrieved May 14, 2019, from http://www.law.northwestern.edu/research-faculty/colloquium/law-economics/documents/Spring18Zingales.pdf

Shermer, M. (2008). Five ways Brain Scans mislead us. *Scientific American, Novembner*, *5*, 1412–1414.

Shi, J., Ausloos, M., & Zhu, T. (2018). Benford's law first significant digit and distribution distances for testing the reliability of financial reports in developing countries. *Physica A*, *492*, 878–888. doi:10.1016/j.physa.2017.11.017

Siegel, J. D. (2010). *Mindsight. Transform your brain with the new science of kindness*. London: OneWorld Publications.

Siegel, J. D. (2017). *Mind. A Journey to the Heart of Being Human*. New York: Norton & Company.

Silver, N. (2012). *The signal and the noise. Why so many predictions fail – but some don't*. New York: Penguin Group Publishing.

Skrynnikova Anastasiya for VC. RU. (2019). *Iz SMI v servis s vy`ruchkoj 1 mlrd rublej v god: e`volyuciya «Banki.ru»* (in Russian). Retrieved from https://vc.ru/finance/67676-iz-smi-v-servis-s-vyruchkoy-1-mlrd-rubley-v-god-evolyuciya-banki-ru

Smith, N. C., & Soonieus, R. (2019). *What's stopping boards from taking action on sustainability? Boards need to look past the low-hanging fruit and start making tough decisions*. Retrieved May 13, 2019, from https://knowledge.insead.edu/responsibility/whats-stopping-boards-from-taking-action-on-sustainability-11436

Smith, P. (1995). On the unintended consequences of publishing performance data in the public sector. *International Journal of Public Administration*, *18*(2/3), 277–310. doi:10.1080/01900699508525011

State of The Advanced Mobility Industry. (2019). *The Drive Towards an Electric and Autonomous Future by GS Capital*. Academic Press.

Stern, J. P. (2016). The English East India Company and the Modern Corporation: Legacies, Lessons, and Limitations. *Seattle University Law Review*, (39), 423.

Stiles, P., & Taylor, B. (1993). Benchmarking corporate governance: The impact of the Cadbury Code. *Long Range Planning*, *26*(5), 61–71. doi:10.1016/0024-6301(93)90078-T

Stilpon Nestor. (2018). *Corporate Governance 2030: Thoughts on the Future of Corporate Governance*. Retrieved from https://corpgov.law.harvard.edu/2018/12/26/corporate-governance-2030-thoughts-on-the-future-of-corporate-governance

Strategy Safari. (1998). *A Guided Tour Through The Wilds of Strategic Management*. Author.

Styhre, A., & Bergström, O. (2019). The benefit of market-based governance devices: Reflections on the issue of growing economic inequality as a corporate concern. *European Management Journal*, *37*(4), 413–420. doi:10.1016/j.emj.2019.01.002

Sumpter, D. (2018). *Outnumbered. From Facebook and Google to fake news and filter-bubbles – the Algorithms that control our lives*. London: Bloomsbury Sigma.

Swaminathan, A., & Herzinger, K. (2018). *Directors and the digital age*. Retrieved October 15, 2019, from https://s3.amazonaws.com/cdn.orrick.com/files/EB-Spring2018-Orrick.pdf

Taleb, N. (2007). *The Black Swan: Second Edition: The Impact of the Highly Improbable*. Random House.

Taleb, N. N. (2005). *Fooled by Randomness. The hidden role of Chance in Life and in the Markets*. New York: Random House Trade Paperbacks.

Taleb, N. N. (2007). *The Black Swan. The Impact of the Highly Improbable*. London: Allen Lane – Penguin.

Taleb, N. N. (2012). *The Antifragile*. Academic Press.

Taleb, N. N. (2018). *Skin in the Game. Hidden Asymmetries in daily life*. New York: Random House.

Tegmark, M. (2016). *Life 3.0. Being Human in the age of Artificial Intelligence*. London: Penguin.

Tenbrunsel, A. E., Diekmann, K. A., Wade-Benzoni, K. A., & Bazerman, M. H. (2010). The Ethical Mirage: A Temporal Explanation as to Why We Are Not As Ethical as We Think We Are. *Research in Organizational Behavior*, *30*, 153–173. doi:10.1016/j.riob.2010.08.004

The Constitution of the Russian Federation. (1993). Retrieved from https://www.dnb.com/about-us/data-cloud.html

The Deep Learning Market Map. 60+ Startups Working Across E-Commerce, Cybersecurity,Sales, And More. (2016). *CB Insights*. Retrieved from https://www.cbinsights.com/blog/deep-learning-aistartups-market-map-company-list

The Digitalisation of the UK Automotive Industry. (n.d.). Retrieved from https://assets.kpmg/content/dam/kpmg/br/pdf/2016/12/smmt-digitalisation-automotive-industry-report.pdf

The WFE Communication Team. (2019). *The World Federation of Exchanges publishes 2018 Full Year Market Highlights*. Retrieved from https://www.world-exchanges.org/news/articles/world-federation-exchanges-publishes-2018-full-year-market-highlightspressrelease

TheJournal.ie. (2016). *Seabirds '10 times' more polluting than humans when it comes to dirtying Ireland's beaches*. Retrieved from https://www.thejournal.ie/seabirds-polluting-humans-beaches-2698817-Apr2016/

Thomas insights. (n.d.). Retrieved from https://news.thomasnet.com/companystory/downtime-costs-auto-industry-22k-minute-survey-481017

Thomas, J. K. (1988). Unusual Patterns In Reported Earnings. *The Accounting Review*, *64*(4), 773. Retrieved from https://ideas.repec.org/p/fth/colubu/fb-_88-34.html

Tononi, G. (2012). *Phi. A Voyage from the Brain to the Soul*. New York: Pantheon Books.

Tractivity. (2018). *Stakeholder Engagement: The Benefits of a Digital Approach*. Retrieved from https://www.tractivity.co.uk/blog/digital-stakeholder-engagement/

Trends in der Transportlogistik. (2017). *Das Logistik-magazin*, 11—12. Retrieved from https://www.verkehrsrundschau.de/fm/3576/WIW_2018.pdf

Tricia, G., & Groysberg, B. (2019). Amazon over the years, based on Jeff Bezos's letters to shareholders. *Harvard Business Review*. Retrieved from https://hbr.org/2019/05/amazons-priorities-over-the-years-based-on-jeff-bezoss-letters-to-shareholders

Tsang, A., Xie, F., & Xin, X. (2019). Foreign institutional investors and corporate voluntary disclosure around the world. *The Accounting Review*, *94*(5), 319–348. doi:10.2308/accr-52353

Ustinov, P. (2017). Are you going to treat us? Robots in white coats. *Forbes*. Retrieved from http://www. forbes.ru/tehnologii/338785-vy-za-nas-eshche-ilechit-budete-roboty-v-belyh-halatah

Valentine. (2014). *Are Boards Flying Blind When it Comes to Enterprise Technology Governance?* doi:10.1080/07366981.2014.881163

Valentine, E., & Stewart, G. (2013, Apr.). The emerging role of the board of directors in enterprise business technology governance. *International Journal of Disclosure and Governance*, 1–17.

Vardi, M. Y. (2019, April 19). Facebook's problem lies in business model. *Houston Chronicle*, p. A19.

Verhezen, P. (2013). Managerial Wisdom in Corporate Governance. In M. Thompson & D. Bevan (Eds.), *Wisdom and Complexity in Organizations*. London: CEIBS & Palgrave. doi:10.1057/9781137002655.0016

Walters, K. (2015, December 1). *Corporate governance in the digital age*. Australian Institute of Company Directors. Retrieved April 20, 2019, from http://www.companydirectors.com.au/director-resource-centre/publications/company-director-magazine/2015-back-editions/december/walters-corporate-governance-in-the-digital-age

Warranty Week. (n.d.). Retrieved from https://www.warrantyweek.com/archive/ww20180405.html

Wathne, K. H., & Heide, J. B. (2000). Opportunism in interfirm relationships: Forms, outcomes, and solutions. *Journal of Marketing*, *64*(4), 36–51. doi:10.1509/jmkg.64.4.36.18070

Weinber, D. (2003). *Small Pieces, Loosely Joined: A Unified Theory of the Web*. Basic Books.

West, S. (2018). Meeting Millennial Expectations in Four Areas of Technology. *Forbes*. Retrieved from: https://www.forbes.com/sites/forbestechcouncil/2018/06/28/meeting-millennial-expectations-in-these-four-areas-of-technology/#3e7c9b244ffc

Whalen, P. (n.d.). *Lehman Brothers and Repo Accounting*. Retrieved from http://sevenpillarsinstitute.org/case-studies/lehman-brothers-and-repo-accounting

What is the difference between artificial intelligence, machine learning and deep learning? (2016). *Nvidia*. Retrieved from http://www.nvidia.ru/object/whatsdifference-ai-machine-learning-deep-learning-blogru.html

Wikipedia. (n.d.). *Gulls*. Retrieved from https://en.wikipedia.org/wiki/Gull

Williams, A., & Zumbansen, P. (Eds.). (2011). *The Embedded Firm: Corporate Governance, Labor, and Finance Capitalism*. Cambridge University Press. doi:10.1017/CBO9780511794537

Williamson, O. E. (1985). The Economic Institutions of Capitalism. Firms, Markets, Relational Contracting. The Free Press.

Wilson, J., & Daugherty, P. R. (2018, July). Collaborative Intelligence: Humans and AI are joining forces. *Harvard Business Review*, 114–123.

Windsor, D. (2009). Tightening corporate governance. *Journal of International Management*, *15*(3), 306–316. doi:10.1016/j.intman.2009.02.003

Windsor, D. (2013). Corporate social responsibility and irresponsibility: A positive theory approach. *Journal of Business Research*, *66*(10), 1937–1944. doi:10.1016/j.jbusres.2013.02.016

Windsor, D. (2019). Influencing MNC strategies for managing corruption and favoritism in Pacific Asia countries: A multiple-theory configurational perspective. *Asia Pacific Business Review*, *25*(4), 501–533. doi:10.1080/13602381.2019.1589769

World Economic Forum Annual Meeting 2016: Mastering the Fourth Industrial Revolution. (2016). *World Economic Forum*. Retrieved from https://www.weforum.org/reports/world-economicforum-annual-meeting-2016-mastering-the-fourthindustrial-revolution

Worldwide desktop market share of leading search engines from January 2010 to July 2019. (2019). Retrieved from https://www.statista.com/statistics/216573/worldwide-market-share-of-search-engines/

Wu, T. (2016). *The Attention Merchants: The Epic Scramble to Get Inside Our Heads*. Vintage.

Xie, J., Nozawa, W., Yagi, M., Fujii, H., & Managi, S. (2019). Do environmental, social, and governance activities improve corporate financial performance? *Business Strategy and the Environment*, *28*(2), 286–300. doi:10.1002/bse.2224

YandexRadar. (2019). *Top Online Projects in Russia*. Retrieved from https://radar.yandex.ru/top_list?month=2019-05

Yang, Y. (2018). *China's WeChat hits 1bn user accounts worldwide*. Retrieved from https://www.ft.com/content/8940f2d0-2059-11e8-a895-1ba1f72c2c11

Yasin, F. M., Muhamad, R., & Sulaiman, N. A. (2014). *Corporate governance research: A review of qualitative literature*. International Conference on Technology and Business Management, University of Malaya. Retrieved May 14, 2019, from http://eprints.um.edu.my/13413/1/D4145-Final.pdf

Yoo, E. (2018). *WeChat mini programs 1 year on: Key figures and trends*. Retrieved from https://technode.com/2018/01/18/wechat-mini-programs-2017/

YutingF. (2018). Retrieved from http://chinafilminsider.com/the-secret-to-wechat-mini-games-success-interview-with-li-qing-director-of-mini-games-department/

Zarkadakis, G. (2015). *In our Image. Savior or Destroyer? The History and Future of Artificial Intelligence*. New York: Pegasus Books.

Zattoni, A., & Cuomo, F. (2010). How independent, competent and incentivized should non- executive directors be? An empirical investigation of good governance codes. *British Journal of Management*, *21*(1), 63–79. doi:10.1111/j.1467-8551.2009.00669.x

Zhang, T., Gino, F., & Bazerman, M. H. (2014). Morality Rebooted: Exploring Simple Fixes to Our Moral Bugs. *Research in Organizational Behavior*, *34*, 63–79. doi:10.1016/j.riob.2014.10.002

ZuckerbergM. (2019). Retrieved from https://m.facebook.com/story.php?story_fbid=10107693323579671&id=4&_rdr

Zumbansen, P. (Ed.). (2011). The Embedded Firm: Corporate Governance, Labor, and Finance Capitalism. Cambridge University Press.

Zumbansen, P. (2011). *The New Embeddedness of the Corporation*. Williams & Peer.

About the Contributors

Mikhail Kuznetsov is a professional corporate director, corporate governance and strategic management expert. Director, System transformation Center, Moscow State University. He has more than 15 years of experience in investment and management consulting, working in one of the largest financial development institutions - IFC, World Bank Group. More than 10 years of experience in the Board of Directors in large and middle-sized companies in finance, energy, transport, food sectors. Founder of the National Association of Corporate Directors (more than 400 participants, 25 cities). He is member of the Expert Committee on Corporate Governance under Federal Agency for State Property Management, Central Bank of the Russian Federation. Candidate of Economic Sciences, MBA lector at RANEPA (Russian Presidential Academy of National Economy and Public Administration), and MSU (Lomonosov Moscow State University), He is a author of 3 books and more than 50 articles on corporate governance and strategic management. Worked with OECD as an expert on the development of national corporate governance standards. Works with the WEF on the topics "Transformation map of Russia", "AI in city governance". The winner of the annual management competition "Leaders of Russia" - 2019.

Maria Nikishova is head of Corporate Governance practice in The Center for Corporate Development "Topcompetence". She is head of the annual research "The National Corporate Governance Index" in Russia. Expert of the System Transformation Center, Moscow State University. IFC Corporate governance consultant. She is a lecturer and PhD-student of the Financial University under the Government of the Russian Federation. She is a author and editor in chief of the media on corporate governance Corpshark.ru. Mrs. Nikishova specializes in digital business transformation, corporate governance and artificial intelligence technologies.

* * *

Mikhail Bakunin is heading Mobility Services Partnerships for the Renault-Nissan-Mitsubishi Alliance with Silicon Valley based partners. His objective is to support the Alliance's strategy of becoming an early provider of driverless vehicles and services, building on the exclusive relationship with Waymo, the Alphabet's company. Prior to Mikhail's assignment in the Silicon Valley office he has been involved in a number of projects related to electric vehicles and e-mobility at Nissan in Europe and Japan. Back in Russia, his home country, Mikhail served in senior management roles in telecom and telecom retail. Mikhail holds a PhD degree in economics from Kazan State University in Russia and an MBA degree from IE Business School in Spain, Madrid.

Sergey Endutkin is the CEO of Right to Development, Head of Legal of Aeroclub JSC. Trainer at Kutafin Moscow State Law University, Moscow Business School, and Russian Management School. Author and trainer at the courses "Corporate Law & Government", "Head of Legal", "Legal Management", and "LegalTech Expert."

Mark Fenwick is a Professor of International Business Law, Faculty of Law of Kyushu University - Graduate School of Law. Mark teaches undergraduate and graduate classes on the following topics: 1 Business crime. 2 Corporate Compliance. 3. Innovation and the law. 4. Entrepreneurship and the law.

Alexander Filatov is a experienced international expert for UNDP projects and IFC short-term consultancy assignments. He is a professional director with experience as an independent director and head of committees of the board of directors in private and public companies in Russia and Kazakhstan. He has fifteen years of experience in management consulting with a focus on corporate governance and business ethics, experience in working with projects of the International Finance Corporation (IFC), OECD (OECD) and UNDP (UNDP).

Helena Coelho Inácio has a PhD in Accounting and Management from the University Autonoma the Madrid, a MSc in Economy by the University of Coimbra and a degree in Accounting and Audit by the University of Aveiro. She is Professor in the University of Aveiro, at the Instituto of Accounting and Administration. She lectures under graduated and graduated courses of accounting and audit. She has a book of Internal Control, communications and publications in audit area. She is a member of the research unit on Competitiveness, Governance and Public Policies (GOVCOPP).

Rui Pedro Figueiredo Marques received the PhD degree in Computer Science in 2014 from the universities of Minho, Aveiro and Porto, three of the top universities in the north of Portugal. In 2008, he concluded his Masters degree in Electronics and Telecommunications Engineering, at the University of Aveiro, and in 2005 he graduated in the same area, also from the University of Aveiro. His main research interests are related to the integration of Information Systems into organizational topics, contributing with solutions to improve the risk management and the organizational efficiency. He is Professor of Information Systems and Technology since 2007 at the Higher Institute of Accounting and Administration, University of Aveiro, Portugal.

Olga Rink is a lecturer at the "Digital Economy" MBA program of MIPT & MGIMO. MSc in Applied Mathematics & Informational Technologies (Moscow Institute of Physics and Technology, artificial intelligence), MBA (Kingston Business School), economist in world economics. Formerly General Manager at Interfax - Dun & Bradstreet, Public Affairs Director at National Settlement Depository, a company of the Moscow Exchange Group. A winner of the EY "Entrepreneurial Winning Women" contest.

Valeria Solovyova is a corporate governance consultant. She specializes in research projects in the field of corporate governance and sustainable development / corporate social responsibility, analysis of the activities of companies. Has experience in participating in projects to evaluate the effectiveness of the board of directors; to assess the effectiveness of the activities of State Development Institutes, companies with state participation; Russian and international benchmarking projects.

Peter Verhezen is a Visiting Professor in Strategy, Sustainability, and Business in Emerging Markets at the University of Antwerp and Antwerp Management School (Belgium), and an Adjunct Professor for Global Corporate Governance, and Business in Asia at the Melbourne Business School. As the Principal of Verhezen & Associates Ltd he advises boards on risk management, strategy and governance in the Asia-Pacific region. He is also a former senior consultant at IFC-WorldBank in Asia-Pacific for Corporate Governance. Peter regularly writes about corporate governance and business ethics in international journals and attempts to share his thought at a variety of international seminars and universities. He co-founded an ICT spin-off from IBM in the early 1990s which he ran for 15 years in Southeast Asia-Australia. During the Asian crisis in 1997, he was a Senior Financial Advisor for IBRA (Ministry of Finance of Indonesia) in collaboration with IMF (from 1998 till 2002) where he successfully restructured more than USD 1.7 billion of corporate debt owned by local but nationalized banks and a number of international bank consortia. He is the author of "Gifts, Corruption and Philanthropy. The Ambiguity of Gift Practices in Business" (Oxford, 2009) and "The Vulnerability of Corporate Reputation. Leadership for Sustainable Long-Term Value", (London, 2015). He also co-authored "Is Corporate Governance Relevant in Indonesia?" (Jakarta, 2012), and "Doing business in ASEAN markets: Leadership challenges and governance solutions across borders" (London, 2016). He studied International Relations and Applied Economics (MA at the University of Antwerp in Belgium) and Philosophy at Leuven University in Belgium (MA & PhD). He took his MBA from Leuven Business School in association with Chicago Booth School of Business.

Erik Vermeulen is a professor of Business and Financial Law at Tilburg University and Tilburg Law and Economics Center in the Netherlands. He is also Head of Governance/Vice-President at Philips Lighting. Erik is best-described as a "global futurist" and "cross-cultural strategic consultant". He is constantly fascinated by technological revolutions and how the on-going digital revolution is changing the way we live, work and learn. He has a particular interest in how new technologies such as artificial intelligence, blockchain and robotics are affecting business, government, and education.

Duane Windsor has a PhD from Harvard University and is the Lynette S. Autrey Professor of Management in Rice University's Jesse H. Jones Graduate School of Business. An undergraduate alumnus of Rice University, his research and teaching emphasize corporate social responsibility, stakeholder theory, environmental sustainability, and anti-corruption reform.

Dmitry Zhdanov was born in 1958 in Moscow. He received higher education in the Moscow Aviation Institute at the Faculty of Economics. From 1985 to the present, he has worked at the Central Economics and Mathematics Institute RAS. In 2000 D.A.Zhdanov got his PhD with the thesis "Problems of Corporate Governance in Russia", and in 2016 he completed his thesis for the degree of Doctor of Economics in the specialty "Low-rational preferences of the dominant shareholders and the organizational structure of Russian industrial corporations". He is actively engaged in teaching, has an academic status of associate professor, is a professor at the Department of Corporate Governance of the Russian Presidential Academy of Economy and Public Administration (RANEPA).

Index

www.ingramcontent.com/pod-product-compliance
Lightning Source LLC
LaVergne TN
LVHW080529300926
849162LV00007B/1569
* 9 7 8 1 7 9 9 8 2 0 1 1 6 *